Sex,
Discrimination,
and the
Division of Labor

Columbia Studies in Economics   8

SEX, DISCRIMINATION, AND THE DIVISION OF LABOR

CYNTHIA B. LLOYD
Editor

COLUMBIA UNIVERSITY PRESS
New York and London   1975

Library of Congress Cataloging in Publication Data

Lloyd, Cynthia B   1943–   comp.
  Sex, discrimination, and the division of labor.

  CONTENTS: Lloyd, C. B. The division of labor between the sexes: a review. Female labor participation, unemployment, and wage differentials: Finegan, T. A. Participation of married women in the labor force. Niemi, B. Geographic immobility and labor force mobility: a study of female unemployment. Polachek, S. W. Discontinuous labor force participation and its effect on women's market earnings [etc.].
  1. Women—Employment—United States—Addresses, essays, lectures.   2. Discrimination in employment—United States—Addresses, essays, lectures.   3. Sex discrimination against women—United States—Addresses, essays, lectures.   4. Feminism—United States—Addresses, essays, lectures. I. Title.
HD6095.L56   331.4′0973   74-32175
ISBN 0-231-03750-3
ISBN 0-231-03751-1 pbk.

To Emily Duane Lloyd

The anticipation of her arrival provided the impetus for this book's completion.

CONTENTS

Preface

UNTIL RECENTLY, economists specializing in the fields of labor and human resources focused their primary research efforts on the American male. This is not entirely surprising, given the clear predominance of men in the labor force as well as in the economics profession in past decades. Theories based on assumptions about typical male behavior were sufficient to explain total changes in the labor force until World War II. Since that time, the dramatic rise in female labor force participation has been the major determinant of changes in the composition of the labor force and in its rate of growth. The need to explain these changes has given rise to a whole new orientation within economic research, which has emphasized the importance of production outside the market sector and of decision making within a family context.

Coincident with this new focus in economic research has been the rise of the Women's Liberation Movement. This movement has affected all strata of social, economic, political, and intellectual life, and has manifested itself within the economics profession in terms of a sudden increase of interest, particularly among young female economists, in research pertaining to all aspects of women's economic role. The Women's Movement has also spurred an interest in undergraduate and graduate courses focusing on women's often-neglected role in all fields within the humanities and the social sciences. At least within the economics discipline, however, the demand for courses on women arose at a time when much research on women was only in its earliest stages.

At Barnard College, where I have been teaching for the last four years, some interested members of the faculty and the administration and some students set up a Women's Center to act as a focal point for much of the activity that was developing on campus. Faculty members were encouraged to develop courses on women within their particular disciplines if enough scholarly material existed. Because of my contact with economists at Columbia who were at work on research dealing with many facets of women's economic role, I initiated a course on "The Role of Women in Modern Economic Life" in the spring of 1972. This experience indicated clearly to me the lack of published material that could be used by undergraduates. Many students with particular research interests were frustrated to find that only highly technical, unpublished manuscripts, on the one hand, or extremely simple-minded popular journalism, on the other, were available for their use.

The idea for this book arose out of this first teaching experience. I was aware of a gap in the literature and was also in contact with many economists who were well equipped to fill it. The collection of essays that follows presents as complete a picture as possible of the new directions in economic research on women. My intent was to choose particularly that research with broad economic and social relevance which might otherwise have been found only in the professional economic journals and expressed in fairly technical language. It is my hope that the authors of these essays have been successful in presenting their work in readable prose without sacrificing any of the rigor of their theoretical or empirical analysis. Although the proportion of contributors who are women is high relative to their proportion in the economics profession at large, this is not surprising in light of their personal identification with many of the questions dealt with. However, this should in no way affect the book's readership; for it is only when both sexes realize equally the importance of this kind of research to their understanding and their lives that the division of labor between the sexes will be elevated from an assumption to a variable in economic analysis.

The essays have been organized according to broad topics to help alert the reader to the kinds of questions the book is attempting to deal with. This should in no way suggest that the selection of essays under each heading presents an exhaustive discussion of the issues involved, nor should it suggest that the research areas delineated by the book's outline are mutually exclusive. My review essay has been written in order to provide the reader with sufficient background to place each of the essays that follow into a larger context. However, each essay can also be read independently. Although no questions have been conclusively answered, many new questions are raised which, it is hoped, will be the stimulus for further research.

Many individuals and past experiences have contributed to the evolution of this book. Obviously only the most important can be noted here. During my years as a graduate student in economics at Columbia University, I had the opportunity to participate in the Labor Workshop, where many of the ideas presented in these essays were first thrashed out. I was fortunate to have had Gary Becker as my teacher in first-year microeconomic theory and to have had Jacob Mincer as my dissertation sponsor. Many of the book's contributors, including myself, owe a great intellectual debt to these two economists, both of whom have been leaders in stimulating economic thought in the research areas covered here.

In addition, my experience teaching at Barnard College has been very valuable in reinforcing my interest in women's studies. The success of the Women's Center and the women's studies program as well as the interest of individual students have encouraged me to undertake this project. My good friend, colleague, and department chairman, Deborah Milenkovitch, has been a constant source of friendly encouragement and sound advice during all the stages of the book's development. A Faculty Research Grant for this academic year has been invaluable in smoothing over all the mechanical hurdles in the process of getting the book to Columbia University Press.

Finally, the importance of the home environment cannot be neglected. Even in today's world of Women's Liberation, few women can hope to have a successful marriage and an interesting and demanding career without the active support and encouragement of their spouses. I have been no exception. My husband has been delighted that I have pursued such an absorbing project and has always helped me to keep my sense of humor through all of its ups and downs.

CONTRIBUTORS

LEE BENHAM

Associate Professor of Economics and
   Preventive Medicine
Washington University
St. Louis, Missouri

ELIZABETH DURBIN

Associate Professor of Economics
New York University
New York City

T. ALDRICH FINEGAN

Professor of Economics
Vanderbilt University
Nashville, Tennessee

ESTELLE JAMES

Professor of Economics
State University of New York at Stony Brook
Stony Brook, New York

GEORGE E. JOHNSON

Associate Professor of Economics
University of Michigan
Ann Arbor, Michigan

SHIRLEY B. JOHNSON

Associate Professor of Economics
Vassar College
Poughkeepsie, New York

ARLEEN LEIBOWITZ

Research Associate
National Bureau of Economic Research
New York City;

Visiting Assistant Professor of Economics
Brown University
Providence, Rhode Island

CYNTHIA B. LLOYD

Assistant Professor of Economics
Barnard College
New York City

Janice Fanning Madden   Assistant Professor of Regional Science
                                 University of Pennsylvania
                                 Philadelphia, Pennsylvania

Beth Niemi   Assistant Professor of Economics
                                 Newark College of Arts and Sciences
                                 Rutgers University
                                 Newark, New Jersey

Solomon W. Polachek   Assistant Professor of Economics
                                 University of North Carolina
                                 Chapel Hill, North Carolina

Mark R. Rosenzweig   Assistant Professor of Economics
                                 Yale University
                                 New Haven, Connecticut

Fredricka Pickford Santos   Assistant Professor of Economics
                                 Graduate School of Economics
                                 Getulio Vargas Foundation
                                 Rio de Janeiro, Brazil, and
                                 University of São Paulo
                                 São Paulo, Brazil

Frank P. Stafford   Associate Professor of Economics
                                 University of Michigan
                                 Ann Arbor, Michigan

Mary H. Stevenson   Assistant Professor of Economics
                                 University of Massachusetts—Boston
                                 Boston, Massachusetts

Myra H. Strober   Assistant Professor of Economics
                                 Graduate School of Business
                                 Stanford University
                                 Stanford, California

Harriet Zellner   Assistant Professor of Economics
                                 Douglass College
                                 Rutgers University
                                 New Brunswick, New Jersey

Sex,
Discrimination,
and the
Division of Labor

"At any rate, when a subject is highly controversial—and any question about sex is that—one cannot hope to tell the truth. One can only show how one came to hold whatever opinion one does hold. One can only give one's audience the chance of drawing their own conclusions as they observe the limitations, the prejudices, the idiosyncrasies of the speaker."

Virginia Woolf,
A Room of One's Own

1

The Division of Labor between the Sexes: A Review

CYNTHIA B. LLOYD

THE CONCEPT of the "division of labor"—the notion that each individual specializes in certain activities and engages in exchange with other individuals rather than each individual producing all the goods and services he or she requires—is one of the oldest and most thoroughly accepted concepts in economics. In fact, it is one of the few concepts which has survived two hundred years of economic thinking virtually intact. It underlies the economic theory of international trade, economic growth, and labor force participation. Its logic is so intuitive that it has not remained the sole purview of economists but has been applied by sociologists and anthropologists to the study of social group interaction and the evolution of sex roles.

The history of thought in the social sciences provides a good example of the development of specialization and the division of labor. The broad social philosophers of the eighteenth and nineteenth centuries—Adam Smith, Thomas Malthus, David Ricardo, John Stuart Mill, Karl Marx— called "political economists" in their day, are today recognized by many separate disciplines in the social sciences as their common intellectual ancestors. But perhaps in the process of specialization, something has been lost. Thus, while John Stuart Mill and Frederick Engels questioned the origin and social consequences of the position of women,[1] contemporary

The author wishes to thank Deborah Milenkovitch, Harriet Zellner, Janice Madden, Fredricka Pickford Santos, Beth Niemi, Arleen Leibowitz, Myra Strober, and Estelle James for helpful comments made on an earlier draft of this paper.

economists rarely concern themselves with such wide-ranging social questions, leaving that task to be parceled out among the other disciplines. Instead, contemporary economists tend to take the present division of labor between the sexes for granted and assume it as given when building economic theories of market as well as household decision making.

At a time of rapid increases in the labor force participation of women and much general discussion of the changing sexual division of labor, it seems appropriate to reexamine the economic concept of the "division of labor" and its applicability to the sexes. This reexamination will make up the first part of this essay. The second and third parts will review the major economic research on women's economic role which antedates the research presented in this volume. This earlier research has focused on two major areas: (1) the effect of economic factors within the household on women's labor force participation and (2) the determinants of the wages of females relative to males in the market as well as of the distribution of workers across occupations by sex. A final section will question some of the consequences for economic research and policy formulation of recent changes in the division of labor between the sexes.

The Economics of the Division of Labor
between the Sexes

Adam Smith's original discussion of the economic advantages to be derived from the division of labor still stands as one of the best. His intricate description of pin production in a small factory illustrates clearly the dramatic increase in output resulting from worker specialization. The advantages of the division of labor are clearly dependent on the size of the market; therefore, the growth in the "wealth of nations" is a cumulative process, with growing population and production providing the basis for further specialization and economic development.

Adam Smith emphasized that the differences in skills between workers arise as a consequence of the division of labor.

The difference of natural talents in different men is, in reality, much less than we are aware of; and the very different genius which appears to distinguish men of different professions, when grown up to maturity, is not upon occasions so much the cause, as the effect of the division of labour. The difference between the most dissimilar characters, between a philosopher and a common street porter, for example, seems to arise not so much from nature, as from habit, custom, and education.[2]

The worker who specializes in one activity for all of his or her life will become particularly good at that through education, training, and long experience. The modern theory of investments in human capital—the notion that expenses incurred for education and training can be regarded as investments which yield returns in the future measured in terms of increased earnings—derives quite simply from this concept of increased productivity through increased specialization.

The economic advantages of the division of labor, however, are not without costs. The worker who has specialized in one function all his life becomes dull and unable to apply his mind to a broader range of interests and problems.

His dexterity at his own particular trade seems, in this manner, to be acquired at the expense of his intellectual, social and marital virtues.[3]

In the long run, this can lead to problems of worker boredom and alienation in occupations which require endless repetition of certain physical functions and little mental effort. Marx described this process as bearing the seeds of the eventual revolution of the proletariat.

Owing to the extensive use of machinery and to division of labour, the work of the proletarians has lost all individual character, and, consequently, all charm for the workman. He becomes an appendage of the machine, and it is only the most simple, most monotonous, and most easily acquired knack, that is required of him.[4]

Similarly, the traditional separation of functions between the sexes has been based on notions of specialization and the division of labor. Many anthropologists in the past observed that the common division of labor in all primitive societies was between man the hunter and provider and woman the gatherer of food and minder of the home.[5] These observations filtered down to us and have become part of the framework within which we view our environment. It came to seem natural that the man should specialize in market activities and the woman in home activities. However, there are many questions to be raised about the true origin of this division of labor and its economic advantages. It is indisputable that certain basic physiological differences between the sexes lead to a natural female advantage in childbearing. In other areas, however, debate arises as to whether there are basic differences in innate abilities between the sexes which always lead to this particular division of labor or whether economic circumstances in the past necessitated a certain division of labor between the sexes which has evolved and been reinforced through the natural economic advantages of specialization.

The noted anthropologist, Eleanor Leacock, writes that

in primitive communal society, the distinction did not exist between a public world of men's work and a private world of women's household service. The large collective household *was* the community, and within it both sexes worked to produce the goods necessary for livelihood.[6]

Despite the lack of distinction between home and market work, however, sharp distinctions between the sexes did exist in terms of tasks performed. Ester Boserup has made a thorough study of different farming systems in the developing countries and has found that each society has a clear sexual division of labor. What is to be noted, however, is that, contrary to common belief, there is no common pattern of sex roles across societies.

Both in primitive and in more developed communities, the traditional division of labor within the farm family is usually considered ''natural'' in the sense of being obviously and originally imposed by the sex difference itself. But while the members of any given community can think that their particular division of labor between the sexes is the ''natural'' one, because it has undergone little or no change for generations, other communities may have completely different ways of dividing the burden of work among the sexes, and they too may find their ways just as ''natural.'' [7]

Agricultural conditions clearly played an important part in determining women's role in the providing of food. In areas of shifting agriculture, where land was cultivated only a few years until the natural fertility of the soil was exhausted, women did most of the farming. Possibly the farming was more complementary than other activities with the woman's childbearing role because of its proximity to home, and, therefore, farming became a feminine occupation. The men concentrated on hunting, the felling of trees, and warfare in order to gain new territory—tasks that were more likely to take them away from the home base. In areas of plough agriculture, where land was cultivated more intensively because of greater population density, men did the farming and women concentrated on home activities. In many cases, the more intensive agriculture involved the work of hired labor on large tracts of privately owned land.[8] For many landless tenants, this created a physical separation between the provision of food and home and probably represents the point from which our traditional sexual division of labor has evolved. This brief description of different agricultural systems fails to support the notion of innate differences between the sexes. However, it should be noted that a common element underlies these alternative forms of the division of labor by sex. Under differing economic circumstances, women's childbearing role constrained them to activities within a narrow radius of home. Hence, both biological and economic conditions played a role in the evolution of a division of labor between the sexes.

Industrialization further accentuated the division of labor between the sexes by creating an even greater physical separation between home and work. As population density increased and the size of the market grew, the division of labor in industry became more sophisticated, thus increasing the relative real income of those participating in market work. Many tasks traditionally done by women in the home were shifted to the male-dominated market sector, where the advantages of the division of labor could be realized. However, many other tasks, such as cooking, cleaning, laundry, and childrearing, were repeated by women in every home. Charlotte Perkins Gilman, an early feminist writer, noted the growing discrepancy between the productivity of home and market work in her book *Women and Economics,* originally published in 1898:

The division of labor of housekeeping would require the service of fewer women for fewer hours a day. Where now twenty women in twenty homes work all the time, and insufficiently accomplish their varied duties, the same work in the hands of specialists could be done in less time by fewer people; and the others would be left free to do other work for which they were better fitted, thus increasing the productive power of the world.[9]

At the same time that this division of labor between the sexes was becoming firmly established in our culture, the proportion of a housewife's time needed to produce the traditional set of household goods and services was declining. The declining birth rate meant that the woman's childrearing responsibilities decreased at the same time that her life expectancy increased many years beyond the end of her reproductive activity. In fact, some have suggested that the dramatic differences between

female and male mortality during the economically most productive decades of life can be attributed to women's less physically demanding
work.[10] In addition, technological change in the home as well as the
increased availability of market substitutes for work traditionally done in
the home reduced the time required to maintain a given-sized household.

With much traditional production withdrawn from the household sector, a wife's responsibilities shifted toward the maintenance of a growing
level of consumption within the household. A rising standard of living
requires the time to maintain it and enjoy it. Rising income has shifted
demand toward a different kind of household production, with higher
standards of quality in terms of children's education, gourmet cooking,
etc. John Kenneth Galbraith expresses this point of view in his most
recent book, *Economics and the Public Purpose*. He suggests that the
weakening economic foundation for the division of labor between the
sexes was strengthened and renewed as it became clear that rising levels
of consumption could not be indefinitely sustained without women, as a
"crypto-servant class," assigned to facilitate them.

With higher income the volume and diversity of consumption increase and there-
with the number and complexity of the tasks of household management. The distribution of time between the various tasks associated with the household, children's education and entertainment, clothing, social life, and other forms of
consumption becomes an increasingly complex and demanding affair. In consequence, and paradoxically, the menial role of the women becomes more arduous
the higher the family income, save for the small fraction who still have paid servants.[11]

This further evolution of the division of labor was not achieved without
cost. Women who specialized in housework and motherhood found that
after many years they did not have enough to keep them occupied full-
time but at the same time they were not suited for many other activities
because they had not developed or maintained any marketable skills. The
tedious and mindless nature of much of women's unpaid work also re-
sulted in alienation and boredom on the part of many housewives. Betty
Friedan in *The Feminine Mystique* described this sense of frustration and
dissatisfaction as the "problem that has no name." [12] An obvious paral-
lel can be drawn here between the revolt of the proletariat predicted by
Marx as the ultimate response to the tedium of overspecialization and the
current revolt of many women against the traditional division of labor be-

tween the sexes in an increasingly affluent and technologically sophisticated society.

Changes in our economic environment as well as the emergence of new attitudes have also had implications for the institution of marriage. Marriage as an institution has evolved from and been reinforced by the original economic advantages of a sexual division of labor. Many centuries of specialization in certain masculine and feminine tasks made a man and a woman into a good working team with complementary skills. In fact, in Gary Becker's new economic model of marriage, the product *"own children"* is considered the main source of complementarity between husband and wife and, therefore, the main source of economic gains.[13] However, as child-care responsibilities have declined with declines in fertility and other forms of household production have become less time-consuming with technological change, the economic underpinnings of marriage have been eroded. The gains from specialization depend on the level of technology and the size of the group involved in exchange, and in today's market an exclusive group of two is too small to reap such gains. Yet marriage remains the major context within which production and consumption decisions take place. Why then does the institution survive? Clearly marriage yields some value or utility to the participants beyond any relative increase in wealth that may be gained through specialization and the division of labor. Even so, it would not be surprising to observe a greater diversity in the composition of households in the future as social and institutional change continues to respond to economic change.

The Modern Theory of the Household and Women's Labor Force Participation

The traditional division of labor between the sexes, although firmly based on economic foundations, represents a constraint not only on economic behavior but also on economic analysis. In the early days of labor market research, there was a clear distinction between labor economics and home economics. Labor economics was a field largely populated by men, who centered their research on labor force patterns of male workers. Home economics was a field with little status mainly populated by women, who dealt with the practical concerns of housewives in managing a household. There was some interest among women economists in women's labor force experience, but the research remained largely descriptive and was not integrated into the mainstream of labor economics.[14] The modern economic theory of the household, best exemplified by Gary Becker's "A Theory of the Allocation of Time," [15] permitted an integration of labor market economics and home economics through a unified theory of economic decision making. Now that the household has gained respectability as a subject of economic analysis, the tools are available for a full study of family decision making and of the determinants of the division of labor between home and market.

The classical theory of labor supply divided time into two alternative uses: paid labor and leisure.[16] The supply of time to the labor market was seen as the complement to the demand for leisure time, and above a certain wage level, which would vary from individual to individual, was expected to decrease with further wage increases. This hypothesis was derived from the substitution and income effects of classical microeconomic theory. A rise in the wage represented not only a rise in the price of an hour of leisure time but also, for a given number of hours of work, a rise in income. It is assumed that any expansion of an individual's real income will lead to an increase in the consumption of all normal goods; in the case of leisure, this would be manifested as a reduction in hours of work. Therefore, the substitution effect, leading to a decline in consumption of the commodity rising in price (in this case, leisure), and the income effect exert opposite influences on labor supply. The net effect is summarized in the theory of the backward-bending supply curve. Perhaps the fact that most women's time was devoted to neither paid work nor leisure time was initially of little concern to economists because women composed such a small minority of the labor force.

The rapid rise in women's labor force participation in the postwar period, particularly dramatic in the case of married women, provided a puzzling paradox to labor economists trained in the traditional school. The theory of the backward-bending supply curve would have predicted that rising income would cause declining labor force participation among both men and women, because leisure is a normal good whose demand rises with income. However, experience seemed to fly in the face not only of traditional theory but also of well-confirmed cross-sectional data which indicated that the percentage of women participating in the labor force varied inversely with their husband's income. The conventional wisdom was that only poor women worked, out of economic necessity, and that as income rose more husbands would be able to afford the luxury of keeping their wives at home, where they could assist in maintaining a higher standard of living. There they would be relieved of the double burden of contributing to family income and taking care of a household, and could resume their traditional specialization in home-related activities.

The growing number of women in the labor force forced some economists to recognize the importance of reconciling the theory with the facts. Jacob Mincer made the first important contribution to our understanding by recognizing the simple fact that women allocate their time in a more complex variety of ways than men.[17] While men's work consists almost exclusively of paid time in the market, women's work often consists of unpaid, nonmarket work which is assigned no value in economic data but which may have immense value to the individual woman or family. Mincer theorized that, although total family income should affect the total amount of time women devote to work (either in the home or in the market), it is the relative productivity of home and market work which should determine where the woman will spend her working day.

Mincer's empirical work, using a variety of data sources, lent support to his extension of the labor supply model to incorporate both home and market work. His statistical analysis showed that, if women's earning power remains unchanged, an increase in family income tends to reduce labor force participation. However, under conditions of unchanged family income and productivity in the home, a rise in the wife's market wage will lead her to reallocate her working time toward the market, where she has become relatively more productive. In fact, his regression results using 1950 census data indicated that a rise in women's own wage, family income remaining unchanged, would, on the average, increase labor force participation four times as much as a similar rise in family income, with wives' wage unchanged, would reduce labor force participation. Within this framework, the rapid postwar rise in women's labor force participation was easily explained in terms of rising wages, despite some uncertainty as to whether women's wages had risen more or less rapidly than men's. Over time, the substitution effect of women's rising wages on their own labor force participation has dominated the long-run income effect.

Mincer also noted the importance of transitory income in explaining the negative simple correlation between husband's income and wife's labor force participation previously observed in cross-sectional data. In order to maintain family consumption levels in line with expectations of permanent family income, families can either save or dissave, with short-run fluctuations in earnings, or they can rely on secondary workers, such as the wife, to adjust labor force participation to suit temporary income needs. In fact, Mincer's statistical analysis indicated that wives' labor force participation is much more responsive to temporary changes in income than to permanent, long-run changes in income. Mincer's results were significant not only in emphasizing the dependency of wives' activities on their husbands' economic conditions but, more importantly, in highlighting the flexibility of the division of labor between the sexes under changing economic conditions. The strong responsiveness of women to changes in their own relative rewards at home and in the market indicated the malleability of the traditionally dichotomous division of labor between the sexes.

Gary Becker, in his "A Theory of the Allocation of Time," directed his attention to the productive aspects of nonworking time. The publication of his article in 1965 represented an important turning point in microeconomic theory, because it opened a whole realm of nonmarket activities to economic analysis. Time and an individual's productivity are the limiting scarce resources in this model. Each individual allocates his or her time among many competing activities both in the market and at home in such a way as to maximize his or her total product or utility. Time can be used to earn money, which can purchase market goods, or can be used in the production and the consumption of commodities at home. Time and market goods are the two major categories of inputs used to produce household commodities, such as cooking, childrearing, and entertaining.

Although the theory itself is completely general and can be applied to either sex individually, its simple rules of allocative efficiency have certain implications for the division of labor within the household:

Instead of simply allocating time efficiently among commodities, multi-person households also allocate the time of different members. Members who are relatively more efficient at market activities would use less of their time at consumption activities [i.e., work in the home] than would other members. Moreover, an increase in the relative market efficiency of any member would effect a reallocation of the time of all other members toward consumption activities in order to permit the former to spend more time at market activities. In short, the allocation of the time of any member is greatly influenced by the opportunities open to other members.[18]

The completely general formulation of the inputs to the household production function for a male–female household would include market goods and both the husband's and the wife's time. Therefore, the combination of inputs chosen for each household activity should depend on the relative efficiency of each of the inputs for that specific activity. Differences in the efficiency of men and women in various household activities are dependent on differences in natural abilities and differences in acquired training. Because of early conditioning as well as school and market training, men tend to specialize within the family in household repairs and family finances, whereas women are more likely to do the cooking and cleaning.

Because of the complex series of input substitutions that are possible as resource productivities change, most economists have made certain simplifying assumptions about the division of labor between the sexes. Men are assumed to work full-time in the market. Women, however, are assumed to distribute their working time between home and market work according to an evaluation of relative productivities. The major input substitution in household production is seen to be between women's time and market goods. Little has been said about changes in men's input of time at home as women's labor force participation increases. Nothing has been said about the dynamics of household decision making in terms of whose preferences dominate or how leisure time is shared. ''The economist does not invade the privacy of the household.'' [19]

The major published studies of female labor supply since Becker's article have focused on the important interdependency between women's labor supply and economic conditions within the home. In Glen Cain's elaboration of Mincer's empirical work, women's labor supply is a function not only of her wage but also of family income, number of children, and the market wage of other family members.[20] In Bowen and Finegan's monumental study of factors affecting labor supply in all population groups, the list of family-related variables affecting women's labor force participation is further expanded.[21] This approach is faithful to Becker's model, which indicates the complete interdependency of household members in time allocation decisions. However, men's labor supply decisions are seen, in their study, as completely independent of any household circumstances. Table 1.1 lists the variables used by Bowen and Finegan to explain male and female labor supply. Essentially, the assumption is that husbands make their decisions, and, once the husband's occupation, employment status, and income are set, women can then make their decisions in the light of their own relative productivities, the family's needs, the availability of substitutes, and possible competition in the female job market.

In order to take full advantage of Becker's theoretical innovations, it is necessary to test the responsiveness of men's labor supply decisions to the economic needs of the family and the characteristics of the wife. The validity of traditional sex-role assumptions will be increasingly brought

TABLE 1.1   Variables Used by Bowen and Finegan
to Explain Male and Female Labor Supply

Variables	Women	Men
Individual Characteristics		
Color	x	x
Marital status	x	x
Schooling	x	x
Age	x	x
Health		x
Other income (husband's)		x
Number of children	x	
Housing circumstances	x	
Occupation	x	
Other family income (total family income minus wife's earnings)	x	
Employment status of husband	x	
Husband's occupation	x	
Labor Market Conditions		
Earnings	x	x
Unemployment	x	x
Male industry mix (percentage of male jobs in SMSA[a])		x
Female industry mix	x	
Female supply (percentage of women in SMSA[a])	x	
Wage of domestics (cost of wife substitute)	x	

SOURCE: William G. Bowen and T. Aldrich Finegan, *The Economics of Labor Force Participation* (Princeton, N.J., 1969).

[a] Standard Metropolitan Statistical Area.

into question as more women spend an increasing amount of time working in the market. A valid test of these assumptions can be made by comparing the response of men and women to these same family characteristics. Some work, so far unpublished, is proceeding along these lines. James Smith estimated the effect of wife's wage, husband's wage, and the presence of children in the home on both male and female labor supply.[22] He found that not only did a rise in husband's wage reduce wife's labor force participation, but that a rise in wife's wage reduced her husband's labor force participation. However, in both cases a change in one's own wage had a stronger effect on labor supply decisions than a similar change in one's spouse's wage. The presence of children in the home is a deterrent to the labor force participation of the wife and an inducement to the labor force participation of the husband. This illustrates that the presence of children, considered to be the main source of complementarity between husband and wife in marriage, reinforces the traditional division of labor that other economic forces appear to be breaking apart. As economic changes (such as productivity improvements in the home, the decline in fertility, and the growing equality in male and female education and training) continue to make men and women more substitutable in household and market production, it will be interesting to observe what changes, if any, evolve in the responsiveness of male and female labor supply decisions to the income, employment status, and occupation of their mates.

Relative Earnings and Occupational Distribution

The division of labor between the sexes extends beyond the household and into the market place. It is manifested in the earnings of women relative to men, in women's positions within the hierarchies of business firms, and in the sharp differences in the occupational distribution of men and women. Until recently few questioned the equity of this division of market tasks and rewards. It was just one of the many economic consequences of a natural evolutionary process from an agricultural to an industrial society.

Recently, some economists have begun to analyze the determinants of wage differentials and occupational distribution. However, no study in this area has yet produced a theoretical framework as cohesive and generally accepted as Becker's theory of the allocation of time. Economic theories of discrimination and human capital are widely applied, but neither separately nor combined do they seem completely capable of explaining the phenomena observed.

The human-capital approach attempts to explain wage differences between individuals and groups in terms of differences in productivity. Because productivity is difficult to measure in many of today's complex industrial processes, level of education, age, and/or years of experience are often used as substitute measures because they are known to be correlated with productivity. Since so many market skills are acquired, developed, and perfected on the job, years of experience has become a particularly important measure of productivity. Unfortunately, however, the measurement of productivity differences between men and women has been hampered by the lack of data on women's job experience. Men's experience can easily be estimated by assuming that they have a continuous attachment to the labor force after completing school. Women's job experience is usually broken into a prechildrearing and a postchildrearing period and cannot be estimated without detailed longitudinal data. Without this information, it is difficult to determine whether or not women's generally lower earnings are the result of differences in productivity or other nonmarket forces.

Several studies have attempted to break down observed wage differentials between the sexes into definable parts. Henry Sanborn, using data from the 1950 census, explained the major portion of the wage differential by adjusting for the fact that men tend to work in higher-paying occupations.[23] The more detailed the occupational breakdown he used, the more of the differential he was able to explain. Sanborn even suggested that that portion of the wage differential which remained unexplained by such factors as differences in education, age (used as a measure of differences in job experience), race, urbanness, and hours of work, could be due to unmeasured productivity differences.

More recent studies, using better adjustments for differences in work experience, have not been able to explain nearly as much of the wage differential as claimed by Sanborn.[24] However, none of these studies has resorted to differences in occupational distribution as a form of adjustment. These studies have made clear that even when one compares women and men with equal education and job experience, women's earnings are significantly less. This appears to be so because of the types of occupations that women enter.

These studies have pointed to the need to explain why women are found in the lower-paying occupations or job classifications. Is it a rational extension of the division of labor between the sexes found in the household or is it a manifestation of some form of discrimination or exploitation? Either hypothesis is plausible, and both together could explain a larger part of the differential. It seems logical that women in the labor force, given their continued commitment to home work, would choose occupations which would provide them with training having some applicability to the home (e.g., teacher, nurse, dietician, waitress). This should be particularly true for those women who expect to have an interrupted career, because then some of the return from any investment in human capital in the form of education or training can be realized in a nonmarket form. This hypothesis may account at least in part for many women's seemingly irrational decision to overinvest in human capital. Although it is true that all jobs permit the acquisition of skills which have some usefulness in nonmarket activities, the historical pattern of women's labor force participation shows a clear relationship between women's jobs in the home and in the market.[25] Not only are women realizing nonmarket returns from skills acquired in the market, but employers have realized returns from the training women traditionally received in the home.

Discriminatory behavior against women in the labor market can be understood within either a utility-maximizing or a profit-maximizing framework. Because of men's dominance in the market, it is clear that they have the power to discriminate. A majority of the labor force is male, almost all employers are male, and, even if housewives are the most vocal consumers, their husbands have the majority of the dollar votes.[26] Their desire to exercise that power may come from a well-evolved culture of expectations about women's place or, alternatively, from a vision of increased profits. Gary Becker's *The Economics of Discrimination* [27] is associated with the former hypothesis, whereas some of the more recent writing on discrimination has leaned toward the latter hypothesis.

Becker's theory was first designed primarily to explain racial discrimination, but it has been applied to sex discrimination as well. In Becker's model, discriminators are those who are not exclusively interested in maximizing money income but are also interested in minimizing their contact with particular groups (e.g., blacks, women). Discriminators in the market can be either employers, employees, or customers, and the degree of their discrimination can be measured by the amount they are willing to pay in terms of higher wages, lower wages, or higher prices in order to hire, work with, or buy from the preferred group.

Although no study has attempted to make a direct estimate of the price discriminators are willing to pay in order to discriminate (sometimes called the "discrimination coefficient"), Victor Fuchs, in his study of wage differentials using individual sample data from the 1960 census, hints at the relative importance of different kinds of discrimination in explaining wage differentials.[28] He found that the female–male ratio of average hourly earnings was lowest among self-employed workers, and in addition, that a much smaller proportion of female relative to male workers are found in the self-employed category. Compared with private wage and salary earners and government employees, the self-employed have the most immediate contact with their consumers. Fuchs concluded that such a pattern of earnings differentials and occupational distribution is "consistent with the hypothesis of discrimination by customers." [29]

The "crowding hypothesis" presents an alternative approach to discrimination not found in Becker's original study. Barbara Bergmann is one of its best-known advocates.[30] In this theory, women are systematically excluded from certain occupations ("masculine occupations") and crowded into other occupations ("feminine occupations").[31] Thus, in the "masculine" occupations, where the supply of women is artificially restricted, the productivity of the marginal worker rises as does the equilibrium wage rate. In the "feminine" occupations, where the supply of workers is artificially expanded, the productivity of the marginal worker falls as does the equilibrium wage rate. The result is that, with the majority of women in "feminine" occupations and the majority of men in "masculine" occupations, the female–male wage ratio is lower than it would have been without occupational entry barriers. If such is the nature of discrimination, productivity differences between men and women, objectively measured, can completely explain wage differences and yet discrimination will be the cause of women's lower relative wages. The effect of such crowding can be compared to the effect of unionization on union versus nonunion wages. The restriction of entry into the union limits the supply of labor in that industry or occupation and forces wages above the competitive level, thus benefiting union members.

Advocates of the crowding hypothesis typically do not use economic analysis to explain the origin of "masculine" and "feminine" occupations. It may be, however, that "masculine" occupations require more on-the-job training, which employers, for various reasons, are reluctant to give to women. This leads to the statistical theory of discrimination, which has been recently developed.

The statistical theory of discrimination explains discrimination as a rational policy on the part of employers to maximize expected profits.[32] The assumption underlying this theory is that employers believe that average labor-force turnover among women is higher than that among men. If this assumption is correct, it is understandable that employers are more hesitant to hire women and to provide them with training, since they believe that their investment in the hiring and training process is more likely to be lost than it would be with a similarly qualified male. Furthermore, it is expensive to acquire extensive information about the reliability and motivation of each individual job applicant; in fact, the cost of acquiring such information about women job applicants may outweigh any gains to the employer in the form of a more certain return on his investment. In this case, discrimination could take the form either of paying equally qualified women less for the same work, in order to force them to finance all the costs of their on-the-job training, or of excluding them from particular jobs.

The fact that, contrary to the beliefs of many employers, separation rates for men and women of similar age and skill employed on similar jobs are about the same [33] does not negate this theory, which is based on expectations and the costs of information and not on statistical reality. That is why the theory is discussed under the heading of discrimination and not under the heading of productivity differences. Discrimination against women may arise out of pure prejudice—as in Becker's model, which assumes utility maximization—or out of a mistaken impression of their abilities and reliability, as in the statistical theory of discrimination. These differences have been well summarized by Harriet Zellner:

Deliberate discrimination is based on a subjective preference for males; that is, it is motivated by some sort of discomfort in dealing with women in certain occupational roles. Erroneous discrimination is based on an underestimation of female capacities in these roles; it is cognitive rather than psychological in origin.[34]

Whatever its motivating force, discrimination clearly accentuates and reinforces the division of labor between the sexes. Although it may enhance the utility or profits of some, it does so at the expense of many others. As women's labor force participation continues to increase both in terms of numbers and in terms of continuity, the importance of understanding the extent and sources of discrimination increases as well. However, this particular kind of research has become exceedingly difficult. Men and women economists, colored by different perceptions of their own sex roles, have been distrustful of each other's premises and conclusions. Male–female wage differentials, unexplained by productivity differences, are often considered a measure of the extent of discrimination. Yet, these estimates vary widely because of differences in data used, and the productivity differences may themselves be an outgrowth of discrimination in access to education and training.

Some Economic Consequences of
a Changing Division of Labor between the Sexes

The Women's Liberation Movement and the recent interest in women's studies have made their mark on the economics profession. The recent publication of a chapter on the "Economic Role of Women" in the President's 1973 *Economic Report* represents an important step in the recognition of women's problems.[35] Prior to this publication, almost all government research on women had been relegated to the Women's Bureau, which seems to stand to one side in the hierarchy of important government agencies. Two of the most important consequences of the upsurge in interest in women's problems among economists may be a reevaluation of the differential impact of laws and governmental policies on men and women, and a growing appreciation of the economic value of nonmarket work.

Recent Congressional hearings have begun to question the impact of Federal income taxes and social security taxes on the take-home pay of married women.[36] It appears that the Federal income tax system and other redistributive schemes that have evolved since its inception (e.g., social security and welfare) have been based on the assumption that the typical American family consists of a working father supporting a dependent wife and children. This assumption is no longer descriptive of social reality. Labor-market statistics for March 1973 indicate that 42.2 percent of the roughly 46.3 million husband-and-wife families had wives in the labor force. An additional 6.6 million families were headed by females, 53 percent of whom were in the labor force.[37] In fact, then, working wives make a substantial contribution to family income. The slight improvement in the distribution of earned income among families between 1958 and 1970 has been mainly attributed to the increasing role of the wife's earnings.[38]

The present income tax and social security systems were designed to aid the man, who, upon marrying, acquired a dependent and experienced no increase in income. To mitigate this additional burden, his total income tax bill was reduced. However, if a married woman works, the rate of tax on her earnings is greater than the rate she would pay as a single taxpayer. As she is a secondary earner, her first dollar of income is taxed at her husband's marginal rate, thus reducing the amount by which her work effort can contribute to family income. In addition, an implicit surtax is imposed on many marriages between working people since the Tax Reform Act of 1969, when the discrepancy between single and married tax rates was somewhat modified.[39] The size of the surtax increases with the size of individual incomes and decreases with the size of the discrepancy between them. The female head of household bears an additional tax burden as well, being required to pay as much as 10 percent more Federal tax than a married couple would pay on the same income.

The social security system also limits the ability of the married working woman to supplement the family's retirement income. A man receives a benefit related to his past earnings and his years of work. A working wife is eligible for the greater of two alternative benefits: one based on her status as a worker and the other based on her status as her husband's dependent. As a wife, she is entitled to 50 percent of her husband's benefit; as a worker she is entitled to a benefit based on her past earnings and years of work. However, in many cases, her benefit as a worker is not as great as the benefit she would be entitled to as her husband's dependent, because of her less continuous labor force participation as well as her lower average earnings. In such cases, her contributions from earnings are providing her certain invalid and death benefits while working but nothing more than she would be entitled to in any case in her old age.[40] Therefore, it is clear that a tax system originally designed to reflect the typical sexual division of labor in the American family and recently revised to alleviate the excessive tax burden formerly placed on the single individual has a perverse effect on the economics of a growing number of American families.

The working-wife problem arises from the definition of income for tax purposes. The value of a housewife's services at home are not included in taxable income. Through the principle of income aggregation, the couple with two incomes is treated as having the same ability to pay as the couple with a single earner and an identical aggregate income. However, the couple with two incomes has the additional expense of buying the services which would be produced at home and be untaxed if the wife did not work.

In fact, the whole emphasis in economics on quantification and market values has misled many of us into giving more emphasis to such measurable quantities as GNP and market earnings and less emphasis to the nonmarket sector.

The labor of women to facilitate consumption is not valued in national income or product. This is of some importance for its disguise; what is not counted is often not noticed. For this reason . . . it becomes possible for women to study economics without becoming aware of their precise role in the economy. This, in turn, facilitates their acceptance of their role.[41]

A recognition of the fact that housewives are not idle and that housework has a real economic value may raise the status of the housewife's occupation. Clearly, during certain periods in the life cycle, particularly when children are young, the economic value families place on a mother's time in the home with her children is so high that, in many cases, no amount of market work by the wife would permit the family to afford a substitute of equal quality. In fact, an improvement in the status of housework may permit men and women to reevaluate their relative nonmarket abilities and lead to a wider diversity of life-styles as men and women increasingly share in both market and nonmarket work. In a society which is experiencing rising real income along with a decline in the work week as well as in the length of the working life, nonmarket time will become the predominant aspect of an individual's life. The freedom to allocate that time without any artificial social constraints will be a liberating experience for both men and women.

Recent economic research on women has clearly increased our understanding of women's role in economic life. In addition, it has already done a lot to extend the scope of the economics field in general. The initial puzzle of women's rising labor force participation forced economists to generalize previous economic theory so as to incorporate the nonmarket sector. This has encouraged economists to move into research areas previously considered beyond the scope of economics. The oft-repeated definition of economics as the study of "how scarce resources are allocated to meet competing ends" is now seen as a mandate to study all kinds of social phenomena, such as the economics of crime, marriage, population, and discrimination and the allocation of time in the nonmarket sector. Thus, the opportunity now exists for economists to liberate themselves from their narrow specialization and division of labor and return to their previous role as political economists and social philosophers. As the division of labor between the sexes becomes more responsive to economic conditions, so the division of labor within the social sciences will be less clearly defined along strictly disciplinary lines.

NOTES

[1] John Stuart Mill, *The Subjection of Women* (London, 1869); Frederick Engels, *The Origin of the Family, Private Property, and the State* (Zurich, 1884).

[2] Adam Smith, *An Inquiry into the Nature and Causes of the Wealth of Nations,* 2 vols. (London, 1930), I: 17.

[3] *Ibid.,* II: 267.

[4] Karl Marx, "Manifesto of the Communist Party," in Robert Freedman, ed., *Marx on Economics* (New York, 1961), pp. 19–20.

[5] Margaret Mead, *Male and Female* (London, 1950), p. 190.

[6] Eleanor Leacock, "Introduction" to Frederick Engels, *The Origin of the Family, Private Property, and the State* (New York, 1972), p. 33.

[7] Ester Boserup, *Women's Role in Economic Development* (New York, 1970), p. 15.

[8] *Ibid.,* pp. 16–35.

[9] Charlotte Perkins Gilman, *Women and Economics* (New York, 1966), p. 245.

[10] Eugene Lewit, "Differences in Male and Female Mortality Rates," in National Bureau of Economic Research, *New Directions in Economic Research* (New York, 1971), p. 130.

[11] John Kenneth Galbraith, *Economics and the Public Purpose* (Boston, 1973), p. 32.

[12] Betty Friedan, *The Feminine Mystique* (New York, 1963), p. 11.

[13] Gary Becker, "A Theory of Marriage: Part I," *Journal of Political Economy,* LXXXI (July/August 1973): 818. The Marxists emphasize the importance of the emergence of private property as an additional element in the evolution of marriage because of the male need to distinguish his own heirs from other children. Marilyn Goldberg, "The Economic Exploitation of Women," *The Review of Radical Political Economics,* II (Spring 1970): 35–47.

[14] For example: Edith Abbott, *Women in Industry* (New York, 1924); Elizabeth F. Baker, *Technology and Women's Work* (New York, 1964); Ivy Pinchbeck, *Women Workers and the Industrial Revolution, 1770–1850* (London, 1930).

[15] *The Economic Journal,* LXXV (September 1965): 493–517. Margaret

Reid's earlier work, *Economics of Household Production* (New York, 1934), was an important precursor to Becker's article.

[16] Lionel Robbins, "On the Elasticity of Demand for Income in Terms of Effort," *Economica*, X (June 1930): 123–29; Alfred Marshall, *Principles of Economics* (London, 1938), pp. 528–29; H. G. Lewis, "Hours of Work and Hours of Leisure," *Proceedings of the Ninth Annual Meetings of the Industrial Relations Research Association* (1957), pp. 196–206.

[17] Jacob Mincer, "Labor Force Participation of Married Women: A Study in Labor Supply," in Universities-National Bureau Committee for Economic Research, *Aspects of Labor Economics* (Princeton, N.J., 1962), pp. 63–106.

[18] Gary Becker, "A Theory of the Allocation of Time," *The Economic Journal*, LXXV (September 1965): 512.

[19] Galbraith, *Economics and the Public Purpose*, p. 35.

[20] Glen Cain, *Married Women in the Labor Force* (Chicago, 1966).

[21] William G. Bowen and T. Aldrich Finegan, *The Economics of Labor Force Participation* (Princeton, N.J., 1969), pp. 88–158.

[22] James P. Smith, "The Life Cycle Allocation of Time in a Family Context" (Ph.D. diss., University of Chicago, 1972).

[23] He started with wage and salary income and then adjusted for differences in hours worked to come closer to a wage variable. Henry Sanborn, "Pay Differences between Men and Women," *Industrial and Labor Relations Review*, XVII (July 1964): 534–50.

[24] Malcolm S. Cohen, "Sex Differences in Compensation," *Journal of Human Resources*, VI (Fall 1971): 434–47; Burton G. Malkiel and Judith A. Malkiel, "Male–Female Pay Differentials in Professional Employment," *American Economic Review*, LXIII (September 1973): 693–705; Larry E. Suter and Herman P. Miller, "Income Differences between Men and Career Women," *American Journal of Sociology*, LXXVIII (January 1973): 962–74; Jacob Mincer and Solomon Polachek, "Family Investment in Human Capital and Earnings of Women," *Journal of Political Economy*, LXXXII, Part 2 (March/April 1974): S76–S108; Isabel V. Sawhill, "The Economics of Discrimination Against Women: Some New Findings," *Journal of Human Resources*, VIII (Summer 1973): 383–96.

[25] Robert Smuts, *Women and Work in America* (New York, 1959).

[26] Clearly, men earn more than women. Although it is often said that women hold the larger share of national wealth, some statistics on the value of estates left by men and women would not suggest this. See, for example, U.S. Congress, Joint Economic Committee, *Economic Problems of Women: Hearings*, 93d Cong., 1st sess., 1973, pt. 2, p. 222.

[27] Gary Becker, *The Economics of Discrimination*, 2d ed. (Chicago, 1971).

[28] Victor Fuchs, "Differences in Hourly Earnings Between Men and Women," *Monthly Labor Review*, XCIV (May 1971): 9–15.

[29] *Ibid.*, p. 11.

[30] Barbara Bergmann, "The Effect on White Incomes of Discrimination in Employment," *Journal of Political Economy*, LXXIX (March/April 1971):

294–313. This article focused only on the black–white problem. See Barbara Bergmann, "The Economics of Women's Liberation," *Challenge* (May/June 1973) for a more popular version of her theory applied to men and women.

[31] These expressions were coined by Harriet Zellner in "Discrimination Against Women, Occupational Segregation, and the Relative Wage," *American Economic Review,* LXII (May 1972): 157.

[32] Edmund Phelps, "The Statistical Theory of Racism and Sexism," *American Economic Review,* LXII (September 1972): 659–61. Isabel Sawhill's approach in her article "The Economics of Discrimination Against Women" (see note 24) also fits the lines of Phelps's arguments.

[33] U.S. Department of Labor, Wage and Labor Standards Administration, Women's Bureau, *Facts About Women's Absenteeism and Labor Turnover* (Washington, D.C., 1969).

[34] Harriet Zellner, "Discrimination Against Women, Occupational Segregation, and the Relative Wage," p. 158.

[35] "The Economic Role of Women," in U.S. President, *Economic Report* (1974), pp. 89–112.

[36] U.S. Congress, *Economic Problems of Women: Hearings,* pp. 221–338.

[37] U.S. Department of Labor, Bureau of Labor Statistics, "Marital and Family Characteristics of Workers," *Special Labor Force Reports* (March 1973).

[38] Peter Henle, "The Distribution of Earned Income," *Monthly Labor Review,* XCV (December 1972): 22.

[39] Even before the 1969 Tax Reform Act, the married working couple was penalized through the loss of one optional standard deduction and the reduced probability that their joint income would entitle them to any child-care deductions. Grace Blumberg, "Sexism in the Code: A Comparative Study of Income Taxation of Working Wives and Mothers," *Buffalo Law Review,* XXI (1971): 49–59.

[40] Carolyn Shaw Bell, "Social Security: Society's Last Discrimination," *Business and Society Review* (Autumn 1972): 46–47.

[41] Galbraith, *Economics and the Public Purpose,* p. 33.

Part 1

Female Labor Participation,
Unemployment, and Wage Differentials

2

Participation of Married Women in the Labor Force

T. ALDRICH FINEGAN

THIS CHAPTER presents an overview of the labor force participation of married women in this country during the years since World War II, with special attention to the impact of labor market conditions on wives' participation decisions. Section I enumerates the many factors that have played a role in the growth of the labor force participation rate (LFPR) of married women during the past twenty-five years. Some of the more interesting cross-sectional relationships between wives' participation and their individual and family characteristics are briefly discussed in Section II. Section III describes a set of intercity regressions which is used to explore the effects of labor market conditions on the LFPR of married women. The results for the specific labor market variables—namely, earnings of women, wages of domestic servants, industry mix, supply of women, and unemployment—are discussed in Sections IV through VII. The essay concludes with a brief summary of its findings.

I. The Increase in
Wives' Participation since 1947

The last quarter century has witnessed a remarkable rise in the labor force participation rate (LFPR) [1] of married women in this country. According

I wish to thank the Princeton University Press for permission to reproduce and summarize some of the material presented in *The Economics of Labor Force Participation* (Princeton, N.J., 1969), by William G. Bowen and myself—hereafter cited as Bowen and Finegan. My to data gathered from a national sample of households by the Current Population Survey of the Bureau of the Census, the percentage of all married women (husband present) who were in the labor force (i.e., employed or seeking work) rose from 20 percent in April 1947 to a shade under 42 percent in March 1972. For married women of working age (20–64), the participation rate increased from about 21 percent to 45 percent during the same period. From a different perspective, in 1947 only one out of every nine members of the labor force was a married woman; by 1972 this ratio had exactly doubled. Put still another way, wives accounted for 46 percent of the growth of the civilian labor force during the past quarter century.

Many factors have contributed to the growing LFPR of married women, including (1) the long-run rise in the real hourly wages that women earn in the labor market, providing an incentive for wives to do more work in the labor market and less at home; (2) the development and diffusion of many labor-saving household appliances and products (e.g., refrigerators and frozen foods) and the partial transfer of certain work from the home to the marketplace (e.g., preparing meals, washing clothes, and child care); (3) the shift of population from rural to urban areas, where jobs for women are more abundant and accessible; (4) the rapid expansion (absolute and relative) of employment in professional, clerical, and service occupations (excluding domestic service), which currently account for two-thirds of all employed women, along with (5) the related shift in the industry mix of nonfarm employment from the goods sector to the services sector (including government)—two ongoing trends which have greatly increased the number of jobs open to women; (6) the decline in length of the average workweek of full-time workers, coupled with an increase in the relative number of part-time jobs—making it easier for wives to reconcile work in the labor market with their homemaking responsibilities; [2] (7) a decline during the last decade in the fraction of married women aged 14–54 with children under six years old,[3] coupled with (8) the growing number of children's day-care centers and the rising percentage of children attending kindergarten—trends having much

distinguished coauthor, now the president of Princeton University, deserves much of the credit for the research reported here. I am also indebted to Mr. James Michael Norris of Vanderbilt University for helpful comments. Responsibility for the shortcomings that remain is mine.

the same effect as the shorter workweek; (9) the ever-rising real-income aspirations of American families; and (10) the slow but steady growth in the average educational attainment of married women, which has probably increased somewhat their "taste" for work in the labor market vis-à-vis work at home.

Changes in employment practices and attitudes have, no doubt, also contributed to the rising LFPR of married women, although it is difficult to isolate their role. The "sex labeling" of jobs by employers and other overt forms of discrimination against women in the labor market seem to have diminished somewhat in recent years, owing in part to the passage of the Civil Rights Act of 1964 (which prohibited job discrimination based on race, color, religion, sex, or national origin) and, more recently, to the repeal or invalidation of many state laws restricting or prohibiting the employment of women in certain occupations. There has also been a marked increase in the social acceptability of the "working wife," although this change in attitudes may be more a consequence of rising participation than a cause. Finally, one can only speculate on the extent to which the Women's Liberation Movement may have enhanced the career ambitions of married women during the past few years.

To enumerate the forces propelling higher market participation by married women is, of course, to look at only one side of the ledger. Some forces have tended to *reduce* wives' LFPR during the period from 1947 to 1972, including (1) the long-run rise in real "other family income" (i.e., total family income minus the wife's earnings), enabling the wife and other family members to afford more leisure time, and (2) the rising relative cost of domestic service.[4]

In any event, the forces pushing wives' labor force rates up have obviously been far stronger than the forces pushing them down, and I see no reason to expect a marked change in this situation during the balance of this decade.[5]

II. The Role of Individual and Family Characteristics in Participation Decisions

Let us turn now to a somewhat different question: What factors are important in shaping a wife's decision to take (or look for) a job in the labor market at any given time? Some of these factors fall under the heading of "labor market conditions," and we shall examine their effects later. But certain characteristics of the individual married woman or her family also play a very important role, and we shall consider them here.

The relationships reported below are based on a multiple regression analysis of data in the 1/1000 sample of the 1960 census. In this analysis, the unit of observation is an individual married woman aged 14–54 who resided in an urban area during the census week; the dependent variable is her labor force status during that week ("1" if she was in the labor force, "0" if not), and the explanatory variables comprise sets of "dummy variables"—one set for various levels of other family income (defined below), another for the educational attainment of the wife, still another for her race, and so on.[6]

Other Family Income (OFI)

This variable is defined as total family income in 1959 minus the earnings (if any) of the wife. The higher a family's OFI, the smaller should be the financial need for the wife to work, all other things being equal. Put differently, if the wife's freedom from market work is a "normal good," we would expect high-income families to "buy" more of it than low-income families. And this is what we find. After adjustment for the effects of differences in color, presence of children, schooling, age, and the employment status of the husband, urban wives aged 14–54 with OFI under $4,000 in 1959 had a census-week participation rate of about 45 percent, compared to a participation rate of less than 10 percent for their more affluent counterparts with OFI of $15,000 or more.

Schooling

The 1/1000 sample reveals a powerful positive relationship between the number of years of schooling a wife had completed and the probability of her being in the labor force: the adjusted LFPR [7] rises steadily from about 20 percent for wives with less than five years of schooling to 38 percent for those with a high-school education, to 47 percent for those with a college degree, and finally to 61 percent for those who attended graduate school. There are at least two reasons for this association: (1) more schooling increases the wage a woman can command in the labor market, thus encouraging her to substitute time in paid employment for some of the time she might have spent working at home; (2) more schooling also increases a wife's access to the cleaner, more pleasant, more interesting jobs. Furthermore, years of schooling may be correlated with an underlying taste for market work as against housework and with certain personal qualities (such as intelligence) which enhance a person's value to an employer; and the experience of education—especially higher education—may increase a woman's desire to work with other people.

Children

The presence of young children, especially those of preschool age, greatly increases the amount of work to be done at home; but it also increases the family's need for money income. These two considerations have opposite effects on the wife's probability of labor force participation, but the data from the 1/1000 sample make it clear that the more-work-at-home factor is much stronger, at least when there are children under six years old to be cared for. The adjusted LFPR for urban wives aged 14–54 *with* children under six was 15 percent, compared to a rate of 36 percent for wives whose youngest children were 6–13 and a rate of 55 percent for wives with no children at home under 14 years of age. However, the presence of older children (14–17) in families with children under six does make it a little easier for the wife to hold down a market job, since the older children can provide some help with certain household tasks. Therefore we find that married women with children under six *and* children aged 14–17 had a LFPR of almost 22 percent, whereas the rate for wives with children under six but *no* children aged 14–17 was only 14 percent.[8]

Color

In every year for which data are available, nonwhite married women have had a substantially higher LFPR than white married women, and the absolute size of this differential has been remarkably trendless since 1948, fluctuating at around 11 to 12 percentage points. Data from the 1/1000 sample reaffirm this differential and help to explain it. For urban wives aged 14–54 in that sample, the crude (unadjusted) LFPR was 47.0 percent for blacks (Negroes) versus 34.7 percent for whites. After we adjust for associated differences in wives' schooling and age, other family income, presence of children in specific age intervals, and the employment status of the husband, the color differential shrinks by almost one-half—i.e., from 12.3 points to 6.8.[9] Taking account of the fact that employed black wives worked, on the average about three fewer hours during the census week than their white counterparts closes the gap still further—to about 3.1 percentage points.[10] What can explain this residual?

Glen Cain has suggested three possible explanations that are not mutually exclusive.[11] One is the lesser degree of job discrimination against Negro women than against Negro men, resulting in a considerably higher ratio of wives' earnings to husbands' earnings for blacks than for whites. This difference should encourage a black family to make some substitution of market work by the wife for market work by the husband. A second factor is the much-discussed matriarchal family structure of Negro society, which Cain relates to the greater degree of marital instability in Negro families, and a consequent incentive for Negro wives to maintain close ties to the labor market as partial protection against the risk of being left self-supporting at some future time. The third reason advanced by Cain springs from differences in the typical housing patterns of white and Negro families, with the greater incidence of crowding and doubling-up in Negro households making it easier for black wives to secure "free" child-care services while at work.

The importance of the third reason is underscored by our finding that the difference in adjusted LFPRs between white and Negro married women is much larger in the subset of wives having children under six years old than in the subset with no children under six.

Employment Status of the Husband

Now suppose that we classify married women into three categories: "husband employed," "husband unemployed," and "husband not in the labor force." It seems plausible to expect that women with unemployed husbands will have a higher LFPR than women with husbands who are employed, since the unemployment of a family's prime breadwinner creates a special need for additional family income. This expectation, which is sometimes called the "additional worker hypothesis," is amply borne out by the data from the 1/1000 sample shown below:

	Labor Force Participation Rate	
Urban Wives, Aged 14–54	Unadjusted	Adjusted
Husband employed	35.0	35.6
Husband unemployed	46.4	41.7
Husband not in the labor force	47.6	37.1

The unadjusted participation rates show about an 11-point difference between the two groups in question; controlling for the effects of wives' schooling, age, color, children, and other family income in the preceding year narrows the gap to about 6 points, which is an estimate of the "pure" additional-worker effect during the census week of 1960.

If we divide our sample of married women into two groups, those who had children under six years of age and those who did not, we find a somewhat larger additional worker effect for the former group than for the latter. The difference between the adjusted LFPR for wives with unemployed husbands and the comparable rate for wives whose husbands were employed is about 9 points for the group with pre-school-age children, but only 5 points for women with no children under six.

Several considerations may help to explain this phenomenon. First, a special intrahousehold substitution effect, whereby the unemployed husband performs certain household chores while the wife works, probably operates with greater force in the case of families with preschool children. Second, wives with young children are themselves younger than other wives, and this fact may make it easier for them to find jobs. Finally, the lower average age of wives with young children suggests that their families have less savings to fall back on and hence a greater need for additional income while the chief breadwinner is out of work.[12]

III. Measuring the Effects of Labor Market Conditions on Wives' Participation

Consider the following two facts. First, in the census week of 1960, the LFPR of married women aged 14–54 years old living in the Charlotte (North Carolina) metropolitan area was almost twice as high as the participation rate for wives who lived in the Pittsburgh SMSA (the two rates were 42.7 and 22.4 percent, respectively). Second, the overall LFPR for all women, aged 16 and over, rose by only 1.2 percentage points between 1958 and 1963, compared to a rise of 3.3 points between 1963 and 1968. The explanation for these seemingly unrelated differentials lies, in large measure, in understanding how various kinds of labor market conditions affect the participation decisions of married women. The balance of this chapter seeks to summarize some recent research findings on these relationships.

The labor market facing married women has many dimensions, and we shall concentrate on five of them: (1) *the earnings of women* (measured by the median annual income of all women who worked 50–52 weeks), (2) *the wages of domestic servants* (measured by an estimate of the median annual earnings of "private household workers, living out" who worked 50–52 weeks), (3) *female industry mix* (a measure of the extent to which the industrial structure of the economy is likely to provide jobs for women), (4) *the supply of women* (measured by the percentage of the total civilian population 14 years old and over who were females—a ratio that varies significantly across metropolitan areas but not over time, wartime periods aside), and (5) *the overall unemployment rate* (the percentage of the civilian labor force of both sexes unemployed during the survey or census week). The expected relationship between each of these variables and the participation decisions of married women is explained in conjunction with the empirical findings presented below.

Most of our evidence on the impact of labor market conditions on wives' LFPR is drawn from a set of *intercity regressions* for the census week of 1960,[13] and a brief explanation of these regressions is needed at this point.

The *unit of observation* in these regressions is a Standard Metropolitan Statistical Area (an SMSA, for short), which consists of one or more contiguous counties containing at least one fairly large city and the surrounding suburbs.[14] An SMSA is probably the best empirical approximation to the "local labor market" of economic theory. In 1960 there were exactly 100 SMSAs with a total population of 250,000 or more in the continental United States, and we used all of them in our "intercity" regressions.[15]

The *dependent variable,* whose variation across SMSAs is what we wish to explain, is the LFPR of a particular group of wives within each SMSA during the 1960 census week.[16] In addition to a "basic regression" for all married women aged 14–54, we also ran similar regressions for numerous subsets of wives classified by narrower age intervals or by presence or absence of small children.

The *independent (explanatory) variables* in the intercity regressions consist of the five *labor market measures* introduced above, plus a set of six *control variables* designed to take account of differences among SMSAs in certain important individual and family characteristics that also affect the labor force participation decisions of married women. The six control variables used in these regressions are the median income of husbands, the mean income from nonemployment sources, the median years of school completed by women over 24, the percentage of wives who were nonwhite, the percentage of wives with children under six years old, and a measure of the net migration of women into (or out of) the SMSA between 1955 and 1960.[17]

All of the statistical relationships reported below between participation rates and labor market variables have been estimated by means of ordinary single-equation, least-squares, multiple-regression techniques. This widely used approach is far from trouble-free, but the results for married women in 1960 are quite impressive, judging from the large number of statistically significant relationships with the expected signs. Indeed, differences among metropolitan areas in labor market conditions in the census week of 1960 were more systematically related to intercity differences in the labor force participation rates of married women than to differences in participation rates of any other major population group.

The specific findings on each of our labor market measures will be presented and assessed on a variable-by-variable basis in the following sections. The complete results of the regression for all married women aged 14–54 are assembled in the Appendix Table.[18]

In Section VII of this chapter we also present the results of several attempts to study the *time-series* associations between unemployment and the LFPR of married women, but it seems best to defer a description of those statistical tests until we are ready to discuss their results.

IV. Earnings of Women

How should an increase in the real wages that a married woman can earn in the labor market, all other things being equal, affect the amount of time she chooses to be in the labor force? The orthodox theory of the supply of labor by an individual returns an uncertain answer. According to this theory, a higher market wage generates both a substitution effect and an income effect. The substitution effect induces the individual to work more, since the higher wage has raised the opportunity cost of leisure time. The income effect, on the other hand, encourages the person to work less, since the higher wage means a higher real income with which the person can now afford to "buy" more leisure time (assuming leisure to be a normal good). The actual change in the quantity of labor supplied depends on the relative strength of these two effects, and the net outcome cannot be predicted on a priori grounds.

This theory requires several modification in the case of the labor force participation decisions of married women, and these modifications lead, fortunately, to a more definite answer.[19] First, the work decisions of family members (like most of their larger expenditures) are usually made by the family, not by the individual alone. The income which is relevant to the demands for leisure by a family member is total family income, and a rise in family income may have quite different effects on the amount of leisure consumed by different family members. Consequently, a rise in the wage offer to a particular family member (the wages of other members remaining the same) need not lead to a reduction in his or her own hours of work, even if the income effect does cause a fall in the aggregate number of hours of work supplied by the family as a whole.

Second, the income effect of higher wages offered to a family member operates only insofar as that person is already devoting some time to work in the labor market. In particular, the income effect of a rise in women's earnings will be nil for a married woman whose only work (thus far) has been in the home, but the substitution effect should operate with as much force on her as on a woman already devoting some time to market work. This point carries special weight in the case of married women, whose overall labor force participation rate is still below 50 percent.[20]

The final and most important modification of the orthodox theory of labor needed here is to recognize that a married woman does not allocate her time simply between leisure and work in the labor market, but among leisure, work in the labor market, and work at home.[21] As Mincer has pointed out,

Work at home is still an activity to which women, on the average, devote the larger part of their married life. It is an exclusive occupation of many women, and of a vast majority when young children are present.[22]

Thus a rise in the real wage that a wife can earn in the labor market will generate, in addition to the ordinary income and substitution effects, a special substitution effect which leads her to substitute work in the market for work at home. The strength of this special substitution effect will depend on many factors, including the ease with which certain market goods (e.g., domestic servants, day care facilities, and restaurant meals) can be substituted for certain home goods (e.g., household cleaning, child care, and cooking done by the wife) and the relative prices and quality of the market goods involved. In any event, the special substitution effect greatly increases the probability that higher market earnings will lead to higher labor force participation by married women—even if their *total* hours of work at home and in the labor market should remain unchanged or decline.

These special considerations, taken together, create a rather strong expectation of a positive association across cities between wives' LFPR and the average annual earnings of women, after all other explanatory factors (including husband's income, the wages of domestics, and our other measures of labor market conditions) have been held constant. The results for this variable from the 1960 intercity regressions for married women are shown in Table 2.1, and they provide impressive statistical support for this expectation.

The highly significant regression coefficient of $+0.47$ from the basic regression indicates that a city with full-year women's earnings \$100 above the mean could be expected to have had a participation rate for married women aged 14–54 about half of one percentage point above average. The *elasticity* of participation with respect to earnings in this regression is $+0.44$; in other words, a 1 percent difference in earnings was positively associated, in partial regression, with a 0.44 percent difference in the participation rate. In 1959 there was a very wide range of female earnings levels among SMSAs (from a low of \$2,320 for Johnstown, Pennsylvania, to a high of \$4,150 for Washington, D.C., with a standard deviation of \$400), and this variable clearly plays an important role in explaining intercity differences in the LFPR of married women.

In a very similar regression designed to predict intercity differences in the LFPR of *men* aged 25 to 54, the regression coefficient for the full-year earnings of men, while statistically significant at the 1 percent level, was very much smaller: namely, $+0.06$. The much larger coefficient for women's earnings in our basic regression for married women aged 14 to 54 is what one would expect, given the much greater opportunities that wives have to substitute work in the labor market for work at home.

Let us now look at the pattern of earnings coefficients as revealed by

TABLE 2.1   Effects of Earnings of Women on
Labor Force Participation Rates of Married Women:
Intercity Regressions, Census Week of 1960

	Earnings of Women [a] (Units of $100)	
	Regression coefficient	t-value
I. Basic regression		
all MW 14–54	+0.47	3.46 *
II. Wives classified by presence or absence of children under 6:		
MW 14+, with children under 6	+0.40	3.48 *
MW 14–54, no children under 6	+0.53	3.31 *
III. Wives classified by age:		
14–19	−0.20	0.94
20–24	+0.16	1.05
25–29	+0.56	4.06 *
30–34	+0.63	4.33 *
35–39	+0.75	5.07 *
40–44	+0.61	3.80 *
45–54	+0.69	4.01 *
55–64 [b]	+0.49	3.75 *

SOURCE: Bowen and Finegan, p. 172 and Appendix Table B-24.

NOTE: MW = married women (husband present).

* Significant at the 1 percent level.

[a] Defined as the median income in 1959 of all women in the SMSA who worked 50–52 weeks that year.

[b] Married women in this age group were not included in the basic regression for all wives aged 14–54, but the results of the regression for this subgroup are included for purposes of comparison.

our subset regressions. There is a small difference in the participation-to-earnings sensitivities of wives with and without children under six, the respective regression coefficients being 0.40 and 0.53. The woman without young children probably finds it easier to substitute market work for work in the home, and thus we might expect her labor force status to be more sensitive to variations in earnings opportunities than the labor force status of a woman with young children.

But it is the difference in earnings coefficients among the subgroups classified by *age* which really stand out. There is a "wrong" sign for teenage wives (the coefficient being nonsignificant, however), a "right" sign but another nonsignificant coefficient for the 20–24 age group, and then a string of highly significant positive coefficients for all of the older groups.

Why do intercity differences in women's earnings have no significant effect on the LFPR of wives aged 14–19 and 20–24? One likely answer is quite simple. Most of these women are too young to have had much previous work experience; at the same time, the economic pressures on some of them to find jobs may be very strong, inasmuch as the earnings of their husbands are relatively low. Thus, what matters for this group is the *availability* of appropriate jobs in the local labor market and the ease with which they can be secured, not how much they pay. This interpretation is supported by the fact that the coefficients for unemployment, female industry mix, and the supply of women (discussed in some detail later on) are all larger than average for these two age groups—and especially large for teenage wives.

V. Wages of Domestic Servants

One of the opportunity costs borne by a wife who takes a market job is that she has less time and energy for the manifold duties of running a home. One way of dealing with this problem is to hire someone to do some of the household chores, usually on a part-time basis. This is not, of course, a costless solution, and whether it is better than the alternatives (not taking the market job, trying to do both kinds of work herself, or drafting other family members into domestic service) depends in part on the price of outside help. Therefore, there ought to be an inverse relationship across cities between the "going wage" for domestic servants and the participation rate of married women, all other things being equal.[23]

To test this expectation, Bowen and I included in our married-women regressions a rough estimate of the median full-year earnings in 1959 of "private household workers, living out"—a variable that had to be constructed in a makeshift way.[24] The results are intriguing. The expected negative relationship holds at a high level of significance not only in the basic regression for all married women aged 14–54 but also for both groups classified by presence or absence of children under six and for all but the two youngest subgroups classified according to age. Furthermore, the pattern of coefficients for the subgroups is remarkably similar to the one observed for women's earnings. So far, so good.

However, the *size* of these regression coefficients is puzzling. In the basic regression, for example, the coefficient for full-year wages of domestics (-0.75) is 1.6 times as large as the one for full-year earnings of women ($+0.47$)—both variables being expressed in hundreds of dollars. This implies that a joint rise of $100 in both types of earnings would have led to a *fall* in wives' LFPR of 0.28 points. When one considers that the typical private household worker nowadays works in several different households each week, that many of these workers are employed by wives who are not in the labor force or by persons living alone, and that many working wives do not have any outside domestic help, one is forced to conclude that the regression coefficient for the wages-of-domestics variable, when interpreted in a straightforward way, is simply too large to be believed.[25]

There is, however, another interpretation of the results for this variable that is easier to reconcile with the size of the observed coefficient—namely, that our measure of the cost of domestic service may be serving as an index of the average cost of a whole array of low-wage, labor-intensive services which are purchased more frequently by families with working wives than by similar families in which the wife stays home.[26] The services provided by day-care centers, laundries, dry cleaners, beauty parlors, and restaurants illustrate the kinds of items we have in mind, and middle-income families spent about seven times as much on the above services in 1960–61 as they spent for domestic help.[27] Given the likely overlap between the local labor market for private household workers and the market for the low-wage workers employed by the above establishments, it seems reasonable to suppose that the prices of such services will be relatively high in cities where the wages of domestics are relatively high. Under this hypothesis, the regression coefficient for the wages of domestics, *now reinterpreted as a proxy for the price of all of these services,* is more believable than it first appeared to be.

VI. Industry Mix and the Supply of Women

We turn now to a pair of labor market variables intended to reflect "structural" differences among SMSAs in the relative availability of jobs commonly held by women: (1) *female industry mix,* which is designed to measure the relative abundance in the SMSA of industries which tend to provide jobs for women, and (2) *the supply of women,* which is intended to reflect the potential relative number of female competitors for these jobs. We discuss these variables together because they play complementary roles in the analysis.

The value of the industry-mix variable for each SMSA is best viewed as a *prediction* of the ratio of female employment to total employment in the SMSA, with this prediction based on two sets of data: the all-U.S. ratio of female employment to total employment within two- and three-digit industries, and the distribution of total employment in the SMSA among these industries. Thus, the industry-mix variable shows what the ratio of female employment to total employment in the SMSA would have been in 1960 had this ratio depended solely on the industry mix of the SMSA and the female employment ratio in each industry for the country as a whole.[28]

We expect, of course, to find a positive association between this industry-mix variable and the LFPR of married women. The higher the value of this variable, the more job opportunities there are likely to be for women in the SMSA and the lower the expected "search cost" of finding one of these jobs, all other things (including unemployment) being equal. Besides, the higher the value of this index, the more likely it is that a given investment in job search will turn up a job which has good working conditions and which is not overly demanding of physical effort.

On the other hand, a city with an unusually attractive industry mix, so far as women are concerned, might also have an unusually large female population (relative to the male population), thus increasing the expected search cost of finding suitable work and consequently discouraging some women from looking for work. That is why the second of these two variables is needed. This variable, which we call "the supply of women," is defined simply as the percentage of the total civilian population 14 years old and over who were females. The higher this fraction, all other things (including industry mix) being equal, the greater should be the competition among women for jobs in the SMSA and therefore the lower should be the LFPR of married women living there.

The results of the intercity regressions for both of these measures of local labor market conditions are presented in Table 2.2. The most strik-

TABLE 2.2   Effects of Female Industry Mix
and Supply of Women on Labor Force
Participation Rates of Married Women:
Intercity Regressions, Census Week of 1960

	Industry Mix, Female [a]		Supply of Women [b]	
	(Both variables in percentage points)			
	Regression coefficient	t-value	Regression coefficient	t-value
I. Basic Regression				
all MW 14–54	+0.91	5.87 *	−0.64	2.10 †
II. Wives classified by presence or absence of children under 6:				
MW 14+, with children under 6	+0.54	4.06 *	−0.68	2.75 *
MW 14–54, no children under 6	+1.18	6.20 *	−0.98	2.77 *
III. Wives classified by age:				
14–19	+1.49	7.17 *	−1.40	3.13 *
20–24	+1.26	8.51 *	−0.88	2.80 *
25–29	+0.83	5.20 *	−0.75	2.39 †
30–34	+0.64	3.76 *	−0.50	1.52
35–39	+0.59	3.44 *	−0.49	1.46
40–44	+0.81	4.25 *	−0.47	1.26
45–54	+1.03	5.16 *	−0.45	1.16
55–64	+0.88	5.91 *	−0.66	2.39 †

SOURCE: Bowen and Finegan, Appendix Tables B-10–B-19 and B-24.

NOTE: MW = married women (husband present).

* Significant at the 1 percent level.

† Significant at the 5 percent level.

[a] The predicted ratio of female employment to total employment in the SMSA based on its industry mix; for details, see the text. Certain coefficients for this variable differ somewhat from those shown on p. 176 of Bowen and Finegan, in that the coefficients shown here are taken from regressions in which the supply-of-women variable was always included (whether statistically significant or not), whereas the coefficients on p. 176 of the book are from "second runs" in which only statistically significant variables were retained.

[b] The percentage of the total civilian population 14 years old and over in the SMSA who were females.

ing feature of these results is that every one of the twenty-two regression coefficients has the predicted sign, and each one for the industry mix measure is easily significant at the 1 percent level. Four of the negative coefficients for the female-population variable are not statistically significant at 5 percent, yet all four have *t*-values larger than 1.0—a *pattern* of results which is much less likely to have occurred by chance than the results for each of these subgroups considered separately.

Two other interesting patterns appear. First, we see larger coefficients for both variables in the regressions for women without small children than in the regressions for women with such children—further evidence that labor market conditions exert, in general, a more powerful influence on the former group of wives than on the latter.[29]

Second, the impact of each labor market variable is greatest on the LFPR of very young wives (aged 14–19 and 20–24). This pattern also seems plausible, since the balance between job openings for women and the potential number of female jobseekers in a metropolitan area ought to be of greatest importance to those wives with very little previous work experience and little information about employment opportunities for women in the community. It is interesting, however, that the sensitivity coefficient for female industry mix makes a comeback in the case of older wives, and we think the explanation lies mainly in the greater willingness of these women to return to work (or to continue working) in industries where the work is generally lighter and more pleasant. A secondary reason may be a greater willingness of employers in industries with a relatively large proportion of female workers to rehire older women.

It is also noteworthy that metropolitan areas in 1960 differed to a much greater extent in the femaleness of their industry mixes than in the femaleness of their populations. The coefficient of variation (defined as the ratio of a variable's standard deviation to its mean) was over three times as large for our measure of industrial composition as for the female population ratio, and this may help to explain why the former variable outperforms the latter in our regressions.

Finally, there is an interesting interaction between these two complementary dimensions of local labor markets. As suggested earlier, SMSAs with above-average employment opportunities for women also tend to have above-average female population ratios. The simple correlation between these two variables is +.59, easily significant at the 1 percent level. This finding suggests that women do tend, on balance, to move to—or at least remain in—those metropolitan areas with relatively high fractions of jobs that are open to them. (Another possible interpretation of this association is that firms with relatively large numbers of jobs for women tend to locate in areas with high female population ratios; there may, of course, be some truth in both of these interpretations.) Insofar as migration is involved, it may be the *single* women who do most of the moving.[30] And, as we would expect, they migrate to cities like Washington, D.C., not to cities like Pittsburgh.

VII. Unemployment

Imagine that the American economy slides into a recession. Real GNP falls or at least stops growing for several quarters, and so does total employment. As a consequence the unemployment rate rises. How will these unwelcome events affect the LFPR of married women?

In spite of the numerous research studies addressed to this question during the past decade,[31] a complete and confident answer still eludes us. The picture that has emerged so far is a collage of seemingly conflicting patterns. Several strands of evidence need to be considered.

Let us begin by returning briefly to the findings from the 1/1000 sample of the 1960 census summarized in Section II. There we saw that wives with unemployed husbands were more likely to be in the labor force than wives with employed husbands. This relationship might suggest that the LFPR of married women would rise in recessions and fall during boom periods, along with the unemployment rate of husbands. Such a conclusion, however, would be unwarranted. The association in the 1/1000 sample tells us only that high unemployment causes *some* wives to enter the labor force—this is the "additional-worker effect" discussed earlier. But there is another effect of high unemployment which pulls the other way—namely, the tendency of high unemployment to discourage *other* wives from looking for work simply by making jobs harder to find. The latter tendency is usually called the "discouraged-worker effect." [32] The key issue is which of these two effects is stronger—a question which the data for individual married women in the 1/1000 sample cannot answer, because these data provide no information on the local labor market conditions these women faced. In short, the classification of wives according to the employment status of their husbands picks up the additional worker effect but ignores the discouraged-worker effect. Thus we must look elsewhere for evidence on the relative strength of these two responses.

Results of Intercity Regressions for 1960

One logical place to look is at cross-sectional data for metropolitan areas. These data should allow both effects free play: cities with a high overall unemployment rate have relatively more unemployed husbands *and* offer more discouragement to would-be jobseekers than do cities where unemployment is low. Thus our intercity regressions provide a setting for what would seem to be a fair test of the relative strength of these two opposing forces. If the additional-worker effect is stronger, the net relationship between the LFPR of married women and the overall unemployment rate in the SMSA should be positive; if the discouragement effect prevails, the relationship should be negative; and a "draw" should manifest itself as no significant association at all.

The results of this analysis, which are presented in Table 2.3, leave not the slightest doubt as to the winner—at least within this setting. In the basic regression for wives aged 14–54 and in every one of the ten subgroup regressions, the net coefficient for unemployment is negative and significant at the 1 percent level. The coefficient of -0.94 in the overall regression signifies that a metropolitan area with an unemployment rate one percentage point above average in the census week of 1960 could be expected to have had an LFPR for its married women aged 14–54 which was nearly one whole percentage point below the all-SMSA average. In sum, this experiment suggests that married women in 1960 were, on balance, much more responsive to the discouragement effect of higher unemployment than to the additional-worker effect. Furthermore, similar intercity regressions for all married women based on data from the 1950 and 1940 censuses yielded similar results, although the regression coefficients for unemployment were somewhat smaller in those years.[33]

The contour of results for our various subgroups of married women in 1960 seems quite consistent with our earlier results, especially the much smaller sensitivity coefficient for wives with children of preschool age. Part of the explanation for this result lies in the larger additional-worker effect for these women, as reported in Section II. But of greater impor-

TABLE 2.3   Effects of Unemployment on
Labor Force Participation Rates of
Married Women: Intercity Regressions,
Census Week of 1960

	Unemployment Rate [a] (percentage points)	
	Regression coefficient	t-value
I. Basic regression		
all MW 14–54	−0.94	4.71 *
II. Wives classified by presence or absence of children under 6:		
MW 14+, with children under 6	−0.51	2.98 *
MW 14–54, no children under 6	−1.37	6.19 *
III. Wives classified by age:		
14–19	−1.48	5.62 *
20–24	−1.01	5.16 *
25–29	−0.97	4.79 *
30–34	−0.81	3.79 *
35–39	−1.08	5.04 *
40–44	−1.07	4.53 *
45–54	−1.12	4.55 *
55–64	−0.93	4.93 *

SOURCE: Bowen and Finegan, p. 180 and Appendix Table B-24.

NOTE: MW = married women (husband present).

* Significant at the 1 percent level.

[a] The percentage of the civilian labor force of both sexes in the SMSA unemployed during the census of 1960.

tance, in all likelihood, is the fact that a smaller fraction of these women are "flexible" with regard to their labor force status. They clearly have a much stronger preference for staying home (as their relatively low LFPR makes clear),[34] and many of those who work anyway do so either because of economic necessity (low family income relative to family needs) or out of a combination of strong career interests and relatively high earnings (as in the case of many professional women). That means relatively few of these wives (compared to those without small children) base their participation decisions on the state of the labor market. In short, the net inverse relationship is smaller for wives with small children because of two reinforcing tendencies: the additional-worker effect is larger and the discouraged-worker effect is smaller.

Why does the discouragement effect of higher unemployment overpower the additional-worker effect? There is an intuitively appealing answer. Think of two metropolitan areas, A and B, which are alike in all relevant respects except that the unemployment rate is 6 percent in A and 4 percent in B. This two-point differential in the overall unemployment rate is likely to be reflected in a roughly similar difference in the unemployment rate for husbands in these two cities. That, in turn, means that the fraction of wives who are *candidates* for additional workers is about 2 percentage points higher in A than in B. However, not every wife whose husband loses his job will enter the labor force! On the contrary, the data in the 1/1000 sample suggest that wives with unemployed husbands in 1960 had an LFPR only about 6 percentage points higher than wives with employed husbands. Thus the fraction of wives who *actually are* additional-worker members of the labor force should be only about 6/100 of 2 percentage points higher in city A than in city B.[35] At the same time, the 2-point difference in the overall unemployment rate will adversely affect the perceived job opportunities of an immensely larger group of wives *whose husbands are employed.* Thus the triumph of the discouraged-worker effect over the added-worker effect is no doubt due mainly to the marked difference in the *number* of wives who are potential members of the two categories.

Analysis of Time-Series Data

A second logical source of information on the relative strength of these two effects is the *time-series data* on the labor force—data gathered each month by the Bureau of the Census from a nationwide sample of households. This is the survey from which the monthly figures on total employment and unemployment are derived, and labor force participation rates by age, sex, and color are also obtained from this source. Unfortunately, we do not have monthly time-series data going back very far on the LFPR of *married* women; but an analysis of such data for *all* women aged 20–64 years old should be an acceptable substitute, since the great majority of these women are married. So the question is this: after the upward trend in women's labor force participation in the period since World War II has been accounted for, what net association do we observe between their LFPR and the national unemployment rate?

To find out, we regressed quarterly averages of the seasonally adjusted LFPR for all women, classified by age, on quarterly averages of the unemployment rate and the ratio of manufacturing employment to total employment (both seasonally adjusted and lagged one quarter); the latter variable serves as an *inverse* measure of the relative abundance of the kinds of jobs open to married women and other secondary-labor-force groups. We also included as controls a pair of time-trend variables. Separate regressions were run for two largely overlapping periods: 1949 (II) (i.e., the second quarter of 1949) to 1965 (III), and 1954 (IV) to 1965 (III). From these regressions we estimated the absolute change in each group's LFPR associated with a one-percentage-point change in the overall unemployment rate *and* the associated cyclical change in the manufacturing-employment ratio, after adjusting for trends.[36] The adjusted regression coefficients for unemployment from these time-series regressions are presented in Table 2.4. For ease of comparison, we also show in this table the weighted averages of the regression coefficients for unemployment constructed from our 1960 *intercity* regressions for various subgroups of women classified according to age and marital status.[37]

One obvious conclusion to be drawn from this table is that the results from time-series analysis are highly sensitive to the particular period analyzed. (To make matters worse, they are also highly sensitive to the choice of explanatory variables and the way one controls for trends.) Thus we see that dropping the early years of the postwar period from the analysis changes the sign of the regression coefficients for women aged 45–54 and 55–64 from positive to negative; it also increases the size of the negative coefficients for women aged 25–34 and 35–44. This comparison suggests that the discouragement effect of high unemployment has grown stronger, relative to the additional-worker effect, during the years since World War II, especially in the case of older women.

But even if we confine our attention to the time-series results for 1954 (IV) to 1965 (III), a period whose midpoint is fairly close to the census week of 1960, there is no escaping the conclusion that the regression coefficients for unemployment from the time-series analysis are much smaller than those from the intercity regressions.[38] For example, the time-series regression for women aged 35–44 during the period from 1954 to 1965 indicates that a one-point rise in the unemployment rate was associated (on the average) with a decline of only one-fourth of a point in this group's LFPR (after controlling for its upward trend); whereas the

TABLE 2.4   Estimates of the Effects of
Unemployment on the LFPR of All Women Aged 20–64
Based on Time-Series Regressions for the
Postwar Period and Intercity Regressions
for the Census Week of 1960

	Regression Coefficients for Unemployment [a]		
All Females,	*Time-series regressions*		*Intercity regressions*
by Age	*1949 (II) to 1965 (III)*	*1954 (IV) to 1965 (I)*	*1960*
20–24	nil [b]	nil [b]	−0.67
25–34	−0.18	−0.25	−0.84
35–44	−0.15	−0.25	−1.00
45–54	0.21	−0.18	−1.01
55–64	0.13	−0.41	−0.87

SOURCE: Bowen and Finegan, Table 16–1, p. 513.

[a] Coefficients from the time-series regressions show the *joint effect* of a one-percentage-point change in the overall unemployment rate and the associated change in the ratio of manufacturing employment to total employment (where this variable is statistically significant) on the LFPR of the subject group over the indicated period, after controlling for trends. Standard errors are not available for these adjusted coefficients; hence we do not know their statistical significance.

The coefficients from the intercity regressions are weighted averages of the net regression coefficients for unemployment from regressions for several marital subgroups of women. Standard errors are not available for these sensitivity estimates either, but most subgroup coefficients were significant at the 1 percent level.

[b] No adjusted regression coefficient is shown for this group because neither the unemployment rate nor the manufacturing-employment ratio was statistically significant at the 10 percent level in the first run.

1960 intercity regressions show a net association between unemployment and this group's labor force participation which is *four times* as large. Why should this be?

The most plausible explanation advanced thus far involves the process by which changes in labor market conditions come to affect individual participation decisions. Just as we expect a rise in the relative price of a consumer good to result in a larger decrease in the quantity of it demanded in the long run than in the short run, so too a given rise in unemployment ought to have a larger discouraging effect on women's labor force participation in the long run than in the short. In both cases, it simply takes time for people to adjust their market decisions to new information concerning costs. According to this explanation, *quarterly time-*

series data pick up mainly the short-run effects of changes in unemployment, whereas the intercity data show mainly the long-run adjustment to different levels of unemployment. [39]

If this explanation is correct, a prolonged change in labor market conditions ought to have a greater impact on women's labor force participation than the short-run changes picked up by our quarterly time-series regressions. How can we test this implication?

A very simple test is to compare the *rate of growth* of women's labor force participation during several subperiods of the past quarter century in which the average level of unemployment has been quite different. Let $\overline{\Delta L}$ be the average absolute year-to-year *increase* in a weighted average of LFPRs for women 20–64 years old during period t, [40] and let $\overline{U}$ be the average rate of unemployment in the economy during the same period. Dividing the years since 1947 into six periods, we obtain the following results:

Period	$\overline{U}$	$\overline{\Delta L}$
1947–52	4.2	0.85
1953–57	4.2	0.83
1958–61	6.1	0.44
1962–65	5.2	0.65
1966–69	3.7	0.98
1970–72	5.5	0.37
1947–72	4.7	0.68

First a word about the characteristics of the particular periods used in this test. Admittedly, this selection is somewhat arbitrary. [41] Each of the first two periods (1947–52 and 1953–57) was characterized by tight labor markets and low levels of unemployment, except for one fairly short recession in each period (in 1949 and 1954, respectively). The interval from 1958 to 1961 began and ended with a recession, and there was only a partial recovery in the two intervening years; unquestionably this was the most depressed period of the six. The years from 1962 to 1965 saw a large rise in employment and a fall in unemployment during the final two years, but there was considerable idle capacity and an excess supply of labor until mid-1965. The years 1966 to 1969 were characterized by increasingly tight labor markets as the economy responded to excess aggregate demand brought on by events related to the Vietnam War. Finally the economy slid into a mild recession in 1970, from which it made a weak recovery in 1971 and a much stronger one in 1972, with unemployment declining to about 5 percent by the end of the latter year.

A glance at the above tabulation leaves no doubt at all that the LFPR of women grew at a markedly faster rate during the three periods of low unemployment (1947–52, 1953–57, and 1966–69) than it did during the three intervals of high unemployment (1958–61, 1962–65, and 1970–72). Furthermore, if we put aside the most recent period (the shortest of the six and hence the most vulnerable to special factors affecting $\Delta \bar{L}$), there is a *perfect inverse rank correlation* between $\Delta \bar{L}$ and $\bar{U}$ among the five remaining periods. This is not to say that unemployment was the sole determinant of the rate of growth of women's labor force participation during the past quarter century; but it does appear to have been a very important influence.

Unfortunately, there is no direct way of comparing the latter findings, which deal with *changes* in the LFPR of women, with our earlier regressions explaining *levels* of participation. But if higher unemployment can cause a marked slowdown in the growth of women's labor force participation over a three-to-five-year period, then the *cumulative* effects of a long period of high unemployment on the *level* of women's labor force participation are obviously much greater than the quarterly time-series regressions would lead us to expect. To put this point another way, quarterly changes in the unemployment rate appear to have only a minor effect on women's LFPR, after accounting for the actual upward trend in their labor force participation; but *prolonged changes in the unemployment rate appear to have a significant impact on this trend itself*. Hence it is not possible to control for this trend and capture the long-run effects of unemployment on women's participation at the same time.

By the same token, the results of the $\Delta \bar{L}$ experiments also suggest that our intercity regressions do not greatly overstate the long-run, economy-wide impact on women's LFPR of a *prolonged* change in the level of unemployment.[42]

Conclusion

Now we are in a better position to hazard an answer to the question posed at the beginning of this section—namely, how is a recession likely to affect the labor force participation of married women? The answer seems to turn on how long the period of higher unemployment lasts. If the economy returns to full employment within a year or so (as happened after the recessions of 1949 and 1954), the net discouragement effect of high unemployment is likely to be small, as the quarterly time-series data suggest. But if the period of high unemployment lingers on for three years or more (as it did following the 1958 and 1961 recessions), then the discouragement effect is likely to be much larger, and the growth in women's labor force participation will be retarded until labor market conditions improve.

VIII. Summary

The rising labor force participation rate of married women is one of the most interesting long-run trends in the American economy. The more important reasons for this trend include the growth in the real wages of women, the development of labor-saving innovations in the home, shifts in the occupational and industrial composition of employment, the shorter workweek, the falling birthrate (since 1960), the earlier school enrollment of children, and the rising educational attainment of married women.

A wife's individual and family characteristics play an important role in determining her labor force status. Data from the 1/1000 sample of the 1960 census of population indicate that a married woman is more likely to be in the labor force the lower her husband's income and the more formal schooling she has had (all other things being equal). The presence of preschool-age children greatly deters her labor force participation, whereas the presence of an unemployed husband tends to encourage it (but not very much). Black married women have a somewhat higher participation rate than white, even after associated differences in the foregoing characteristics have been adjusted for.

Labor market conditions also matter. Inter-SMSA regressions indicate that high female wages and an industry mix that provides many jobs for women both serve to increase the percentage of married women in the labor force, whereas a high cost of domestic service (and related labor-intensive services) and a high female population ratio both serve to reduce it. A high overall unemployment rate also discourages married women from participating in the labor force, but time-series data suggest that the strength of this effect largely depends on how long high unemployment lasts.

APPENDIX TABLE   Multiple Regression Equation
Used to Explain Intercity Differences
in Labor Force Participation Rates
of Married Women (husband present), Aged 14–54,
Census Week of 1960

Independent Variables	b	(s)	t
Unemployment (%)	−0.94	(0.20)	4.71 *
Income of husbands ($100/yr.)	−0.20	(0.10)	1.97
Earnings of females ($100/yr.)	0.47	(0.14)	3.46 *
Other income ($100/yr.)	−1.40	(0.53)	2.65 *
Schooling (yrs.)	0.73	(0.41)	1.78
Wages of domestics ($100/yr.)	−0.75	(0.25)	3.04 *
Industry mix, female (#)	0.91	(0.16)	5.87 *
Supply of females (%)	−0.64	(0.30)	2.10 †
Color (% nonwhite)	0.08	(0.04)	1.89
Children under 6 (%)	−0.55	(0.11)	4.96 *
Migration (#)	0.12	(0.06)	2.05 †

Other Data

Dependent Variable $L_{MW14-54}$.	
Mean	34.1
Standard Deviation	4.1
Constant Term	61.3
Standard Error of Estimate	2.4
Number of Observations	100
R^2	0.69

NOTE: Units of measurement are shown in parentheses following variables.

# means that the unit cannot be abbreviated readily (see definitions of variables below).
b = Net (partial) regression coefficient.
(s) = Standard error of the regression coefficient.
t = t-value of the regression coefficient (b/s); t-value may differ from b/s ratios in table owing to rounding.

* Significant at the 1 percent level.
† Significant at the 5 percent level.

DEFINITION OF VARIABLES:
   $L_{MW14-54}$: percentage of all married women, husband present, aged 14–54, in the total population, who were in the labor force during the Census Week.
   Unemployment: percentage of the civilian labor force unemployed during the Census Week.
   Income of Husbands: median income in 1959 of all men married with wife present.
   Earnings of Females: median income in 1959 of all females who worked 50–52 weeks that year.

Other Income: mean income from nonemployment sources in 1959 per recipient of *any kind* of income.

Schooling: median years of school completed by all females aged 25 years and older.

Wages of Domestics: estimate of average annual earnings of domestics obtained by calculating median weekly earnings in 1959 of female private household workers (living out) and multiplying this figure by 52.

Industry Mix, Female: a measure of the percentage of jobs in each SMSA which we might expect to be held by women; based on the industry mix of the SMSA.

Supply of Females: percentage of the total civilian population aged 14 years and older who were females.

Color: percentage of all married women who were nonwhite.

Children under 6: percentage of married couples with one child or more under 6 years of age.

Migration: net migration (+ = in, − = out) between 1955 and the 1960 Census Week of all females aged 30 to 54 years, divided by the total population of that group in the 1960 Census Week. (Members and former members of the armed forces and inmates of institutions are included in both numerator and denominator.)

NOTES

¹ According to current official definitions, the labor force consists of persons who were *employed* or *unemployed* during the survey week. The *employed* consist of those persons who worked at least one hour for pay or profit or at least fifteen hours in a family business or on a family farm during the survey week, plus those with a job but not at work during that week because of vacation, illness, bad weather, a labor–management dispute, or personal reasons. The *unemployed* comprise those persons who actively looked for work during the preceding four weeks, those on layoff from their present jobs, and those waiting to start a new job within the next thirty days. A group's *labor force participation rate* is simply the percentage of that group that was in the labor force during the survey week. For further information on labor force definitions and data, see the Technical Note in the back of any recent issue of *Employment and Earnings* (published monthly by the Bureau of Labor Statistics, U.S. Department of Labor).

² A full-time worker is defined as one who worked 35 hours or more in the labor market during the survey week; part-time workers put in fewer than 35 hours. The Current Population Survey indicates that 72 percent of all employed wives worked full-time in 1972, while 28 percent worked only part-time. The average (mean) workweek was 40.4 hours for wives on full-time schedules, 19.4 hours for those working part-time, and 34.5 hours for all working wives. Comparable data for married women are not available for the late 1940s or early 1950s, but the average workweek of all employed women 25–64 years old fell from about 39 hours in 1950 to 35.5 hours in 1972, while the fraction of these women working part-time rose from about 20 percent to 25 percent.

³ As a consequence of the postwar "baby boom," this fraction increased from about 40 percent in 1948 to about 42 percent in 1960. But more recently, in response to a declining birthrate, the relative number of married women under 55 with pre-school-age children has been falling, so that by 1972 this fraction stood at only 35 percent. A decrease in this ratio tends to increase the overall LFPR of married women because wives with very young children have a much lower participation rate than other wives of the same age—a point documented later in this section.

[4] According to the Department of Commerce, the average cost of domestic service rose by 137 percent from 1947 to 1970, compared with a 74 percent rise in the overall Consumer Price Index. However, the adverse effect on wives' LFPR of the rising relative cost of domestic service has been at least partly offset by a declining relative price of household appliances (goods of a labor-saving nature): the price index for the latter commodities rose by only 11 percent from 1947 to 1970.

[5] For a more detailed analysis of the rise in the LFPR of married women, including an heroic effort to estimate the quantitative contributions of many of the foregoing factors to this rise, see chapter 7 of Bowen and Finegan.

[6] A dummy variable takes only the values of one or zero. For example, our set of dummy variables for the educational attainment of the wife includes one variable for 0–4 years of school completed, another for 5–7 years, still another for 8 years, and so on. A dummy variable is assigned the value of 1 if the individual wife falls in that particular category and 0 if she does not. The categories are always defined in such a way that each individual can be placed in only one category. For further details, see Appendix A of Bowen and Finegan.

[7] As indicated above, the adjusted participation rates for wives classified by a given socioeconomic variable (such as years of school completed) indicate the partial association between their labor force participation and different categories of that characteristic after the effects of other variables in the regression have been held constant.

[8] The probability that a wife with children of preschool age will be in the labor force also rises with the age of her youngest child. See Bowen and Finegan, pp. 102–3.

[9] The adjusted participation rates are 42.0 for Negroes, 35.2 for whites. These two rates purport to show what the LFPRs of white and black wives would have been if each group had been the same (i.e., at the national average) with respect to other family income, schooling, age, children, and husband's employment status. The compression of this differential is due mainly to the fact that black wives are heavily concentrated at the lower end of the other-family-income distribution.

[10] The latter figure is the difference between the adjusted participation rates for black and white married women expressed in terms of "full-time-equivalent participants" per week.

[11] See Glen Cain, *Married Women in the Labor Force* (Chicago, 1966), pp. 83, 85–89, and 101 ff. Cain considers each of these explanations in some detail, and the discussion that follows is nothing more than a brief summary of the hypotheses he advances and supports.

[12] Jacob Mincer was the first to point out that the added-worker response is an alternative to dissaving by the household, and that transitory reductions in OFI should give rise to larger added-worker effects than permanent differences. See his pathbreaking paper, "Labor Force Participation of Married Women," in Universities-National Bureau Committee for Economic Research, *Aspects of Labor Economics* (Princeton, N.J., 1962), pp. 63–97.

[13] The results of these regressions are explained in more detail in chapter 6 of Bowen and Finegan. We also ran comparable regressions for the census weeks of 1950 and 1940, which produced findings generally similar (in the case of all married women) to those presented here. It would be instructive to have the results of a similar set of regressions for the census week of 1970, but the complete data needed have only recently been published by the Bureau of the Census.

[14] For the exact (and exhausting) official definition, see U.S. Census, 1960, Final Report PC(1)-1D, pp. ix–x.

[15] We use the terms "city" and "intercity" as shorthand substitutes for "SMSA" and "inter-SMSA," respectively.

[16] As suggested earlier, there was considerable variation across SMSAs in the LFPR of married women in 1960. In the case of all wives aged 14–54, the mean LFPR was 34.1 percent and the standard deviation 4.1 percent.

[17] The two income variables, taken together, are viewed as a fairly good substitute for other family income (OFI), for which data by SMSA are not available. The migration variable is needed to control for the likelihood that women with a strong attachment to the labor force will be overrepresented among women who have recently migrated to a city (relative to the female population as a whole). As Mincer puts it, "migration to better job opportunities is an alternative to dropping out of the labor force. . . ." (See his widely quoted review article, "Labor Force Participation and Unemployment: A Review of Recent Evidence," in Robert A. Gordon and Margaret S. Gordon, eds., *Prosperity and Unemployment* (New York, 1966), pp. 79–81.) It is true that in some cases the decision of a family to move from one city to another is really made by the company that employs the *husband,* and in other cases the husband's prospects for finding a job (or a better job) is the sole consideration. But it seems likely that the employment prospects of the wife are taken into account in a good many migration decisions. Thus we would expect to find a higher LFPR of married women in cities which gained population because of migration between 1955 and 1960 than in cities experiencing a net outward migration, and that is exactly what our intercity regressions show. (See the Appendix Table.)

[18] Space does not permit presentation of the complete results of the subgroup regressions for married women in this chapter. These results may be found in Bowen and Finegan, Appendix Tables B-11–B-19 and B-24.

[19] For a precise and comprehensive statement of the theory of choice applicable to the participation decisions of married women, see Jacob Mincer, "Labor Force Participation of Married Women," pp. 63–68.

[20] It is, however, a mistake to interpret the labor force participation rate for married women to mean that a certain fraction of these women are in the labor force all year while the rest of them are outside it all year. There is a good deal of turnover among the wives who hold market jobs. For example, while 23 million married women held a market job at some time during 1970, only 17.5 million were employed during the survey week in March of that year.

[21] For the record, two other possible uses of a married woman's time should be mentioned: additional formal education, and unpaid work for a wide variety of civic, political, charitable, and religious organizations. Neither the wife who is enrolled in school nor the one who is engaged in volunteer work is counted as being in the labor force (on that account), but both types of activity clearly enhance economic welfare in a larger context—as does work in the home.

[22] Mincer, "Labor Force Participation of Married Women," p. 65. While Mincer's statement, made in 1961, still holds true, it is interesting to see that the largest *relative* increase in labor force participation during the last twenty-five years has occurred among married women *with* children under six years old—the rate for this subgroup having risen from 11 percent in April 1948 to 30 percent in March 1972. (The LFPR for wives with children aged 6–17, but with none under six, rose from 26 to 50 percent over the same period.)

[23] The latter prediction requires two caveats. First, it is implicitly assumed that intercity variations in the wages of domestic help are not due mainly to differences in the *demand* for such help by working wives: in that case, a *positive* relationship between these wages and wives' LFPR might well appear. A more important qualification to our basic expectation (i.e., a negative association between wives' participation rate and the wages of private household workers) is that it cannot be applied to blacks and other disadvantaged minority groups, since domestic service is an important (albeit diminishing) source of employment for women in these groups.

[24] The values of this variable had to be estimated from two statistics for each SMSA: (1) Y, the median earnings in 1959 of all females in this occupation who were in the labor force during the census week and who received *some earnings* that year; (2) f, the fraction of women in this occupation with some earnings in 1959 who worked 50–52 weeks that year. Letting E stand for our estimate of full-year earnings of these women, we used the formula

$$E = 52\left[\frac{Y}{f(51) + (1-f)(28)}\right],$$

which reflects the admittedly arbitrary assumption that the mean number of weeks worked by those domestics who worked fewer than 50 weeks in 1959 was 28 weeks in every SMSA. (The actual all-U.S. average was 27 weeks, but the true figure undoubtedly varied to some extent across SMSAs.)

[25] The same "credibility gap" applies, of course, to the coefficients for this variable in the subgroup regressions, and that is why I do not present those coefficients here. (They can be found in Bowen and Finegan, p. 167.)

[26] We are indebted to Professor Albert Rees of Princeton University for suggesting this interpretation.

[27] This conclusion is based on data in the Bureau of Labor Statistics, *Survey of Consumer Expenditures* for 1960–61, Supplement 3, Part B, Table 30C.

[28] It would not have been legitimate, in constructing this explanatory variable, to use the *actual* ratio of female employment to total employment in each SMSA, since the actual ratio will depend, in part, on the LFPR of married women in the city, which is what we are attempting to explain. For a detailed account of the construction of this variable, see Bowen and Finegan, pp. 772–76.

[29] The reader may be wondering how it is possible for the supply variable's regression coefficient to be larger in both of these two subgroups than in the basic regression for all women aged 14–54. The explanation is twofold. First, we had to use a different control variable for children in the two subgroup regressions (namely, the average number of children under 18 years old per married couple with one or more children) from the one used in the basic regression (namely, the percentage of married couples with children under six). Second, interactions among the other variables, the presence of children under six, and the LFPR of married women could generate higher labor-supply coefficients for the two subgroups than for the basic group, even if identical sets of explanatory variables had been used in each regression.

[30] However, a number of the SMSAs with high female population ratios have large military establishments (San Diego and Norfolk-Portsmouth are examples). This is not surprising when we remember that men in the Armed Forces are excluded from the denominator of our female population ratio, whereas their civilian wives are included in the numerator (if they live in an SMSA). This fact suggests that the migration of servicemen and their wives may account for a good portion of the intercity differences in our supply-of-women variable.

[31] For a critical review of these studies, see Mincer's essay, "Labor Force Participation and Unemployment" in Gordon and Gordon, *Prosperity and Unemployment* (see note 17), and Bowen and Finegan, pp. 609–26.

[32] This terminology is somewhat misleading, because it suggests that persons must actually experience a period of unemployment before they become discouraged about the prospects of finding a job. There is no reason why this need be the case. Just as persons act on the basis of their expectations concerning wages and other conditions of employment, they may decide not to look for work at all simply on the basis of their expectations as to the probability of finding a satisfactory job in a reasonable period of time.

[33] See the "comparability regressions" on pp. 190–96 of Bowen and Finegan.

[34] In the 1960 census week, the overall LFPR for married women (aged 14–54) in urban areas with children under six was roughly 19 percent, compared to a rate of 47 percent for urban wives without small children.

[35] For reasons explained in Bowen and Finegan, pp. 183–85, data from the 1/1000 sample probably underestimate somewhat the size of the additional-worker effect associated with *intercity* differences in unemployment, but a correction of this understatement (which would raise the fraction cited in the text to perhaps 18/100 of 2 percentage points) would not alter the general argument presented in this paragraph.

[36] The rationale for this particular regression model as well as its limitations are discussed at length in chapter 16 of Bowen and Finegan.

[37] Only the intercity regressions for married women were reported earlier in this essay, but we also made similar tests for other marital categories (such as divorced women, widowed women, and never-married women). The results of the latter regressions are discussed in chapters 8 and 10 of Bowen and Finegan.

To save space, only the *adjusted* regression coefficients for unemployment from the time-series regressions are shown in Table 2.4. The complete results of these regressions appear in Appendix Tables D-2 and D-4 of Bowen and Finegan.

[38] For another study of the time-series data that reaches the same conclusion, see Peter S. Barth, "Unemployment and Labor Force Participation," *Southern Economic Journal*, XXXIV (January 1968): 375–82.

[39] Jacob Mincer was the first person to suggest this interpretation; he has also provided some supporting evidence by showing that there is a high positive correlation between unemployment rates in the same local labor markets in widely separated years. See his "Labor Force Participation and Unemployment," in Gordon and Gordon, *Prosperity and Unemployment,* pp. 79–81.

[40] The weighted average used here is based on annual average LFPRs for all women aged 20–24, 25–34, 35–44, 45–54, and 55–64, with each groups's LFPR in each year weighted by its population in 1960. The use of a weighted average controls for movements in the overall (unweighted) LFPR due to changes over time in the relative number of women in different age categories.

[41] In selecting these intervals I have avoided using any year as both the end of one period and the beginning of another. This procedure increases the economic homogeneity of each period and minimizes the distortions in $\Delta \bar{L}$ that might result from unusual events in a particular year. Also, two of the breaks (those between 1952 and 1953 and between 1961 and 1962) happily coincide with changes in the Current Population Survey that caused minor losses of historical comparability.

[42] Additional support for this interpretation of the intercity regressions is presented in chapter 17 of Bowen and Finegan. There we estimate the amount of "induced participation" caused by the economic recovery and boom of 1963–67, where "induced participation" is defined as the *difference* between the *actual* change in the size of the total labor force during this period and the *projected* change based on an extrapolation of trends in group-specific labor force participation rates during the preceding period of high unemployment—specifically, the period from 1959 (I) to 1963 (IV). The estimate of induced participation for the entire expansion of 1963 to 1967 comes to 1.6 million persons (one million females and 600,000 males), whereas the unemployment coefficients from the 1960 intercity regressions would have predicted an induced expansion of the labor force of roughly 1.9 million persons (1,040,000 females and 850,000 males) during this period.

3

Geographic Immobility and Labor Force Mobility: A Study of Female Unemployment

BETH NIEMI

WOMEN ARE SUBJECT to more unemployment than men. The female unemployment rate has been consistently higher than the male rate over the past twenty-five years, and the gap has somewhat widened recently. An understanding of these unemployment patterns and trends is a necessary component of a more complete picture of women's economic role and the division of labor by sex.

Although this gap between the unemployment rates of men and women has been obvious for many years, it has only recently received much attention. The sharp rise in unemployment in 1970–71 made unemployment rates, including those of women, a focus of interest and controversy. Unfortunately, some of the resulting discussion of the high unemployment rate of women has not been particularly enlightening. There has been a regrettable tendency to dismiss female unemployment as somehow less important than male unemployment. Various attempts have been made to minimize the seriousness of the high level of unemployment in recent years by drawing attention to the changing composition of the labor force, specifically the growing proportions of women and young people among the unemployed.

The current trouble is laid mainly to changes in the makeup of the nation's labor force. More and more teenagers and women have been taking jobs or seeking them, and experts . . . have found these groups more vulnerable to unemployment than adult men even in good times. . . . These two groups are described as being "loosely attached" to the labor force for such reasons as inexperience and less need to be breadwinners than most adult men. Both groups typically have much higher jobless rates than adult males even in good times.[1]

It is true that women constitute an increasing fraction of the total labor force. It is also the case that the female unemployment rate is less closely tied to the ups and downs of the business cycle than the male unemployment rate. However, to say that much of female unemployment is not cyclical is not the same thing as saying that it is not a serious problem. The observation that the unemployment rate of adult men has not shown any upward trend should not lead us to the conclusion that the aggregate unemployment rate "has increasingly become a misleading measure of economic distress." [2] This line of reasoning has led to the following policy recommendations with respect to unemployment among women:

> George Hagedon, vice president and chief economist of the National Association of Manufacturers, urges the administration not to base policy on the "purely mythical" goal of 4% [aggregate unemployment rate]. And Thomas F. Johnson, research director of the American Enterprise Institute, suggests that the White House should instead shoot for subtotal targets such as 3.2% for adult men and perhaps *6% to 8% for women.*[3] (Italics added.)

Such blatantly prejudiced policy proposals have not gone unprotested. The contention that unemployment among women is far less serious than among men has been challenged by some economists, who have emphasized the important contribution of working women to both the level of national income and the standard of living of individual families.[4]

Obviously, female unemployment is more in the limelight today than in the past, and it is of crucial importance at this point to understand why women have a higher rate of unemployment than men. This is especially true in view of the distressing fact that this unemployment gap continues to widen. Most of the attention given to economic inequality between the sexes has concentrated on wage differentials—the question of why women earn substantially less than men. A complete understanding of the economic disadvantages to which women are subject requires that equally careful attention be given to the sex differential in unemployment rates.

Patterns and Causes of Unemployment among Women

Figures 3.1–4 provide a summary of the post–World War II unemployment patterns for men and women. The male and female unemployment

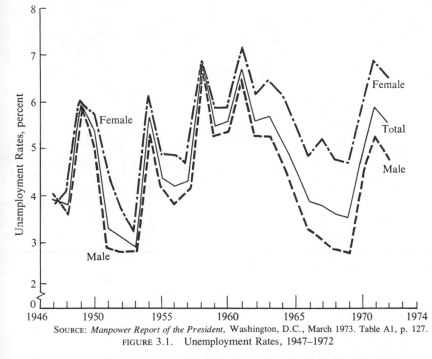

SOURCE: *Manpower Report of the President,* Washington, D.C., March 1973. Table A1, p. 127.

FIGURE 3.1.   Unemployment Rates, 1947–1972

rates have followed the same general cyclical pattern, but the difference between them has narrowed during recessions. That is, the female unemployment rate is consistently higher but exhibits a lesser amplitude of cyclical fluctuation than the male rate. This relationship between the two unemployment rates has also held for three major subgroup classifications—men and women aged 25 and over, married men and women, and white men and women. Recently the gap between the female and male unemployment rates has widened.

Within three groups—nonwhites, teenagers, and those aged 20–24—pre-1962 unemployment rates did not follow the general pattern of a higher rate for females than for males. However, this situation changed when the 1962–69 expansion began, and since 1962 the female unemployment rates have been higher than those for males among teenagers and nonwhites. For men and women aged 20–24, the female unemployment rate exceeded that for males from 1962 through 1969. When aggregate unemployment rose sharply in 1970–71, the unemployment for men in this age group again rose above that for women, but another

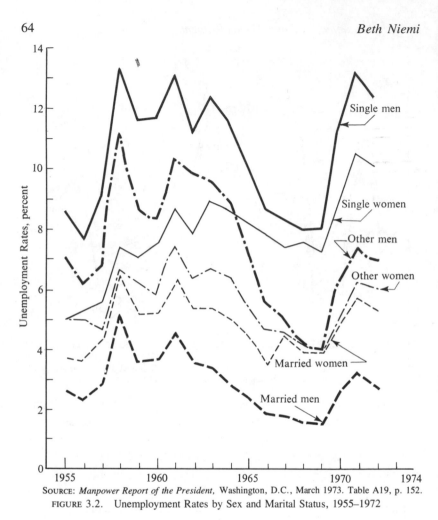

Source: *Manpower Report of the President,* Washington, D.C., March 1973. Table A19, p. 152.
Figure 3.2.   Unemployment Rates by Sex and Marital Status, 1955–1972

reversal occurred in 1972 with the improvement that year in the overall unemployment situation. (These relationships can be seen in Figures 3.3 and 3.4.) It appears that the 1962 reversal of the relative incidence of unemployment for men and women within these three groups is a specific and striking example of a more general phenomenon—the worsening of the relative unemployment position of women in recent years. For the bulk of the labor force this deterioration took the less dramatic form of a widening of the already existing gap between the unemployment rates of women and men.

The purpose of this study is to explain the relatively high unemployment rates of women. The divergence from this pattern within the young and nonwhite groups and the recent deterioration in the relative unemployment status of women will also be considered.

The standard Department of Labor approach to unemployment divides unemployment into three categories: [5]

1) *Frictional* unemployment is transitional in nature, resulting from the fact that some time is usually required for an unemployed person to find a suitable job, even when such a job is available.

2) *Cyclical* unemployment occurs in recession periods and is the result of deficient aggregate demand and a consequent reduction in employment opportunities.

3) *Structural* unemployment results from long-term declines in specific geographic areas, industries, or skills, and is exacerbated to the extent that the affected workers tend to be geographically or occupationally im-

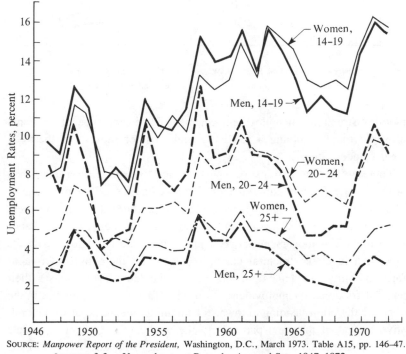

SOURCE: *Manpower Report of the President,* Washington, D.C., March 1973. Table A15, pp. 146–47.

FIGURE 3.3. Unemployment Rates by Age and Sex, 1947–1972

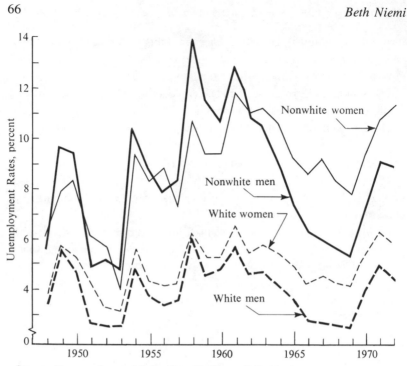

SOURCE: *Manpower Report of the President,* Washington, D.C., March 1973. Table A14, p. 145.

FIGURE 3.4.   Unemployment Rates by Race and Sex, 1948–1972

mobile. Structural unemployment can be viewed as a type of frictional unemployment involving a relatively high cost of movement (between areas or occupations).

There are several reasons to expect women to experience a more than proportionate share of all three of these categories of unemployment. Their relative lack of training, particularly in specific skills, makes them susceptible to cyclical layoffs and unemployment; their low intra–labor force mobility—movement between jobs within the labor force—results in a high level of structural unemployment; and their high inter–labor force mobility—movement in and out of the labor force—raises their level of frictional unemployment. Two other factors exert pressure in the opposite direction, tending to lower the unemployment rate of women relative to that of men and particularly the cyclical component of female unemployment. These are (1) the different industrial distributions of the male and female labor forces, with women tending to be concentrated in less cyclically volatile sectors, and (2) the flexibility and positive cyclical sensitivity of the female labor force, which expands in prosperity and shrinks during recessions.[6]

The three factors that tend to raise the female unemployment rate are interrelated and, in fact, stem from a common source, which involves the woman worker in a vicious circle with respect to training, labor force status, earnings, and unemployment. The "normal" role for a woman is still seen to be that of a wife, often out of the labor force entirely, or at most a secondary worker with substantial nonmarket responsibilities. Thus women are conditioned to expect to spend considerable amounts of their working lives outside the labor force, and are implicitly or explicitly discouraged from investing heavily in market-oriented skills and career preparation. Actual discrimination against women in the labor market reinforces this effect, and helps to make this socially conditioned expectation of secondary labor-force status a self-fulfilling prophecy.

Human Capital and Female Unemployment

An understanding of women's relative lack of specific training and their intra–labor force immobility can be derived from the theory of investment in human capital.[7] Both training and migration are forms of investment in human capital which may be undertaken in response to future income prospects. Because of systematic differences by sex in the costs of and returns from such investments, women will generally make these investments less readily than men. While the average adult male remains in the labor force throughout his working life, the typical woman is in the labor force for approximately only half this period.[8] Thus the relevant time period over which the returns from any investment in training or mobility are realized is shorter for a woman than for a man, and the expected net gain from a given investment is correspondingly reduced. The fact that female labor force participation also tends to be intermittent makes investment in migration or in specific training even less profitable for the woman worker. This section examines the actual position of women with respect to both specific training and geographic mobility, and the ways in which this affects the female unemployment rate.

Specific Training

While formal education costs are not much smaller for women than for men, women's investment in on-the-job training comes to only a fraction of the amount invested by males.[9] Women invest less in market-oriented training because they generally expect to have a shorter duration of labor force attachment than men. Even when an individual woman plans to remain in the labor force throughout her working life, an employer may estimate the probability of her remaining in his employ not from his knowledge of her, but from his experiences with or beliefs about turnover among women workers in general.[10] He will therefore hesitate to invest in specific training for her. Women will hence have less specific training than will men, and less of their training will be financed by the employer.

In April 1962, the Bureau of Labor Statistics (BLS) made a detailed survey of a sample of persons who had experienced five or more weeks of unemployment in 1961. The completed survey included 3013 individuals, of whom 945, or just over 30 percent, were women, and included information on training received in addition to formal schooling. These data reveal that a greater proportion of the men than the women in this group had received some special training. Thirty-five percent of the men and 25 percent of the women had acquired some training, while 7 percent of the men and 3½ percent of the women had received more than one course of training, either on the job or in special schools. Special training was positively correlated with educational attainment for both men and women. For men, the proportion with training ranged from 22 percent for those with only an elementary school education to 55 percent for college graduates, while the corresponding percentages for women were 9 and 47 percent. At each level of educational attainment, relatively more men than women had some special training.[11]

The relative lack of specific training on the part of women implies susceptibility to cyclical unemployment. If specific training were the only important factor determining the relative cyclical unemployment of men and women, it would be expected that the female unemployment rate would be more volatile over the course of the business cycle than the male unemployment rate. However, the male unemployment rate has the greater amplitude of cyclical fluctuation. This in itself, of course, does not constitute evidence that the specific-training hypothesis is incorrect, but it does indicate that the specific-training effect is possibly outweighed by other factors. One factor to consider is that women tend to be concentrated in those sectors less affected by cyclical declines; this might partially counteract the effect of lack of specific training on the susceptibility of women workers to cyclical layoffs. One would expect, however, that the specific-training effect would cause women in industries affected by cyclical declines to be more likely to be laid off than men. This expectation was tested with data from the 1/1000 sample of the 1960 census. Unemployment rates calculated for men and women and classified by industry are presented in Table 3.1.

TABLE 3.1 Unemployment Rates
by Industry and Sex, April 1960

	Male (%)	Female (%)
Agriculture, forestry, fisheries	3.0	6.0
Mining	8.6	3.4
Construction	10.6	3.3
Durable manufacturing	5.4	8.5
Nondurable manufacturing	4.1	8.5
Transportation and communication	4.2	3.2
Trade	4.1	6.3
Finance, real estate, insurance	1.5	2.4
Service	4.0	3.5
Public administration	5.4	4.8

SOURCE: U.S. Census, 1960, 1/1000 sample.

The female unemployment rate was higher than the male rate in exactly half of the ten industries. However, some of the industries in which women had a lower unemployment rate than men are those that include only a minute percentage of the female labor force. Only 0.1 percent of the female labor force is in the mining industry, and the construction industry accounts for only 0.8 percent. Four industries account for over three-fourths of the female labor force: service (36 percent), trade (20.4 percent), nondurable manufacturing (13.4 percent), and durable manufacturing (8.4 percent). These same four industries include almost 60 percent of the male labor force. Although the male unemployment rate is somewhat higher than that for females in the service industry, women do have a substantially higher rate of unemployment than men in durable and

TABLE 3.2   Cyclical Fluctuations in Employment

Year	Actual Employment (thousands), A	Trend Value (thousands), T	Deviation of Actual Employment from Trend, $A - T$	Cycles in Employment $\frac{A - T}{T} \times 100$
A. Total Female Employment				
1947	16,683	16,391.4	+291.6	+1.8
1948	17,351	16,946.4	+404.6	+2.4
1949	17,806	17,501.4	+304.6	+1.7
1950	18,412	18,056.4	+355.6	+2.0
1951	19,054	18,611.4	+442.6	+2.4
1952	19,314	19,166.4	+147.6	+0.8
1953	19,429	19,721.4	−292.4	−1.5
1954	19,718	20,276.4	−558.4	−2.8
1955	20,584	20,831.4	−247.4	−1.2
1956	21,495	21,386.4	+108.6	+0.5
1957	21,765	21,941.4	−176.4	−0.8
1958	22,149	22,496.4	−347.4	−1.5
1959	22,516	23,051.4	+535.4	−2.3
1960	23,272	23,606.4	−334.4	−1.4
1961	23,838	24,161.4	−323.4	−1.3
1962	24,047	24,716.4	−669.4	−2.7
1963	24,736	25,271.4	−535.4	−2.1
1964	25,443	25,826.4	−383.4	−1.5
1965	26,232	26,381.4	−149.4	−0.6
1966	27,333	26,936.4	+396.6	+1.5
1967	28,395	27,492.4	+903.6	+3.3
1968	29,242	28,046.4	+1095.6	+3.9
B. Total Male Employment				
1947	44,258	44,365.4	−107.4	−0.2
1948	44,729	44,737.2	−8.2	−0.01
1949	45,097	45,109.0	−12.0	−0.01
1950	45,446	45,480.8	−34.8	−0.1
1951	46,063	45,852.6	+210.4	+0.5
1952	46,416	46,224.4	+191.6	+0.4
1953	47,131	46,596.2	+534.8	+1.1
1954	47,275	46,968.0	+307.0	+0.7
1955	47,488	47,339.8	+148.2	+0.3
1956	47,914	47,711.6	+202.4	+0.4
1957	47,964	48,083.4	−119.4	−0.2
1958	48,126	48,455.2	−329.2	−0.7
1959	48,405	48,827.0	−422.0	−0.9
1960	48,870	49,198.8	−328.8	−0.7

Table 3.2 (continued)

Year	Actual Employment (thousands), A	Trend Value (thousands), T	Deviation of Actual Employment from Trend, $A - T$	Cycles in Employment $\dfrac{A - T}{T} \times 100$
B. Total Male Employment (continued)				
1961	49,193	49,570.6	−377.6	−0.8
1962	49,395	49,942.4	−547.4	−1.1
1963	49,835	50,314.2	−479.2	−1.0
1964	50,387	50,686.0	−299.0	−0.6
1965	50,946	51,057.8	−111.8	−0.2
1966	51,560	51,429.6	+130.4	+0.3
1967	52,398	51,801.4	+596.6	+1.2
1968	53,030	52,173.2	+856.8	+1.6
C. Female Employment, Service Workers Other than Private Household				
1958	2841	2875.6	−34.6	−1.2
1959	3050	3022.2	+27.8	+0.9
1960	3233	3168.8	+64.2	+2.0
1961	3361	3315.4	+45.6	+1.4
1962	3426	3462.0	−36.0	−1.0
1963	3590	3608.6	−18.6	−0.5
1964	3699	3755.2	−56.2	−1.5
1965	3825	3901.8	−76.8	−2.0
1966	4032	4048.4	−16.4	−0.4
1967	4255	4195.0	+60.0	+1.4
1968	4383	4341.6	+41.4	+1.0
D. Male Employment, Service Workers Other than Private Household				
1958	2681	2677.2	+3.8	+0.1
1959	2704	2745.6	−41.6	−1.5
1960	2818	2814.0	+4.0	+0.1
1961	2865	2882.4	−17.4	−0.6
1962	2934	2950.8	−16.8	−0.6
1963	3051	3019.2	+31.8	+1.1
1964	3153	3078.6	+65.4	+2.1
1965	3155	3156.0	−1.0	−0.03
1966	3276	3224.4	+51.6	+1.6
1967	3301	3292.8	+8.2	+0.2
1968	3273	3361.2	−88.2	−2.6

SOURCE: Employment figures taken from *Statistics on Manpower,* a supplement to the *Manpower Report of the President* (Washington, D.C., March 1969), Table A-1, p. 1, and Table A-9, p. 11.

nondurable manufacturing and in trade, three industries which are relatively severely affected by cyclical declines in demand.

Female labor force turnover is a second factor which may dampen the effect on unemployment of women's lack of specific training. The effect of female labor force turnover can be eliminated by looking at cyclical variations in employment rather than unemployment by sex. If female employment fluctuates relatively more over the business cycle than male employment, there is evidence in favor of the specific-training hypothesis. Women may be considerably more subject to cyclical disemployment than men, because of their paucity of specific training, but they may not show up as unemployed to any great extent because of their tendency to leave the labor force during periods of recession.

I computed the cycles in total employment for both men and women for the period 1947–68, adjusting for the trend of secular growth. I also applied the same technique to the employment data for a particular occupation—services (other than private household)—for the period 1958–68. The latter analysis eliminates not only the effect of high labor force turnover among women, but also the effect of the different occupational distributions of the male and female labor forces. The results of this analysis are presented in Table 3.2.

Female employment did display greater variability over the course of the business cycle than male employment. The percentage deviations from trend—and often the absolute size of the deviations as well—were larger for female than for male employment. No clear pattern emerges for employment in services, probably because data broken down by both occupation and sex is available for only a limited number of years. The greater cyclical volatility of female relative to male employment during the post–World War II period does support the hypothesis that women workers tend to receive less specific training than their male counterparts, and are therefore more susceptible to cyclical layoffs. Although there is evidence in support of this hypothesis, this relative lack of specific training makes little quantitative contribution to the observed female–male unemployment differential.

Intra–Labor Force Immobility

The geographic and occupational mobility of women workers tends to be low. Such investment in human capital is more likely the larger the average wage differential to be gained, the longer the time period over which the gain will be realized, the lower the discount rate, and the smaller the direct and opportunity costs of the venture.[12] There are systematic differences by sex in both the relevant time period and the level of costs which cause women to make such investments less readily than men. The likelihood that a woman will remain in the labor force for a shorter period of time than a man lowers her expected return on any form of market-oriented investment.

It is highly unlikely that migration for the purpose of seeking employment will be feasible for married women, because the total cost of such movement must include the opportunity cost incurred by their husbands. A married woman's geographic location is a function of her husband's employment rather than her own personal job opportunities. Geographic mobility may be random for such a woman in one of two ways. She may find herself unable to migrate in response to her personal opportunities for employment, or she may be forced to migrate when her husband changes jobs. This second case can be viewed as an involuntary job shift, analogous to a layoff.

Intra–labor force immobility is strongest in the case of the geographic immobility of married women. In the case of occupational mobility for which some retraining may be required but for which migration is not necessary, the opportunity costs incurred by other family earners are not considered. However, occupational mobility and migration may tend to go together. If a change to a new occupation involves moving to a new location, the geographic immobility of female workers will decrease their occupational mobility as well. This lack of intra–labor force mobility will increase the rate and duration of female unemployment, but it may also lead to withdrawal from the labor force.

Data on potential occupational and geographic mobility are available for that subgroup of the Bureau of Labor Statistics sample, described in the section on specific training, who were unemployed at the time of the survey, in April 1962. These individuals, who constitute over 25 percent of the entire sample, were asked about their willingness to take a job in another area of the country and their interest in retraining.

Table 3.3A gives the percentage distribution of answers to the question "Would you accept a job in another area?" Table 3.3B gives the distribution of responses to a query on interest in being trained. In the case of

Beth Niemi

TABLE 3.3 Potential Geographic and
Occupational Mobility of Unemployed
Individuals in the BLS Sample, April 1962

A. Interest in a Job in Another Area

	Men			Women		
	Yes	It depends	No	Yes	It depends	No
Total	34.6	24.7	40.7	12.9	11.2	75.9
White	32.5	24.5	43.0	10.6	10.3	79.1
Nonwhite	43.3	25.4	31.3	19.4	13.9	66.7
Married	29.9	29.9	40.2	8.2	9.8	82.0
Single	41.9	12.8	45.3	21.3	18.0	60.7
Other	48.1	16.9	35.0	19.0	10.5	70.5
18–24	41.3	16.7	42.0	11.8	11.8	76.4
25–54	36.0	26.5	37.5	12.6	11.1	76.3
55 +	26.1	26.7	47.2	15.6	10.9	73.5

B. Interest in Training

	Men			Women		
	Yes	It depends	No	Yes	It depends	No
Total	79.3	6.5	14.2	76.7	6.2	17.1
White	76.8	7.5	15.7	71.7	7.3	21.0
Nonwhite	89.8	2.3	7.9	91.0	3.0	6.0
Married	78.6	7.7	13.7	73.6	7.8	18.6
Single	83.4	4.6	11.9	88.1	0.0	11.9
Other	74.7	4.0	21.3	77.1	6.2	16.7
18–24	86.7	5.5	7.8	80.3	4.9	14.8
25–54	82.4	6.4	11.2	79.5	6.4	14.1
55 +	65.8	7.7	26.5	58.9	7.2	33.9

SOURCE: U.S. Department of Labor, Bureau of Labor Statistics (BLS) Survey of Unemployment in 1961. For a more detailed account of this survey, see BLS, "Survey of the Work History of the Unemployed," *Monthly Report on the Labor Force,* March, May, and August, 1963, pp. xiv–xxi, 16–24, and 15–27, respectively; or Robert L. Stein, "Work History, Attitudes, and Income of the Unemployed," *Monthly Labor Review,* 86, No. 12 (December 1963): 1405–13.

geographic movement, the unemployed were asked if they would accept a job in another area at the same wage as they had received when they last worked. In this case, expected wage differentials between areas are to be seen mainly as the result of variation in the probability of obtaining employment. Training, on the other hand, can be assumed to affect both the actual wage and the probability of obtaining it.

It appears that the unemployed are reluctant to migrate in order to obtain employment. Only 35 percent of the men and 13 percent of the women said that they would definitely be willing to move if offered a job in another area of the country. As predicted, women are much less interested than men in investing in such a move. Whites and nonwhites exhibited similar patterns of geographic mobility by sex, with nonwhites of both sexes being more willing to move than their white counterparts. Over 40 percent of the nonwhite men and almost 20 percent of the nonwhite women were ready to accept a job in another area.

About one-fourth of the men said they would consider taking a job in another area under certain conditions, while 40 percent claimed that they had no interest in moving. The men who were unwilling to move placed greatest emphasis on the presence of home, family, and relatives in explaining their disinclination to migrate. Only 3 percent of the men who did not want to move mentioned their wives' jobs in the present area as a possible deterrent.

In contrast to the men, over three-fourths of the women were definitely unwilling to move; only 11 percent expressed willingness to move under certain conditions. Married women were predictably the least mobile. Only about 8 percent of the married women were definitely willing to move, while 28 percent were not willing to migrate under any circumstances. In contrast, 21 percent of the single women were willing to move. One-fourth of the married women cited their husbands' jobs in the present area as a factor making migration impossible for them.

A great proportion of both the men and the women expressed an interest in training; the inquiry was phrased to determine interest in a hypothetical training program which would provide for some payment to the trainees. Many more people were interested in being trained than in moving to another area, and the differences between male and female responses were much smaller. Single women were again more interested than married women in obtaining training.

The proportions who said that they would be interested in training under certain conditions were relatively small. Those in this group who mentioned specific conditions tended to emphasize the kind of training provided. Those who were not interested in training explained this in terms of either being too old for training or being satisfied with their usual occupation.

The BLS survey information indicates that women are potentially less mobile within the labor force, both geographically and occupationally, than men. But this alone is not conclusive evidence that women's intra–labor force mobility is lower than that of men. Actual mobility patterns may diverge from attitudes toward mobility as expressed in response to the BLS questionnaire. Hence the actual incidence of intra–labor force mobility must also be analyzed. Some information on job changes and occupational mobility in 1955 and 1961 is presented in Table 3.4.

It is clear from Table 3.4A that women change jobs less frequently than men. In addition, Tables 3.4B and 3.4C indicate that, when women do change jobs, they show a greater tendency than men to remain within the same occupation.

Clear and interesting evidence that geographic mobility tends to be involuntary or exogenous for women can be found in unemployment rates for men and women cross-classified by geographic mobility, computed from 1960 census data. Individuals were classified as nonmobile (same address in 1955 and 1960) or mobile (change of address between 1955 and 1960), with a subcategory among the mobile for those who moved from one state to another between 1955 and 1960. The following unemployment rates were obtained:

	Nonmobile	Mobile	Different State
Men, 14+	4.6	5.1	4.4
Women, 14+	4.5	6.3	7.1

For male workers, interstate mobility had the effect of decreasing the unemployment rate. However, geographic mobility, especially long-distance mobility, decidedly worsened the unemployment situation for women, indicating that such migration was governed by factors other than personal economic opportunity.

The geographic immobility of women raises their rate and duration of unemployment relative to those of men. However, the more viable alternatives to labor force participation available to women tend to decrease the duration of female unemployment via the exit of unemployed women from the labor force. The average duration of unemployment is longer for men than for women, both in periods of prosperity and during recessions. For example, in 1961, a year of high unemployment, 34.7 percent of all unemployed men were unemployed more than 15 weeks and 18.6 percent were unemployed more than 27 weeks; the corresponding percentages for unemployed women were 26.9 and 13.5. In 1968, a very prosperous

TABLE 3.4   Job Changes in the United States,
1955 and 1961

A. *Rate of Job Changing, 1955 and 1961*
   (numbers in thousands)

	1961			1955		
		Changing Jobs			Changing Jobs	
	Total Working	Number	%	Total Working	Number	%
Total	80,287	8,121	10.1	75,353	8,366	11.1
Men	49,854	5,509	11.0	47,624	5,940	12.5
Women	30,433	2,612	8.6	27,729	2,426	8.7

B. *Distribution of Job Changes in 1955*

	Number (thousands)			Percentage Distribution		
	Total	Male	Female	Total	Male	Female
Total job changes	13,324	9,448	3,876	100	100	100
Same occupation	5,417	3,832	1,585	41	41	41
Different occupation	6,087	4,519	1,568	46	48	40
Job left, no other						
started	1,820	1,097	723	13	11	19

C. *Pattern of Job Changes in 1961*
   (numbers in thousands)

		Percentage Distribution of Pattern of Changes				
Job Changes by	Number [a]	Total	SS	SD	DS	DD
Men	7,539	100	33.5	17.6	10.0	38.9
Women	3,329	100	34.7	21.3	9.9	34.2

SOURCES: "Job Mobility of Workers in 1955," Current Population Reports Series p-50, no. 70, Table 15, p. 27; and Gertrude Bancroft and Stuart Garfunkle, "Job Mobility in 1961," *Monthly Labor Review*, 86, No. 8 (August 1963): 898, 905.

NOTE: SS = same occupation and some industry
   SD = same occupation and different industry
   DS = different occupation and same industry
   DD = different occupation and different industry

[a] Persons making four or more changes excluded.

year, long-term unemployment was much less in evidence: 16 percent of all unemployed men and 13.2 percent of all unemployed women were unemployed for more than 15 weeks, and the duration of unemployment extended beyond 27 weeks for only 6.7 percent of the men and 4.2 percent of the women.

One important problem with data on the duration of unemployment for men and women is that they include some women whose attachment to the labor force is weak, and who seek work for a short period and leave the labor force without becoming employed. Their presence in the unemployment figures obviously lowers the average observed duration of unemployment for women. It also makes it very difficult to use information on duration of unemployment to ascertain whether unemployed women have more difficulty than unemployed men in finding new jobs.

The effect on unemployment duration of the high labor force turnover of these marginal female labor force participants may be partially eliminated by separating labor force entrants from those who lost or quit a previous job. Then the duration of unemployment for men and women can be classified by reason for unemployment. Such information for 1968 is given in Table 3.5.

Not only do unemployed men average a longer duration of unemployment than unemployed women, but this relation also holds within each category of reason for unemployment. However, the difference in duration is greatest among labor force entrants; the duration of unemployment among women who lost or left a job approaches that of their male coun-

TABLE 3.5 Percentage Distributions of
Unemployed Persons by Sex,
Reason for Unemployment, and Duration,
1968 Annual Averages

Reason and Sex	Number of Unemployed (thousands)	Percentage Unemployed				
		<5 wks	5–14 wks	15–26 wks	≥27 wks	Average Weeks
Male, 20 +	993	49.6	30.9	10.8	8.6	10.9
Job losers	599	46.6	32.4	12.2	8.8	11.3
Job leavers	167	56.3	26.3	9.0	7.8	9.8
Entrants	227	52.9	31.3	7.9	7.9	10.0
reentrants	205	53.2	30.7	7.8	7.8	9.9
new workers	22	n.a.	n.a.	n.a.	n.a.	n.a.
Female, 20 +	985	58.2	27.0	9.7	5.1	8.7
Job losers	341	48.4	31.7	13.5	6.2	10.2
Job leavers	167	57.5	26.3	9.6	6.6	9.3
Entrants	477	65.2	24.1	6.9	3.8	7.3
reentrants	422	66.1	24.2	6.4	2.2	7.0
new workers	55	58.2	23.6	10.9	5.5	8.8

SOURCE: Kathryn D. Hoyle, *Job Losers, Leavers, and Entrants: A Report on the Unemployed*, Bureau of Labor Statistics, Special Labor Force Report No. 106 (Washington, D.C., 1969), Table 7, p. A-1.

terparts. It is possible that availability of unemployment insurance may be increasing the duration of unemployment among women who have lost or left a job. Among job losers and job leavers, a greater proportion of women than of men experienced unemployment of 15 to 26 weeks in duration, but a higher proportion of men than of women were unemployed more than 26 weeks. Perhaps women who are eligible for unemployment insurance remain in the labor force for as long as they can collect such benefits (usually a maximum of 26 weeks), but tend to leave the labor force if they fail to find employment within a short time after the exhaustion of benefits.

A study published by the Bureau of Employment Security in 1958 indicates that women covered by unemployment insurance are more likely to exhaust their benefits than their male counterparts.[13] Data for the United States as a whole and for individual states show a greater proportion of women among exhaustees than among total claimants for the 1954–56 period; women constituted 36 percent of total claimants and 42 percent of total exhaustees.

Women are less mobile than men within the labor force, geographically and occupationally, because of systematic differences by sex in the total cost of a given move and the expected period over which returns will be reaped. Because an unemployed woman's range of choices is more restricted than that of her male counterpart, it will be more difficult for her to find employment. This structural factor raises the female unemployment rate. However, when faced with the prospect of very long-term unemployment and a very low expected gain from continued job search, women are more likely than men to leave the labor force; more acceptable nonmarket uses for time tend to be available to women than to men. Consequently, the impact of women's immobility within the labor force on the female–male unemployment differential is small. The most important factor in raising the unemployment rate of women relative to that of men is the high level of female labor force turnover, which is the subject of the following section.

Inter–Labor Force Mobility

The most striking characteristic of female labor force participants is their high inter–labor force mobility. The rate of labor force turnover for women is close to ten times as great as that for men. Almost 55 percent of the women in the country were in the labor force at some time during 1972, but less than 45 percent are in the labor force at any moment.

It has already been demonstrated that men have a higher rate of intra–labor force mobility than women, and a great number of studies on job changing confirm this.[14] Since women have a higher rate of inter–labor force turnover, it is possible that the total rate of turnover (intra– plus inter–labor force) is similar for men and women.[15] If the total turnover rates for the male and female labor force are comparable, but relatively more inter–labor force turnover exists among women and relatively more intra–labor force turnover among men, this difference in the composition of total turnover would tend to raise the unemployment rate of women relative to that of men. According to the BLS definitions of employment and unemployment, transitional unemployment is more likely to occur when an inter–labor force move is made than when an intra–labor force move is made.

It is necessary to recognize that a great deal of productive work takes place outside the labor market in our economy, with the bulk of this non-market production still being done by women. A housewife is counted as not in the labor force by the BLS, but this certainly does not imply that she does not do any work. In a very real sense, then, a shift from outside the labor force into paid employment can be viewed as analogous to an interindustry job change.

There are two possible ways of making any job shift. The first is to engage in job search as a full-time activity until an acceptable job is found, after first leaving one's old job. Either an intra–labor force or an inter–labor force shift made in this fashion involves a transitional period of unemployment while the search is taking place. The more common method of job changing, however, is to engage in job search as a part-time activity, leaving one's old job only after a new one has been ob-tained. In the case of a shift from one market job to another this second type of job shift does not involve transitional unemployment, for having a job takes precedence over seeking work in the BLS definitions of employ-ment and unemployment. On the other hand, a housewife who is seeking employment in the market is defined as unemployed, with her search for a job taking precedence over her nonmarket work. Thus, with the excep-tion of the possible case where an individual is offered a job without seeking one and moves directly from outside the labor force into employment, inter–labor force mobility necessarily involves transitional unemployment, and differences by sex in the type of job mobility are one factor contributing to the higher unemployment rate of women.

In an earlier study, I computed total annual turnover rates for men and women.[16] These results indicate that, although men are more mobile within the labor force than women, the very great amount of inter–labor force movement of women relative to men leads to a rate of total mobility for women that is considerably greater than that for men. This raises the unemployment rate of women relative to that of men.

The relationship between labor force participation and unemployment is generally an inverse one, both cross-sectionally across groups within the labor force and over the course of the business cycle. Cross-sectionally, a lower rate of labor force participation has generally been accompanied by greater labor force turnover, and therefore by a higher rate of unemployment. Men and women in the labor force provide an obvious example of this relationship.

A good index of labor force turnover is the ratio of the proportion of the population who were in the labor force at any time during the year (the labor force experience rate, or LFE) to the average labor force participation rate of the population for that year. This ratio must have a value of 100 or more; the larger the value of this index, the more labor force turnover exists. A turnover index equal to 100 represents the absence of any labor force turnover; in this case the same people are always in the labor force, and no one enters or leaves the labor force during the year. At the other extreme, the upper limit on the value of this index is equal to 100 divided by the labor force participation rate, and one would expect a negative correlation between the actual turnover index and the labor force participation rate. Labor force turnover is necessarily low for a group with a high rate of labor force participation, as there is little leeway for inter–labor force mobility when 90 percent of the population is in the labor force at any moment. On the other hand, labor force turnover is most likely, but not necessarily, high for groups with low labor force participation rates. For example, the upper limit on the value of the turnover index is 105 if the labor force participation rate is 95 percent, 133 if the labor force participation rate is 75 percent, and 300 if the labor force participation rate is 33 percent.

Actual labor force participation rates, labor force experience rates, and labor force turnover indices for men and women are given in Table 3.6. Average annual labor force turnover lies in the range 10–12 percent, with the female labor force exhibiting annual turnover of roughly 30 percent and the male labor force only 2 percent. In addition to being very low, the turnover rate of the male labor force has been fairly constant over time, while female labor force turnover has shown a slight decrease, as female labor force participation and permanency of labor force attachment have increased.

The effect of this inter–labor force turnover on unemployment can be observed in data on the sources of unemployment (job loss, quitting, labor force entry and reentry), collected by the BLS since 1964. The data reveal that 37 to 52 percent of the unemployment of women aged 20 and older is the result of entry or reentry into the labor force. Table 3.7 shows

TABLE 3.6   Labor Force Participation Rates,
Labor Force Experience Rates,
and Labor Force Turnover Indices
for the Population Aged 16 and Over, 1957–71

	Total, 16 +			Men, 16 +			Women, 16 +		
Year	LFP	LFE	$\dfrac{LFE}{LFP}$	LFP	LFE	$\dfrac{LFE}{LFP}$	LFP	LFE	$\dfrac{LFE}{LFP}$
1957	58.7	65.2	111.1	82.7	84.1	101.6	35.9	47.3	131.9
1958	58.5	64.6	110.5	82.1	82.6	100.7	36.0	47.4	131.8
1959	58.3	64.4	110.5	81.7	82.4	100.9	36.1	47.4	131.1
1960	58.3	65.6	112.4	81.2	83.1	102.4	36.7	49.0	133.4
1961	58.0	64.1	110.5	80.3	81.4	101.4	36.9	47.7	129.3
1962	57.4	64.5	112.4	79.3	81.3	102.5	36.7	48.7	132.7
1963	57.3	64.4	112.3	78.8	80.8	102.5	37.0	48.9	132.1
1964	59.6	66.5	111.6	81.9	83.4	101.8	38.7	50.7	130.8
1965	59.7	66.0	110.5	81.5	82.5	101.2	39.3	50.0	127.3
1966	60.1	66.7	111.0	81.4	82.2	101.0	40.3	52.2	129.6
1967	60.6	67.1	110.7	81.5	82.1	100.7	41.2	53.1	129.0
1968	60.7	67.5	111.1	81.2	82.1	101.2	41.6	53.8	129.3
1969	61.1	67.9	111.2	80.9	82.5	102.0	42.7	54.4	127.3
1970	61.3	68.0	111.0	80.6	82.5	102.3	43.4	54.6	126.0
1971	61.0	68.2	111.8	80.0	83.0	103.7	43.4	54.6	125.6

SOURCES: Labor force and population figures are taken from the *Manpower Report of the President* (Washington, D.C., March 1972), Table B-1, p. 192. Labor force experience figures are taken from BLS Special Labor Force Reports Nos. 11, 19, 25, 38, 48, 62, 76, 91, 107, 115, and 127.

NOTE: The figures for 1957–63 are for the population aged 14 and over.

TABLE 3.7   The Sources of Unemployment for Men and Women

Date	Men, 20 +				Women, 20 +			
	Total	Job Loser	Job Leaver	Entry	Total	Job Loser	Job Leaver	Entry
June 64	3.6	2.3	0.5	0.8	5.2	2.2	0.9	2.0
Dec. 64	3.8	2.5	0.4	0.8	4.1	1.7	0.8	1.6
June 65	2.9	1.8	0.4	0.7	4.8	2.1	0.9	1.8
Nov. 65	2.5	1.6	0.4	0.5	4.3	1.4	0.9	2.0
Jan. 66	3.4	2.3	0.5	0.6	4.2	1.7	0.8	1.7
June 66	2.3	1.2	0.4	0.7	3.9	1.1	1.0	1.8
1967	2.3	1.5	0.4	0.5	4.3	1.6	0.7	2.0
1968	2.2	1.3	0.4	0.4	3.8	1.3	0.6	1.8
1969	2.1	1.2	0.4	0.6	3.7	1.2	0.6	1.9
1970	3.5	2.2	0.4	0.8	4.8	1.9	0.8	2.1
1971	4.4	2.9	0.5	1.0	5.7	2.5	0.8	2.5
1972	4.0	2.5	0.5	1.0	5.4	2.2	0.9	2.4

SOURCES: 1964–66: Kathryn D. Hoyle, "Why the Unemployed Look for Work," *Monthly Labor Review*, 90, No. 2 (February 1967), 35.
1967–68: *Employment and Earnings*, January 1969, Table A-10, p. 121.
1969–70: *Employment and Earnings*, January 1971, Table A-10, p. 123.
1971–72: *Employment and Earnings*, January 1973, Table 10, p. 130.

NOTE: The figures for 1967–72 are annual average rates.

total unemployment rates and the division of the total rates into job loser rates, job leaver rates, and entry and reentry rates for men and women.

The high entry and reentry rates of women, from two to four times as great as those for men, account for much of the difference in unemployment rates between the sexes. However, even if the rate of unemployment resulting from labor force entry were as low for women as for men, the female unemployment rate would still exceed the male rate for seven of the twelve dates surveyed. Job leaver rates tend to be 1½ times to twice as high for women as for men, while the female job loser rate exceeds the corresponding male rate on only two of the twelve dates.

It is clear from these statistics that women do have a much greater rate of inter–labor force mobility than men, and that this high rate of labor force turnover makes a substantial contribution to the female–male unemployment differential. In fact, this is by far the most important reason for the relatively high unemployment rate of women, with female intra–labor force immobility and lack of specific training having only a minor effect in raising the female unemployment rate.

Recent Changes in Differential Unemployment

Not only do women have higher rates of unemployment than men, but the unemployment situation of women has worsened over time. This can be clearly seen in Figure 3.1. In fact, the aggregate unemployment rate has risen over time in part because women and young people, with above-average unemployment rates, make up an increasing proportion of the labor force. The unemployment rates of young workers and women have also risen over time, although the average unemployment rate of adult men has shown no upward trend. Teenagers of both sexes have suffered from rising unemployment, but girls more so than boys. A similar pattern has prevailed among nonwhites—higher unemployment for both sexes, and a worsening of the relative position of females.

Two factors that have undoubtedly affected these changes in differential unemployment are the rising trend in school enrollment and the minimum wage. Growing school enrollment has raised the unemployment rate of teenagers as a result of the larger amount of frictional unemployment that occurs every June as more and more students enter the labor force temporarily. The minimum wage increases in the past twenty-five years have led to an upward drift in the actual ratio of the minimum to the average wage, which has had an adverse effect on the unemployment position of less skilled groups in the labor force. Burns found that the ratio of the teenage unemployment rate to the rate for adults was invariably higher during the six months following an increase in the minimum wage than during the preceding six months; the same was true of the ratio of the female to the male unemployment rate.[17]

As was discussed earlier, there are three groups—nonwhites, teenagers and those aged 20–24—for whom pre–1962 unemployment rates did not follow the general pattern of a higher rate of unemployment for women than for men. However, there were exceptions to the general pattern of higher male than female unemployment rates within these groups before 1962. An examination of these exceptions will aid in formulating an explanation of the 1962 reversal for these specific groups, and of the widening gap between female and male unemployment rates for the labor force as a whole. The male unemployment rate fell below the female rate in one or more of the three groups in 1951, 1952, and 1956—three years at the peaks of business cycles. In addition, 1951–52 coincided with the

Korean conflict and the consequent heightened demand for military man-power, and is therefore comparable in this respect as well to the 1965–67 period, when the Vietnam War exerted similar pressures.

It appears that a disproportionate concentration of cyclical unemployment among nonwhite men and young men kept their rates of unemployment above those of their female counterparts throughout most of the 1947–62 period. This is confirmed by the fact that the excess of male over female unemployment rates within these groups was greatest at business cycle troughs (1949, 1954, 1958), and that the exceptions occurred at the peaks of business cycles. During the 1960s, economic expansion caused unemployment to fall continuously and substantially. Unemployment fell more for men than for women during this period, since a greater proportion of the original male unemployment was of a cyclical nature. The relatively large frictional element in female unemployment remained constant or even rose as the growing demand for labor induced increases in the female labor force. In addition, the military demand for manpower, which was concentrated among males aged 18–26, tightened the labor market for this group to a degree that almost eliminated growth in the male civilian labor force.[18] Draft deferments for those enrolled in school accelerated the upward trend in school enrollment for young men, increasing the negative effect of the draft itself on the male civilian labor force.

In a detailed econometric study,[19] I have examined the actual effect of the business cycle, the upward trend in female labor force participation, the military demand for manpower, and changes in school enrollment on the trend over time in the male–female unemployment differential. It is clear from these results that the business cycle had the dominant effect on this differential in the younger age groups, while the growth in female labor force participation is of at least equal importance in explaining the worsening of the relative unemployment position of women aged 25–54, among whom the bulk of the increase in the female labor force has been concentrated.

Conclusions

The positive female–male unemployment differential and the widening of this gap over time are closely related to women's status as secondary workers in our economy. Women receive relatively little specific training and also have a low rate of intra–labor force mobility. However, these two factors actually have only a small net positive effect on the female unemployment rate. It is the high *inter*–labor force turnover of women that accounts for most of the sex differential in unemployment rates.

The high rate of female labor force turnover, however, is considerably less satisfactory as an explanation for the recent deterioration in the unemployment situation of women. It is indeed ironic that the contention that unemployment among women is of minor importance should be encountered with such frequency at just the time when the unemployment position of women relative to men is obviously getting worse.[20]

Some of the observed deterioration is the result of the continuous expansion of the 1960s, which lowered the unemployment rate of men relatively more than that of women, because the female unemployment rate has such a large frictional component. However, the positive relationship between female labor force participation and the female–male unemployment differential is somewhat disturbing. While the interpretation of this relationship is not entirely clear, it definitely cannot be explained solely in terms of labor force turnover. As larger numbers of women participate at least intermittently in the labor force, it is possible that labor force turnover and frictional unemployment might increase. This would be the case if a large part of the growth in participation took place among those groups of women displaying the most intermittent behavior. However, the data on labor force turnover over time in Table 3.6 are not consistent with this hypothesis. If anything, there is some evidence at this point that female labor force turnover may be starting to decrease slightly as the labor force attachment of women grows. Perhaps employment discrimination directed against women is a significant factor in the widening unemployment gap. Women are still very heavily concentrated in the same clerical and service occupations to which they were restricted twenty years ago. It has been suggested that overcrowding in these occupations as the female labor force increases results in both low wages and high unemployment rates for women workers.[21] The recent trend in differential unemployment is consistent with this hypothesis.

Fairly drastic changes in the current labor force behavior and commitment of women would be necessary to bring the labor force turnover among women and the resulting frictional unemployment into line with those of men. A significant trend toward more permanent labor force attachment would be expected to shrink the female–male differential in unemployment rates eventually. However, the degree of employer discrimination against women and the speed with which we can expect these attitudes to change will have an important effect in determining the possibilities for narrowing the gap in unemployment rates.

NOTES

[1] Richard F. Janssen, " 'Full Employment' Remains a Nixon Target But Chances of Achieving It Appear Slight," *Wall Street Journal,* January 21, 1972, p. 30.

[2] "Living with a Higher Jobless Rate," *Business Week,* December 25, 1971, p. 37.

[3] Janssen, " 'Full Employment,' " p. 30.

[4] Carolyn Shaw Bell, "Unemployed Women: Do They Matter?" *Wall Street Journal,* March 15, 1972, p. 18.

[5] U.S. Congress, Senate, *Special Committee on Unemployment Problems, Report No. 1206,* 86th Cong., 2d Sess., 1960, p. 36.

[6] Jacob Mincer, "Labor Force Participation and Unemployment: A Review of Recent Evidence," in Robert A. Gordon and Margaret S. Gordon, eds., *Prosperity and Unemployment* (New York, 1966), p. 100.

[7] As developed by Gary S. Becker in *Human Capital: A Theoretical and Empirical Analysis with Special Reference to Education* (New York, 1964), Part 1.

[8] Howard Hayghe, *Marital and Family Characteristics of Workers, March 1972,* Bureau of Labor Statistics, Special Labor Force Report No. 153 (Washington, D.C., 1972), p. 35.

[9] Jacob Mincer, "On-the-Job Training: Costs, Returns, and Some Implications," *Journal of Political Economy,* LXX (October 1962 Supplement): 67.

[10] Cf. Edmund S. Phelps, "The Statistical Theory of Racism and Sexism," *American Economic Review,* XLII (September 1972): 659.

[11] Beth Niemi, *Sex Differentials in Unemployment in the U.S. and Canada* (Ph.D. diss., Columbia University, 1970), p. 65 and Table 34, p. 190.

[12] *Ibid.,* pp. 23–24.

[13] U.S. Department of Labor, Bureau of Employment Security, *Adequacy of Benefits under Unemployment Insurance* (BES No. U-70 [R], October 1958).

[14] For example, see Robert L. Bunting, "Labor Mobility: Sex, Race, and Age," *The Review of Economics and Statistics,* XLII (May 1960): 229–31; R. L. Bunting, Lowell D. Ashby, and Peter A. Prosper, Jr., "Labor Mobility in Three Southern States," *Industrial and Labor Relations Review,* XIV (April 1961):

432–45; Paul Eldridge and Irwin Wolkstein, "Incidence of Employer Change," *Industrial and Labor Relations Review,* X (October 1956); *Minnesota Manpower Mobilities,* University of Minnesota Industrial Relations Center, Bulletin 10 (1950).

[15] Suggested by a comment by Jacob Mincer in Mark Perlman, ed., *Human Resources in the Urban Economy,* (Baltimore, 1963), p. 116.

[16] Beth Niemi, "The Female–Male Differential in Unemployment Rates," *Industrial and Labor Relations Review,* XXVII (April 1974): 334.

[17] Arthur F. Burns, *The Management of Prosperity* (New York, 1966), p. 47.

[18] Jacob Mincer, "The Short-Run Elasticity of Labor Supply," *Industrial Relations Research Association Proceedings* (1966), p. 225.

[19] Beth Niemi, "Recent Changes in Differential Unemployment," mimeographed (1973).

[20] Professor Bell highlights this irony in her description of the attitude of some economists that "we should pay less attention to the total unemployment rate, including all those women, and concentrate more on the more favorable-looking rate for married men. Or in other words, we should pay less attention to unemployment among women precisely because they have become a more important factor in the workforce." Carolyn Shaw Bell, "Unemployed Women: Do They Matter?" p. 18.

[21] Barbara R. Bergman, "Curing High Unemployment Rates Among Blacks and Women," testimony prepared for delivery before the Joint Economic Committee, U.S. Congress, 92d Cong., 2d Sess., October 17, 1972, p. 11

4

Discontinuous Labor Force Participation and Its Effect on Women's Market Earnings

SOLOMON W. POLACHEK

THE QUESTION of woman's role as a wage earner has become an issue of growing social, economic, and political importance in the United States today. The rapid rise in female labor force participation has led to an increased awareness among women of their status within the economy relative to males. Research in economics and other social sciences into the nature and scope of the employment and earnings differentials existing in the labor market today has been spurred on by women's claims of unequal treatment. Although discrimination may be an important determinant of women's present social and market position, economic analysis shows the phenomenon to be a far more complicated one.

In 1959, the working female earned, on the average, 53 percent as much as her male counterpart. Even on an hourly basis, the wage differential was over 30 percent. Corroborating sets of data indicate a certain consistency of these wage differentials over the last several decades (Table 4.1). Yet, because these raw differentials may overstate the real difference in wages by not comparing men and women with similar labor market attributes, the present study was designed to make more refined

The theoretical framework as well as the statistical results reported in this paper largely derive from a paper this author coauthored with Jacob Mincer of Columbia University and the National Bureau of Economic Research. This paper, which was presented at the Population Conference II in Chicago on June 4–5, 1973, is entitled "Family Investments in Human Capital: Earnings of Women." The author wishes to acknowledge the intellectual debt he owes to Jacob Mincer while at the same time taking full responsibility himself for any errors which he might have made. He also wishes to acknowledge the substantial editorial assistance received from Cynthia B. Lloyd, editor of this volume.

estimates of such wage differences as well as to shed light on their causes.

It is observed that important family characteristics, such as marital status, family size, and child spacing, have systematically different effects on the labor force participation and earnings of men and women.[1] According to Figure 4.1, wage differentials are greatest between married males and married females and smallest between single males and single females. Further analysis reveals that for single males and single females of the same age and level of education, hourly wage differentials average only 18 percent, while being over 50 percent for married males and females. Similarly, when comparing the wages of working females with

TABLE 4.1   Male–Female Wage Differentials

	1959		1966a		1966b
	Yearly	*Hourly*	*Yearly*	*Hourly*	*Yearly*
Male earnings	$4,491	$2.63	$6,870	$3.06	$5,693
Female earnings	2,391	1.81	2,390	1.99	2,149

SOURCES: 1959: Computed from U.S. Census, 1960, 1/1000 sample.
1966a: Computed for males and females 30–44 years of age from the 1966 Survey of Economic Opportunity Data.
1966b: U.S. Census, 1960, *Current Populations Reports* P-60, No. 53—median wage and salary income for persons 14 years of age and over.

children and those without children, it is found that each additional child reduces the female wage by up to 7 percent, depending on the age of the child. The spacing of children is also important. Empirically it can be shown that even when comparing women with the same number of children, the more widely spaced the children (i.e., the greater the range in the ages of the children), the lower the wage rate of the working mother. Thus, the mother of twins earns, on the average, 1.2 percent more than the mother whose children were spaced two years apart. At the same time, children have a positive although less profound effect on their father's earnings, thereby further increasing the wage gap. These effects are shown in more detail in Appendix Table 4.1.

This paper focuses upon the following question: Why do these family characteristics have such a pronounced influence on the size of the male–female wage differential? In answering this question, this study will demonstrate that family characteristics are, in fact, proxies for lifetime and

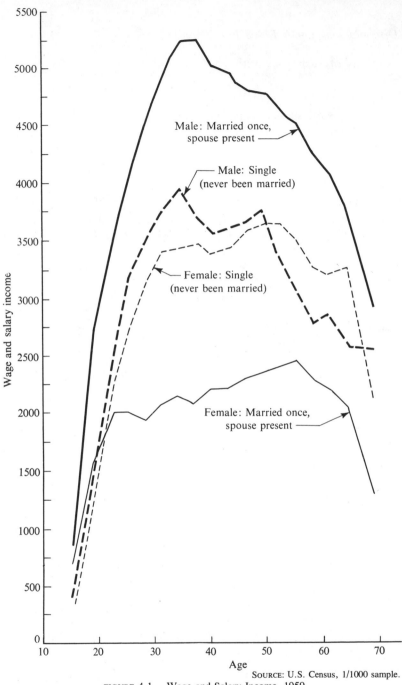

SOURCE: U.S. Census, 1/1000 sample.

FIGURE 4.1.   Wage and Salary Income, 1959

life-cycle variations of labor force participation. In addition, these differences in expected and actual labor force participation will be shown to affect the amount of individual human capital investment on and off the job, which in turn affects the wage rate received for market work.

Facts about Women's Labor Force Participation

To analyze the effects of differing male–female labor force participation patterns on earnings, definitions must be established concerning the measurement of the participation variable. Traditionally, most studies of labor force behavior have measured the extent of labor force participation either by whether or not the person was in the labor force during a given survey week or by the number of weeks or hours spent at work per year. Although such measures are important in understanding aggregate male and female labor force participation, they are less useful when analyzing wage differentials. Instead, overall life-cycle labor force commitment, or the proportion of time worked from period to period over an entire lifetime, would be the more relevant variable.

Little comprehensive data is available from which one can obtain individual work history information. Until recently, the two most comprehensive sources of individual labor market data for males and females were the *United States Census of Population and Housing* and the *1967 Survey of Economic Opportunity* (SEO). Unfortunately, neither of these Bureau of Census sources contains retrospective information on labor force participation. However, the *1967 National Longitudinal Survey of Work Experience for Females 30–44 Years of Age* (1967 NLS) which has just recently been made available, does present such work histories for a sample of females.

Although the Bureau of the Census does not collect work history data over an individual lifetime, certain life-cycle implications may be pieced together from available respondents' work habits during the census survey week. These patterns emerge by utilizing the data on each individual and aggregating them over age, sex, and marital status categories. First, labor force participation of females is less than half that of males.[2] Second, the age–participation profile of married females is characterized by a double peak, with the probability of working in the labor force highest before and after the child-bearing ages and lowest within the prime childbearing ages. This pattern is even more apparent when levels of schooling are taken into account. During the child-bearing period of the life cycle, even those females with the very highest levels of education drop out of the labor force to the same extent as females with the lowest levels of schooling.[3] Third, the life-cycle labor force participation patterns of single males and females show roughly similar characteristics.[4] Generally, single males and single females have lower labor force participation rates than married males, but much higher rates of participation than married females.

The National Longitudinal Survey [5] is more complete. For a sample of over 5,000 females, it presents individual information on current labor force status, work experience in 1966, work experience before 1966, attitudes toward work and women's role, marital and family history, health, education, income, wealth, and transfer payments. For each respondent, a history of work experience was computed from the time formal schooling was completed. This work history contains the number of years the respondent worked six months or more during the intervals between the following points in the life cycle (see Figure 4.2): (1) the completion of

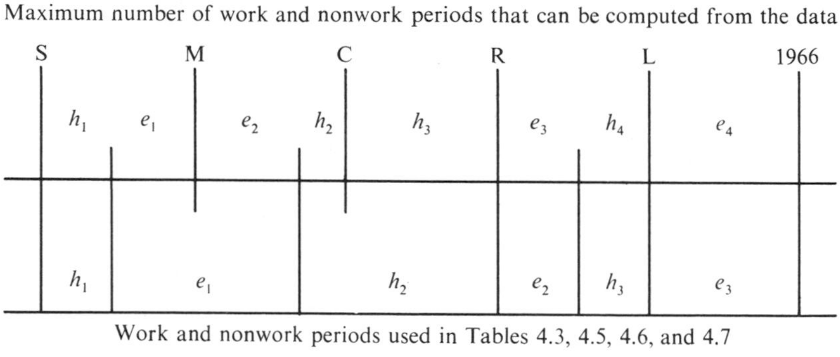

Maximum number of work and nonwork periods that can be computed from the data

Work and nonwork periods used in Tables 4.3, 4.5, 4.6, and 4.7

Source: NLS survey

KEY:

    S = year schooling ended
    M = year first marriage
    C = year first child born
    R = year of reentry into the labor force
    L = year current job began
    e_i = periods of market work in the labor force
    h_i = periods not at work in the labor force

FIGURE 4.2. Work History Information from NLS Survey

TABLE 4.2 Labor Force Participation of Mothers
(white married women, with children, spouse present)

| Proportion Working: | *Percentages* | | | |
	In 1966	*After first child*	*Ever*	N
Age 30–34	43	64	82	925
$S < 12$	46	63	75	294
$S = 12$	43	63	84	446
$S > 12$	40	59	88	185
Age 35–39	47	67	87	945
$S < 12$	45	66	82	336
$S = 12$	49	68	88	422
$S > 12$	47	67	92	187
Age 40–44	53	70	88	1078
$S < 12$	52	72	78	465
$S = 12$	54	70	91	446
$S > 12$	51	68	93	167

SOURCE: *1967 National Longitudinal Survey of Work Experience of Females 30–44 Years of Age;* hereafter cited as 1967 NLS.

NOTE: S = years of schooling.
N = number in sample.

formal schooling (S), (2) the time of the first marriage (M), (3) the birth of the first child (C), (4) the time of reentry into the labor force after the first child (R), and (5) the time when the last or current job was started (L). The patterns of labor force experience are enumerated in Tables 4.2 to 4.7, and confirm the patterns already encountered in the census data.

Table 4.2 indicates that, although close to 90 percent of all mothers in the sample worked at least some time since leaving school, only about two-thirds had returned to the labor market since the birth of their first child. A certain intermittency of labor force participation among these workers is indicated, in that only about 50 percent worked in 1966—the year prior to the survey. Table 4.3 indicates the difference in lifetime labor force participation between married women with and without children as well as between married and single women. Never-married women spent 90 percent of the time since they left school in the labor market, whereas married women with children spent less than 50 percent of their time in market work. Childless women, those with children but without husbands (widowed, divorced, and separated), and those who married more than once spent less time in the labor market than never-

TABLE 4.3   Work Histories of Women, Aged 30-44, by Marital Status (average number of years)
(See Figure 4.2 for key to symbols)

	h_1	e_1	h_2	e_2	h_3	e_3	Σe	Σh	S	N_c	N
White, with Children											
Married once, spouse present	.57	3.55	6.71	1.14	1.22	1.69	6.4	10.4	11.8	3.16	2398
Remarried, spouse present	.54	2.43	7.85	2.60	2.02	2.00	7.1	10.3	10.6	3.28	341
Widowed	1.11	4.25	9.37	1.51	1.44	2.56	8.4	11.9	12.0	2.44	45
Divorced	.94	2.96	6.54	4.24	2.38	2.92	10.1	9.8	10.8	2.98	133
Separated	.74	3.97	7.81	2.71	1.14	2.08	8.7	9.6	10.1	2.86	65
White, Childless											
Married once, spouse present	1.01	5.18		4.39	3.35	4.90	14.5	3.3	11.7		147
Never married		7.08			1.46	7.48	14.5	1.5	12.9		153
Black, with Children											
Married once, spouse present	1.12	3.00	7.12	2.95	2.14	3.26	9.1	10.3	10.0	4.59	563
Remarried, spouse present	.96	2.44	7.43	4.93	2.05	3.36	10.7	11.7	9.6	4.22	170
Widowed and divorced	1.19	2.23	7.67	4.36	1.90	3.68	10.3	10.8	9.8	4.20	149
Separated	1.28	2.86	6.24	5.57	2.38	2.81	11.2	9.8	9.4	4.22	191
Black, Childless											
Married once, spouse present	2.33	4.75		3.83	4.53	4.77	13.4	6.9	10.9		71
Never married		7.15			4.74	6.45	13.6	4.7	10.9		47

SOURCE: 1967 NLS.

NOTE: Because of coding errors in the currently available NLS versions, certain individuals listed as not having worked in 1966 were inadvertently listed as having not worked throughout their lifetime. This error in the NLS tapes means that the estimates of Σh relative to Σe in this table, Table 4.4, as well as for the second row of Tables 4.5 through 4.7, are biased upward. The remainder of the tables are based on data for those in the labor force in 1966, and therefore do not contain this bias.

S = years of schooling.
N_c = family size.
N = number in sample.

married women, but more than mothers who were married once with spouse present.

The amount of time spent in and out of the labor force also depends on the level of education. Table 4.4 indicates that the total number of years spent in the labor force, represented as a fraction of the total possible years that could be spent at work, varies not only with marital status but also with education. The higher the educational attainment, the greater the commitment to the labor force. Among females of all marital status categories (including blacks), those who attended graduate school spent,

TABLE 4.4   Percentage Lifetime Labor Force Participation
by Marital Status and Education

Marital Status	Elementary	High School	College	Graduate School
Married, spouse present	27.4%	33.8%	36.4%	50.0%
Married, spouse absent	28.3	33.4	54.1	NC
Widowed	31.7	32.4	44.9	56.5
Divorced	38.1	51.8	62.4	50.0
Separated	46.1	47.5	49.6	68.2
Never married	28.2	66.9	88.9	97.2
Total	30.1	36.9	41.4	59.1

SOURCE: 1967 NLS.

NOTE: Lifetime Labor Force Participation = total years worked divided by total exposure (age minus education minus 6) to the labor force.

NC = not calculated (too few observations)

on the average, 60 percent of their working life at work, while those with lower levels of education spent only about a third of their total possible working life in the labor force. If the sample is restricted to never-married females, these percentages are much higher. In fact, never-married women who have attended graduate school work almost 100 percent of the time.

As indicated, male–female wage differentials are greatest for married females with children. A detailed analysis of their life-cycle participation is given in Tables 4.5–4.7. The major stages of labor market activity and nonmarket activity are shown chronologically as the length of nonparticipation during the interval between leaving school and marriage (h_1), the years of market work between school and the birth of the first child (e_1), and an uninterrupted period of nonparticipation, starting just before the

TABLE 4.5   Work Histories of Married Women,
Aged 30–34, by Education and Current Work Status
(See Figure 4.2 for key to symbols)

Worked in 1966	h_1	e_1	h_2	e_2	h_3	e_3	Σe	Σh	N_c	N
$S < 12$	1.93	2.37	5.80	3.18	2.20	1.90	7.45	9.93	3.42	135
$S = 12$–15	.90	2.84	5.41	2.21	1.39	2.31	7.36	7.70	2.89	233
$S \geqslant 16$	.37	2.57	2.65	2.22	1.22	2.00	6.79	4.24	2.39	35
Did not work in 1966, but worked since birth of first child										
$S < 12$	1.67	2.23	6.29	1.31	5.09		3.54	13.05	3.50	68
$S = 12$–15	.81	2.90	4.65	1.23	4.75		4.13	10.21	3.49	93
$S \geqslant 16$	.50	1.85	3.57	1.71	3.57		3.56	7.64	3.00	14
Hasn't worked since birth of first child										
$S < 12$	4.54	1.42	9.64				1.42	14.18	3.24	85
$S = 12$–15	2.28	3.21	7.93				3.21	10.21	3.03	211
$S \geqslant 16$	1.95	1.11	7.20				1.11	9.15	3.14	34

SOURCE: 1967 NLS.

NOTE: S = years of schooling.
N_c = family size.
N = number in sample.

TABLE 4.6   Work Histories of Married Women,
Aged 35–39, by Education and Current Work Status

Worked in 1966	h_1	e_1	h_2	e_2	h_3	e_3	Σe	Σh	N_c	N
$S < 12$	1.94	2.78	7.98	3.47	2.78	3.40	9.65	12.70	3.37	152
$S = 12$–15	.98	3.42	6.85	3.09	2.01	3.70	10.21	9.84	2.99	250
$S \geqslant 16$	1.01	2.95	4.72	2.04	1.25	5.46	10.45	6.98	2.72	43
Did not work in 1966, but worked since birth of first child										
$S < 12$	2.15	2.96	9.00	1.80	6.40		4.76	17.55	3.70	65
$S = 12$–15	1.20	3.74	7.42	1.18	5.94		4.92	14.56	3.51	101
$S \geqslant 16$	.38	5.75	6.50	1.15	2.62		6.90	9.50	2.87	8
Hasn't worked since birth of first child										
$S < 12$	4.23	3.54	13.53				3.54	17.76	3.58	113
$S = 12$–15	2.97	3.85	11.62				3.85	14.59	3.16	170
$S \geqslant 16$	1.88	2.65	10.15				2.65	12.03	3.50	26

SOURCE: 1967 NLS.

NOTE: S = years of schooling.
N_c = family size.
N = number in sample.

TABLE 4.7   Work Histories of Married Women,
Aged 40–44, by Education and Current Work Status

Worked in 1966	h_1	e_1	h_2	e_2	h_3	e_3	Σe	Σh	N_c	N
$S < 12$	2.41	3.29	10.38	3.94	2.95	4.93	12.16	15.74	3.18	240
$S = 12$–15	1.55	4.16	8.74	3.57	2.63	4.43	12.16	12.92	2.72	297
$S \geqslant 16$	.93	3.20	6.89	3.06	1.86	4.89	11.15	9.68	3.65	29
Did not work in 1966, but worked since birth of first child										
$S < 12$	2.35	3.31	12.95	1.51	6.89		4.82	22.19	3.41	89
$S = 12$–15	1.39	3.68	10.43	1.24	8.23		4.92	20.05	3.36	82
$S \geqslant 16$	3.19	1.19	9.80	1.34	4.80		2.53	17.19	3.59	5
Hasn't worked since birth of first child										
$S < 12$	6.23	2.63	17.66				2.63	23.89	3.93	130
$S = 12$–15	3.36	4.88	15.12				4.88	18.48	3.12	141
$S \geqslant 16$	3.03	2.67	13.35				2.67	16.38	2.96	31

Source: 1967 NLS.

Note: S = years of schooling.
   N_c = family size.
   N = number in sample.

first child was born (h_2), followed by periods of intermittent participation
and nonparticipation (e_2 and h_3), and finally by e_3, the present job tenure of
women working at the time of the survey.

   It is clear from the tabulations that, after their schooling, the life cycle
of married women features several stages which differ by age, education,
and current work status in the nature and degree of labor market and
home involvement. There is usually continuous market work prior to the
birth of the first child. The second stage, lasting between five and ten
years, is a period of nonparticipation in the labor force on account of
childbearing and child care, followed by intermittent participation before
the youngest child reaches school age. For many the third stage is a more
permanent return to the labor force, though for some it is still of an intermittent nature. In the NLS data, which is restricted to women less than 45
years old, only the beginning of the third stage is visible.

   All of these tables point to the fact that the proportions of time spent
working and not working vary among females. As indicated, much of this
variation depends upon differences in home responsibilities. The married
woman with many children and little education spent the most time out of
the labor force. Since each additional child causes a decrease of lifetime

labor force participation, females with high levels of education tend to have less children and to space them more narrowly than do mothers of low education.

Although sex, labor force participation over the life cycle, and wages may all be related, these data certainly do not prove that such a relationship exists. By applying the human capital theory of income determination, a causal link between these three factors will be established.

Theoretical Framework

The theory of human capital evolved as an interest developed in explaining not only the distribution of earnings between the basic factors of production (capital and labor), but the narrower problem of the distribution of earnings within the labor sector itself. In this regard, it became clear *not* only that individuals differ in terms of basic attributes such as ability, but that, through their own decisions, they can play a major role in determining the nature and extent of their human capital as measured by their levels of health, education, job training, etc. Investments in developing and maintaining such stocks of human capital yield a return in terms of increased market and/or psychic income. However, like any other form of capital, the stock of human capital will depreciate if not maintained and will fail to grow unless current investments exceed the rate of depreciation. The advisability of such investments can be determined by weighing the costs against the returns: i.e., the present costs of investments (both direct costs and any foregone market earnings) against the discounted stream of future increments in income.[6]

Normally, for those who have a lifetime commitment to the labor force, job-related investment activity is concentrated in the early years and tapers off at older ages. At least two reasons can be given for the prevalence of such patterns of human capital investment. First, because there is only a finite life span over which the returns from investment can be reaped, investments made at older ages produce returns over shorter periods and, hence, have a smaller payoff to the individual. Second, time, measured in terms of foregone market earnings, becomes more valuable as one grows older. Since time is an important component of self-investment, such investment becomes more costly, and hence less profitable, at older ages. Hence, at older ages both the returns fall and the costs rise, so that investment can be expected to decline.

A typical male age-earnings profile (i.e., a graph of the logarithm of hourly wages plotted against age) is illustrated in Figure 4.3. The profile is characterized by a steady rise in the hourly wage rate from entry into the labor force until just prior to retirement. Associated with rising wages is an increasing stock of human capital over the life cycle. This represents the netting out of two effects: (1) gross human capital investment, or the accumulation of earnings power; and (2) gross human capital depreciation, or the decline of earnings power. Net investment is the sum of these

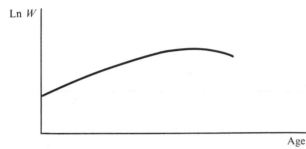

FIGURE 4.3.   A Typical Age-Earnings Profile

two effects. The diminishing rate of increase in earnings with age can clearly be related to the typical decline in net investment with age.[7]

Figure 4.4 depicts these concepts graphically. The upward-sloping marginal cost (*MC*) curve implies a rising cost for each additional unit of human capital purchased per time period. Further, the marginal return in period i from each additional unit of human capital acquired (MR_i) is the present value of additional wages generated in each succeeding period of the working life from human capital investment.[8] Since the gains from investment decline over the life cycle, *MR* shifts down from period to period, MR_{i+1} being lower than MR_i.[9]

In equilibrium one purchases human capital up to the point that marginal revenue equals the marginal cost of the last unit purchased. Diagrammatically, the quantity of human capital purchased in each period can be read off the horizontal axis at I_1, I_2, I_3, etc., finally reaching zero at retirement from the labor force. By projecting these gross investments across a 45° curve, it becomes apparent that gross investment declines with age. As indicated, such an investment pattern gives rise to an earnings function of the type pictured in Panel D of Figure 4.4: steeper at

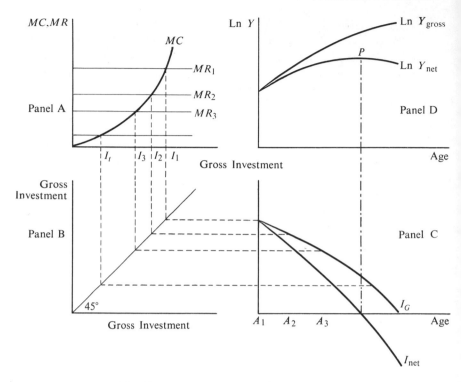

FIGURE 4.4.   The Human Capital Model of Earnings Determination

younger ages, at which investment is greater, and flatter at older ages, at which investment is smaller.

If depreciation of skills (because of either age or obsolescence) occurs, then the net investment (I_{net}) will be lower than gross investment. At the age when I_{net} intersects the horizontal axis capital stock begins to decrease, and earnings are at a maximum (P on the corresponding age–earnings profile). This analysis of the costs and returns of investment, although implicitly derived for males, can be applied to female earnings patterns as well.

Females differ from males in their expectations of lifetime labor force participation. According to Tables 4.2 through 4.7, the female, especially the married female, tends to participate in the labor force more intermittently than her male counterpart. About ten years, on the average, are spent out of the labor force to bear and raise children. Still more time (about four years) is spent in intermittent participation as children are

growing up. The effect of these periods is to lower the gain from investment. That is, because monetary gains from investment cannot be reaped
when not at work, the average married female's returns from investment
are reduced by the present value of the extra earnings from investment
she would have earned had she continued to work instead of staying at
home.

If a comparison is made of the *MR* curve of the female out of the labor
force for ten years (between the ages of 22 and 32) and that of one who
works continuously (Figure 4.5), we find a large initial difference in returns from investment. Although, as indicated in this diagram, positive

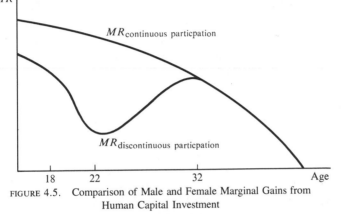

FIGURE 4.5.   Comparison of Male and Female Marginal Gains from
Human Capital Investment

returns from investment exist while the female is out of the labor force,
positive net investment need not occur. If postschool human capital investment in part consists strictly of on-the-job training, then the costs of
investment become higher when the female is out of the labor force and
investment is thereby reduced.[10] Thus this analysis predicts little, if any,
positive net investment during the home time and intermittent participation segments of the female life cycle. Greater investment would occur
during the periods of full-time work, when the marginal returns of investment, *MR*, are relatively high and the marginal costs, *MC*, are relatively
low.

Thus, since the returns from investment are in part based on the duration and continuity of labor force participation, any group expecting relatively low lifetime labor force participation would realize a smaller gain
from investment and hence, all other things being equal, would invest
less. As a consequence, they would be expected to have lower and flatter

earnings profiles than those with a relatively more continuous labor force participation.

Empirical Analysis and Results

Regression analysis can be used to determine how varying degrees of life-cycle labor force participation affect subsequent wage rates. This procedure entails the specification of a functional relationship between wages earned and time spent working or not working during the life cycle.[11] It is hypothesized that an individual's wage rate is functionally related to the amount of schooling, the number of years of work experience, and the extent of home time, as well as to other indices of human capital such as specific job training and certification, mobility, health, number of children, and current weeks and hours of work. This function is fitted to data in the following form:

$$\ln w = c + a_1 S + a_2 e + a_3 h + a_4 x + u, \tag{1}$$
where w is the observed hourly wage rate;

  c is a constant term
  S is the years of schooling;
  e is a vector of work experience segments;
  h is a vector of home time segments;
  x is a vector of other indices of human capital investment, as
    well as of other related variables; [12] and
  u is the statistical residual, assumed to have a zero mean and
    to be independently distributed with a constant variance.

With the semilogarithmic specification used, coefficients a_i can be interpreted as partial elasticities, thereby yielding the percentage change in hourly wages, given a unit change in the associated independent variable.

The results of these regressions are presented in Appendix Tables 4.2 through 4.4. The first table presents these findings stratified by marital status and presence of children, the second by level of schooling, and the third by lifetime work experience. In these tables, work experience is divided into three segments: e_1, which equals years worked between school and birth of the first child; e_2, which equals years worked after child rearing but before current job, and e_3, which equals years worked on current job. Time out of the labor force is consolidated into two segments: h_1, which equals home time after the first child, and h_2, which equals all other home time.

The coefficients of these variables give an indication of the effects of discontinuous labor force participation on earnings. A priori, because more investment occurs on the job than off the job, we expect the coefficients for the home time variables to be smaller in magnitude than those for the experience variables. Similarly, when the job is more permanent (i.e., before the first child and after the completion of childrearing), the rates of investment should be higher than in the periods of intermittent employment. Since the coefficients represent the relative change in earnings during these periods (i.e., the slope of the age–earnings profile), and hence represent the rate of investment, human capital accumulation should be highest for e_1 and e_3 and lowest for h_1 (the longest period out of the labor force).

Generally, the coefficients of e_1 and e_3 exceed the coefficients for e_2 implying that intermittent labor force participation does little to increase the respondent's wages. Hence, little human capital investment occurs during such periods of labor force participation. Wages rise faster, with more investment occurring, when the job is expected to be of longer duration. In most cases, extra experience in one's current job is more important with respect to earnings growth than is earlier experience, thereby implying that in the prechildrearing period women invest less, because of their expectation of being out of the labor force in subsequent periods.

Because labor force attachment is higher for those females without children than for those with children, on-the-job human capital investment should be higher for the former group. The regression results confirm this expectation, thereby indicating that over the life cycle hourly wages rise faster for those with greater labor force attachment. Similarly, classification of women by schooling and by lifetime work experience (Appendix Tables 4.3 and 4.4) illustrates that those with a stronger labor force commitment invest more heavily while at work.

The coefficient of home time is negative, indicating a net depreciation of earning power during time out of the labor force.[13] On the average, for each extra year spent at home, female earnings are lowered by 1.5 percent. This rate is smaller for those without children and those never married. Perhaps these latter groups of females devote some of their time out of the labor force to human capital investment in the form of job search.

Similarly, those females who have spent more than half the total possible years after the end of school working have greater losses from being out of the labor force than those with less of a labor force commitment. If we distinguish between h_1 and h_2, we find the rate of depreciation of earnings to be higher when time is taken off from work during the period of childbearing than when time is taken off during other life-cycle phases.

The implication of these results is that when comparing two individuals at work in the labor force, both with the same actual on-the-job experience, the worker who achieved this experience more continuously would have the higher earnings. Thus, not only is the length of labor force experience important in determining wages, but so also is the continuity of this experience.

Other variables known to affect earnings were also included in the regressions in order to isolate the effects of the human capital variables which are of particular interest in this study. For most of the equations, positive coefficients for additional training and certification variables indicate that the rate of increase of earnings is greater when special training is obtained. It was also found that the longer the length of residency in a county or metropolitan region, the higher the earnings of married women (spouse present) and the lower the earnings of single women. In economic theory, migration is usually seen as a response to better earnings opportunities elsewhere. However, in the case of married women, a move is usually motivated by better job opportunities for the husband and may result in unemployment or lesser earnings for the wife.[14] As expected, the duration of any illness as well as family size are negatively related to earnings, while the size of the place of residence (a measure of job opportunities) has a positive effect on earnings.

In summary, the coefficients of the job experience and home time variables show that intermittent labor force participation is associated with nonmonotonically declining investment behavior. Not surprisingly, the greatest investment and hence the greatest rise in earnings occur when labor force participation is most steady. In fact, during home time, the amount of depreciation caused both by aging and by nonuse of skills outweighs the appreciation of human capital stock from market investment occurring at home. Other measures of job intermittency yielded the same results. Those females who enter and exit the labor force frequently earn less than those with a strong commitment; and those who follow their husband by moving from a county or SMSA also suffer, in general, a loss of earnings. In short, we have found that a high continuous labor force participation has the greatest impact on raising female wages.

Despite the fact that being out of the labor force has a negative effect on female earnings, maternal and family responsibilities deter most women from making a more complete commitment to the labor market.[15] Thus, it is presumably because of these responsibilities that married females tend to work shorter hours, and closer to their home, and to move when their husbands migrate to new jobs. Yet, as we have seen, such behavior is costly in terms of limiting investment and hence earnings on the job.

This discontinuous participation has both direct and indirect effects. The direct effects can be determined from the coefficients of the home time variables. For example, from Appendix Table 4.3 those females with more than a high school education who are out of the labor force after their first child suffer a direct loss in earnings of 4.3 percent a year. For those of lower education as well as during other home time periods, these rates of depreciation are not as great. Without the responsibilities of child care, however, these women could have spent this same time continuing to work in the labor force. Thus, one indirect cost of discontinuous work experience is the loss of potential earnings that could have been generated if the time spent at home had been spent in market work, with a concomitant continuing accumulation of additional experience and human capital. For these same women, this work experience would have yielded an average annual increase of 2.1 percent in earnings. Thus the total earnings loss would be the sum of the direct and indirect effects, or 6.4 percent per year.[16] Yet, this estimate of the potential loss in earnings may still be an underestimate. To the extent that women anticipate leaving the labor force to raise a family, their investment decisions while in the labor force may be affected. Perhaps without this expectation of being out of the labor force, women's investment during their first period of participation would approach that of males.

These effects of intermittent labor force participation are illustrated graphically in Figure 4.6. The vertical axis represents the loss in earnings from being out of the labor force. For women with at least one year of a college education ($S \geq 13$), five years out of the labor force would result in more than a 30 percent drop in earnings potential. For less educated

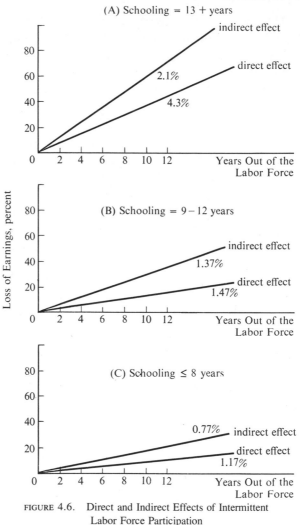

FIGURE 4.6.   Direct and Indirect Effects of Intermittent
Labor Force Participation

groups—those with more intermittent life-cycle labor force participation—the annual rates of loss are lower but total years out of the labor force tend to be higher.

The Male–Female Wage Gap

These results establish that, along with levels of schooling, life-cycle labor force participation patterns are the primary determinant of postschool investment and hence of wages. All other things being equal, those with more continuous labor force experience earn higher wages, while those who take time out from work tend to earn less. One application of these findings is to determine the proportion of male–female wage differentials that can be explained by the intermittent labor force participation patterns of female workers.

To do this, the two female home time periods were consolidated into one (H), and the three job experience segments were divided into experience prior to the current job (E_1) and experience on the current job (E_2). In regressions using the SEO data for males and the NLS data for females, these three variables were used as the primary variables explaining percentage variations in income. The results of these regressions are illustrated in Figure 4.7. As expected, higher and steeper male age–earnings profiles are observed.[17]

In Figure 4.7, GF represents the earning profile (in logarithms) for males. Somewhat below this male profile is the female profile, $ABHE$. The negatively inclined segment of this curve, BH, is the net depreciation of earnings occurring during home time. The rising regions, AB and HE, are of different slopes, illustrating the differing rates of human capital investment in E_1 and E_2. Presumably because E_2 is more permanent than E_1, greater investment occurs during the former period.

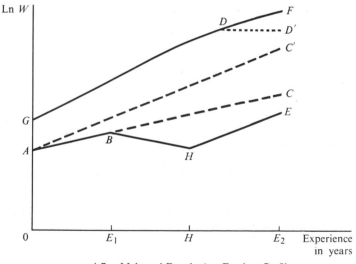

FIGURE 4.7.   Male and Female Age-Earnings Profiles
Computed from Regression Results

If females had the continuous labor force experience of males, their earnings profile would then continue along the dotted extension of the first segment AB up to the point C. This construction assumes that the anticipation of home time decreases the initial rate of investment. On the other hand, the profile AC' assumes that women have experience comparable to that of men and do not reduce their initial rate of investment in anticipation of future departures from the labor force. The gap between these curves ($C'F$) represents a measure of the unexplained portion of the male–female earnings differential. This method of assigning male experience to the female equation explains up to 50 percent of the differences in male–female hourly earnings. Alternatively, by assigning female experience to the male equation and assuming the male rate of investment, we can represent potential female earnings by point D. Because this latter method assumes the male rate of investment and hence neglects the effect of expectations of intermittent labor force participation on investment, the resultant gap (ED') overestimates the unexplained wage differential.

By accounting for factors other than labor force experience, a greater proportion of the wage gap would be explained. For example, wives and mothers often settle for lower-paying jobs in order to work closer to home or at more convenient hours, while factors such as geographic mobility of husbands may interrupt or curtail their wives' job advancement.

The data on work histories show a trend suggesting a prospective narrowing of the wage differential. Tables 4.5–4.7 show that the home time period starting just prior to the birth of the first child (h_1) has been shrinking when older women are compared to younger ones. Women aged 40–44 who had their first child in the late 1940s stayed out of the labor force about five years longer than women 30–34 years old whose first child was born in the late 1950s. Family size is about the same for both age groups but is higher for the middle group, aged 35–39, whose fertility marked the peak of the baby boom. Still, the "home time" interval in that group is shorter (by about two years) than in the older group and longer than in the younger group. Thus, the trend of increased labor force participation of young mothers is persistent. If by the time the women aged 30–34 get to be 40–44 (1977) they have had four more years of work experience than the older cohort, their wages should be 8–10 percent higher than those of the latter, due to less depreciation and longer work experience. Thus, the total observed wage gap between men and women aged 40–44 should narrow by about one-fifth, while the gap due to work experience should be reduced by one-fourth.[18]

Conclusions

Despite the unexplained gap in wages between males and females, to my knowledge no other study of national scope has yet accounted for as large a proportion of the differential.[19] Nevertheless, it should be emphasized that one can conclude from these results neither that the "unexplained" portion of the wage gap is attributable to discrimination, nor, for that matter, that the "explained" portion is not affected by discrimination. More precisely, if a distinction were made between direct discrimination (the payment of differing wage rates for the same work) and indirect discrimination (the subtle socialization process of the division of labor within the household, which discourages most women from making a complete commitment to the labor market), we would find that the "unexplained" wage gap is an upper limit of direct discrimination, while the total wage gap is a reflection of discrimination in its indirect form. Obviously, if the division of labor within the family is equated with discrimination, then no studies of wage differentials would be necessary because all differentials would, by definition, be caused by discrimination.

In conclusion, the importance of continuous work experience as the major causal factor determining male–female wage differentials must be emphasized. The fact that females are, on the average, out of the labor force over ten years causes a decline in their initial human capital investment as well as a depreciation of already existing earnings potential. The result of this discontinuous labor force participation is that females both enter occupations requiring lesser amounts of training and train less even when in professions typified by much on-the-job training. As a result, we observe females being overrepresented in lower-paying occupations while also receiving lower pay in the higher-paying professions.

While I do not, in this paper, discuss a particular policy for achieving equality of wages, it is obvious that, if such is the desired social goal, legislation should be introduced easing the barriers that cause females to devote relatively less time to market work. Fully subsidized family planning services (including abortion), subsidized child care, and the adoption of tax and pension schemes that do not discriminate against the supplementary earnings of married women are all examples of steps that can be taken in this direction. Because the lifetime labor force participation of women has been increasing slowly while so far affecting mostly the younger cohorts, not much discernible change has been observed in the male–female wage differential. On the other hand, discernible progress has been made for the younger cohort. It is to be hoped that this progress will continue.

APPENDIX TABLE 4.1 Percentage Effect of Indicated Variables on Wages

Population:	Sex	Years Married	Number of Children			Existence of Children>18	Spacing of Children (standard deviation change)
			<6	6–11	12–17		
1. Single (never been married) males and females	−.187 *						
2. Married once, spouse present, males and females	−.616						
3. Married once, spouse present, males [a]		0.0039 *	0.0240 *	0.0301 *	0.0115 *	0.0064	
4. Married once, spouse present, females [a]		−.0032	−.0548	−.0669 *	−.0252	−.0112	
5. Married once, spouse present, males							
1–2 children less than 18 [b]		0.0034 *					0.0064
3 or more children less than 18 [b]		0.0019					−.0023
6. Married once, spouse present, females							
1–2 children less than 18 [b]		−.0081 †					−.0065
3 or more children less than 18 [b]		−.0092					−.0167

SOURCE: Computed from U.S. Census, 1960, 1/1000 sample, for those white individuals under age 65 at work with positive earnings.

NOTE: The percentages are coefficients of regression equations of the indicated independent variable on ln(wages/year) for the given population subgroup.

* Significant at greater than the 1 percent level.
† Significant at greater than the 10 percent level.
[a] In addition standardizing for education, exposure to the labor force, hours of work, occupation, and industry.
[b] In addition standardizing for education, exposure to the labor force, hours of work, region of country, and size of city.

APPENDIX TABLE 4.2 Earnings Functions of White Women by Marital Status and Presence of Children

| | | | Married | | | | | Never Married | |
| Variable | | | Children | | Married | | No Children | | Never Married | |
	coefficient	t-statistic	coefficient	t-statistic	coefficient	t-statistic	coefficient	t-statistic	coefficient	t-statistic
Constant	.38		.21		.09		−.42		.55	
S	.076	11.5	.063	10.5	.064	12.0	.081	4.4	.077	4.9
$(A - S - 6)$	−.064	−3.8								
$(A - S - 6)^2$	.001	4.2								
e_1			.021	2.8	.008	2.8	.014	1.6		
e_2			.012	1.6	.001	.3	.011	1.3		
e_3			−.0002	−.5	.012	2.7	.015	2.2	.009	1.5
$e = e_1 + e_2 + e_3$									.026	1.5
$(e)^2$			−.0008	−1.9	−.012	−2.5			−.0007	−1.1
$(e_3)^2$					−.003	−.7				
h_1										
h_2										
$h = h_1 + h_2$			−.007	−1.5			−.005	−1.5	−.009	−.6
$(h)^2$			.000	.2			.002	.7		
etr					.0002	1.5	.0003	2.4	.0003	1.7
ect					.010	3.2	−.003	−1.2	−.011	−1.8
hlt					−.0003	−1.3	−.002	−1.3	−.0008	−1.2
res					.001	1.2	.006	1.7	−.012	−2.2
loc					.044	2.7	−.021	−.4	−.02	−.3
$\ln hrs$					−.11	−3.7	−.15	−1.6	−.43	−4.4
$\ln wks$					.03	1.6	.25	2.2	.21	1.4
N_c					−.008	−1.0				
R^2	.16		.25		.28		.39		.41	
N	993		993		993		147		138	

SOURCE: 1967 NLS.

NOTE:
C = intercept
S = years of schooling
A = age
e_1 = years of market work between school and first child
e_2 = years of market work after first child and before commencement of current job
e_3 = current job tenure
e = total years of work
h_1 = home time after first child
h_2 = other home time

h = total home time
etr = experience x training (months)
ect = experience x certificate (dummy)
hlt = duration of illness (months)
res = years of residence in county
loc = size of place of residence at age 15
ln hrs = (log of) hours per week on current job
ln wks = (log of) weeks worked per year
N_c = family size
R^2 = coefficient of determination
N = sample size

APPENDIX TABLE 4.3 Earnings Functions of White Married Mothers, Spouse Present, by Schooling

	S ≤ 8				S 9–12				S ≥ 13		
	b	t	b	t	b	t	b	t	b	t	b	t
s	.049	1.6	.044	1.3	.051	3.2	.055	3.4	.068	2.8	.079	2.7
e_1	.007	.4	−.002	−.4	.013	1.7	.012	1.5	.021	1.4	.018	1.2
e_2	−.004	−2.1	−.028	−1.8	.009	1.6	.003	.6	−.020	−1.5	−.020	−1.4
e_3	−.002	−.3	−.008	−.5	.013	.7	.009	.5	.009	+2.0	.011	2.2
h_1	−.011	−1.5	−.007	−1.2	−.014	−1.3	−.010	−1.6	−.043	−3.1	−.031	−2.8
h_2	−.006	−.4	−.003	−.2	−.002	−.4	−.002	−.4	−.005	−.4	−.004	−.3
hlt			−.0007	−.7			−.0011	−2.3			−.009	−.6
ln hrs			−.050	−.7			−.090	−1.8			−.130	−1.1
ln wks			−.070	−.6			.060	1.6			.090	1.2
N_c			−.008	−.2			−.019	−.4			−.010	−2.0
R^2	.26		.32		.21		.26		.27		.33	
N	182				593				218			

NOTE: For key, see Appendix Table 4.2.
  b = regression coefficient
  t = t-ratio

APPENDIX TABLE 4.4 Earnings Functions of
White Mothers, Spouse Present,
by Lifetime Work Experience

Variable	Worked More Than Half of Years		Worked Less Than Half of Years	
	Coefficient	t-statistic	Coefficient	t-statistic
Constant	−.28		−.10	
S	.073	9.4	.059	7.9
e_1	.009	2.1	.003	.4
e_2	.006	1.4	−.005	−.6
e_3	.017	2.0	.022	3.8
e_3^2	−.002	−.7	−.001	−1.5
h_1	−.014	−2.3	−.010	−2.6
h_2	.011	1.7	−.004	−.9
hlt	−.0008	−2.1	−.0001	−.3
res	.002	1.1	.002	1.0
loc	.064	2.8	.024	1.0
$ln\ hrs$	−.08	−2.0	−.13	−4.4
$ln\ wks$	.07	1.9	.023	1.0
N_c	−.015	−1.4	−.001	−.2
	$R^2 = .22$		$R^2 = .21$	
	N = 536		N = 604	

NOTE: For key, see Appendix Table 4.2.

NOTES

[1] Contrary to what many believe, the following statistics indicate that the male–female difference in occupational distribution is not as important a factor in defining the size of wage differentials as are family characteristics. Index-number computations were used to estimate what women would earn on the average if their distribution among occupations was the same as that of men, assuming that they would continue to earn average female wages in each occupation. The same calculation was made for men. The results, tabulated below, demonstrate that, on the average, male–female wage differentials are larger within occupations (even on as detailed a basis as the 1960 U.S. Census classification of 297 occupations) than between occupations. From these computations, it is clear that, if males had a female occupational distribution and females a male occupational distribution, the hourly wage differential would be reduced by only 12 percent.

Indices of Occupational Segregation as a Determinant
of Male–Female Wage Differentials

	Yearly	Hourly
Mean female earnings $[Y_F]$	$2,391	$1.81
Mean male earnings $[Y_M]$	4,941	2.63
Mean female earnings with male occupational distribution $[Y_{FM}]$	2,706	1.87
Mean male earnings with female occupational distribution $[Y_{MF}]$	4,372	2.49

SOURCE: U.S. Census, 1960, 1/1000 sample.

When this same index-number calculation is applied to the subgroup of single (never-been-married) males and females, we find that wage differentials would widen if males had a female occupational distribution and females had a male occupational distribution.

[2] For a more detailed analysis of male–female differences in labor force participation, see T. Aldrich Finegan's paper "Participation of Married Women in the Labor Force" in this volume.

[3] Arleen Leibowitz, "Education and Allocation of Women's Time" (Ph.D. diss., Columbia University, 1972). Also see her paper in this volume.

[4] For an analysis of life-cycle aspects of labor force participation, see: G. Ghez and G. Becker, "The Allocation of Goods and Time Over Time" (New York, forthcoming); James Heckman, "Three Essays on Household Labor Supply and the Demand for Market Goods" (Ph.D. diss., Princeton University, 1971); and James P. Smith, "The Life Cycle Allocation of Time in a Family Context" (Ph.D. diss., University of Chicago, 1972).

[5] This survey is described in great detail in Herbert S. Parnes et al., *Dual Careers* (U.S. Department of Labor, 1970).

[6] For a detailed definition and theoretical and empirical discussion of human capital, see the now classic book: G. Becker, *Human Capital: A Theoretical and Empirical Analysis with Special Reference to Education* (New York, 1964). For detailed theoretical and empirical analyses of postschool investment, see J. Mincer, "Investment in Human Capital," *Journal of Political Economy,* Vol. LXVI (August 1958); "On the Job Training: Costs, Returns, and Implications," *Journal of Political Economy,* Vol. LXX (October 1972 Supplement); and "The Distribution of Labor Incomes: A Survey with Special Reference to the Human Capital Approach," *Journal of Economic Literature,* Vol. VIII (March 1970). T. W. Schultz, *Human Capital: Policy Issues and Research Opportunities* (New York, 1972), contains an excellent description of the directions of human capital analysis.

[7] Yoram Ben Porath, "The Production of Human Capital and the Life Cycle of Earnings," *Journal of Political Economy,* LXXV (August 1967): 352–65, describes in detail why human capital investment declines with age.

[8]
$$MR_t = \sum_{i=0}^{T-t} \frac{\Delta W}{(1+r)^i} N_i,$$

where W = the additional wage in each year due to human capital investment;

T = year of retirement, assumed to be known with certainty;

t = period in which investment is made;

r = rate of discount; and

N_i = labor force participation in period i, which is assumed to be constant.

[9] The *MR* curve is horizontal in each period because ΔW is assumed to be constant and invariant with respect to quantity of human capital purchased. Clearly in reality, this need not be the case. However, whether the *MR* curve is downward sloping or horizontal, the fact remains that if labor force participation is constant in each period, marginal revenue declines over the life cycle.

[10] The implication is that since it becomes more difficult to obtain training, the MC' curve (see graph) shifts up to MC', further reducing investment (I to I').

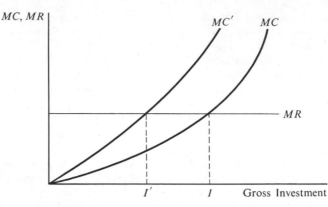

[11] Such a functional specification of the relation between the logarithm of earnings and linear values of schooling and experience variances can be theoretically derived from a recursive model of human capital investment.

Let E_i = gross earnings (or earnings capacity) before investment in period i;

C_i = net investment in period i;

$k_i = C_i/E_i$ = fraction of earnings invested in period i (or "time-equivalent" of investment period i); and

r = rate of return on investment.

Beginning from period 0, if E_0 = given innate initial earnings power, then

$$E_1 = E_0 + rC_0.$$

Thus, if C_0 dollars were invested in the initial period, then earnings capacity in the following period would be increased from the initial earnings by the return on initial investment. By definition,

$$C_0 = k_0 E_0,$$

implying by substitution that

$$E_1 = E_0 + rk_0 E_0 = E_0(1 + rk_0).$$

If in this period C_1 dollars are invested (or k_1, if expressed as a fraction of earnings capacity), then observed earnings (designated by Y_1) would be

$$Y_1 = E_1 - C_1 = E_1 - k_1 E_1 = E_1(1 - k_1) = E_0(1 + rk_0)(1 - k_1),$$

and capacity earnings in the next period would be

$$E_2 = E_1(1 + rk_1) = E_0(1 + rk_0)(1 + rk_1).$$

If this process is followed sequentially, then in period m,

$$E_m = E_0(1 + rk_0)(1 + rk_1) \cdots (1 + rk_m) = E_0 \prod_{i=1}^{m} (1 + rk_i),$$

or

$$ln\ E_m = ln\ E_0 + \Sigma\ ln\ (1 + rk_i).$$

Since $ln\ (1 + rk) = rk$ when rk is small,

$$ln\ E_m = ln\ E_0 + r\ \Sigma k_i,$$

and

$$ln\ Y_m = ln\ E_0 + r\ \Sigma k_i + ln\ (1 - k_m).$$

When we designate Σk_i (the sum of time-equivalent investments) as years of schooling, years of experience, years of home time, and the other variables representing investment, we obtain this semilogarithmic specification of the equation for $ln\ w$ that follows in the text.

[12] The vector of variables, x, is defined as follows:

1. Training and certification variables: *etr*, which represents the product of total work experience and, non-school training (in months) for the individual; *ect*, which represents the product of total work experience and whether the individual has earned a training certificate.

The coefficients of these training and certification variables can be interpreted as the additional percentage that earnings would rise per additional year of experience, given an additional month of nonschool training or a training certificate.

2. *hlt*, which represents the duration of any illness (in months);

3. *res*, which represents years of residency in the county in which one lives;

4. *loc*, which represents the size of the place of residence when respondent's wage age is 15;

5. *ln hrs*, which represents (log of) hours per week on current job;

6. *ln wks*, which represents (log of) weeks per year on current job;

and

7. N_c, which represents the number of children.

[13] Since over the life cycle both positive investments and depreciation occur simultaneously, a negative coefficient implies that the depreciation is greater in magnitude during the home time period. Thus, although one may be investing during the home time period (e.g., in keeping up with one's skills or in scanning the job market), the natural depreciation of aging as well as that of not using one's training dominate and cause a net decrease in earnings potential.

[14] See Beth Niemi, "Geographic Immobility and Labor Force Mobility: A Study of Female Unemployment" in this volume for a further elaboration of this point.

[15] This fact is confirmed in many attitudinal surveys. For example, in Dykman and Stalnaker, "Survey of Women Physicians Graduating from Medical School, 1925–1940," *Journal of Medical Education* (March 1957), 57 percent of the female physicians as compared to 0.1 percent of the male physicians gave family responsibilities or problems (including pregnancy) as the reason for curtailing medical activity. Of those that did curtail their medical activity in any way, 74 percent of the married women while only 1.5 percent of the males gave reasons involving family responsibility.

[16] These rates represent averages over the periods in and out of the labor force. For example, it is thus true that, during a period out of the labor force, depreciation may be greatest the first year and decline for each additional year. For such a case, added time out of the labor force would be less costly for each succeeding year.

[17] A comparison of the relevant variables indicates the following:

A Comparison of Mean Data Values by Data Source

	SINGLE			MARRIED		
	SEO		NLS	SEO		NLS
	Males	*Females*	*Females*	*Males*	*Females*	*Females*
Education	11.57	12.62	12.75	11.63	11.40	11.75
A-S-6	18.69	18.52	15.99 [a]	19.36	20.36	9.69 [a]
ln (wks)	3.83	3.86	3.88	3.89	3.64	3.49
ln (hrs)	3.72	3.66	3.68	3.77	3.47	3.47
No children		0.16	0.033		2.58	2.35
Health	0.90	0.91	0.92	0.93	0.93	0.87
ln (w/yr)	8.49	8.25	8.35	8.83	7.78	7.48
ln (w/hr)	5.54	5.34	5.41	5.76	5.28	5.21

[a] Actual years of experience.

Analysis was performed on the data of the husbands of the married females in the NLS data. However, it was thought that their characteristics were not equivalent to those of the control group, in that some were more than 44 years old.

[18] Two opposing biases mar this conjecture. On the one hand, since the decline in home time is overestimated, too great a narrowing of the wage gap is predicted. On the other hand, since the amount of home time is declining, investment during the working phases of the life cycle would be greater than estimated, thereby causing a downward bias in the projection of the wage gap. It is encouraging to find that in recent work by Victor Fuchs, "Short-Run and Long-Run Prospects for Female Earnings," *American Economic Review,* LXIV (May 1974): 236–42, a narrowing of the male–female wage gap was found, consistent with this study's prediction.

[19] The several studies that explain a greater proportion of male–female wage differentials concentrate on narrower segments of the economy, such as particular occupations or firms. For example, see the paper by George Johnson and Frank Stafford in this volume, "Women and the Academic Labor Market" as well as Berton G. and Judith A. Malkiel, "Male–Female Pay Differentials in Professional Employment," *American Economic Review,* LXIII (September 1973): 693–705; Donald J. McNulty, "Differences in Pay between Men and Women Workers," *Monthly Labor Review,* LXL (December 1967): 40–43; and Henry Sanborn, "Pay Differences Between Men and Women," *Industrial and Labor Relations Review,* XVII (July 1964): 534–50.

Part 2

Discrimination
and Occupational Segregation

5

The Determinants of Occupational Segregation

HARRIET ZELLNER

THE STATISTICS on occupational distribution present a rather extreme picture of occupational segregation by sex. For example, although women represented only 33 percent of total employment in 1960, most of them were concentrated in occupations in which they made up a large majority of those employed. As can be seen in Table 5.1, 47 percent of employed women in 1960 were in occupations in which women represented 80 percent or more of total employment; only 2 percent of employed men were in these same occupations. Whereas only 20 percent of employed women were in occupations in which they represented less than 33 percent of total employment, almost 90 percent of employed men were in these occupations.

Moreover, it is likely that a finer statistical breakdown of occupations would reveal an even greater degree of segregation than that shown in Table 5.1. For example, until 1960 barbers, beauticians, and manicurists were lumped together into a single category; for the 1960 census, this category was broken down into two separate ones: "hairdressers and cosmetologists" and "barbers." Although women represented 57 percent of employment in the grosser category in 1960, using this figure to measure the degree of sex segregation in these trades would give a highly misleading picture, for while women represented 89 percent of hairdressers and cosmetologists, they made up only 3 percent of the barbering trade. Just as the finer breakdown of the 1960 figures yields a more extreme picture of segregation than do the grosser 1950 categories, further refinements

TABLE 5.1   Proportion of Employed Women and Men
by Proportion Female of Occupation in Which
They Are Employed

	Females 100%	Males 100%
Proportion of Occupation that is Female (%)		
80–100	47	2
50–79	22	5
33–49	11	6
0–32	20	87

SOURCE: U.S. Census, 1960, PC(2), 7A, *Occupational Characteristics*, Table 21.

are very likely to produce further increases in the degree of segregation measured.

The difference in occupational distribution between males and females may be attributable to market discrimination, to "objective" (i.e., non-discriminatory) market processes, or to some combination of both. Determining the relative significance of discrimination in generating the observed segregation is extremely important and extremely difficult. There are two alternative strategies open to the researcher attempting to do so. One is to determine how well objective market processes can account for segregation before constructing a theory which assumes discrimination. The other is to reverse the procedure, building and testing a discrimination model first. I have adopted the former strategy because the first question a practitioner of any science should ask about a phenomenon presented for analysis is: "How well can our current theory or models derived from that theory explain it?" If the answer is "Not very well," the need for a new theory is obvious. Even if the answer is "Quite well," nothing stands in the way of constructing a new theory, since it might do still better. But the question should be answered one way or another before proceeding further; this paper is concerned with doing just that.

Development of a Model

Economists assume that the process of occupational choice is rational in that people know the money wage and nonpecuniary characteristics associated with each occupation, and choose that occupation the pursuit of which maximizes their utility. As a first step in the choice process, people must be able to rank occupations according to the expected financial reward associated with each. They may not choose the occupation with the highest expected wage; they may decide rather to forego some income in order to indulge a preference for a certain type of work. But if the choice process is to be considered a rational one, they must be presumed to know just how much this indulgence will cost them.

Suppose there are two occupations, F and M, requiring equal years of schooling. Suppose the wage paid in occupation M increases with the hours worked per week, weeks worked per year, and years of experience in M while in occupation F wage rates are independent of participation levels. The situation is as pictured in Figure 5.1.

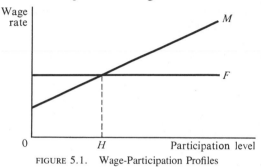

FIGURE 5.1.   Wage-Participation Profiles

At some particular participation level, the wages paid in M and F may be the same. But for higher participation levels the wage in M rises above that in F; for lower participation levels, the opposite situation obtains. The order, then, in which an individual ranks occupations according to expected wage rate is itself a function of the pattern and extent of participation that he or she envisages. For example, any person who intends to supply less than the amount of time indicated by OH will rank F above M; a person intending to supply more than this amount of time will rank M above F. We can assume that occupations are distributed along a continuum with respect to the steepness of the relationship between wage and participation level, the wage rate increasing sharply with participation in some while increasing little or not at all in others.[1]

If individuals do not differ with respect to their labor supply intentions, differences across occupations in the steepness of the wage–participation relationship will be irrelevant to the occupational choice process.[2] In particular, if women on average intend to supply as much time to the labor market as do men, differences among occupations in the extent to which the wage rate varies with the participation level will be irrelevant to an explanation of differences between the sexes in occupational distribution.

However, because males and females do on average differ significantly with respect to the extent and continuity of their labor force participation, the wage that an average male can expect to earn in each occupation will differ from the wage that an average female can expect to earn. The sexes will, therefore, differ in their ranking of occupations by expected wage. This difference in ranking by expected wage will, in general,[3] imply a difference in ranking by utility, which will in turn imply some difference in occupational distribution. It will, moreover, imply the *observed* difference in occupational distribution if the following conditions obtain:

1) the more female-dominated occupations do in fact offer a higher wage than the more male-dominated occupations for lower levels of participation (and, of course, a lower wage than the male-dominated occupations for higher levels of participation);

2) the women who enter the more female-dominated occupations do in fact intend to work less in the market than persons who enter the more male-dominated occupations; and

3) not only are their intended levels of participation lower than those of persons in the more male-dominated occupations, but they are *sufficiently* lower as to make pursuit of a more male-dominated occupation relatively unprofitable (i.e., their intended participation level falls to the left of OH in Figure 5.1).

All three of these conditions must obtain if male–female differences in intended labor force participation are to explain the observed difference in their respective occupational distribution. Only if the more female-dominated occupations are in fact characterized by a flatter wage–participation relationship will these occupations be preferred by individuals intending to supply relatively less time to the labor market. Moreover, the existence of a flatter wage–participation relationship in the more female-dominated occupations will be useful in explaining occupational segregation only if women entering these occupations do in fact intend to supply relatively less time to the labor market than do women entering more male-dominated occupations. If they intend to supply as much or more time to the market, the existence of a flatter wage–participation relationship in more female-dominated occupations should serve as a deterrent rather than as an incentive to entering these occupations. Finally, only if women in more female-dominated occupations would earn lower wages at their intended participation levels in more male-dominated occupations can these participation levels be said to dictate the pursuit of a more female-dominated occupation.

Since the theory of occupational segregation developed above is dependent on all three of these conditions obtaining simultaneously, it may be tested by testing any one of them. In the remainder of this paper I will be concerned with testing the hypothesis that women who enter the more female-dominated occupations do intend to supply less time to the labor market than those who enter more male-dominated occupations (condition 2). Before proceeding to an empirical test of the theory, however, it will prove useful to demonstrate its generality by examining several apparently alternative explanations.

One apparent alternative is that women choose those occupations requiring the least amount of training, either on-the-job or in school, because the expected return to investment in training is lower the shorter the amount of time spent in the labor force, and women in general supply less time to the labor force. But this "investment" explanation of occupational choice is not in any sense a genuine alternative to the theory of occupational choice developed thus far. The hypothesis that women choose occupations requiring less training because they intend to work less in the market assumes that labor supply intentions govern occupational choice; it merely specifies one channel through which the supply effect may operate. Labor supply intentions are assumed to influence desired investment levels, which in turn influence occupational choice. The primary determining factor remains supply intentions.[4]

Another apparent alternative to the labor supply model is that female occupational choices are governed (far more strongly than are male occupational choices) by considerations of domestic productivity. If two occupations, F and M, pay the same wage and are alike in all other respects except one—that skills learned in F increase domestic productivity more than those learned in M—then women (who it is assumed intend to spend more time than men in nonmarket production) will tend more toward occupation F than toward occupation M.[5] Once again, the implications to be drawn from this "domestic productivity" hypothesis are for the most part identical to those derived from the labor supply model. This should not, of course, be surprising, since the domestic productivity explanation assumes that those entering the more female-dominated ("domestic productivity–increasing") occupations intend to supply less time to market activities than do those entering the more male-dominated occupations.[6]

Finally, it could be hypothesized that women choose to enter more female-dominated occupations simply because they have a taste for the work performed in them, whereas males prefer to do the sort of work performed in the more male-dominated occupations. The problem with this sort of explanation is that it is largely untestable (by economists). Unless the theory provides a way of predicting (independent of information provided by the occupational distribution itself) those occupations for which women have a greater taste than do men, we cannot test for the impact of differential tastes on occupational choice. A model of taste formation is required if tastes are to serve as an explanation rather than merely as an interpretation of the observed data. However, economists are not generally in the business of theorizing about taste formation because economics does not equip them to do so (though sociology or psychology might). Economics concerns itself rather with analyzing the consequences of some change in incentives given a set of tastes, however these tastes were generated.

It is clear, then, that the above explanations of occupational choice are not really alternatives to the labor supply model. The first two depend upon the assumption that the more female-dominated occupations are chosen by persons who intend to supply less time to the labor force than do those who enter the more male-dominated occupations; the third, based upon hypothesized taste differences, is interpretive rather than explanatory.

A Test of the Labor Supply Hypothesis

At first sight it might appear that the best way to test the hypothesis that women who enter the more female-dominated occupations intend to work less in the market than those who enter more male-dominated ones would be to estimate (using multiple regression analysis) the relationship between the proportion of an occupation that is female (hereafter referred to as "proportion female") and the actual participation level across occupations. This procedure would not provide an unambiguous test of the hypothesis, however, because the relationship observed at any point in time between actual participation level and proportion female is a product of demand as well as of supply conditions. For example, if the more male-dominated occupations are subject to greater cyclical instability on the demand side than are the more female-dominated occupations, the observed relationship between actual participation level at any point in time and proportion female will represent a biased estimate of the relationship between intended participation level and proportion female.

One course of action would be to estimate the relationship between proportion female and participation level while controlling for all demand factors that might operate differentially (and systematically) across occupations. An alternative approach, adopted here, is to test the labor supply hypothesis by relating factors known to influence female participation levels, rather than the actual participation levels themselves, to the proportion of an occupation that is female. For example, suppose a negative relationship between husband's income and wife's intended labor supply has been repeatedly observed. Then women with higher-income husbands should be more likely to enter the more female-dominated occupations, since women with higher-income husbands (all other things being equal) are expected to supply less time to the labor market. In fact, the logic of the labor supply model implies that any factor which is negatively related to intended labor supply should in general be positively related to the proportion female of the occupation chosen; conversely, any factor which is positively related to intended labor supply should in general be negatively related to proportion female of the occupation chosen.

Estimating the relationship between factors influencing female participation levels (rather than their actual participation levels) and proportion female of the occupation chosen will provide an unambiguous test of the labor supply model. If it is found, for example, that women in the more female-dominated occupations tend to have (all other things being equal) higher-income husbands, it would imply that women who enter these occupations intend to supply less time to the labor market—a result predicted by the theory. If it is found instead that husband's income (all other things being equal) is unrelated or negatively related to proportion female, it would imply that women who enter more female-dominated occupations intend to supply as much or more time to the labor market than do other women—a result contradictory to the theory. In either case, however, there is no need to speculate about whether the estimated relationship is in actual fact a reflection of variation in demand conditions across occupations.

The hypothesis that women who enter more female-dominated occupations intend to supply less time to the labor market will be tested by determining whether factors affecting the labor supply of married (spouse present) women in one direction affect proportion female of the occupations these women enter in the opposite direction. The first empirical task of this paper will be to ascertain the sign, size, and statistical significance of the former set of relationships.

The Supply Equation

What factors, then, are known to influence the labor supply of married women? A good deal of theoretical and empirical work has been done in this area.[7] As a result, the wife's potential wage and her schooling, her

TABLE 5.2   Estimated Supply Equations
for Married Women (spouse present)

Independent Variables	Expected Sign	Dependent Variable = "Weeks Worked in Year"		Dependent Variable = "Labor Force Stability"	
		Estimated coefficient	t-value	Estimated coefficient	t-value
(1)	*(2)*	*(3)*	*(4)*	*(5)*	*(6)*
Wife's potential wage	NP	+0.1910	5.7888	+0.0033	3.9058
Wife's nonlabor income	(−)	−0.2772	−5.1916	−0.0036	−2.6395
Husband's actual income	(−)	−0.0482	−7.6663	−0.0014	−8.4675
Husband's schooling	(−)	−0.0291	−0.5331	−0.0019	−1.3465
No. children 0 to 5	(−)	−4.3190	−11.7938	−0.0897	−9.6401
No. children 6 to 11	(−)	−1.3321	−3.9212	−0.0025	−0.2884
No. children 12 to 19	NP	−0.4000	−1.4540	+0.0112	1.6077
Wife's age	NP	+0.7011	5.6388	+0.0346	10.9475
Wife's age squared	(−)	−0.0076	−4.9574	−0.0004	−9.6822
Wife's schooling	NP	+0.0580	0.5814	+0.0001	0.0525
		$R^2 = .119.$		$R^2 = .114.$	

SOURCE: U.S. Census, 1960, 1/1000 sample. Regressions were run on white married, spouse present, women, 18 years of age and over, nonfarm, not enrolled in school, employed in 1959 as private wage and salary workers.

NOTE: NP = No prediction.

husband's income and schooling, nonlabor income, the number and age of children in the home, and the wife's age are expected to be important determinants of her labor supply.

Table 5.2 lists these variables in column 1 and states in column 2 the expected sign of the relationship between each variable and wife's labor supply. The relationship actually estimated (using multiple regression analysis) between each variable and weeks worked in 1959 is reported in column 3 along with its *t*-value in column 4. Column 5 reports the relationship estimated between each variable and another measure of labor supply, "labor force stability," (a variable which for each woman takes on the value of 1 or of zero; 1 if she was still in the labor force in April 1960, having worked in 1959, and zero if she had worked in 1959, but had left the labor force by April 1960). Column 6 reports the associated *t*-values.[8]

WIFE'S WAGE

The net impact on wife's labor supply of increases in her potential wage cannot be predicted a priori but depends upon the relative strength of the negative income and positive substitution effects associated with a change in wage rate. An increase in wife's wage (husband's income held constant) represents an increase in family income. Increases in family income are expected to increase the wife's (and family's) demand for "leisure" (assuming it to be a normal good), thus reducing the wife's labor supply.[9] On the other hand, an increase in wife's wage makes any time spent by her in nonmarket activity more costly, inducing a substitution of market goods (or the time of other family members) for her own time in nonmarket activity and thereby an increase in the time she supplies to the labor force. If this positive substitution effect outweighs the negative income effect, an increase in wife's wage will be associated with an increase in her labor supply. If the income effect outweighs the substitution effect, a negative relationship between wife's wage and her labor supply will be observed.

As can be seen in Table 5.2, the substitution effect clearly outweighs the income effect; wife's wage is positively and significantly related to both measures of labor supply.[10] It is expected, therefore, that a negative relationship between wife's wage and proportion female of the occupation she enters will be observed.

WIFE'S NONLABOR INCOME [11]

Increases in wife's nonlabor income can be expected to increase her (and the family's) demand for leisure, and since no change in the price of wife's time has occurred (her wage is held constant), there is in this case no positive substitution effect to weigh against the negative income effect. Increases in wife's nonlabor income should, therefore, reduce her labor supply. As can be seen in Table 5.2, the empirical results support this prediction. Wife's nonlabor income is negatively and significantly related to both measures of her labor supply.[12]

Since the relationship between wife's labor supply and her nonlabor income is negative, the relationship between this variable and the proportion female of the occupation in which she is employed is expected to be positive.

HUSBAND'S INCOME

It will prove useful to this analysis to separate husband's income into two components: "permanent" and "transitory" income. "Permanent" income can be thought of as the income an individual expects to earn on the average; "transitory" income represents temporary departures (in a positive or negative direction) from this expected level of income. Husband's transitory income is, then, equal to the amount he is currently earning minus the amount he is expected to earn normally. In years when actual income is above expected income, the husband is receiving positive transitory income or positive "income transitories." In years when actual income is below expected income he is receiving negative transitory income or "negative income transitories."

In the empirical work presented here, husband's permanent income is represented by his level of educational attainment. Transitory income is represented by differences in actual income amongst men who have had the same years of schooling (and therefore presumably have the same permanent income). Both components of husband's income are expected to have a negative influence on wife's labor supply, since both represent increases in family income and hence in each family member's demand for leisure. Since the wife's wage is held constant, there is no positive substitution effect to weigh against the negative income effect on wife's labor supply of increases in husband's income.[13] As can be seen in Table 5.2, husband's transitory income is negatively (as expected) and very significantly related to both measures of wife's labor supply, while husband's permanent income is not significantly related to weeks worked by the wife in 1959 and only approaches significance in its relationship to her labor force stability.[14]

Since husband's permanent income is not significantly related to wife's labor supply, no prediction is made with respect to the sign of its relationship to proportion female of the occupation she enters. Husband's transitory income, although also negatively related to wife's labor supply, is expected to be negatively related to the proportion female of the occupation she enters. The reason for this "perverse" expectation with respect to the sign of the occupation–transitory income relationship lies in the nature of wife's labor supply response to transitory changes in husband's income. Women responding to a transitory decrease in husband's income presumably view their increased levels of labor supply as only temporary. They are, therefore, unlikely to change occupation if already employed; if they were not previously in the labor force, but now enter it intending to work for only a short period, the labor supply model implies that they would do better (financially) to choose one of the more female-dominated occupations. We should, therefore, observe that women whose husbands are experiencing negative income transitories concentrate in the more female-dominated occupations, thus imparting a negative tendency to the relationship between husband's transitory income and proportion female of the occupation entered by the wife.

CHILDREN

The next set of variables refer to the presence of children in the home. Three separate variables are defined: the number of children less than 6 years of age, the number of children aged 6 to 11, and the number of children aged 12 to 17. The wife's labor supply is expected to vary negatively and most sharply with the number of preschoolers in the home, since preschoolers make the greatest demands on the wife's time, and negatively but less strongly with the number of children aged 6 to 11. A prediction with respect to the sign of the relationship between wife's labor supply and number of children aged 12 to 17 cannot be made a priori. While children in the latter age bracket make demands upon the mother's time, they can also substitute for her in the performance of some household and child-care chores. The net effect of children in this age range may, therefore, be either positive or negative.

As can be seen in Table 5.2, wife's labor supply varies (as predicted) negatively and most strongly with the number of children less than 6 and negatively but less significantly with the number of children aged 6 to 11. The effect of the number of children aged 12 to 17 on wife's labor supply is positive when the dependent variable is "labor force stability" and negative when the dependent variable is "weeks worked." It appears, then, that the positive effects of substitution between wife's time and that of older children in household production are reflected in greater labor force stability on the part of the mother, but are not strong enough to outweigh the negative effect on total weeks worked of the additional child-care responsibilities represented by children in this age bracket.

It is expected, therefore, that the number of preschool children will be positively related to proportion female of the occupation in which the mother is employed, as will the number of children aged 6 to 11. No prediction is made with respect to the relationship between the number of children aged 12 to 17 and proportion female because one supply relationship is positive while the other is negative, and it cannot be stated a priori whether one is more important for occupational choice than the other, and if so, which one.

WIFE'S AGE

The effect of changes in wife's age (all other things being equal) on her labor supply cannot be predicted a priori. Changes in intended participation with age will be influenced (over the early and middle stages of the life cycle) by changes in domestic productivity. Just as market productivity increases with labor force experience, so domestic productivity is expected to increase with experience in home production; and experience in home production should (all else constant) vary directly with age. Since wife's wage is held constant in the equation, increasing age represents increases in the productivity of her time in the home relative to its productivity in the market. Increases in the relative productivity of wife's time in home production will generate both negative substitution and positive income effects on intended labor supply; the net effect depends, of course, on which is stronger.[15] As middle age approaches, changes in domestic productivity are likely to become relatively unimportant; beyond that point in the life cycle, the relationship between age and intended participation level will be governed by other factors. Since aging is associated with declining physical strength and vigor, the disutility of working may increase with age. Husband's retirement from the labor force may increase the utility of wife's leisure time (though the opposite has been known to occur), encouraging the wife's withdrawal from, or reduction of time supplied to, the labor market.

As can be seen from Table 5.2, the relationship between age and labor supply is highly significant; up to approximately 44 years of age participation level increases with age; beyond 44, the relationship turns negative. It would appear from these results that the positive income effect of increases in the relative productivity of wife's time in home production with increases in her age outweighs the negative substitution effect up to approximately 44 years of age, and that past 44 the substitution effect and the other labor supply reducing factors noted above combine to produce a negative relationship between wife's age and her labor supply. It is expected therefore that the relationship between wife's age and the proportion female of the occupation in which she is employed will be positive up to approximately 44 years of age and negative thereafter.

WIFE'S SCHOOLING

The sign of the relationship between wife's schooling and her labor supply (all other things being equal) cannot be predicted a priori. In this case as well, there are forces operating in both a positive and a negative direction. Higher levels of schooling may be associated with stronger tastes for market work; we would expect, of course, that individuals with stronger tastes for market work would, all other things being equal, supply more time to the labor market. However, increases in education may also reflect increases in nonmarket relative to market productivity (since the market wage is held constant). As discussed with respect to the age variable, increases in domestic productivity may have a negative or a positive impact on labor supply, depending on whether the substitution effect or the income effect is dominant.

As reported in Table 5.2, wife's schooling is positively but not significantly related to her labor supply. It appears, then, that the positive-taste-for-market-work effect and the positive real income effect of increased domestic productivity are just about offset by the negative substitution effects. Since wife's schooling is not significantly related to her labor supply, no prediction is made with respect to the sign of its relationship to proportion female in the occupation in which she is employed.

Having derived the expected sign of the relationship between proportion female of the occupation in which the wife is employed and each of the independent variables, the next task is to estimate the relationships empirically and compare these expectations to the estimates obtained.

The Occupational Choice Equation

Proportion female of the occupation in which each of the married women in the sample was employed was regressed on the supply variables discussed above. In Table 5.3 these independent variables are given in col-

TABLE 5.3   Estimated Occupation Equation
for Married Women (spouse present)

Independent Variables	Expected Sign	Dependent Variable = Proportion Female	
		Estimated coefficient	*t-value*
Wife's potential wage	(−)	−0.0016	−2.8349
Wife's nonlabor income	(+)	+0.0006	+0.6587
Husband's actual income	(−)	+0.0001	+1.2753
Husband's schooling	NP	+0.0054	+5.8361
No. children under 6	(+)	−0.0186	−2.9817
No. children 6 to 11	(+)	−0.0063	−1.0814
No. children 12 to 17	NP	−0.0115	−2.4503
Wife's age	(−)	−0.0104	−4.8974
Wife's age squared	(+)	+0.0001	+4.3957
Wife's schooling	NP	+0.0122	+7.1538
		$R^2 = .037.$	

SOURCE: U.S. Census, 1960, 1/1000 sample. Regressions were run on white married, spouse present, women, 18 years of age and over, nonfarm, not enrolled in school, employed in 1959 as private wage and salary workers.

NOTE: NP = No prediction.

umn 1; column 2 lists the expected sign of the relationship (derived for each variable in the preceding section); columns 3 and 4 report, respectively, the estimated coefficient and its associated *t*-value. Table 5.4 repeats the information given in Table 5.3, listing first those variables that had the sign predicted by the theory, then those variables having a sign opposite to that predicted by the theory, and finally those variables for which no prediction was made.

TABLE 5.4

Variables Having Predicted Sign	(t-value)
Wife's potential wage	(−2.8349)
Wife's nonlabor income	(+0.6587)
Wife's age	(−4.8974, +4.3957)
Variables Having Wrong Sign	
No. of children under 6	(−2.9817)
No. of children 6 to 11	(−1.0814)
Husband's actual income	(+1.2753)
Variables for Which No Prediction Was Made	
Husband's schooling	(+5.8361)
Wife's schooling	(+7.1538)
No. of children 12 to 17	(−2.4503)

Discussion of Results

Variables Having the Predicted Sign

The significant relationship between proportion female and wife's potential wage and between proportion female and wife's age provide the clearest support for the labor supply model. The relationship between proportion female and wife's nonlabor income provides no real support for the labor supply model; a *t*-value of .6587 or greater would be observed about 50 percent of the time if wife's nonlabor income and proportion female were completely unrelated.

Variables Having the Wrong Sign

The fact that number of children less than 6 does not have its predicted sign is particularly damaging to the labor supply model. Number of preschoolers in the home is the most important variable influencing wife's labor supply; for women employed in 1959, each child under 6 reduced weeks worked by four and reduced the probability of still being in the labor force in April of 1960 by about 9 percentage points. Yet of women who were employed in 1959, those with small children were more likely to be in male-dominated occupations. It is important, therefore, to speculate on the forces that may be producing this relationship.

Having preschoolers at home is a powerful deterrent to the mother's labor force participation; women who remain employed when they have small children may (all other things being equal) have relatively strong tastes for market work. If, additionally, women with relatively strong tastes for market work tend to enter more male-dominated occupations, we might observe a negative relationship between number of small children at home and proportion female of the mother's occupation simply because women in more male-dominated occupations are more likely to remain employed when they have small children than are women in more female-dominated occupations.

The fact that the observed relationship between number of preschoolers at home and proportion female of the mother's occupation is negative may, alternatively, be due to the impact of either "general" or "firm-specific" training on the behavior of both employees and employers. "General" on-the-job training raises the market productivity of workers and therefore the wage they can earn in any firm; "firm-specific" training raises employees' productivity, and therefore their wage, only in the firm providing it. Women who have invested more in either type of training have more to lose by leaving the labor force than women who have invested less. Moreover, employers generally share the cost of firm-specific (although not of general) training and, thus, they also stand to lose if the employee leaves. They may therefore be more willing to work out arrangements whereby women with small children may remain with the firm. If male-dominated occupations are characterized by more on-the-job training than are more female-dominated occupations, we might observe that women with small children are likelier to be in the former occupations. While women in general may wish to reduce their labor supply when they have small children, doing so will be costlier to women in more male-dominated occupations, while the difficulties of remaining employed may be reduced for them by employers anxious to protect the firm's investment.

The fact that the sign of the estimated relationship between husband's actual income and proportion female is positive (rather than negative as predicted) may represent a failure of the model or may be attributable to measurement problems. Variation in husband's actual income, with schooling levels held constant, was presumed to represent transitory income variation. The accuracy with which it does so depends, of course, on the accuracy with which schooling level represents permanent income. While husband's schooling is a good indicator of his permanent income, it is not a perfect one; some men have permanent incomes well above those of others who have had the same amount of schooling. Therefore, even with husband's schooling level held constant, some of the variation in husbands' actual income will in fact represent variation in their permanent income. Because permanent income is positively related to proportion female of the occupation entered by the wife, any variation of permanent with actual income will impart a positive tendency to the measured relationship between actual income and proportion female.

Variables for Which No Prediction Was Made

Although husband's schooling was not found to be significantly related to wife's labor supply (see Table 5.2) it is very significantly related to the proportion female of the occupation she enters. It may be that husband's schooling has a sufficiently strong negative impact on some other dimension of labor supply (such as total years in the labor force) to account for its very strong positive relationship to wife's occupation. Or it may be that husband's schooling affects wife's occupation through some channel other than (or in addition to) labor supply.

The very strong positive relationship between wife's schooling and proportion female of the occupation in which she is employed points to some serious omission in the formulation of the model. It seems unlikely that schooling has a negative impact on some other dimension of labor supply (not measured here) sufficiently powerful to explain the observed positive relationship of schooling to proportion female. One possible explanation is that discrimination against women in more male-dominated occupations increases with their level of educational attainment. If women can more easily gain employment in those male-dominated occupations that are relatively low-skilled, we might observe a positive relationship between a woman's schooling and proportion female of the occupation she enters. Of course, it is possible that a woman's schooling affects her occupational choice through some channel other than labor supply and other than discrimination. As with all the other variables discussed in this section, only further research can yield more definitive conclusions.

The fact that number of children 12 to 17 years of age is negatively and significantly related to proportion female of the mother's occupation may be attributable to what can be called the ''second career effect.'' Women whose eldest children are in the 12-to-17-year-old range are more likely to have achieved their desired family size than women whose eldest children are under 12. They may therefore have expectations of a fuller and more continuous attachment to the labor force than women whose eldest children are in the lower age intervals, and may for this reason be likelier to enter more male-dominated occupations.

A Digression

The observed relationship between a woman's age and the proportion female of the occupation in which she is employed is, as reported above, in accord with that implied by the labor supply model. Of course many theories can explain the same phenomena and it may be appropriate here to offer an alternative hypothesis with respect to the determinants of the observed age-occupation relationship. It may be due primarily to the impact of World War II labor market conditions on the occupational distribution of women. Between 1941 and 1945 business actively recruited women for employment in the more male-dominated occupations. The results reported in this paper show that the women most likely to be in more male-dominated occupations in 1960 were around 52 years of age; [16] they would have been around 32 in 1940. It may have been these women who answered the ads for "Rosie the Riveter." Women younger than this probably had small children to care for, while women somewhat older may have already established themselves in more traditionally female jobs by the time the war began. The women who entered these traditionally male-dominated occupations probably received a good deal of on-the-job training (since the duration of the war was uncertain), and were therefore likely to remain in them after the war ended. A survey done by the Bureau of Labor Statistics on job tenure by period current job started lends some support to this hypothesis. For example, of women employed in 1951, 46.8 percent of those who got their current job before January 1942 and 37 percent of those who got their job between January 1942 and September 1945 were still with their original employer in 1963, whereas of those who got their job after the end of the war (October 1945 to June 1950), only 17.5 percent were still with their original employer in 1963. [17] The age–occupation relationship observed in the 1960 data may be attributable, then, to purely secular phenomena: a combination of relatively low hiring rates of women in more male-dominated occupations before and after World War II and an unusual period of active recruitment during the war years.

Conclusions

It is clear that a good deal of work is required in order to develop a satisfactory explanation of occupational segregation. The failure of the labor supply model to predict occupational affiliation as well as one might have expected could be attributed to a number of factors. Some have already been noted in the discussion of variables having the wrong sign. It may also be that assumptions (1) or (3) of the model (which were not tested in this paper) do not hold; the more female-dominated occupations may not, in fact, be characterized by a flatter wage–participation relationship; even if they are, it may be that the participation level at which most male-dominated occupations become more remunerative is so low that female labor supply intentions are not relevant to their occupational choice decision. Finally, it may be that discrimination plays a significant enough role in determining occupational distribution that failure to specify and control for its operation prevents us from observing some of the relationships implied by the labor supply model.

NOTES

[1] Steeper wage–participation level relationships imply greater returns for continuous high-level participation. Occupations characterized by higher "tooling-up" costs (i.e., by higher levels of short- and long-term on-the-job investments) should therefore be characterized by steeper wage–participation level relationships. Since occupations vary with respect to the former, they should vary with respect to the latter.

[2] This assumes also that people do not differ with respect to their preference for current over future income.

[3] This assumes that men and women do not differ in their tastes for types of work in just such a way as to offset differences in expected wages.

[4] The investment hypothesis does of course yield an additional prediction: viz., that female-dominated occupations will be characterized by lower average skill levels as well as by lower levels of participation.

[5] In fact, under these circumstances women (or any group of individuals intending to spend relatively more time in nonmarket activities) would be willing to work in F for a somewhat lower wage than in M. Increases in domestic productivity represent increases in real income. The greater the proportion of working time applied by individuals to nonmarket production, the greater the amount by which the money wage in F relative to that in M understates the real wage in F relative to M.

[6] The explanation via domestic productivity does imply one result which the basic labor supply model does not: viz., that the absolute level of money wages may be lower in the more female-dominated occupations because part of the remuneration for participation in these occupations is in the form of an (unmeasured) increase in domestic productivity.

[7] Jacob Mincer, "Labor Force Participation of Married Women," in Universities—National Bureau Committee for Economic Research, *Aspects of Labor Economics* (Princeton, N.J., 1962); Gary Becker, "A Theory of the Allocation of Time," *Economic Journal,* LXXV (September 1965): 493–517; Glen Cain, *Married Women in the Labor Force* (Chicago, 1966); William G. Bowen and T. Aldrich Finegan, *The Economics of Labor Force Participation* (Princeton, N.J., 1969).

[8] It will be noted that only measures of current labor supply are used in estimating these supply equations; the 1960 census, the data source upon which the empirical work in this paper is based, provides no information on lifetime labor supply. The accuracy with which occupational affiliation can be predicted from current labor supply depends upon the relative importance of current vs. lifetime labor supply decisions in determining current occupational affiliation and the degree to which current and lifetime labor supply decisions are correlated.

[9] The term ''leisure'' is used throughout this paper as a convenient rubric for all nonmarket activity. It is assumed that income of all family members is pooled and that the leisure enjoyed by each family member is a function of total family income.

[10] Since wife's wage is endogenous to the model, the wage variable entered in the supply equation is estimated using a two-stage, least squares procedure.

[11] Wife's rather than family nonlabor income is used here because husband's nonlabor income is already included in the husband's income variable.

[12] Part of this negative relationship may be spurious since unemployment compensation is included by the Census Bureau in the category of nonlabor income.

[13] Insofar as increases in husband's income are due to increases in his wage rate (rather than in his nonlabor income), substitution of wife's for husband's time in home production will contribute to the size of the measured (negative) income effect.

[14] These results (a stronger transitory than permanent income effect) are consistent with the results Mincer reports in ''Labor Force Participation of Married Women.''

[15] We expect a negative substitution effect because an increase in the productivity of wife's time in the home induces a substitution in consumption toward more time-intensive home goods and substitution of wife's time for market inputs in the production of each of these home goods. Both these substitution effects in production and consumption reduce the time available for market work. We expect a positive income effect because increases in the productivity of wife's time in domestic production represent increases in real income. These real income increases should increase the demand for all (noninferior) commodities. Since the market wage is held constant, only an increase in family labor supply can produce the extra money income necessary to purchase additional market goods.

[16] This is the age at which the partial relationship between proportion female and age reaches a minimum.

[17] U.S. Department of Labor, Bureau of Labor Statistics, *Special Labor Force Reports,* No. 36 (October 1963).

6

Discrimination—
A Manifestation of Male Market Power?

JANICE FANNING MADDEN

IN RECENT YEARS, measurement of the wage differential between the sexes has dominated economic research on sex discrimination. Relatively little attention has been focused upon the application of economic theories to the study of the economic forces which lead to sex discrimination. Whether this results from a belief that the analytic tools previously developed to deal with race discrimination are directly applicable, that the studies of female participation in the labor market fully explain the income differentials involved, or that sex discrimination itself is an insignificant problem; or whether it is because most economists are male, the silence is surprising. Sex discrimination has profound economic implications and is worthy of economic analysis as to its causes within and its effects upon the marketplace.

In economic terms, discrimination occurs whenever market allocations are affected by nonpecuniary or extraneous factors such as sex. Operationally, discrimination can be classified into three types: wage discrimination; occupational or job discrimination; cumulative discrimination.

Wage discrimination occurs when wage differentials are not based on productivity differentials. As Figure 6.1 indicates, *D*, the demand curve of labor, is different from *MRP*, the marginal revenue product of labor. (Marginal revenue product is the amount added to total output by the last worker hired multiplied by the price at which this output sells.) This type

The author wishes to thank Bruce Fitzgerald, Clifford Hawley, Jay Salkin, and the editor, Cynthia Lloyd, for the comments they made on earlier drafts of this paper.

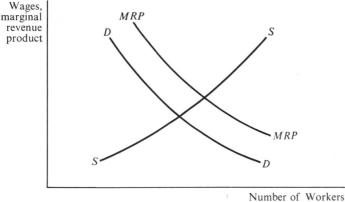

FIGURE 6.1.   Wage Discrimination

of discrimination occurs when women performing the same work as men have different job titles and lower pay.

Occupational or job discrimination occurs when criteria other than productivity are used in determining the number of workers hired. As Figure 6.2 indicates, barriers to entry are placed on some jobs, with the result that *S,* the supply curve, is shifted to the left, *S'*, for these jobs and to the right, *S"*, for the remainder of jobs. (This is distinguishable from wage discrimination in that it involves movement along the demand curve for labor rather than a shift of the demand curve.) Different sex patterns in occupations are indicative of this type of discrimination: for example, the

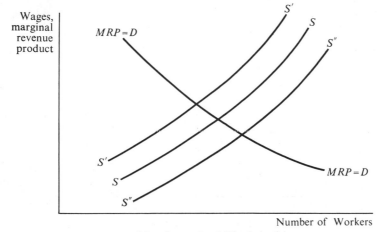

FIGURE 6.2.   Occupational Discrimination

fact that there are almost no women airline pilots and few women doctors, and that almost all telephone operators are women.

Cumulative discrimination occurs when a worker has a lower level of productivity due to past discrimination. As Figure 6.3 indicates, the demand curve for labor is the marginal revenue product of labor, but the *actual* marginal revenue product has shifted downward due to previous patterns of discrimination. For example, this type of discrimination occurs when the choices that younger women make concerning types of training and levels of education are affected by the job patterns of older women who have been victims of discrimination.

There are two different premises from which one can construct an economic model of sex discrimination. One can take prejudice, defined as a preference for not associating with women under some circumstances, as *given* and explain how this prejudice interacts with market forces to produce the observed discrimination. Alternatively, one can construct a model in which prejudice is the *result* of group behavior rather than its cause. In this case, the causes of discrimination are not attributed to the subjective feelings of the parties involved; rather, discrimination is viewed as a rational act within the objective self-interests of the discriminators. That is, discrimination is a manifestation of male economic power, not a product of male preferences.

It is important to distinguish among the different types and causes of

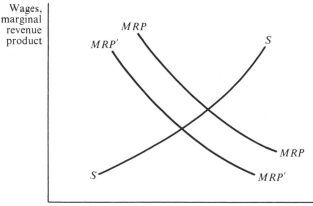

FIGURE 6.3.   Cumulative Discrimination

discrimination because, as discussed in the last section, different policy measures are appropriate for each.

The Becker Model: Discrimination as Taste

The most comprehensive theoretical treatment of discrimination is Gary Becker's *Economics of Discrimination*.[1] Becker's model is a "preference" model which concentrates on wage discrimination. He assumes the existence of prejudice. The emphasis of the analysis is clearly on race discrimination, but Becker maintains that the model is applicable to sex discrimination.[2] The model provides a convenient starting point in analyzing the problems that a sex discrimination model should explain. It also provides a contrast to the suggested male power alternative.

Becker hypothesizes that prejudice, which he labels a "taste for discrimination," affects the economic decision making of employers, co-workers, and consumers within a free and competitive market. (This hypothesis represents an extension of the usual economic behavioral postulates that economic agents maximize profits in production and maximize utility in consumption.) In the Becker model, each economic agent maximizes utility, which is a function of profits and of the expression of prejudice. Becker maintains that these two goals are incompatible, so that utility maximization necessitates trade-offs between profit maximization and discrimination.

Following the Becker formulation, if an employer has a taste for discrimination against women, then he must be compensated for hiring women. The net addition to product made by women hired must exceed their wage rate. Thus, the demand curve for female labor will be to the left of the marginal revenue product curve, as illustrated in Figure 6.1. The greater the prejudice, the larger the shift in the demand curve. Each employer hires females as if the female wage were the market wage plus some amount compensating for the distaste of associating with women. All those employers for whom the male–female wage differential is not sufficient compensation will hire only men at higher salaries, thus paying for their discriminatory behavior.

If co-workers are prejudiced against women, they must receive higher wages for working with women than for working in an all-male establishment. Employers would respond to these employee tastes by hiring sexually segregated work forces, thus avoiding payment of any wage premiums for prejudice. No wage differential would result if employers themselves do not discriminate, but there would be job segregation by sex (assuming that males and females are continuously substitutable in the work force).

If consumers discriminate against goods and services produced by females, they must be compensated for buying female-produced goods and services by lower prices than exist for similar, male-produced items. As a result of consumer preferences, the revenue produced by the output of female labor is less than that for male labor, so the employer offers lower wages to females.

The actual incidence of consumer discrimination is considered [3] insignificant as an explanation of wage differentials, since the production of most goods does not involve contact between employees and consumers and it is difficult to tell merely from looking at a product whether it was produced by males or by females. While service occupations are more contact-oriented, sexual preference can work both ways: for example, women are preferred as Playboy bunnies, airline stewardesses, and lingerie salespeople, while men seem to be preferred as tire salespeople, stockbrokers, and truck drivers. In any case, consumer discrimination causes occupational segregation rather than wage differentials. If the female wage decreases as the amount of consumer contact required by a job increases, women seek employment in jobs where consumer contact is minimal and wages are higher. Only if there are not enough non–consumer-contact jobs for working women, forcing them to seek employment in consumer-contact jobs, would consumer discrimination be responsible for wage differentials. Since most jobs do not require consumer contact, consumer discrimination would segregate women into these jobs, but would not *cause* wage differentials. Empirical studies [4] have shown that wage differentials are greater in consumer-contact occupations than in other occupations. But this research only indicates a correlation between consumer contact and wage differentials; it does not demonstrate that one factor is the cause of the other. There is no theoretical basis to the claim that consumer discrimination is the *cause* of the sex–wage differential. Rather, the problem is to determine why women remain employed in these consumer-contact occupations. Why haven't they moved to occupations involving less consumer contact? Employer and/or employee discrimination must be responsible.

Discrimination by both employers and employees is necessary for the model to predict the three types of discrimination defined above. Discrimination by employers results in wage discrimination; discrimination by fellow employees and consumers results in occupational or job discrimination. Cumulative discrimination results from a tradition of wage and job limitations that affects expectations and, therefore, credential-attainment patterns of younger women.

The implication of the Becker model is actually quite optimistic. As Becker suggests, if competition exists in the labor market and if the cost of discriminatory behavior is borne by the discriminators, then non-discriminators will be more efficient producers and will expand relative to discriminators. Therefore, wage differentials and discrimination will decrease over time.

But such a prediction does not accord well with a casual observation of data. Between 1939 and 1971, the median wage and salary income of females employed full-time year-round declined in relation to male income. The change was from 60.8 percent of male income in 1939 to 59.5 percent in 1971.[5] Though males may have gained in skills and training relative to females, the persistence of this sex–wage differential suggests that labor markets may not be competitive and/or that discriminators may not be making trade-offs between the exercise of prejudice and the attainment of profits.

An Alternative Model: Discrimination as Power

An alternative model is based on the premise that prejudice and discrimination are the result of group behavior. Prejudice is explained by the model, not assumed as a given. Discrimination is assumed to be a manifestation of male power, rather than a manifestation of male tastes. It is hypothesized that the female labor market is not competitive, but rather is controlled by male interests. There are no trade-offs between tastes and profits. Instead, fulfillment of the ''taste'' for discrimination is hypothesized to be compatible with the profit-maximization objective. From this perspective, there is not necessarily a decrease in discrimination over time, for there are no profit incentives toward the elimination of discrimination.

Specifically, it is contended that males, acting as employers and as employees, have power over the female labor market. For expository purposes, let us first examine the case of employer monopsony power. A *monopsony* exists when there is only one employer in the labor market who, due to the lack of competition for labor, has market power over both male and female labor. (Subsequently, male worker power will be added to the model.) An employer monopsony construct of the type first suggested by Joan Robinson is adapted.[6] The assumptions necessary to the model are: (1) employer monopsony power exists; (2) the labor force can be clearly differentiated by sex; (3) employers perceive that the supply of female workers is less responsive to wage changes than is the supply of males. In economic terms, the elasticity of the female labor supply to the firm is less than that of male labor supply, where elasticity is defined as the percentage change in employment divided by the percentage change in wages. Given these assumptions, the employer's demand for workers is determined by labor supply conditions as well as by the worker's productivity.

Figure 6.4 illustrates the labor market that the hypothetical employer faces. There are two labor supply functions, S_f and S_m, differentiated for males and females. *MRP* represents the marginal revenue product of labor, assuming for graphical simplicity that male and female labor are equally efficient.[7] The employer's demand for male and female labor does not reflect the productivity of that labor; rather, it is responsive to the conditions of labor supply. The amount of labor employed, T, is such that the marginal cost of the total amount of labor employed,[8] MC_t, is equal to its marginal revenue product and to the marginal costs of male and female labor, MC_m and MC_f respectively. In other words, the employer keeps hiring workers from the female (male) labor pool until the amount which the last female (male) worker hired contributes to the firm's revenue equals the change in the amount the firm must pay in total wages to the female (male) labor pool. The wages of males and females are then determined by the supply price of the number of males (M) and females (F) employed. Wages are set at whatever level it takes to get the required number of females (males) to work.

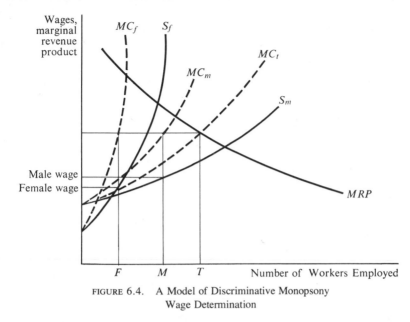

FIGURE 6.4.   A Model of Discriminative Monopsony
Wage Determination

This situation is in contrast to a competitive market, where workers are paid according to their productivity. In a competitive market, wage and employment levels would be determined as illustrated in Figure 6.5. The employers' demand for labor is equivalent to the marginal revenue product curve (MRP). Competition drives wages to the level where the amount of labor demanded equals the amount supplied, as indicated by the intersection of MRP and S_t, the total-labor-supply curve (a horizontal summation of S_m and S_f). S_m and S_f determine the number of males, M, and of females, F, hired. In a competitive market, the differences in the supply of labor by sex do not affect wage levels by sex.

In a monopsony market, if females are less responsive to wage changes than are males (that is, if the wage elasticity of the male-labor-supply curve is greater than that of the female supply curve), the employer will pay females less than equally productive males simply because women are willing to work for less. However, both males and females are paid less than their productivity.

If male workers have monopoly power of their own through unionization while female workers do not, this result changes. In this case, male workers are paid their marginal revenue product, while nonunionized

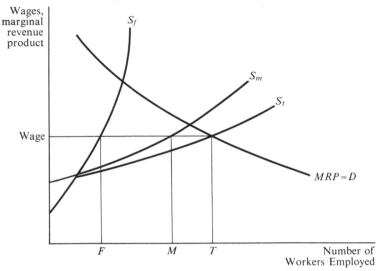

FIGURE 6.5.   A Model of Competitive Wage Determination

female workers are paid their supply price regardless of the relationship by sex between the elasticities of the aggregate supply curves.

As shown in Figure 6.6, the male union negotiates a wage, $\overline{W}_m$, at which the employer can hire as many male workers as he wants up to point $Q_m{}^*$. Beyond $Q_m{}^*$, the aggregate male labor supply curve (S_m) is operative. The monopsonist employer, then, perceives his effective male supply curve to be $\overline{W}_mQS_m$. Male workers are paid the negotiated $\overline{W}_m$, while nonunionized female workers are paid their supply price. This result is illustrated in Figure 6.7, which combines the unionized male-worker-supply curve of Figure 6.6 with the employer-monopsony model of Figure 6.4. In Figure 6.7, as in Figure 6.4, the total number of workers hired, T, is indicated by the point at which the marginal cost of hiring an additional worker, MC_t, equals the worker's marginal revenue product, MRP. The employer equates the marginal cost of hiring an additional female worker, MC_f, to MC_t to determine F, the number of female workers hired. The female wage is the supply price of F. The number of male workers hired is derived by subtracting F from T. The male wage is that set by the union, $\overline{W}_m$, which is also equal to the marginal revenue product of their workers' labor.

This is a simplistic description of the workings of the power model. The key element is that discrimination is a tool of profit maximization

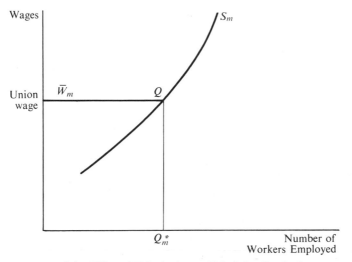

FIGURE 6.6.   Effect of Unionization on Male Labor Supply Curve

that is based on the power of some groups within the economy. The wage differentials which result are based on labor supply differences between the sexes and not on shifts in the demand curve, which are necessary in the Becker model.

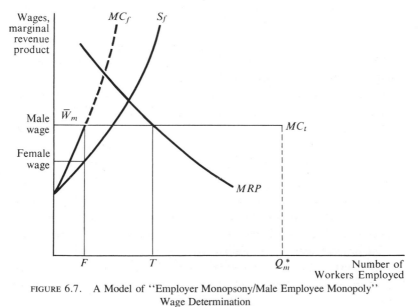

FIGURE 6.7.   A Model of "Employer Monopsony/Male Employee Monopoly" Wage Determination

Monopsony and a Sex-Stratified Labor Market

A more detailed discussion of the three assumptions mentioned above will add to the comprehensiveness of the model. First, let us examine the assumption that male employer monopsony power and male employee monopoly power exist.

The Case for Male Market Power

The term "monopsony power" is used in a liberal sense, analagous to "imperfect competition." The concept of a monopsonist as an employer who faces an upward-sloping supply curve is maintained and is extended from simple monopsony to cover more complicated monopsonylike structures (employment cartels, wage leadership, oligopsony, etc.). Thus the bases of this market power are intended to be more diverse than the literal definition of monopsony as a market in which there is only one buyer. Insofar as males exert economic and/or extraeconomic influence over females, males and females are not independent and competitive outcomes will not correspond to actual results.

While the existence of such influence or power is obvious to even the casual observer, the exposure of such sexual power has been the avid concern of the leaders of the women's liberation movement.[9] The argument against the assumption of female–male independence is supported by analyses of family structure, legal codes, and female corporate activity. Such arguments have been well advanced in previous studies; only highlights will be presented here.

The relationship between males and females is obviously different from the relationship between blacks and whites. Males and females alter their independent status through the institution of marriage. Women are the only "oppressed group" in history to live with the "oppressors." As illustrated by female labor force participation studies [10] and as proposed in the early feminist and Marxist literature,[11] marriage and the number of children are the prime determinants of female labor supply. Thus the "interaction" of males and females in the noneconomic sphere of the family affects the female's decision to work. Family decision making may facilitate the enforcement of discrimination.

Economists know very little about the family decision-making process. Full treatment of the respective roles of male and female family members in such decision making should be an integral part of any comprehensive theory of sex discrimination. The monopsony model of discrimination, in particular, is based on differences between male and female labor supplies to different occupations. These supply differences are determined by family decisions, both as to participation in the labor force and as to specific occupations entered and left. These decisions are directly affected by the nature of the individual utility functions, by the method of aggregating individual utility functions into the family utility function, and by the implicit price ratios of female labor to male labor, to household goods, etc. If male dominance over this process is extensive, it constitutes a means of maintaining male power in the labor market.

The available evidence suggests (not surprisingly) that a husband's attitude toward working wives is highly correlated with whether his wife works.[12] This evidence is consistent with two hypotheses: 1) that career-oriented wives choose husbands with favorable attitudes toward working wives; and 2) that husbands' attitudes affect wives' decisions to work.

Family customs affect economic outcomes in still other ways. In particular, family bonding restrains the female's ability to react to discrimination. Juanita Kreps, for example, contends that the class, status, and income a woman achieves are dependent primarily on the success of her father or husband.[13] Therefore, she has every reason to promote his cause even when it conflicts with her own career interests, as it often may. Kreps concluded that marriage does weaken the basis for any concentrated action of one sex group against the other.

The economic exchange between males and females is also altered by government legislation. The Becker model hypothesizes that males maximize a utility function which is a function of profit and of discrimination. Under the assumptions of this model, over time the smallest taste for discrimination among males governs.[14] If a higher taste for discrimination is legally enforced, then the actual discrimination is greater than that which the Becker model yields. Legal sanctions on females further negate the independence of males and females.

The government has made itself a partner in the establishment of sexual power through the enactment and enforcement of protective labor legislation. This legislation includes regulation of hours worked, of minimum wages, of equal pay, of work before and after childbirth, of occupations, and of working conditions. Though these laws may have originally been written to protect females, they do not consider individual abilities and preferences, and, therefore, tend to discriminate as well as to protect by limiting the job opportunities open to females.

State protective legislation has acted as a constraint on female workers. This can be demonstrated by a survey of cases filed with the Equal Employment Opportunity Commission (EEOC) and with state human rights commissions.[15] Cases in which state protective legislation is used by employers to defend discrimination against females have become significant enough to warrant a revision of EEOC *Guidelines on Discrimination Because of Sex,* such that state protective legislation is now prohibited when it operates to include sex as a bona fide occupational qualification.[16] Nonetheless, the state laws still exist and act as a constraint on female employment opportunities relative to male employment opportunities.

Legal sanctions enforce male power in yet other ways. The Committee on Civil and Political Rights of the President's Commission on the Status of Women [17] has constructed a complete survey of such laws, which include the vesture of control of all property in the husband and other limitations on a wife's legal capacity.

The imprecision with which the term ''monopsony power'' has been employed indicates that we really are not describing a one-employer market but rather a market in which an implicit, collusive sexist agreement (gentlemen's agreement?) exists between employers, so that they act as one. This model emphasizes the *group* interests of employers rather than the individual interests emphasized by the Becker model. Economic models have traditionally emphasized the motivations of individual employers unless group interests were defined in some explicit, legally enforceable form such as government price regulation, union contracts, or occupational licensing. As Kenneth Arrow has argued,[18] however, there is little distinction between legal contracts and other social pressures in terms of their effects on the market. If group interests can lead to legislation, there is no reason to believe that these same pressures could not operate in less explicit ways. American law has long recognized that collusion without express agreement is feasible in fixing prices and restricting output. For example, when firms in an industry recognize that price cutting induces counteractions from rivals which, in the end, leave the entire industry worse off, mutual restraint follows. This behavior is called "conscious parallelism." Industries that have been prosecuted under the Sherman Antitrust Act for conscious parallelism include lumber dealers, motion picture distributors, tobacco manufacturers, and pharmaceutical companies.[19] Conscious parallelism is as possible in labor markets as it is in product markets.

In labor markets, the gain from discriminating must be made greater than the profits to any *single* employer cheating on the agreement. The enforcement of sex-discriminatory norms depends, then, on weakening the individual profit motivation and strengthening the discrimination motivation and the *group* profit motivation.

The government can provide enforcement by restricting the occupations open to females. By not permitting women to be employed in jobs that require night work, overtime, weight lifting, standing, and industrial homework; by requiring firms that hire females to provide special meal or rest periods, lunch rooms, and women's rest rooms or dressing rooms; and by outlawing employment of females in "dangerous" occupations, the government restricts individual employers from profiting by hiring the "discriminated against." The government formalizes the gentlemen's agreement to employ females only in "women's jobs," thus overcrowding the female occupations by shifting their supply curve and lowering marginal productivity and wages in female jobs, while having the reverse effect on male jobs. The government's "protective legislation" thus enforces occupational discrimination and, by this restriction on female employment alternatives, weakens the bargaining position of female workers vis-à-vis their employers.

The cumulative discriminatory effects of the socialization process also eases the enforcement of discrimination among individual employers. Few employers are ever confronted with the actual choice of hiring females into "male" jobs at lower wages. Educational discrimination, in terms of both the courses females are encouraged to take in school and the on-the-job training they seek, control entry into "male" skilled jobs. Employers seldom see a qualified female. Both the social identification of certain prestigious jobs as "male" and the absence or paucity of female role models in these occupations discourage females from training or applying for such jobs. An employer is likely to view the individual profit lost from not employing females to be minimal if few qualified females actually seek such employment.

The employer may be further discouraged from hiring females in male jobs by the pressure and power of male-dominated labor unions. The power to discriminate against female workers may be a result of the monopoly power of male workers as well as the monopsony power of employers. The union seldom if ever seeks wages or employment levels that maximize firm profits; rather, it advocates female and male wages and employment levels that maximize the welfare of the union.

While it is not clear whether unions maximize their membership's welfare by maximizing the wage level, total employment, total membership income (wages times total union employment), or some other factor, it is clearly to the advantage of any single union member to block the entry of other workers into his labor market. While there are numerous ways to exclude competitive workers from the market (license requirements, entrance fees, prolonged apprenticeships), discrimination against any particular competitive group (such as females) can be a more efficient barrier to entry, if there is emotional support from union members. Not only is sex discrimination an administratively easy form of exclusion, but it also provides psychic income to workers who would rather not associate with the excluded group at equal occupational levels. Unions may accomplish the exclusion of women by negotiating with employers to set up job requirements which effectively exclude women. Thus they would, for example, support the bargain for a wage structure tied to seniority, for discrimination against part-time workers, for equal pay for females, for excluding women from jobs requiring weight lifting, night hours, or overtime, etc.

When discrimination against females takes this form, we would expect union-dominated occupations to be predominantly male occupations. Females within these occupations would, however, be expected to receive the same pay as men receive. Unions support occupational discrimination against females but not wage discrimination, since a difference in wages would induce employers to hire females rather than union members and thus destroy union power. Wage discrimination, on the other hand, may be monopsony-motivated, since it is to the advantage of employers more than male employees. However, unions can ease the enforcement of occupational discrimination among employers and, through this further differentiation of the labor force, create more opportunities for the employer to wage-discriminate profitably between occupations.

In conclusion, these analyses of the organization of the family, of the nature of the socialization process, and of legal codes and extralegal pressures all conform to the hypothesis of male domination, although other interpretations are not excluded.

Separability of the Labor Market by Sex

We have demonstrated in the discussion of the general monopsony model that for a monopsonist to discriminate, the labor market must be separable into two or more distinguishable labor pools with different elasticities of supply. This section discusses the methods of separating the labor force into male and female components.

It is obviously an easy task for an employer to distinguish his female from his male employees, but employment policies which are based only on a sexual difference may not be optimal methods of exercising discriminatory monopsony power. To avoid moral and legal outrage and to encourage peaceful coexistence among his employees, an employer may classify his workers by "objective" standards that are in fact highly correlated with sex differences. It is clear that males and females seldom work at the same job for the same firm. Even at more aggregated levels of occupational divisions, the separation is clear. Few occupations employ large numbers of both sexes. Most men work in occupations that employ very few women; a significant proportion of women work in occupations that employ very few men.[20] This division by sex can be encouraged in many ways: (1) particular occupations are assigned to one sex for biological reasons; (2) general conditions of employment consistent with the life-styles or lifetime working cycles of only one sex are specified; and (3) particular occupations are assigned to one sex because of socially induced differences in attitudes and motivation between the sexes.

There are certain biological differences in the capacities of males and females that can logically be expected to affect their relative distribution among occupations. Assignment of males to jobs which biologically require males (and vice versa) does not involve any occupational discrimination. At the same time, the sexual classification of jobs often subdivides the labor pool and may be the vehicle by which a monopsonist discriminates in wages. While it is obvious that biology explains a reluctance to employ female sperm donors or male wet nurses, it is not at all clear how it affects most other occupations. There is no apparent physical reason why most accountants and auditors are male and bookkeepers female, or why clergymen are male and religious workers female, or why elementary-school teachers are female and college teachers male. The major female occupations are not apparently restricted to the female sex for physical or biological reasons.

The reader may wonder if the biologically based ability differences between males and females might be intellectual as well as physical.[21] If such an intellectual difference exists, the distribution of sexes among occupations might reflect inherent differences in intellectual as well as in physical capacities, so that the monopsonist is able to subdivide his labor pool by sex, utilizing the intellectual as well as the physical requirements of various occupations.

Such a justifiable division by occupation need not indicate occupational discrimination. But in practice, this "natural" division merely furthers a discriminatory wage structure. To say that males and females are physically or intellectually different does not imply that either has inferior abilities. Males and females can contribute with equal efficiency (if in different ways) to the final product. The monopsonist pays different wages because the abilities which are different enable him to separate his labor pool, and the elasticities of labor supply are different between the pools. The differences in pay to males and females are not, in this case, based on any differences in the value of their productivity.

Consistent with this line of thought, Juanita Kreps [22] has suggested that salary differentials in academe reflect differences in the sex typing of particular positions rather than differences in levels of ability. Maintaining that teaching is a relatively female occupation and research a relatively male occupation, Kreps concludes that teaching is rewarded less than research because it is a more female occupation than is research. Kreps, without formulating any monopsonistic theory of the educational complex, does not provide any empirical basis for her conclusion. In the absence of objective measures of academic competence, there also seems to be no way to test her conclusions statistically. Only judgment is involved in determining the productivity of college professors; it is impossible to determine if this judgment is based on sexist notions of the value of female work or on actual differences in the value of their product.

On the other hand, if monopsony power exists to any important degree, the employer is motivated by profit considerations to differentiate his work force in such a way that he can lower his wage bill by wage discrimination. If men and women do different jobs (though their respective marginal revenue products are equal in their different endeavors), a means is provided for the monopsonist to differentiate his work force (and for the econometrician to explain discrimination on occupational grounds).

If "natural" differences between males and females are not sufficient for achieving the desired degree of occupational segregation by sex the monopsonist may induce greater occupational sex differentiation by setting sex-linked requirements for a particular job. He may foreclose any significant female interest in the job he is offering by making it inconsistent with the female life-style and working cycle. Given biology and the current status of social attitudes, female life-styles are distinguished from male life-styles by special responsibilities in the bearing and rearing of children. This has predictable effects on the female work life, which becomes discontinuous and, often, part-time. Therefore, if job requirements are structured so as to preclude part-time work or to require career continuity with one employer, such a job will never be a female occupation. If such requirements could be eased but are not, effective occupational discrimination is occurring along with potential wage discrimination.

Thus, if a monopsonistic employer wishes to separate his workers by sex covertly and pay differential wages, he may simply offer lower salaries to part-time workers and to workers unable to work during the peak performance period of 20 to 35 years of age. Setting job requirements so that part-time work is available only in the lowest-paid occupations and only in the lowest ranks of the more prestigious occupations limits large numbers of females to such jobs.

Differences in life-cycle participation can separate the labor force in another way if promotions are based on performance during any period between the ages of 20 and 35. Such rigidity places females at a comparative disadvantage, since these years are also their peak years of childbearing and childrearing. To deny upper-echelon jobs to those workers who do not meet performance requirements within a period that must fall between the ages of 20 and 35 is to deny upper-echelon positions to married woman and to relegate these women to subordinate positions.

Social custom reinforces different types of motivation among males and females, which adds to the occupational division by sex. Because men are expected to be sources of both their own support and that of their families, they are motivated toward careers from infancy. The female role is projected as that of housewife and mother, usually subordinate to the male "head of household." Females are less frequently motivated to think in terms of careers. They are regarded by the society primarily in domestic roles and only secondarily as workers.

Historically, as production moved from the home to the factory, female workers changed their workplace from the home to the factory.[23] But the female role of housewife and mother was also carried from home to factory. When women entered the labor force, they naturally sought jobs similar to those in which they had domestic experience. As women sewed and knitted in the home, they entered the labor force as textile workers and clothing salesclerks; as women taught and reared their own children, they entered the labor force as elementary-school teachers and baby-sitters; as women prepared meals for their families, they entered the labor force as waitresses, food packers, and cooks; as women served as "helpmates" to their husbands, they entered the labor force as secretaries, stenographers, and administrative assistants to male management; as women nursed their families in sickness, they entered the labor force as nurses; as women kept their own homes, they entered the labor force as private household help.

Social projections of "proper" female and male roles alter the distribution of the sexes among occupations by creating an artificially high correlation between motivations and sex and between specific types of training and sex. These social norms act to create a threat of social ostracism for females who demonstrate "male" motivation or seek training for "male" occupations. These psychic costs form another barrier to female entry into male occupations, in that a monopsonist can discriminate against females by differential pay schedules between jobs which require socially identified male traits (career motivation and training interests) and those which are socially identified with female traits. The stronger the social pressure, the easier it is for the monopsonist to separate his labor pool by sex through occupational distinctions.

Elasticity of Labor Supply by Sex

In applying a monopsony model to sex discrimination, it is also necessary to consider whether the third condition for discrimination (that the female labor supply elasticity be less than the male elasticity) can be met.

Within the general model, the ability of the monopsonist to separate the labor market by sex would imply wage discrimination against females only if their labor supply to the firm was less elastic than the male labor supply (see Figure 6.4). On the other hand, if the male supply were less elastic, the model would predict wage discrimination against males.

Time-series data clearly indicate both increasing labor force participation of women and decreasing working hours of men during time periods of generally increasing income. It may be concluded that the male-labor-supply curve is backward-bending while the female supply curve is positively related to wage rates. Mincer and Cain have studied the relationship between the labor force participation of married women, their median income, and their husband's income.[24] Both studies (using cross-sectional data) indicate that the effect of wives' own income is positive and twice the size of the effect of husbands' income in determining the probability of wives' labor force participation. Bowen and Finegan,[25] studying the direct relationship between the labor force participation of men and women and their respective incomes, have found that the labor force participation of married women is much more responsive to wages than is the participation of men. These results would appear to be inconsistent with the elasticities hypothesized in the discriminatory monopsony model.

Empirical studies measure the labor supply functions for the economy as a whole but not for individual firms, industries, or occupations. However, the supply curves of concern in the discriminatory monopsony model *are* those to occupations, industries, and firms. The supply curves illustrated in Figures 6.4, 6.5, and 6.6 are the supply curves perceived by an employer, not by the entire economy. Any introductory economics text distinguishes (for sellers' markets) between the industry's demand curve for output and the firm's demand curve.[26] It is that type of distinction that is made here for a buyer's market.

There are two ways in which an inelastic "aggregate male supply function" may actually be elastic relative to the elastic "aggregate female supply function" at the disaggregated firm level. Males may be unionized, and/or there may be relatively more competition for male workers among employers. In both cases, the male labor supply curve faced by the individual employer is more elastic than the aggregate male labor supply curve.

Simply, the firm views the male wage as parametric and the female wage as variable. As an example, a hospital perceives that a ''union,'' the American Medical Association, has set the rate at which physicians can be hired. This wage is viewed as parametric in that no matter how many doctors the hospital employs, the wage is the same. Nurses, on the other hand, are attracted into their jobs from their alternative occupation as housewives. The number of nurses who seek employment with the hospital depends on the wages offered. Nurses' wages, then, are treated as a variable by the hospital, since these wages may be varied by the hospital as the number of nurses hired varies. In a similar manner, a business firm perceives that its competition in hiring for junior executive is so strong that the firm has no control over wages. The competitively determined wage is taken as a parameter. However, secretarial salaries are viewed as variable in the same sense as were nurses' salaries. In both examples, the supply of male labor to the firm is more elastic than the supply of female labor.

The ideal way to test this hypothesis empirically is to examine the changes in employment by sex which are indicated by changes in recruitment expenditures and wages offered by individual firms.[27] If the male wage elasticity is greater than the female elasticity, a firm which increases (decreases) its wages and recruitment expenditures should attract (lose) proportionately more male workers than female workers. Unfortunately, wage and employment data are not currently available on a firm-by-firm basis; rather, it is collected on individuals. From this type of data it is impossible to gauge the effect of changes in wages by particular firms.

Developments in economic theory guide the manner in which data are collected. For macroeconomic questions, wage and employment statistics aggregated over individuals are appropriate. Since microeconomic labor market theory has traditionally explained wage differentials in terms of differences in individual productivities, individual statistics have also been appropriate. For our microeconomic analysis, however, firms are hypothesized to have latitude in setting wages, at least vis-à-vis the female labor force, so that wages should differ over firms even when worker quality is held constant.

Our theory is clearly testable but a direct test cannot be presented here; we must await the accumulation of appropriate data. This has often been the case in the testing of new theoretical models.[28] But this does not mean that we cannot present some indirect evidence of the hypothesized elasticities. If either competition or a union has made the male supply curve to the firm more elastic, then competition or unionization must not operate on the female supply curve to the same extent.

In the case of competition in the male market, the employer competes with other employers for male workers, but similar competition does not occur in the female labor market. For female workers the employer competes with domestic duties. To employ men, he must pay the going, competitively determined wage. In perfect competition, this wage is unique. Since no employer can individually influence the market, no worker would work for less than he could earn elsewhere. Likewise, no employer would pay more than the going rate, since he could hire sufficient help at that level.

For female workers, the employer must pay a wage which is more attractive than the value placed on work in the home. He does not compete with other employers so much as with household chores. The value placed on housework, however, is not uniquely determined. There is no market in which the value of a wife's services are exchanged. Her work is not paid; it has only implicit value. This implicit value differs from household to household.[29] Varying opportunity costs [30] of female workers prompt an upward-sloping female labor supply curve to the employer, while the constant opportunity costs of male workers prompt a horizontal male labor supply curve.

The method by which unionization of males can make the male supply curve elastic relative to the female supply curve is explained above. Likewise, the statistical evidence suggests that unions are in the control of males.[31]

If unionization and/or employer competition has made the male labor supply curve more elastic than the female supply curve, then we should observe greater variance between employers in female wage rates than in male wage rates. Once again, we do not have the employer data to verify such a hypothesis.

But less direct evidence supports this contention. Beth Niemi's work, reported elsewhere in this volume, indicates that women who change their labor force status are four times more likely than men to do so by moving in or out of the labor force itself and only one-third as likely to do so by changing employers. Other studies of labor mobility are consistent with these results.[32] Furthermore, casual observation of the geographic labor market indicates that males face a more competitive labor market than females. Even within the same occupation and wage categories, males work for a more spatially dispersed group of employers than females.[33] This indicates that there is a larger potential number of employers competing for males than for females.

The problem with these interfirm mobility studies is that they show movement only between firms. They don't relate worker movement to changes in wages, which would be of particular interest for our purposes. In studies where mobility rates have been examined in relation to wage changes,[34] there has been no study of differences by sex. Nonetheless, the evidence that is available is consistent with the contention that employers compete with other employers for male workers and with household activities for female workers.

In conclusion, a clear test of the elasticities of labor supply by sex is impossible at the present time, due to a lack of data. Nonetheless, implications of the hypothesis that the employer's supply of male labor is more elastic than his supply of female labor are consistent with empirical observations.

A Comparison of Policy Implications

The expected effectiveness of policies to alleviate sex discrimination depends on the model used to analyze discrimination. In the Becker model, sex discrimination is represented by wage differentials and occupational segregation based on taste; in the noncompetitive power model, sex discrimination is a set of wage differentials between occupations, with the occupational classification biased against women and based on power. Thus, the Becker and the noncompetitive models suggest different viewpoints toward equal pay legislation, antidiscrimination in hiring legislation, affirmative action programs, and quota systems, depending on the effectiveness of each policy in limiting power or changing tastes, and in stopping wage or occupational discrimination. In this section, we analyze each of these policies and suggest some alternatives.

Since equal pay laws are meaningless without antidiscrimination legislation with regard to hiring, we discuss these alternatives as a single plan.

For the Becker competitive model, the effect of such legislation depends directly on the extent to which the costs of discriminatory practices are raised. To the extent that it is possible to evade the antidiscrimination laws, firms forced to pay one wage will hire only one sex—either males at the value of their marginal product or females at the value of their marginal product less the amount of the discrimination coefficient. Equal pay laws prompt occupational segregation. If antidiscrimination legislation is strictly enforced, the wage discrimination of the competitive model is alleviated, since occupational segregation is not seen as the cause of wage differentials. In the noncompetitive model, strict enforcement will also eliminate intraoccupational wage discrimination, but will not eliminate (and may even increase) interoccupational wage discrimination. In this model, the wage differential between occupations reflects the sexual composition of occupations as well as productivity differences, so that the interoccupational wage differences are a substantial part of wage discrimination. Equal pay and antidiscrimination legislation could prompt greater occupational differentiation through greater use by employers of sex-correlated artificial job requirements.

An affirmative action program goes beyond the requirements of an antidiscrimination law. It requires employers and/or unions to take positive steps to employ females and to give preference to qualified females over equally qualified males. As with antidiscrimination laws, this action is more potent if discrimination is interoccupational rather than intraoccupational, and if it is based on power rather than taste. Affirmative action programs are the next step after antidiscrimination laws in pulling women into male jobs and corroding sex-based power. Employers are required to acquaint women with job opportunities and to hire qualified respondents. As "male" occupations lose their sex identity through an increase in female supply, sex discrimination through interoccupational wage discrimination is impossible. The power of males to exclude females is limited.

A quota system requires that employers and/or unions employ females at some given percentage of the work force in each occupation, regardless of qualification. Such a policy is certainly capable of pulling women into "male" occupations, depending on how fine an occupational breakdown is utilized. However, if less qualified women are hired to replace qualified men, total production must decrease since less productive factors are employed. Furthermore, income is transferred from the qualified men, who are now forced into lower paying jobs (or unemployment), to the less qualified women who take their former jobs.

As a means of eliminating discrimination, the quota system is much more effective in the monopsony model, where discrimination depends on occupational differentiation and the power of the discriminator. If discrimination is primarily wage discrimination (as the Becker model postulates) the quota system is ineffective, as quotas do not eliminate salary differentials.

Since the main employment disadvantage of women is their unfavorable occupational distribution, more innovative proposals directed at this particular aspect of the woman problem are necessary. For example, to require all employers to verify that all job requirements are performance requirements could potentially open more jobs to women. There is some potential disadvantage to highly bureaucratized organizations who have found that, in their case, rigid rules are the most efficient way to govern decision making. This legislation could complement the present antidiscrimination legislation by outlawing occupational discrimination as a means to circumvent Title VII of the Civil Rights Act.

Of course, a reform of the process of socialization into sex roles could have pervasive effects greater than any of the remedial actions suggested above. If responsibilities for housekeeping and childrearing are shared, the male and female life cycles may not be so distinct, since females do tend toward greater participation in the labor market when their homemaking duties are diminished, i.e., before the birth of their children and after their children are of school age. As the life-cycle characteristics of men and women become more alike, the ability of the employer to act on a life-style characteristic as a sex indicator is diminished. Likewise, the profit motive for such discrimination would be eliminated as the wage elasticity of the labor supply curve becomes similar for both sexes.

It is not clear, then, that there can be any reasonable expectation of short-term changes in sex roles. We do not even know which aspects of feminine and masculine roles are cultural and which are biological. Nonetheless, if sex roles become less distinct, there will be less basis for sex discrimination in the labor market.

The sex problem is not the same as the race problem and will not be solved by adding the word "sex" to racial legislation. Such an addition to Title VII of the Civil Rights Act of 1964 was suggested in hopes of blocking the legislation and was met with Congressional laughter and ridicule. The extent of our commitment to the elimination of discrimination will determine who laughs last.

NOTES

[1] Gary Becker, *The Economics of Discrimination,* 2d Edition (Chicago, 1971).

[2] *Ibid.,* p. 11.

[3] Kenneth J. Arrow, "Some Models of Racial Discrimination in the Labor Market," The Rand Corporation, RM6253-RC.

[4] Victor R. Fuchs, "Differences in Hourly Earnings between Men and Women," *Monthly Labor Review,* XCIV (1971): 9–15; Henry Sanborn, "Pay Differences between Men and Women," *Industrial and Labor Relations Review,* XVII (July 1964): 534–50.

[5] U.S. President's Council of Economic Advisors, *Economic Report of the President* (Washington, D.C., 1973), 103.

[6] Joan Robinson, *The Economics of Imperfect Competition* (London, 1934), pp. 301–4.

[7] For a discussion of the same problem complicated by relaxing the assumption that male and female labor are equally efficient, see Janice F. Madden, *The Economics of Sex Discrimination* (Lexington, Mass., 1973), pp. 61–64.

[8] This is a measure of the rate of increase in the total wage bill incurred by increasing employment. If the supply of labor curve for the relevant pool is upward-sloping and if all workers in this labor pool are paid equally, increasing employment increases the total wage bill by the amount paid in wages to the new worker hired plus the amount of increase paid to the incumbents.

[9] See Kirsten Amundsen, *The Silenced Majority: Women and American Democracy* (Englewood Cliffs, N.J., 1971); Caroline Bird, *Born Female: The High Cost of Keeping Women Down* (New York, 1968); Kate Millett, *Sexual Politics* (New York, 1969); Georgene H. Seward and Robert C. Williamson, eds., *Sex Roles in a Changing Society* (New York, 1970); Carol Andreas, *Sex and Caste in America* (Englewood Cliffs, N.J., 1971); Edmund Dahlstrom, ed., *The Changing Roles of Men and Women* (London, 1962).

[10] Glen G. Cain, *Married Women in the Labor Force* (Chicago, 1966); Clarence D. Long, *The Labor Force under Changing Income and Employment* (Princeton, N.J., 1958): Jacob Mincer, "Labor Force Participation of Married Women," in Universities-National Bureau Committee for Economic Research,

Aspects of Labor Economics (Princeton, N.J., 1962); William B. Bowen and Aldrich T. Finegan, *The Economics of Labor Force Participation* (Princeton, N.J., 1969).

[11] Frederick Engels, *The Origin of the Family, Private Property, and the State* (Zurich, 1884); August Bebel, *Woman and Socialism* (New York, 1938); Karl Marx et al., *The Woman Question* (New York, 1951); Charlotte P. Gilman, *Women and Economics* (Boston, 1898); John Stuart Mill, *The Subjection of Women* (London, 1869).

[12] Leland J. Axelson, "The Marital Adjustment and Marital Role Definitions of Husbands of Working and Non-Working Wives," *Marriage and Family Living,* XXV (May 1963): 189–95; Mildred W. Weil, "An Analysis of the Factors Influencing Married Women's Actual or Planned Work Participation," *American Sociological Review,* XXVI (February 1961): 91–96.

[13] Juanita Kreps, *Sex in the Marketplace: American Women at Work* (Baltimore, 1971), p. 105.

[14] Becker does point out that at any given point in time, the level of effective discrimination is dependent on the distribution of tastes for discrimination and the relative proportion of "discriminated against" workers in the labor force. However, over time the smallest taste should govern, since employers with the smallest taste for discrimination will have the greatest profits and, consequently, will expand. *Economics of Discrimination,* p. 43.

[15] See, for example: *Rosenfeld* v. *So. Pacific Company,* 293 F. Supp. 1212 (C.D. Calif. 1968); *Richards* v. *Griffith Rubber Mills,* 300 F. Supp. 338 (D.C. Ore. 1969); *Bowe* v. *Colgate-Palmolive Company,* 416 F. 2d 711 (7th Cir. 1969); *Caterpillar Tractor Company* v. *Grabeic,* 63 LC 9522, 2 FEP Cas. 945 (S.D. 711, 1970).

[16] 29 C.F.R. 1604.1 (1970).

[17] U.S. President's Commission on the Status of Women, *Report of the Committee on Civil and Political Rights* (Washington, D.C., 1963).

[18] Arrow, "Some Models of Racial Discrimination."

[19] *Eastern States Retail Lumber Dealers' Association* v. *U.S.,* 234 U.S. 600 (1914); *Interstate Circuit, Inc., et al.* v. *U.S.,* 306 U.S. 208 (1939); *American Tobacco Co. et al.* v. *U.S.,* 328 U.S. 781 (1946); *U.S.* v. *Charles Pfizer & Co., Inc., et al.,* 281 F. Supp 837 (1968).

[20] Fuchs, "Differences in Hourly Earnings," p. 14; McNulty, "Differences in Pay Between Men and Women Workers," *Monthly Labor Review,* XC (December 1967): 545; Valerie K. Oppenheimer, *The Female Labor Force in the United States* (Berkeley, 1970), pp. 64–116.

[21] For a survey of psychological studies of the differences in abilities between males and females, see Edwin C. Lewis, *Developing Woman's Potential* (Ames, Iowa, 1968). The studies indicate that, for example, girls of school age tend to be superior to boys in tests of verbal ability, perceptual speed, memory, and artistic ability, while males excel in tests of mechanical ability, numerical ability (as adults), spatial relations, and scientific aptitude.

[22] Kreps, *Sex in the Marketplace,* pp. 55–62.

[23] For a history of industry's adaption to the female worker, see Elizabeth Baker, *Technology and Women's Work* (New York, 1964).

[24] Cain, *Married Women in the Labor Force;* Mincer, "Labor Force Participation of Married Women."

[25] Bowen and Finegan, *Economics of Labor Force Participation.*

[26] See, for example, Paul A. Samuelson, *Economics,* 8th ed. (New York, 1970), p. 432.

[27] For an explanation as to why recruitment expenditures as well as wages must be included, see George J. Stigler, "Information in the Labor Market," *Journal of Political Economy,* LXX (October 1962): 94–105.

[28] This has been a serious problem, for example, in testing regional and urban economic theories.

[29] For a discussion of how this work is evaluated, see Kreps, *Sex in the Marketplace,* pp. 66–73; Colin Clark, "The Economics of Housework," *Bulletin of the Oxford Institute of Statistics,* XX (1958); Ismail H. Siregeldin, *Non-Market Components of National Income* (Ann Arbor, Mich., 1969).

[30] "Opportunity cost" is defined as the value of the benefit which is given up to perform one job as opposed to another.

[31] See Madden, *The Economics of Sex Discrimination,* p. 57; Bessie Hillman, "Gifted Women in the Trade Unions," in Beverly Cassara, ed. *American Women: The Changing Image* (Boston, 1962), p. 99.

[32] For example, see Donald J. Bogue, *A Methodological Study of Migration and Labor Mobility in Michigan and Ohio in 1947* (Oxford, Ohio, 1952); Robert L. Bunting, "Labor Mobility: Sex, Race, and Age," *The Review of Economics and Statistics,* XLII (May 1960): 229–31; Robert L. Bunting, Lowell D. Ashby, and Peter A. Prosper, Jr., "Labor Mobility in Three Southern States," *Industrial and Labor Relations Review,* XIV (April 1961): 432–45; Paul Eldridge and Irwin Wolkstein, "Incidence of Employer Change," *Industrial and Labor Relations Review,* X (October 1956): 101–7; *Minnesota Manpower Mobilities* (University of Minnesota Industrial Relations Center, 1950).

[33] For example, see Richard A. Lester, "Wage Diversity and Its Theoretical Implications," *The Review of Economics Statistics,* XXVIII (August 1946): 152–53; Richard A. Lester, *Hiring Practices and Labor Competition* (Princeton, N.J., 1954); Charles A. Myers and W. Rupert Maclaurin, *The Movement of Factory Workers* (New York, 1943); Lloyd G. Reynolds, *The Structure of Labor Markets* (New York, 1951); Lloyd G. Reynolds and Joseph Shister, *Job Horizons* (New York, 1949).

[34] This conclusion is supported by Fuchs, "Differences in Hourly Earnings," p. 10, and by Albert Rees and George P. Shultz, *Workers and Wages in an Urban Labor Market* (Chicago, 1970), p. 66.

7

Relative Wages and Sex Segregation by Occupation

MARY H. STEVENSON

For many years, economists all but ignored the issue of wage differences between men and women. Recently, however, the issue has received more attention, and there has been a revival of interest in the "crowding hypothesis," a concept expounded in the 1920s in England. This hypothesis argues that the major reason for the low wages of women workers is that, by being denied access to many occupations, they are crowded into a limited number of remaining occupations.[1] Because women must compete with each other for jobs that are within the small range of occupations in which women are deemed acceptable, the supply of labor to these occupations is artificially enlarged, and the remuneration is therefore less than it otherwise would be. Correspondingly, men in many occupations are protected from competition for jobs on the part of women workers, so that the supply of labor in men's occupations is artificially reduced, and their remuneration is therefore higher than it otherwise would be. Removal of discriminatory barriers would reduce competition for jobs in female-dominated occupations and increase competition for jobs in male-dominated occupations, resulting in pay increases in the former and pay reductions in the latter.

The empirical work discussed in this paper applies the theoretical framework of the crowding hypothesis to an examination of occupational categories based on job requirements. Previous studies of occupational wage differences between men and women have defined occupations either too narrowly or too broadly. Neither approach gives a clear impression of the extent of discrimination against women.

Studies that use a narrow definition of occupation generally compare men and women within a specific occupation (e.g., accounting clerk). Male–female wage differentials are generally much smaller within specific occupations than across the labor market as a whole. McNulty found that women working in establishments that hire both men and women for a specific occupation fare better than women in establishments that hire women only.[2] Rees and Schultz found that substantial male–female wage differentials persisted after differences in human capital were controlled for within occupations.[3] While some very useful information has emerged from studies using this approach, the major problem with such an approach is that it encompasses only a small segment of the labor force. Most occupations are not integrated by sex, and by the time a researcher has focused in on those men and women who work in the same, narrowly defined occupation, a major source of wage differentials has already been eliminated—those differentials that arise when women do not have access to all occupations on an equal basis with men.

The other approach has been to compare earnings between men and women in broadly defined occupations (e.g., clerical workers, service workers).[4] Such an approach was used in a *New York Times* article of July 26, 1970,[5] which referred to the substantial earnings differentials within broad occupations as evidence of a ''double standard'' or of ''unequal pay scales.'' Inferences that differences in pay within these broad occupations are a measure of discrimination are grossly inaccurate, since each of these broad occupations is composed of a variety of specific jobs, which may require vastly different amounts and combinations of education and training. The specific jobs done by men and women within these broad occupations may therefore not be comparable at all.

If narrowly defined occupations encompass only a small segment of the labor force, and if broadly defined occupations do not provide a sensible basis for comparison, then perhaps a meaningful way to categorize occupations would be in terms of clusters of specific occupations that all require similar amounts of human capital, as measured by the education and training necessary to perform the job. In this way, earnings of men and women doing jobs that require similar amounts of human capital can be compared, even though the men and women are not necessarily doing exactly the same job. A formulation very much like this was proposed by Sir Roy Harrod in 1945:

I shall use the term "category" of billets or jobs. I say that two jobs are in the same "category" if they require the same amount of general education, specialized training, apprenticeship and experience for their efficient execution. But the specific nature, as distinct from the amount, of the training, etc., need not be the same. Thus a certain grade of administrative billet and a certain grade of school teaching billet might be in the same category. In the long run, subject, of course, to frictions and irregularities, persons of similar aptitude may expect to get similar pay in billets of the same category.[6]

Although Harrod's formulation was purely hypothetical, this paper uses his concept of occupational categories based on human capital requirements. The U.S. Department of Labor's *Dictionary of Occupational Titles (DOT), 1966 Supplement* provides estimates of the general educational development (cognitive skill) and specific vocational preparation (training time) necessary to perform specific jobs. Specific occupations were grouped together on the basis of the DOT's estimated requirements, and seventeen distinct job categories were created, with each category representing jobs requiring similar educational development and training time. The categories were numbered from one to seventeen, and the entire categorization was called Occlevel.[7] In general, high-number occlevels correspond to greater education and training requirements. However, Occlevel is not a strictly ordinal measure, since in some cases a higher occlevel may represent requirements for more education but less skill than a lower occlevel.

Since specific jobs within an occlevel all require similar amounts of education and training, people who hold jobs within an occlevel ought, in theory, to be capable of holding any other job in that occlevel. In reality, other job requirements may intervene, so that complete interchangeability may not be possible. For instance, some jobs within an occlevel may have a further requirement that, in addition to a given level of education and skill, a worker must have perfect eyesight. The assumption of interchangeability is probably more valid at lower occlevels than at higher ones. A person who works as an electrician may also have the aptitude to be a plumber, but a person who works as a lawyer may not be as likely to have the aptitude to be a doctor.[8] To the extent that there are significant training costs involved in preparing for a specific occupation, these training costs may create mobility barriers that further reduce the likelihood of interchangeability.

The data used in my analysis come from a variety of sources. The sample population was drawn from the 1967 Survey of Economic Opportunity (SEO) and includes black and white adults who worked full-time full-year (defined as at least 30 hours a week for at least 40 weeks) and were at their usual job when the survey was taken. Average hourly wages (before deductions) for this population were $3.48 for white males, $2.33 for black males, $2.24 for white females, and $1.75 for black females. If an hourly wage of $2.25 were designated as the boundary between high-wage and low-wage jobs,[9] then about a fifth of the white males, almost half of the black males, about three-fifths of the white females, and over three-fourths of the black females earned low wages. Therefore, women who work full-time, full-year, have lower average wages than men and have a disproportionate share of low-wage employment.

The SEO listed the specific occupation and industry in which each worker was employed. Other data about the characteristics of those occupations and industries [10] was merged with the SEO file, so that the data set included information about the individual worker as well as information about the occupation and industry in which the worker was employed.

The Occlevel categorization and the merged SEO data set were used to test two hypotheses about women workers: 1) within occlevels, women would have more years of schooling but lower average pay than men; and 2) within occlevels, women would be crowded into fewer specific occupations than men, and that crowding would be related to wage differences. White men are used as a benchmark group with which to compare white female and black female workers, since it is presumed that white men do not suffer from racial or sexual discrimination in the labor market.

Wages and Education

The first hypothesis argues that women are at a disadvantage in the labor market because, when job requirements are held constant, women do work similar to that of men who have fewer years of schooling than they do. In this way, the return on women's investment in education is reduced, since it would appear that women need higher educational achievements than men in order to perform the same kind of work. Restricting women with a certain number of years of schooling to the same range of occupations as men with fewer years of schooling is one way in which discrimination may occur; another way would be to pay women less than men for the same quality work.

It should be noted that this hypothesis relates occlevel only to formal years of schooling. The lack of information on a worker's labor force experience represents a major shortcoming of the data used in this study. To the extent that men, on the average, have more job experience than women, the findings relating formal education to occlevel may be overstated. If, within an occlevel, women have more formal education but men have more experience, then it is possible that men could have equivalent or greater amounts of human capital than women. A recent study by Solomon Polachek attributes from 15 to 50 percent of the hourly wage differential to the fact that, while men have steady exposure to the labor force, women's labor force exposure is segmented and interrupted by time spent at home.[11] In recent years, many economists have argued that across all occupations, women's stock of human capital is lower than men's both because of fewer years of job experience and because of depreciation of market skills with a lack of continuity of labor force participation.

However, the direction of causation between experience and wages is far from clear. The traditional view would be that since some women prefer to leave the labor force to attend to family duties, their lower amount of experience explains the lower wages they receive. In the context of the crowding hypothesis, women receive lower wages because of labor market segregation, and those lower wages induce some women to leave the paid labor market for the alternative of unpaid household work. It remains an open question whether women receive lower wages as a result of less experience or whether they wind up with less experience as a result of lower wages.

The relationship between occlevel, mean education level, and average wage is presented in Tables 7.1 and 7.2. Table 7.1 indicates that for each race/sex group, higher occlevels tend to be accompanied by higher levels of education and higher wages. Within each occlevel, white men consistently received the highest wages. They were generally followed by white women, with black women usually in last place. Although white men in an occlevel consistently receive the highest wages, they are not always the most highly educated group.

In order to compare education and wage levels of white men to those

TABLE 7.1   Mean Education and Average Wage by Occlevel

| Occlevel | White Male | | White Female | | Black Female | |
	Mean education (Years of schooling)	Avg. wage	Mean education (Years of schooling)	Avg. wage	Mean education (Years of schooling)	Avg. wage
1	8.95	2.27	8.74	1.62	7.98	1.05
2	9.51	2.30	9.05	1.56	9.04	1.39
3	a	a	a	a	a	a
4	a	a	a	a	7.46	.52
5	9.96	2.79	10.22	2.03	10.48	1.89
6	9.95	2.83	9.65	1.82	10.85	1.80
7	10.17	3.07	11.48	2.11	11.75	1.78
8	10.58	3.08	9.75	2.21	a	a
9	9.77	3.20	a	a	a	a
10	12.12	3.16	11.80	2.27	12.28	2.43
11	12.17	3.39	11.59	2.01	11.94	1.96
12	10.95	2.99	12.05	2.25	9.61	1.57
13	10.87	3.47	11.32	2.27	10.46	2.01
14	11.27	3.54	a	a	a	a
15	14.04	3.99	15.01	3.08	15.71	3.41
16	14.68	4.70	14.19	3.01	15.41	3.03
17	17.00	4.93	15.19	4.06	a	a
Total	11.39	3.33	11.57	2.22	10.25	1.73

NOTE: a = less than 0.5% of race/sex group in the occlevel.

of the female groups, an index was constructed which measures the ratio of percentage differences in wages between white males and each of the female groups to percentage differences in education (see Table 7.2). When the index has a value between 0 and 1, percentage differences in education are greater than percentage differences in wages. When the index has a value greater than 1, percentage differences in wages are greater than percentage differences in education. When the index has a negative value, either the female group is lower paid and better educated than the white males, or the female group has higher pay but less education than white males. In this analysis, a negative value always refers to the former possibility, since the latter does not occur.

The numbers in Table 7.2 may be interpreted as follows: in occlevel 1, a white male with 1 percent more education than a white female could expect to receive wages that are 12.24 percent higher than hers; in occlevel 5, a white male with 1 percent less education than a white female would nevertheless receive 10.44 percent higher wages.

An index value between 0 and 1 does not occur. The comparison of

TABLE 7.2   Ratio of Percentage Difference in
Wages between White Males and Each Female Group
in Occlevel to Percentage Difference in Education

Occlevel	White Female	Black Female
1	12.24	4.96
2	6.66	8.01
3	*a*	*a*
4	*a*	*a*
5	−10.44	−6.18
6	11.85	−4.03
7	−2.43	−2.71
8	3.61	*a*
9	*a*	*a*
10	10.67	−17.50
11	8.55	22.44
12	−2.46	3.88
13	−8.37	11.16
14	*a*	*a*
15	−3.30	−1.22
16	10.80	−7.15
17	1.66	*a*
Total	−21.09	4.80

NOTE: *a* = less than 0.5% of race/sex group in the occlevel.

wage differences and educational differences between white men and
white women indicates that in a majority of cases within occlevels, white
men earn higher wages and are better educated, although percentage
wage differences are larger than the percentage differences in education.
In a substantial minority of cases within occlevels (five out of the thirteen
for which data were recorded), white women received lower pay even
though they had more years of schooling. It can be seen from Table 7.1
that this pattern was also true for white women across all occlevels. The
pattern for black women was similar to that of white women within
occlevels, though information for fewer categories could be recorded. For
the sample as a whole, on the average, black women were lower paid and
had fewer years of education as compared with white men, but percentage differences in wages were larger than percentage differences in education.

These tables indicate that men and women in the same occlevel do not
have the same education level, and that even when women were more
highly educated, they received lower pay than men. When men had

higher education levels, their wage advantage far exceeded their educational advantage. Since, in the sample population, average wages among women workers with less than a high-school diploma were extremely low ($1.29 for black women and $1.85 for white women, as compared with 2.85 for white men), it may be surmised that some of the difference in wages between men and women is a result of women being constrained to compete against men with less education for a given range of jobs, and in any case not receiving wages commensurate with their education level. This form of discrimination is not as blatant as, for instance, having two wage scales for a given occupation, and it may be easier to enforce because it may be more difficult to detect. Equal pay legislation provides that workers doing substantially the same jobs should get the same pay, but it does not specify that equally talented workers should have equal access to jobs.

Occupational Distribution by Sex

The second hypothesis states that, of those performing jobs with similar human capital requirements, the women are concentrated in fewer distinct occupations, and specifically in those occupations with the lowest wages.

Differences in the occupational distribution of women vis-à-vis that of men may be clearly seen in several of the tables to be presented here. Table 7.3 shows the distribution of each race/sex group across occlevels. An index of segregation may be created, this index being a measure that indicates what percentage of each female group would have to change occlevels in order that their distribution across occlevel would be the same as that of white males. The index of segregation[12] may be measured as

$$\frac{\sum_{i=1}^{n} \left| x_1 - x_2 \right|}{2},$$

where x_1 = percentage of white males in an occlevel;
  x_2 = percentage of each female group in an occlevel; and
  n = number of occlevels.

The following example shows how the index works: Assume all men and women are in three occupations, A, B, and C. Thirty percent of women

TABLE 7.3   Distribution of Race/Sex Groups
across Occlevel

Occlevel	White Male	White Female	Black Female
1	5.7%	3.2%	28.1%
2	2.1	2.9	10.3
3	0.2	0.1	0.0
4	0.1	0.4	0.7
5	16.2	19.6	14.8
6	7.7	7.9	11.8
7	3.5	4.1	2.0
8	3.4	0.5	0.1
9	2.9	0.2	0.4
10	4.6	13.3	7.5
11	8.1	13.4	3.5
12	1.9	16.7	9.3
13	23.5	3.0	2.2
14	1.0	0.0	0.0
15	9.2	11.1	7.5
16	5.3	2.8	1.5
17	4.6	0.8	0.3
Total	100%	100%	100%
N	5485	2611	1843

are in A, 45 percent in B, and 25 percent in C; 40 percent of the men are in A, 25 percent in B, and 35 percent in C. In order for the two distributions to match, either 20 percent of the women would have to move from B (10 percent to A and 10 percent to C) or 20 percent of the men would have to move to B (10 percent from A and 10 percent from C). Therefore, 20 percent of the men (or the women) would have to change occupations, and the index of segregation would be 20 percent. Using the formula, the absolute differences in distribution are summed across occupations: 10 percent in A + 20 percent in B + 10 percent in C = 40 percent. The calculation of the sum of *absolute* differences without regard to sign means that the percentage of women (or of men) needing to change occupations has actually been counted twice, and it is therefore necessary to divide by 2, yielding the correct answer, 20 percent.

The index of segregation across occlevels is 36 percent for white females and 46 percent for black females. The distribution of black women across occlevels, compared with the distribution of white men, is most dramatically different at the lowest levels. These levels contain a small fraction of the white men but a substantial portion of the black women.

Therefore, the index of segregation is showing the effect of fewer years of schooling and perhaps poorer-quality schools in relegating a disproportionate number of black women to the lowest occlevels. This is not the case for white women. The index of segregation between white men and white women seems to reflect a preponderance of "men's" jobs or "women's" jobs between occlevels 10 and 13, and would therefore seem to be less related to differences in education between white men and white women.

Another index of segregation was used to measure the degree of segregation between white men and other race/sex groups *within* occlevels. In this case, the index of segregation was calculated for each occlevel as

$$\frac{\sum_{i=1}^{n} \left| x_1 - x_2 \right|}{2},$$

where x_1 = percentage of white males in the occlevel in a specific occupation;

   x_2 = percentage of each female group in the occlevel in a specific occupation; and

   n = number of specific occupations in the occlevel.

These indexes are presented in Table 7.4. Since occlevel is a method of categorizing occupations according to the amount of education and training needed to perform a job, the index of segregation within occlevel is measuring effects *other* than differences between race/sex groups in education and specific vocational preparation. As explained earlier, one can say, at least on a conceptual level, that an individual in an occlevel should be capable of performing any job in the occlevel, unless other job requirements (in addition to education and training) preclude it. It is striking to note, therefore, that for women, both black and white, the index values for segregation *within* occlevels are fairly consistently higher than the measures of segregation *across* occlevels.

Measuring segregation is one way of quantifying "crowding." However, it is really a measure of the wide differences between the jobs that most men and most women have. The proportion of specific occupations in each occlevel which have at least one person of a given race/sex group can also be used as a measure of "crowding." Examination of the data showed that black females appeared in the fewest number of specific oc-

TABLE 7.4   Index of Segregation within
Occlevels, between White Males and Each Female Group

Occlevel	White Male–White Female	White Male–Black Female
1	77.21	89.97
2	56.89	73.41
3	a	a
4	a	a
5	44.42	36.56
6	82.19	87.46
7	92.68	89.76
8	47.88	a
9	a	a
10	15.76	5.94
11	51.36	52.71
12	82.50	66.68
13	67.36	70.84
14	a	a
15	64.43	70.41
16	47.43	77.28
17	51.24	a

NOTE: a = less than 0.5% of race/sex group in the occlevel.

cupations, followed by white females; white males appeared in the largest number of specific occupations. This pattern generally held within each occlevel as well as across all occlevels. A third indication of sex differences in occupational distribution would be shown by a tally, for each occlevel, of the number of specific occupations that have white males as well as black or white females, those with white males only, and those with no white males but only black or white females. Such a tally shows that the bulk of specific occupations in which there are no white males, but only white females and/or black females, occur at the lower occlevels. The bulk of the white-male-only occupations occur at the higher occlevels. The fact that there are so many occupations in which there are only white males, and another handful in which there are no white males, is significant not only because it demonstrates occupational segregation, but also because it makes some standard analyses impossible to do.

All of the measures presented above show the differences between the sexes in occupational distribution. A fourth way of gauging "crowding" would be to measure the concentration of each race/sex group in specific occupations within an occlevel. Since a small number of people of a

TABLE 7.5 Percentage of Each Race/Sex Group in the Three Most

Occlevel	White Male			1st
	1st	1st + 2d	1st + 2d + 3d	1st
1	58.33%	78.85%	84.94%	40.96%
2	26.72	42.24	56.90	30.67
3	a	a	a	a
4	a	a	a	a
5	64.23	71.99	79.75	38.79
6	50.82	64.24	72.00	51.71
7	32.81	49.48	63.54	33.02
8	42.33	65.08	79.37	75.00
9	54.78	78.98	86.62	a
10	78.40	95.20	99.60	86.49
11	69.73	87.89	92.60	37.71
12	20.00	35.24	45.71	76.43
13	19.86	36.15	45.69	29.49
14	67.86	85.71	92.86	a
15	15.45	25.55	35.05	38.49
16	24.06	42.27	54.64	24.66
17	16.80	33.20	43.60	42.86

NOTE: *a* = less than 0.5% of race/sex group in the occlevel.

given race/sex group within an occlevel may give a distorted impression of ''crowding'' (e.g., if there is only one black female in an occlevel, necessarily 100 percent of black females in the occlevel will be in only one specific occupation), results are not reported in cases where less than 0.5 percent of a race/sex group is in a given occlevel. Table 7.5 shows, for each occlevel, the proportion of each race/sex group in the most concentrated, the two most concentrated, and the three most concentrated occupations. In general, white males seem to be the least concentrated, followed by white females and then by black females, who are the most concentrated. Although this measure of concentration, like the earlier measures of segregation, refers to the occupational distribution of the sexes, there are conceptual differences between them. Segregation measures the degree of difference in the way that men and women are distributed across specific occupations; concentration measures the proportion of a race/sex group in any given occupation. For example, if 80 percent of the men were in occupation A, 10 percent in B, and 10 percent in C, while 80 percent of the women were in C, 10 percent in B, and 10 percent in A, they would be equally concentrated (80 percent in the most

Concentrated Occupations of Each Occlevel

White Female			Black Female	
1st + 2d	*1st + 2d + 3d*	*1st*	*1st + 2d*	*1st + 2d + 3d*
61.45%	74.70%	66.22%	84.94%	90.93%
53.33	64.00	51.85	82.01	92.59
a	*a*	*a*	*a*	*a*
a	*a*	100.00	100.00	100.00
52.83	65.50	45.42	58.97	69.23
74.63	86.34	46.33	71.10	89.45
59.43	82.08	30.56	55.56	72.22
91.67	100.00	*a*	*a*	*a*
a	*a*	*a*	*a*	*a*
98.56	100.00	72.46	90.58	99.28
75.14	89.43	44.62	81.54	93.85
85.13	89.70	48.84	68.60	88.37
55.13	71.80	53.66	82.93	87.81
a	*a*	*a*	*a*	*a*
64.95	79.73	44.60	65.47	82.73
47.95	58.91	55.56	74.08	81.48
57.14	66.67	*a*	*a*	*a*

populated occupation for each) but highly segregated (70 percent of the men or the women would have to change occupations in order that their distributions match).

The Relationship between
Relative Wages and Occupational Distribution

It is clear from the data presented above that women are in fewer occupations than men, that they are in different occupations than men, and that they are more concentrated in a subset of occupations than are men. These tendencies are apparent within occlevels as well as across all occlevels. The fact that these tendencies can be seen even among occupations categorized according to education and skill requirements—which are therefore, at least to some degree, theoretically interchangeable—is striking.

What remains to be demonstrated is the relationship between relative wages and occupational distribution. At a very general level, it may be observed that the same rank ordering of the race/sex groups holds on several dimensions, within and across occlevels. Ranking wages from high to low and concentration from low to high, white men have the highest wages (see Table 7.6) and are the least concentrated in specific occupations; white women rank second in wages and second in concentration (i.e., their wages are lower than men's, their concentration higher), and they are segregated from white men occupationally; black women have the lowest wages and are the most concentrated, and their occupational distribution is most unlike the distribution of white men. These general observations suggest an inverse relationship between relative wages and concentration, or between relative wages and segregation, and would be consistent with the crowding hypothesis.

Problems arise, however, in translating the crowding hypothesis into a more exact operational test. In the analyses presented below, results are often contradictory and reflect a very complex set of relationships. Part of the difficulty arises from applying a *ceteris paribus* equilibrium model to a set of data which reflects a nonequilibrium real world, in which all else *cannot* be held equal. Several attempts to relate relative wages to mea-

TABLE 7.6   Average Wages and Wage Ratios
by Occlevel for Race/Sex Groups

| | Average Wages | | | Wage Ratios | |
Occlevel	White Male	White Female	Black Female	WF/WM	BF/WM
1	$2.27	$1.62	$1.05	.71	.46
2	2.30	1.56	1.39	.68	.60
3	*a*	*a*	*a*	*a*	*a*
4	*a*	*a*	.52	*a*	*a*
5	2.79	2.03	1.89	.73	.68
6	2.83	1.82	1.80	.64	.64
7	3.07	2.11	1.78	.69	.58
8	3.08	2.21	*a*	.72	*a*
9	3.20	*a*	*a*	*a*	*a*
10	3.16	2.27	2.43	.72	.77
11	3.39	2.01	1.96	.59	.58
12	2.99	2.25	1.57	.75	.53
13	3.47	2.27	2.01	.65	.58
14	3.54	*a*	*a*	*a*	*a*
15	3.99	3.08	3.41	.77	.85
16	4.70	3.01	3.03	.64	.64
17	4.93	4.06	*a*	.82	*a*

NOTE: *a* = less than 0.5% of race/sex group in the occlevel.

sures of "crowding" will be described, and the contradictory outcomes will be interpreted.

One way of demonstrating the effect of occupational segregation on wages is to hold average wages for each race/sex group in each occlevel constant, but to assume a distribution of each of the female groups across occlevels identical with that of white males. This shows how different wages would be if the female groups had the white male distribution. Alternatively, the occupationl distribution of each of the female groups may be held constant, while white male average wages are substituted for the wage rates of the other groups. This demonstrates how different wages would be if no one changed occlevels but everyone in an occlevel got paid at the white male average rate. The results of these two exercises are

TABLE 7.7 Average Wages across Occlevel,
and Computed Wages If Female Groups Are
Given White Male Occlevel Distribution or
White Male Average Wages

	Average Wages across Occlevel	*Average Wages across Occlevel, if Given Own Wages and White Male Occlevel Distribution*	*Average Wages across Occlevel, if Given White Male Average Wages and Own Occlevel Distribution*
White Male	$3.33	$3.33	$3.33
White Female	2.22	2.28	3.16
Black Female	1.73	2.14	2.81
WF/WM	.67	.68	.95
BF/WM	.52	.64	.84

found in Table 7.7. Each female group is helped more by receiving white male wages in their own occlevels than by being distributed across occlevels in a manner similar to white men. The most interesting results are those for white women. Changing their distribution across occlevels to match that of white males would do virtually nothing to boost their relative wages. Giving white women the white male average wages in each occlevel would bring white women very close to parity with white men.

The implication of this analysis is that for white women, almost all of the difference in wages vis-à-vis white men may be attributed to occupational segregation *within* occlevels, or differences in wages within specific occupations; none of the wage difference is attributable to the difference in distribution across occlevels. For black women, some portion of the difference in wages vis-à-vis white men was a result of the difference in distribution across occlevels (presumably related to differences in quantity and quality of schooling, as well as discrimination), but a larger portion was related to occupational segregation *within* occlevels or wage differences within specific occupations.

Therefore, some evidence relating to wages and occupational segregation may be obtained from the device described above and reported in Table 7.7. Although it would be desirable to apply these devices to occupations within an occlevel in order to sort out the effect of occupational segregation versus the effect of wage differences within an occupation, several problems arise in so doing. In Table 7.8, white male average wages for an occupation are substituted for the wages of the female groups. Ordinarily, this would be taken as a gauge of how much average wages would be raised if everyone in an occupation got the same pay as

TABLE 7.8   Average Wages by Occlevel and
Calculated Average Wage Weighted by
White Male Wages in Occupations

	White Male	White Female		Black Female	
Occlevel	Avg. wage	Avg. wage	Avg. wage if paid WM wages	Avg. wage	Avg. wage if paid WM wages
1	$2.27	$1.62	$2.47	$1.05	$2.31
2	2.30	1.56	1.97	1.39	1.88
3	a	a	a	a	a
4	a	a	a	a	a
5	2.79	2.03	3.03	1.89	2.89
6	2.83	1.82	2.48	1.80	2.24
7	3.07	2.11	2.88	1.78	2.84
8	3.08	2.21	3.42	a	a
9	3.20	a	a	a	a
10	3.16	2.27	3.10	2.43	3.11
11	3.39	2.01	3.48	1.96	3.64
12	2.99	2.25	3.35	1.57	2.75
13	3.47	2.27	3.46	2.01	3.18
14	3.54	a	a	a	a
15	3.99	3.08	3.39	3.41	3.38
16	4.70	3.01	3.84	3.03	3.60
17	4.93	4.06	5.05	a	a

NOTE: Empty white male cells receive average white male wages for the occlevel.

a = less than 0.5% of race/sex group in the occlevel.

white males—i.e., how much of the wage difference is attributable to within-occupation, as opposed to within-occlevel or across-occlevel, differences. However, the results of this exercise raise some questions of interpretation. In six cases out of thirteen, white women would have wages higher than those of white men if they were paid the same white male wages within occupations. Black women would, in three cases out of eleven, earn more than white men, but in one case they would have earnings below their original earnings. Therefore, the results of this exercise are ambiguous, and seem to be not only indicating the effect of intraoccupational wage differences, but also suggesting that the distribution of the female groups is such that a higher proportion of them than of white males are in jobs that pay better-than-average wages to white males, although these are not necessarily high-paying jobs for women.

The other part of this exercise would be to give the white male occupational distribution to the female groups, weighted by their own wages. This would ordinarily show the result of occupational segregation within occlevels. However, this exercise could not be done at all, since a significant portion of the white males are in occupations in which there are no women, so that no wage weights are available. The fact that the distribution of the women is so different from that of white males makes the measuring of the impact of that difference on relative wages even more difficult.

In many cases, there is no such thing as a "good" (high-paying) occupation or a "bad" (low-paying) occupation, defined independently of particular race/sex groups. An occupation that pays white males more than their occlevel average wage may pay female groups less than their occlevel wage, and vice versa. Table 7.9 lists the number of such asymmetric occupations. The fact that some occupations are neither "good" nor "bad" in the abstract underlies the confusing results of Table 7.8 and would also underlie the analysis described above that could not be performed. It is intriguing to speculate about what role asymmetry plays in maintaining the occupational distribution of each race/sex group. For those occupations that pay higher-than-average wages to white men but lower than average wages to women, asymmetry may be a means of deterring women from these occupations. (It may also be a manifestation of greater hostility toward women in these occupations.) For those occupations that pay lower than average wages to white men but higher than

TABLE 7.9   Asymmetric Occupations: Wages above
Occlevel Mean for White Men but below Occlevel
Mean for Women; Wages below Occlevel
Mean for White Men but above Occlevel Mean for Women

| | White Male–White Female | | White Male–Black Female | |
Occlevel	High WM/Low WF	High WF/Low WM	High WM/Low BF	High BF/Low WM
1	1	1	0	2
2	0	3	0	2
3	*a*	*a*	*a*	*a*
4	*a*	*a*	*a*	*a*
5	2	2	1	0
6	0	4	1	1
7	2	1	0	2
8	2	1	*a*	*a*
9	*a*	*a*	*a*	*a*
10	0	0	1	0
11	1	2	3	0
12	0	1	0	2
13	3	2	1	1
14	*a*	*a*	*a*	*a*
15	1	6	3	2
16	0	5	0	3
17	2	2	*a*	*a*
Total	14	30	10	15

NOTE: *a* = less than 0.5% of race/sex group in the occlevel.

average wages to women, asymmetry may be a means of attracting
women to occupations that are relatively undesirable to white men.

An alternative approach to testing the relationship between relative
wages and "crowding" would be to examine occupational concentration,
rather than occupational segregation. A simple correlation between relative wages and concentration, as measured by the proportion of each
female group in the two most concentrated occupations in each occlevel
(see Table 7.5), turned out to be very low: .078 for white females and
.152 for black females. In fact, the most concentrated occupations in each
occlevel do not necessarily pay lower-than-average wages to any of the
race/sex groups. In some occlevels the highest paying occupation is also
the most populated for each race/sex group. However, it seems entirely
rational that people in an occlevel would go into the highest paying job
within that occlevel, and this is in no way inconsistent with the crowding
hypothesis. It may simply mean that although the most populated occupa-

tion pays higher than average wages in the occlevel, these wages would be even higher in the absence of crowding. Even a higher than average female wage within an occlevel is often well below the male average wage.

The question then becomes: if concentration is sometimes associated with higher than average wages and sometimes not, what role does concentration play for each different race/sex group? Table 7.10 compares wages in the most concentrated occupation (the most populated if it accounts for over 50 percent of the race/sex group, otherwise the two most populated) with average wages for each race/sex group in each occlevel. Concentration does pay in some cases for each race/sex group, but concentration pays off the most for white men. In four occlevels, white women gain more (or lose less) from concentration than white men; in all other cases white men are the beneficiaries. Wages are lower in the concentrated occupations as compared to the occlevel average wage in four

TABLE 7.10   Ratio of Wages in Most
Concentrated Occupation(s) in Occlevel to
Average Wage in Occlevel

Occlevel	White Male	White Female	Black Female
1	1.13	1.00	.83
2	1.07	.88	.99
3	a	a	a
4	a	a	a
5	1.01	1.00	1.01
6	1.02	.99	1.03
7	1.03	1.08	.79
8	.94	1.07	a
9	1.05	a	a
10	1.02	1.01	.95
11	1.07	.95	1.03
12	.85	1.08	.90
13	.98	.90	.82
14	1.05	a	a
15	.93	.98	1.03
16	1.01	1.01	1.02
17	1.15 *	1.13	a

NOTE: *a* = less than 0.5% of race/sex group in the occlevel.

* Clergymen are excluded from this measure, since their wages are unrepresentative of the occlevel and highly deviant.

cases out of fifteen for white men, but in five out of thirteen cases for white women and six out of eleven cases for black women.

In a final attempt to sort out the nature of the relationship between wages and crowding, a correlation coefficient was calculated between the index of segregation and relative wages within occlevels. The relationship for black women was inverse, -.497, but fell short of statistical significance. Part of the failure to reach significance may be attributed to the small number of observations for this race/sex group (as Table 7.10 shows, data for black women could be recorded for only eleven occlevels, as opposed to thirteen occlevels for white women). The results for white women appear puzzling: relative wages and the index of segregation seem to be completely unrelated to each other, with a correlation of .0001. To the extent that large portions of white men and women within an occlevel are in the same occupation and receive dramatically different wages, relative wages and the index of segregation would both be expected to be low. In the case of white women within occlevels, three occlevels had unusually low segregation indexes and unusually low relative wages. On examination, one occlevel contained salesworkers not elsewhere classified; another contained clerical workers not elsewhere classified; the third contained accountants and auditors. In all three cases, significant portions of white men and white women were in these occupations, and the wages were dramatically higher for white men than for white women. The first two categories may contain men and women doing different work, as they are broadly defined. The third category is well-defined, and reflects intraoccupational wage differences that may arise from sex segregation according to firm or industry, rather than sex segregation by occupation. In Rees and Schultz's study of the Chicago labor market, female accountants were paid less than men even though the females had more seniority. Rees and Schultz concluded that women accountants were not hired in the most prestigious firms, so that the wage difference was due to sex segregation by firm.[13]

When the correlation is repeated without these three occlevels, the new correlation coefficient is -.51. Because of the reduced number of observations, this falls short of statistical significance. To the extent that black women are also affected by this intraoccupational parity problem, the correlation reported for them is artificially low. The difficulty with the above correlations is that the presence of intraoccupational wage differences affecting large portions of an occlevel dilutes the effect of any correlation between segregation and relative wages. To the extent that intraoccupational wage differences reflect sex segregation on the firm or industry level, one form of labor market segregation masks the effect of another.

To sum up the findings on hypothesis II: it has been shown that women are distributed differently across occupations and are "crowded" into fewer occupations. It has been shown indirectly that there is an inverse relationship between occupational concentration and relative wages, and between segregation and relative wages. This could not be shown directly because of the data problems described above.

Proposals for Change

What needs to be done in order to improve women's relative wages and erode occupational sex segregation? In addition to policies designed to promote more continuous labor force participation among women (e.g., day care facilities, flexible hours, broader opportunities for part-time employment), there must be policies designed to reduce occupational segregation. Two related yet distinct tasks must be accomplished: 1) women must enter formerly male occupations, and 2) men must enter formerly female occupations.

In order to induce men to enter women's occupations, these occupations will have to become equal in attractiveness to the occupations that men now choose (perhaps even more than equal, at first, if there are psychological barriers against men doing "women's" work). One route toward improving the "image" of women's occupations might be through unionization and attempts to gain better wages by means of collective bargaining. The sex composition of elementary and secondary school teaching has been changing, and men now constitute a majority of secondary-school teachers. The fact that this change has parallelled the growth of unionization and even militancy among teachers is suggestive, though by no means conclusive. The stereotypic view of women and unions is that women do not want to join unions, and are hard to organize because they see themselves as only peripherally attached to the labor force. Yet a recent article by Lucretia Dewey stated that "recent data on NLRB white-collar elections indicate that, when the opportunity was available, women in these occupations did not differ significantly from men in their preference for union representation." [14]

A tight labor market, with shortages in many occupations, would facilitate the movement of women into occupations outside the traditional women's sphere. In addition, something resembling current "affirmative action" programs is probably necessary. A *New York Times Magazine* article of August 1971 introduced the "Galbraith Plan" to promote minorities.[15] Essentially, this plan calls for integration of jobs paying over $15,000 with representation of minority groups being proportional to their representation in the local labor force. Firms employing over 2,000 workers would have from ten to thirteen years to meet this requirement, but they could file their own planned timetable for compliance. A government agency, the Minorities Advancement Commission, would oversee the progress of the Galbraith Plan, and would impose penalties on firms that failed to meet their own timetables. The Galbraith Plan, therefore, extends the affirmative action approach of Executive Order 11246 (which applies only to firms with government contracts) to all firms employing over 2,000 workers, including state and local governments as well as private employers. Nevertheless, the Galbraith Plan is meant to apply to only a small portion of the work force. The $15,000 floor was chosen because it represented 150 percent of median earnings, and the plan is meant to apply only to top levels of employment. Unless the results of the Galbraith Plan are expected to "trickle down" by some unexplained mechanism, this plan leaves most of the labor force unaffected, and does nothing to aid the lowest-paid minority workers.

The policy to be proposed here involves extending the jurisdiction of Galbraith's Minorities Advancement Commission to apply to the entire labor force, rather than only to those workers with the highest levels of earnings. The Minorities Advancement Commission itself could be incorporated into the Equal Employment Opportunities Commission (EEOC), which would also be given a broader range of powers.

Currently, the EEOC has a mandate to collect information on employment practices, and to publish such information in periodic reports. It also has the power to investigate charges of denial of equal employment opportunity when such charges are filed in writing by an aggrieved party or by a member of the Commission. Upon investigating a charge of denial of equal employment opportunity, the Commission determines whether or not the charge is true and reports its findings. If it finds that denial of equal employment opportunity has occurred, it can try to remedy the situation through informal conciliation between the complainant and the respondent. If such conciliation fails, the EEOC has no further power. The only recourse left for the complainant (or in cases of major importance the EEOC itself) is to initiate a civil action in court and have the court decide the case and prescribe remedies where necessary.

The EEOC's powers should be expanded beyond conciliation to include the ability to prescribe remedies when it is found that equal employment opportunity has been denied. In this respect, its powers for dealing with denial of equal employment opportunity would be similar to the powers the National Labor Relations Board (NLRB) has in dealing with unfair labor practices under the National Labor Relations Act. Like the NLRB, the remedies prescribed by the EEOC would be enforceable by the courts.

My final policy proposal deals with changing the expectations of the public, and especially those of many women, regarding the proper role of women workers. As Janice N. Hedges points out, the expected demand through the 1970s for workers in traditional women's occupations is not great enough to absorb the expected number of women workers, especially those with college degrees.[16] The implication is clear: women with college degrees need to stop thinking only in terms of being teachers, nurses, and social workers and start thinking about careers as doctors, dentists, engineers, and architects. Below the college-degree level, Hedges advises women that strong labor force needs in the 1970s will be for mechanics and repairmen.

There is an urgent need for changing expectations, not only regarding what women workers can do, but also regarding the probability that a woman will be in the labor force. Women's Bureau publications point up the inconsistency of a situation in which 90 percent of the girls today will be working women at some point in their lives, and yet "most girls have a romantic image of life: school, marriage, a family—and they live happily ever after."[17]

Given the realities of women's labor force participation, it is clear that there is a misallocation of resources resulting from faulty counseling and mistaken expectations. Public policy in this case could take the form of legislating funds for programs to train and/or retrain school counselors and professionals in vocational education, in order to make them aware of the likelihood of women's labor force participation and the disadvantages of traditional sex-stereotyped training programs.

NOTES

[1] An early statement of the crowding hypothesis was by F. Y. Edgeworth in "Equal Pay to Men and Women for Equal Work," *Economic Journal,* XXXII (December 1922): 431–47 Recent work on the crowding hypothesis as applied to blacks as well as women has been done by Barbara R. Bergmann at the University of Maryland.

[2] Donald McNulty, "Differences in Pay Between Men and Women Workers," *Monthly Labor Review,* XC (December 1967): 40–43.

[3] Albert Rees and George P. Schultz, *Workers and Wages in an Urban Labor Market* (Chicago, 1970).

[4] See for instance, U.S. Department of Labor, Women's Bureau, *1969 Handbook on Women Workers,* p. 139.

[5] "Why Women Complain," *New York Times,* July 26, 1970.

[6] R. F. Harrod, *Economic Essays* (New York, 1952), pp. 45–46.

[7] This occupational categorization was developed in 1971 at the Institute of Labor and Industrial Relations, Ann Arbor, Michigan, by Barry Bluestone and Mary Stevenson.

[8] In addition to Occlevel, another categorization was developed. This categorization, Occgroup, was designed to exclude from Occlevel those occupations which require heavy lifting or work in very hazardous surroundings. The rationale for excluding such occupations from comparison is that women might reasonably not be expected to work in those occupations, because of either physical strength limitations or protective state labor laws. Occgroup defined clusters of occupations more narrowly, so that they reflect not only given education and skill requirements but also the number of adverse working conditions (according to the DOT, adverse working conditions include exposure to: extremes of cold plus temperature changes; extremes of heat plus temperature changes; wet and humid environment; noise and vibration; hazards of bodily injury; fumes, odors, toxic conditions, dust, poor ventilation). Occgroup is meant to be used as a check on the Occlevel results, to ensure that such results are not merely artifacts produced by the fact that men, on the average, are stronger than women. The findings for Occgroup were generally consistent with the Occlevel findings.

[9] For an explanation of the choice of the $2.25 hourly wage as the cutoff point between high-wage and low-wage jobs, see Barry Bluestone, William Murphy, and Mary Stevenson, *Low Wages and the Working Poor,* Institute of Labor and Industrial Relations (Ann Arbor, Mich., 1973). For a full-time, year-round worker, an hourly wage of $2.25 yields an annual income of $4,500. This income level, for an urban family of four with no other income sources, is at approximately the level of the Social Security Administration's "low-income" line.

[10] Sources for occupational and industrial data included: U.S. Department of Labor, Bureau of Employment, *Dictionary of Occupational Titles, Supplement* (Washington, D.C., 1966); U.S. Department of Labor, Bureau of Labor Statistics, *Employment and Earnings for the United States 1909–1968,* Bulletin No. 1312-6 (Washington, D.C., August 1968); U.S. Department of the Treasury, Internal Revenue Service, Statistics Division, *Corporation Source Book of Statistics of Income* (Washington, D.C., 1953–54, 1958–59, 1961–62, and 1965–66); U.S. Department of Commerce, *Census of the Manufactures and Mineral Industries* (Washington, D.C., 1953, 1958, and 1963).

[11] See Solomon Polachek's article in this volume, "Discontinuous Labor Force Participation and Its Effect on Market Earnings."

[12] This index is taken from Edward Gross, "Plus Ça Change . . . ? The Sexual Structure of Occupations Over Time," *Social Problems,* XVI (Fall 1968): 198–208.

[13] Rees and Schultz, *Workers and Wages,* p. 94.

[14] Lucretia Dewey, "Women in Labor Unions," *Monthly Labor Review,* XCIV (February 1971): 44.

[15] John Kenneth Galbraith, Edwin Kuh, and Lester Thurow, "The Galbraith Plan to Promote Minorities," *New York Times Magazine,* August 22, 1971.

[16] Janice N. Hedges, "Women Workers and Manpower Demands in the 1970's," *Monthly Labor Review,* XCIII (June 1970): 19–29.

[17] U.S. Department of Labor, Women's Bureau, "Expanding Opportunities for Girls: Their Special Counseling Needs," revised (Washington, D.C., 1971).

8

Women and the Academic Labor Market

GEORGE E. JOHNSON AND FRANK P. STAFFORD

DURING THE PAST FEW YEARS, a great flurry of activity has centered around the question of discrimination against women faculty in higher education. Executive Order 11246 of 1968, Title VII of the Civil Rights Act of 1964 as amended in 1972, the Equal Pay Act of 1963, which was amended to apply to higher education in 1972, and Title IX of the Education Amendments of 1972 all addressed themselves to the question. Provisions of these acts are enforced by a number of government agencies—the Office of Civil Rights of the Division of Higher Education of HEW, the Office of Federal Contract Compliance of the Employment Standards Administration of the Department of Labor, and the Equal Employment Opportunity Commission. Numerous individual actions to gain promotion and back pay have been instituted, and a number of institutions have made "equity adjustments" to their women faculty. It has not been uncommon for universities to grant across-the-board increases of $100–2,000 to all women faculty so that they can receive "equal pay for equal work." [1]

It seems fair to say that a great deal more effort has been expended in upgrading the labor market status of academic women than on any other group of employed women—certainly in per capita terms. It is interesting to point out, therefore, that even prior to these acts of policy, women's earnings in academia were much higher relative to men than in most other industries or occupations. In the economy as a whole, women earn about 60 percent of what men earn,[2] but in academia the percentage salary disadvantage is less than half of this. Furthermore, employment in higher education is a very small fraction of total employment. In 1960, for example, only 11 out of every 10,000 employed women (and 26 out of every 10,000 employed men) were college instructors. Moreover, the absolute number of women involved is rather small: during the 1960s only 17,929 women earned doctorates (compared to 154,111 men). Thus, governmental policies to enhance the status of women in universities will benefit very few women, and these women are already in the upper end of the income distribution.[3]

Male–female differences in academic salaries are often attributed almost wholly to discrimination. An alternative explanation is that the differential is, to a large extent, generated by the market's reaction to choices by females with regard to lifetime labor force participation and on-the-job training. Because a division of labor between the husband and wife is characteristic of most families, married women, including those who are highly educated, work less during the time when small children are present.[4] One would expect that a period of reduced market activity associated with childbearing and child care would result in some obsolescence of skills for a faculty member as well as a narrowing of her opportunities for professional development.

One can raise questions about whether child care by women reflects completely voluntary choices. Does society, in some sense, force women to specialize in this activity to a greater extent than would be economically "rational"? Questions such as these, though very important, are generally beyond the scope of this particular paper.[5] We take the division of labor between the sexes as given and seek to explain its potential influence on male–female salary differences in academia. While we believe that we have provided support for what can be termed the "division-of-labor hypothesis," this does not *prove* that labor market discrimination does not exist in academia.

Earnings Differences between Men and Women Academics

In this section we report evidence on the pattern of earnings of male and female academics in 1964 and 1970. Our data source is the National Science Foundation Register for each year, and the sample is restricted to individuals who have received a Ph.D. and who are teaching full time in an academic institution. We also restrict our attention to four disciplines—economics, sociology, mathematics, and biology—but the same patterns have been observed in all other disciplines we have studied, and we suspect that they apply to all disciplines.

In order to estimate the earnings patterns of academics, we related the nine-month salary level of each individual in the sample to the following variables: (1) years since the Ph.D.; (2) years of working experience prior to the degree; (3) a variable denoting the "quality" of the institution from which the Ph.D. was received; and (4) the sex of the individual.[6] Because there are reasons for supposing that the relationship between salary and years since the doctorate is different for males and females, our statistical procedure allowed for this possibility. The estimated pattern of nine-month salaries for academics with four years of predegree experience (the average amount) who did not attend a "top ten" graduate school in their discipline [7] (approximately 30 percent of academics did their graduate work at one of the ten highest ranked universities) is presented for 1964 in Table 8.1 and for 1970 in Table 8.2.

The most striking features of these results are: (1) beginning salaries for females are not substantially less than for male academics; and (2) the rate at which salaries increase with years since the Ph.D., or what we call potential postdegree experience, is much greater for male than for female academics. From Table 8.1, the estimated salary for a new Ph.D. in economics in 1964 was $7,690 for males and $7,500 for females; women earned $190 or 2.5 percent less than men.[8] This is a relatively trivial difference and certainly not one worth employing federal inspectors to eliminate. However, after twelve years of potential experience, women earned $2,210 or 23 percent less than men, and this is not a trivial difference.

TABLE 8.1   Estimated Nine-Month Salaries
of Male and Female Academics by Years Since Receipt
of Doctorate for Four Disciplines, 1964

	Economics		*Sociology*		*Mathematics*		*Biology*	
Years Since Doctorate	*Male*	*Female*	*Male*	*Female*	*Male*	*Female*	*Male*	*Female*
0	7,690	7,500	7,210	6,840	7,650	7,130	6,910	6,500
6	9,610	8,400	8,970	8,030	9,780	8,210	8,670	7,680
12	11,360	9,180	10,530	9,050	11,680	9,070	10,280	8,660
18	12,700	9,810	11,690	9,800	13,410	9,600	11,510	9,350
24	13,430	10,240	12,260	10,200	13,560	9,740	12,180	9,640
30	13,440	10,450	12,160	10,200	13,190	9,470	12,180	9,500

TABLE 8.2   Estimated Nine-Month Salaries
of Male and Female Academics by Years Since Receipt
of Doctorate for Four Disciplines, 1970

	Economics		Sociology		Mathematics		Biology	
Years Since Doctorate	*Male*	*Female*	*Male*	*Female*	*Male*	*Female*	*Male*	*Female*
0	11,610	11,000	10,560	10,130	10,510	9,860	9,680	8,580
6	14,480	13,010	13,330	12,150	13,830	11,830	12,370	10,600
12	17,010	14,810	15,770	13,860	16,980	13,480	14,880	12,390
18	19,070	16,220	18,000	15,380	20,800	14,810	16,880	13,690
24	20,160	17,090	18,180	15,500	20,720	14,970	18,020	14,300
30	20,170	17,330	17,720	15,190	20,600	14,610	18,120	14,140

The same pattern is revealed in each of the four disciplines reported and in both time periods. This is most clearly seen in Table 8.3, where the ratios of female to male academic salaries are given. The percentage salary disadvantage of women in a particular category can be obtained by multiplying (1 − the pertinent ratio) by 100. In all cases the percentage salary disadvantage increases with potential postdegree experience (years since the Ph.D.), at least up to eighteen years of professional experience (this corresponds to between 45 and 50 years of age). Thereafter, the relative position of female academics holds steady or improves slightly. In 1970, the largest salary disadvantage at eighteen years of postdegree experience was 29 percent, in mathematics, and the smallest was 15 percent, in economics and sociology.

TABLE 8.3   Ratio of Estimated Salaries of
Female to Male Academics by Years Since Receipt of
Doctorate for Four Disciplines, 1964 and 1970

	Economics		Sociology		Mathematics		Biology	
Years Since Doctorate	*1964*	*1970*	*1964*	*1970*	*1964*	*1970*	*1964*	*1970*
0	.97	.95	.95	.96	.93	.94	.94	.89
6	.87	.90	.90	.91	.84	.86	.89	.86
12	.81	.87	.86	.88	.78	.79	.84	.83
18	.77	.85	.84	.85	.72	.71	.81	.81
24	.76	.85	.83	.85	.72	.72	.79	.79
30	.78	.86	.84	.86	.72	.71	.78	.78

Interpretation of the Evidence

Earnings over the Life Cycle

That the salaries of female academics relative to those of male academics decline with years since receipt of the Ph.D. up to about age 45 is a matter of fact; what prudent persons will disagree on is just what this evidence means. The two principal alternative explanations are that the sex difference in salaries reflects either (a) differences in acquired skill and productivity between men and women; or (b) direct labor market discrimination against women by male-dominated university faculties and administrations. It is, of course, also possible that the salary disadvantage of women is due to a combination of both of these.

Before offering an assessment of the relative merits of these alternative explanations, it is useful to review those elements of economic theory which explain the variation of wages and incomes over the life cycle in the absence of discrimination or family obligations. The basic notion is that individuals make decisions concerning the acquisition of new skills and the sharpening up of old ones so as to increase (or maximize) their long-run total income. For an academic, the costs of learning a new technique or of writing a significant article are represented by foregone consulting income or a reduction in leisure. Also, new Ph.D.'s often choose to teach in large, research-oriented departments even though these universities pay young faculty poorly compared with schools which are less prestigious. The benefits to these "investment" activities subsequent to the receipt of the Ph.D. degree accrue later in life, primarily in the form of higher salaries but also in the form of increased status and better working conditions. The most important implication of this theory is that younger academics are likely to spend more time investing in their skills than older academics. The reasoning behind this is quite straightforward: a 25-year-old assistant professor has about forty years to amortize an investment; a 64-year-old professor has only one year to do so and—unless he greatly enjoys the acquisition of new knowledge for its own sake—has much less motivation to take time away from consulting or leisure-time activities.[9]

To a large extent, professors are paid in proportion to their academic reputation. Therefore, if the amount of time devoted to skill improvement and upkeep declines with increasing age, we would expect the annual salary increases of younger professors to be larger than the salary increases of older professors. This is indeed the case—at least for male academics. Table 8.4, which is derived from information contained in Tables 8.2 and 8.3, shows the percentage change in salaries over the six-year period from 1964 to 1970 for selected years since receipt of the doctorate in 1964. For example, a new male Ph.D. in economics earned $7,690 in 1964; in 1970 the same person earned $14,480. This represents an increase over the six-year period of 88 percent. Notice that, in all cases ex-

TABLE 8.4   Estimated Percentage Change in Nine-Month Salaries from 1964 to 1970 for Male and Female Academics by Years Since Receipt of Doctorate in 1964 for Four Disciplines

Years Since Doctorate in 1964	Economics		Sociology		Mathematics		Biology	
	Male	*Female*	*Male*	*Female*	*Male*	*Female*	*Male*	*Female*
0	88	73	85	78	81	66	79	63
6	78	76	76	73	74	64	72	61
12	68	77	71	70	78	63	64	58
18	59	74	55	58	54	56	57	53
24	50	69	44	49	52	50	49	47

cept one (mathematicians with twelve years of postdegree experience in 1964), percentage salary increases for male academics decline with years since the doctorate. The decline in the rate of growth of earnings is, in fact, so precipitous that the earnings of younger academics catch up and in some cases eventually surpass those of older academics.

This pattern of earnings growth is quite consistent with the economic theory we sketched above. The young biologist is motivated to spend 400 hours working on his paper, "Some Strangely Neglected Aspects of the Molecular Structure of the Brain of the Butterfly," but his senior colleague, who is five years away from retirement, is likely to ask, "What's the point?" and—correctly, from an economic point of view—leave the butterfly problem to the aspiring assistant professor. Two years later, the younger biologist is now recognized as one of the world's leading experts on butterfly research and may receive offers to switch universities at a substantial increase in salary. The older biologist has not improved his skills or reputation; they may even have depreciated over the period. Hence, the younger biologist gains in his salary position relative to the older biologist.

The Division of Labor and Acquired Market Skills

As is also shown in Table 8.4, this same pattern of earnings growth subsequent to receipt of the doctorate is *not* consistently observed for women academics. During the six years from 1964 to 1970, the earnings of male economists who received their doctorates in 1964 rose by 88 percent, but for women the increase was only 73 percent. The corresponding figures for the other fields are consistent with this pattern. As a result, referring to Table 8.3, the ratio of female to male salaries for the class of 1964 fell from .97 in 1964 to .90 in 1970 in economics, from .95 to .91 in sociology, from .93 to .86 in mathematics, and from .94 to .86 in biology. The diminished relative salaries of women also occurred in the six-to-twelve years of postdegree experience range, but the quantitative magnitude of the retardation was much smaller. Thereafter, increases for men and women were not substantially different.

This evidence provides the basic starting point for the differential market productivity interpretation of the difference between the salaries of male and female academics. But to complement our discussion of the potential relevance of the division-of-labor hypothesis, we also need to review the evidence on labor force behavior of women academics. Since our N.S.F data do not contain information on marital status and family obligations of women doctorates, we turn to the study by Helen Astin that does have this information.[10]

There are two important characteristics of women doctorates which mitigate against obsolescence and limitation of professional development through lack of labor market participation and on-the-job training. First, there is a much lower marriage rate for women doctorates than for other women in their age cohort. Only 55 percent of the women doctorates in a 1965 survey were or had been married. "In a comparable age group (40–44 years) in the general population, . . . 86 percent were married."[11] Second, "Among women of comparable ages in the general population only 45 percent worked as compared with 91 percent of the women in this sample."[12]

Despite this evidence of strong career commitment on the part of

women doctorates, Astin found evidence consistent with other studies of
the labor market in general and of educated women in particular: namely,
for those women who are married there exist substantial family influences. Reduced labor market activity in the form of part-time employment was most strongly influenced by present marital status (as well as by
husband's income level) and the presence of preschool-age children.[13] In
addition, Astin also found women doctorates distributed their labor market hours differently than men.

With respect to her work activities, the typical woman doctorate in the sample
spent about half her working time in teaching and about one-fourth in research.
. . . Harmon's data (1965) showed that men doctorates, on the other hand,
devoted a comparatively large proportion of their time to research and administration (research, 41 percent; teaching, 31 percent; administration, 20 percent; other,
8 percent).[14]

These comparisons are not perfectly suited to our discussion because they
do not apply exclusively to academia, but to the extent that there is inter-
sectoral migration over the career and to the extent that most doctorate
holders are in academic employment, there is considerable validity to the
comparison.

Given the lack of information on marital status and number of children
in the Register data, we can rely only on indirect evidence on the labor
force behavior of female relative to male academics to supplement Astin's findings. First, the NSF data also show that women are more likely
than men to work part time. For example, for biologists between the ages
of 30 and 34, 11.8 percent of women versus 1.1 percent of men worked
part time in 1970. Between the ages of 35 and 44 the figures were 7.2
percent versus .5 percent. Second, according to information in the 1960
census, the "labor reserve" for women college professors totaled 13,441,
as compared with 38,367 in the labor force.[15] This means that 26 percent
of women who had experience within the preceding ten years as college
professors were out of the labor force at the time of the sample. The corresponding figure for men was only 6 percent. Third, in 1960, 34.5 percent of women college professors worked 50–52 weeks per year, compared with 58.3 percent of men. Furthermore, in the sample week the
average reported workweek for women in college teaching was 35.0
hours versus 42.3 hours for men.[16]

If one accepts the evidence on differential labor force activity of men and women doctorates, then one would predict that women, particularly those who are married and have children, would not experience a growth in skills at as rapid a rate as their male counterparts during the first ten years or so after receipt of the Ph.D. (Table 8.4). This is the basic evidence which can be given and which is consistent with the division-of-labor hypothesis. What is also quite clear is that information on lifetime participation and earnings of single women should be compared with that for men. In this case the family role should not result in the same lowered rate of increase in salary and other forms of compensation.

While the data on earnings for doctorates in given fields by sex and marital status are very scant, there are some data on one form of compensation—promotion rates—for men and for married and single women. And given the importance of family roles in the division-of-labor hypothesis, it is useful to examine these data, limited though they may be. For doctorates in a cohort centered in 1940 who remained in academic employment and were sampled in a study of Ph.D.'s, about 85 percent of the males were at the rank of full professor twenty years later. Of the married women, only 46 percent were at the rank of full professor; but 70 percent of the single women had attained this rank.[17] This evidence is consistent with the division-of-labor hypothesis but is subject to some important qualifications. To begin with, the sample sizes were small, but beyond this problem there are others.

First, should one really compare single women to what are for the most part married men? It seems plausible that marriage and family obligations would induce a greater work effort by the major earner regardless of sex, just as marriage and family responsibilities would presumably induce a greater effort at home productivity by the major nonmarket (home) producer. After all, this is the essence of the gains from specialization inherent in the family division of labor. Without this division of labor effect, married men would presumably expend a lessened effort on the job. Accordingly, married men would be more comparable to single women, if somehow this division of labor effect could be allowed for. One comparison that suggests itself is between single men and single women, but the number of single men in academia at advanced career points is not large, at least in terms of the number in the study to which we have been referring.

Second, women tend to be in the fields where the promotion rates and salaries are lower. To the extent that these fields are chosen voluntarily rather than through some form of occupational segregation, we would expect women, regardless of marital status, to have a lower rate of promotion than men.

To summarize, the evidence reviewed on salaries and labor force participation differences is, for reasons already noted, not sufficiently unambiguous that we can readily identify the precise relative importance of the division of labor versus other effects. Yet the evidence does provide fairly clear support for the view that a substantial portion of the wage differential can be attributed to differences in labor supply behavior and choices concerning on-the-job training on the part of women. *On the average,* a year of potential postdegree experience is not the same for a female academic as it is for a male, and the salaries of women reflect this.

Discrimination Hypotheses

We now turn to the question of the ways in which the observed salary differentials between women and men can be interpreted as evidence of discrimination. There are actually several approaches to a discrimination interpretation of the evidence. The three general approaches which we will discuss are direct discrimination, discrimination through crowding, and societal discrimination; within each of these approaches one can develop several different variants. We will start by outlining the different forms of direct discrimination.

First, women may face what can be termed employer/employee discrimination by (male) deans and faculties. If the dean and the faculty do not like to work with women or for some reason feel threatened by female intellectuals, they will be willing to forego a better department or even higher salaries to escape having to interact with women. For example, they may refuse to hire a woman who is as able as or even more able than the best male candidate because they feel uncomfortable discussing their discipline with a woman for fear that she may be as smart as they are. Worse yet, it may even be obvious that she is smarter. (Here we must distinguish between fear of being embarrassed by a smart woman as distinct from the general fear of being embarrassed by a smart person, regardless of sex.) To submit to this prejudice and to hire the less competent male means that the department would have a weakened position in terms of teaching or research, but it would have been "worth it" to the male discriminators.[18]

Another possibility is customer (student) discrimination. In cases where the students in a class are at least 50 percent women, this seems a bit far-fetched. But suppose the field in question is currently a "man's subject" and most of the students are men. Then it can be argued that the students feel (more) uncomfortable hearing truths from women rather than from men.[19] If such preferences by faculty and students characterize most of the institutions in the market, then there will be a differential in compensation between men and women because of differing enrollments in classes taught by men and women.

Implicit in our argument about discrimination by employers and employees is that there is a willingness to forego departmental output for the sake of having male colleagues—and this can be termed discrimination against women. Another possibility that would result in a male–female salary differential is *positive* discrimination in favor of less competent males, and this can be made clear by an imaginary example. Suppose the chairman of a biology department hires three professors: two men engaged in what appears to be promising research on butterflies and a young woman who says frankly that she has interests in teaching but cannot spend much time on research because of household commitments. Time passes, and one of the males publishes a number of papers on his research which, although they fall short of earning him the Nobel Prize, establish his reputation. The other male is, quite frankly, disappointing. Although he publishes a few papers, they fail to advance the state of knowledge in any way. All three, including the woman, teach satisfactory courses in elementary biology, and carry their share of departmental and administrative responsibilities.

How does the department chairman distribute salary increases to these three people? The first professor has had offers from Yale and UCLA, and they have to be matched. The woman professor receives cost-of-living increases, because her productivity has not really changed greatly. The chairman was able to tell her that she should get only somewhat more than a new assistant professor gets, because after a year or so of experience, a new assistant professor could teach almost as well as she can. What does the chairman do with the second male professor, who may well be convinced that his own research represents the most important insight since *The Origin of Species?* There is no outside demand for his services. His research productivity is, in fact, no greater than that of the woman professor. What probably will happen, of course, is that the second professor will be paid somewhere between what the first professor and the woman professor are paid. The chairman would find it extremely distasteful to tell the second professor that his research is hopeless and that he will receive only what the woman is paid. On "equity" grounds, therefore, the less competent male professor is paid more than he is worth. There is (or *was,* prior to the HEW pressure) little such pressure to pay the woman more than she is worth.

A second form of the discrimination hypothesis is the crowding hypothesis.[20] The basic argument is that exclusion of a group from a certain labor market results in higher pay for those already in that market and correspondingly lower pay in the labor markets into which the group is crowded. Here women can be viewed as excluded from the academic labor market for Ph.D.'s and crowded into lower-paying occupations, such as grade-school teaching, or into the particular occupation of housewife. This results in high-paying male jobs and low-paying women's work.

A third version of the discrimination hypothesis relates to the fact that women have traditionally been expected to perform roles as wives and mothers and thus subordinate their own career goals to the interests of their husbands and children. This could be considered a form of societal discrimination. It used to be the case—and except for the upper middle classes is probably still the case—that a woman with clearly defined career aspirations was considered rather odd and had to overcome various degrees of social ostracism in order to accomplish her objectives. We recognize this phenomenon but we will concentrate on the question of the existence of direct discrimination and occupational crowding.

If there is direct labor market discrimination against women, what form does it take? In order to be consistent with the evidence, it is clear that one must stress the denial of advancement opportunities for women, for, as we have noted above, the starting salaries of men and women academics are not much different. If there are no skill differences between men and women given the number of years since the Ph.D., we would expect the woman biologist to be just as likely as the man biologist to do *the* definitive research on butterflies and hence have as high a productivity over her entire career. However, if the observed pattern of salary differences is due to discrimination, universities will not bid for her services as eagerly as they would for the services of the male butterfly expert. One would then have to ascribe the following motivation to (male) university decision makers: they have no problems with the presence of women in junior positions, but they feel threatened when women demonstrate their competence and push for senior positions at salaries comparable to their own.

If the preceding argument is correct, we would expect that women would have lower promotion rates. This is, in fact, true. As we have noted, the National Academy of Sciences study found that women had lower promotion rates (though the differences were smaller for single women), and these patterns can also be observed from the Register data. In biology in 1970, for example, 41.7 percent of males and 19.5 percent of females attained the rank of full professor ten to twelve years after receipt of the doctorate. These figures changed to 80.6 and 39.3 percent for sixteen to nineteen years after the Ph.D. Similar results obtained for each of the other disciplines studied. This could be interpreted as reflecting a reluctance on the part of the senior faculty to allow women into the "club." The problem with this interpretation is that promotion to a higher rank and acquisition of tenure are based on the same sort of considerations as salary—publications, market value, etc. Thus, evidence that women are subject to lower rates of promotion is consistent with both the acquired-skill-differences explanation and the denial-of-advancement-opportunities explanation.

To summarize the direct discrimination discussion, what is often argued as per se evidence of discrimination can be interpreted as reflecting differences in life-cycle accumulation of professional skills. To resolve this question, it would be necessary to examine the earnings patterns of women who do work full time throughout their careers and should therefore have comparable levels of acquired skill. Studies of the regular labor market offer considerable support for the view that the potential role of direct discrimination against women is much smaller than is suggested by the wage differential unadjusted for detailed work history.[21] However, to our knowledge, the relevant data have not yet been gathered for Ph.D.'s by field of study in the academic labor market.

A second view of discrimination is the crowding hypothesis. The first kind of evidence which can be reviewed is that the percentage of women in the different fields we have studied is negatively related to earnings level. There are proportionately fewer women in the higher-paying disciplines, such as physics, economics, and mathematics. Yet, more is required to establish the crowding hypothesis; what is needed is complementary evidence that women are less likely than equally qualified men to be offered fellowships and admission to programs. A number of research efforts are currently underway, and the evidence to date does not generally show obvious discrimination against women.[22] However, it is a possibility that graduate programs may recognize differential rates of completion on the basis of sex. Obviously, admission committees generally look at past attrition rates of graduates to form an estimate of the likely completion rates of admittees in the near future. If women have *changed* career commitments, sole reliance on past behavior may in fact be viewed as a form of entry limitations against women.

One piece of evidence which has been derived from our study relates to the representation of women within the various subspecialties of biology. We studied biology because it has a rather large proportion of women Ph.D.'s. What we observed is that there was no tendency for women biologists to be overrepresented in the lower-paying specialties.[23] While we do not feel that the issue of crowding is even near to being resolved, it should be noted that evidence for the hypothesis must be carefully interpreted. If women (or men) anticipate a major commitment to household production and family responsibilities they will quite reasonably be expected not to make as great a commitment to the labor market and will then seek to find employment in lower-paying, "crowded," but less demanding employment.

Another variant of the crowding hypothesis that seems to be prevalent in discussions of women's earnings relates to the role of research as a determinant of academic salary. In this view it is argued that research is often vastly overrated as a measure of an individual's contribution to academic life and that there would be, up to a point, a high payoff in terms of productivity to substitution away from research and toward teaching— at least in numerous cases. Because married women find it difficult to develop a research output comparable to that of males, published output becomes, at least in part, a convenient mechanism for limiting entry of women to higher-paying jobs. This is a difficult proposition to test be-

cause of the necessary ambiguity involved in defining what academic output "should be." This is particularly true since it is often argued that
research is a public good which generates indivisible benefits and needs
to be subsidized.

Additional Evidence and Interpretation

We have thus examined the evidence on the lifetime salary patterns of
male and female academics and found that it is generally consistent with
what one would expect on the basis of the economic theory of life-cycle
investments in skill acquisition. The data are also consistent with a special case of the model of direct labor market discrimination. Specifically,
they are consistent with the hypothesis that women are denied opportunities for advancement because male-dominated university power structures feel threatened by ambitious and well-trained women. We have
argued that at least some of the wage disadvantage of female academics is
due to acquired skill differences, for the average woman spends a smaller
fraction of her time in work pursuits than a man, and this means that
women get less experience per year since the Ph.D. However, it is clearly
possible that the effect of these skill differences on relative salaries is exacerbated by discrimination. In this section we examine an additional
piece of evidence and relate it to the question at hand.

A rather striking feature of the data for each of the disciplines is that
women academics are concentrated at colleges and universities which
exphasize teaching as opposed to research. In mathematics in 1970, for
example, 5 percent of the entire sample were women. For those universities which were ranked in the top twenty in terms of the quality of graduate program, less than 2 percent of the sample were women. For a sample
of high-quality small private colleges (Amherst, Oberlin, and the like),
6 percent of the sample were women. The same differences are observed
in a comparison of the University of California and the California State
College systems, the former having 2 percent women on the faculty and
the latter 10 percent.

By the acquired-skill-differences explanation of the male/female salary
differential, the reason for the fact that women are less likely to teach at
the research mills is that *on the average* they are less likely to have
engaged in skill acquisition activities subsequent to receipt of the doctorate. By the direct labor market discrimination explanation one would

have to argue that the Harvards and the Berkeleys have a stronger dislike for females who are as well qualified as men than do schools with less prestige.

Throughout our presentation we have talked about the "typical" male and the "typical" female. In part this is due to the fact that our data do not go much further than identifying whether the person is male or female—in addition to a few other characteristics. The implication of the preceding section is that, on the average, males are more likely to be demanded by the high-paying research universities than are females. This is probably due to the fact that—at least historically—men have made a more total commitment to their careers than women, for most women have been delegated the major share of household responsibilities as well. Again, there will be many exceptions to this rule; we are talking only about averages.

Conclusions

Utilizing data from the National Science Foundation Register for Ph.D.'s by academic discipline, we have shown that while women Ph.D.'s start out at salaries only somewhat lower than those of men, their relative salary position erodes with years of potential experience. This we interpret as evidence which is consistent with the hypothesized effects of the division of labor within the household on market and nonmarket activity of married women. Specifically, those women who are married are most likely to drop out of full-time employment, particularly when preschool-age children are present in the household. This is shown in Helen Astin's study, and she has also shown that a higher income level for the husband reduces the labor force participation of the wife. Consequently, the reduced labor force activity and corresponding erosion of skills should result in lowered earnings when women return to full-time employment. While our data do not contain information on marital status or children, other studies of the labor market have had access to such data. From this evidence and some limited evidence on promotion differentials, we do believe that there is no reason to suppose that the division-of-labor/acquired-skill hypothesis is not important in explaining much of the salary disadvantage of women faculty.

In reviewing possible discrimination hypotheses used to explain the earnings and promotion differentials between men and women faculty, we noted that many of these explanations could also be thought to be consistent with current evidence on lifetime earnings. As a result, reasonable persons might have quite different positions on the relative role of discrimination vis-á-vis acquired skill differences. However, it would be our hope that those who do place close to sole reliance on either interpretation would have come to appreciate the potential relevance of the other interpretation. The importance of the distinction is that if the discrimination interpretations are by and large correct (particularly the direct discrimination interpretation), then current Federal efforts can be viewed as in some ways desirable. On the other hand, suppose the division of labor interpretation is by and large correct. Then differentials arising through part-time work experience need not be interpreted as simply due to male prejudice. Further, intrafamily choices of market and home production, which are much less subject to direct policy action, are going to be more important in determining the academic salary structure of men and women in the long run.

NOTES

[1] See Association of American Colleges, Project on the Status and Education of Women, *On Campus with Women* (Washington, D.C., May 1973).

[2] U.S. President, *Economic Report of the President* (January 1973), p. 103.

[3] That such policies benefit the relatively well-off doesn't necessarily distinguish them from many other public policies.

[4] See, for example, C. Russell Hill and Frank P. Stafford, "Allocation of Time to Pre-School Children and Educational Opportunity," *Journal of Human Resources*, IX (Summer 1973): 323–41.

[5] Recent theoretical work has dealt directly with analyzing various aspects of the mutual gains from marriage. See Gary S. Becker, "A Theory of Marriage: Part I," *Journal of Political Economy*, LXXXI (July/August 1973): 813–46. One of the major points of this theory is to demonstrate that this division of labor is *not* fixed but depends on the ratio of men to women, for example.

[6] For details on the choice of independent variables, functional form, and statistical procedures employed in this analysis, see our "The Earnings and Promotion of Women Faculty," *American Economic Review*, LXIII (December 1974). The simpler approach of comparing cell means could not be used because of the small numbers of female respondents in some fields (notably, economics and mathematics).

[7] Our procedure was as follows: those respondents who received their doctorates prior to 1940 were assigned the ranking from the Hughes study of 1925; for graduates in the 1940–59 period, the rankings of the 1957 Keniston study; and for 1960–70 graduates, the 1964 Cartter ranking. In this way the individual's rank depends on both the school attended and his vintage. Those schools with top ten ranks were combined into a single variable. These data are found in A. M. Cartter, *An Assessment of Quality in Graduate Education*, (Washington, D.C., 1966), p. 35. This procedure had to be modified for biology, since it comprises several disciplines that are ranked separately in the Cartter volume. Basically, the biology rankings were weighted averages of the separate subdisciplines in 1964, because historical data were not consistently available.

[8] It should be stressed that these figures and all other figures in the paper refer

to *average* salaries. Some academics made more than that predicted in Tables 8.1 or 8.2 and others made less.

[9] It should be pointed out that the above discussion refers to the *typical* case; there are certainly many exceptions to the rule.

[10] See Helen S. Astin, *The Woman Doctorate in America* (New York, 1969).

[11] *Ibid.*, p. 26.

[12] *Ibid.*, p. 58.

[13] *Ibid.*, p. 63. Here she finds that marital status, husband's income, and presence of preschool-age children all contribute to part-time employment.

[14] *Ibid.*, p. 73.

[15] U.S. Census, 1960, *Occupational Characteristics,* Subject Report PC(2)-7A. "Labor reserve" is defined as comprising those qualified for employment by past experience but not currently seeking work.

[16] While differences in weeks worked can be thought of as primarily measuring differences in summer employment, hours per week are less likely to be subject to this problem.

[17] National Academy of Sciences, *Careers of Ph.D.'s: Academic Versus Non-academic,* (Washington, D.C., 1968), pp. 21, 71, 85. "Single" is defined as never married and "married" is defined as ever married.

[18] See Gary S. Becker, *The Economics of Discrimination,* 2d ed. (Chicago, 1971).

[19] Alternatively, the (male) students may prefer a half-truth spoken by a male to a full-truth spoken by a female.

[20] See Barbara Bergmann, "The Effect on White Incomes of Discrimination in Employment," *Journal of Political Economy,* LXXIX (March/April 1971): 294–313.

[21] See, for example, Burton G. Malkiel and Judith A. Malkiel, "Male–Female Pay Differentials in Professional Employment," *American Economic Review,* LXII (September 1973): 693–705.

[22] See Lewis C. Solmon, "Women in Graduate Education: Clues and Puzzles Regarding Institutional Discrimination," *Research in Higher Education* (1973), pp. 299–332.

[23] See Johnson and Stafford, "Earnings and Promotion of Women Faculty." In fact, there was a weak positive relation between percentage of women in a specialty and earnings level.

Part 3
Economic Aspects of
Women's Nonmarket Activities

9

Women's Work in the Home

ARLEEN LEIBOWITZ

DRAMATIC CHANGES over the last thirty years in the amount of time married women spend in the labor force are well documented. While only 15 percent of married women were in the labor force in 1940, the comparable figure for 1950 was 24 percent, for 1960, 31 percent, and for 1972, 41.5 percent.[1] These changes in labor force participation have, of necessity, affected the allocation of time to various activities in the household as well. The accompanying changes in the nature of production within the household are not as well understood and have only recently come to the attention of economists.

A comparison of time budget studies over a fifty-year period shows that while the total amount of time spent in household work by urban nonemployed women has remained virtually constant at approximately 53 hours per week, the proportion of time spent in cooking and cleaning has decreased, while the proportion spent in child care has increased.[2] Today as in the past, employed women, on the average, spend less time in household production than nonemployed women. Since the proportion of women in the labor force has been rising, the average time input to household tasks has been declining over the last fifty years.

Valuable insights into the labor force behavior of married women have

Some of this material has appeared in Arleen Leibowitz, "Education and Home Production," *American Economic Review*, LXIV (May 1974): 243–50. This research has been supported by a grant from the National Institute of Child Health and Human Development received by the National Bureau of Economic Research. The following paper is not an official National Bureau publication since the findings reported herein have not yet undergone the full critical review accorded National Bureau studies, including approval of the Board of Directors.

been gained by analyzing the problem within a household production context. Jacob Mincer pioneered this approach, in which women are seen as choosing not simply between work and leisure, but between work in the home, work in the market, and leisure.[3] While income affects the total amount of work, the division of work between home and market depends on wage rates, productivity in the home, and the price and availability of substitutes for the wife's labor in the home.

Women's increasing schooling over the last fifty years has been a major factor in increasing their productivity in the market relative to that in the home, thereby drawing them into the labor force. But what has been the effect of schooling on production *within* the home? Some recent studies by economists on various aspects of human capital investment have shed light on the relationship between women's education and their productivity within the household. Grossman has analyzed the relationship between schooling and the production of health by the household, arguing that the productivity of wives' time input should affect the production of their husbands' health.[4] He finds that wife's schooling has a significant, positive impact on health which is as great as the effect of husband's schooling on his own health level. Benham postulates a model in which human capital is accumulated within the home as well as in school and on the job.[5] Thus the wife's education affects her husband's stock of human capital. He finds support for this hypothesis in the positive relationship between the earnings of married men and their wives' schooling.

Household Production and Education

Household production analysis, which has been so fruitful in explaining female labor supply, is based on the concept that time and market goods are combined in the household to produce the commodities which are desired. "Dinner" is an example of a commodity that can be produced with some purchased goods and the addition of one's own time.

Because both time and goods are used to produce commodities, the price of a commodity consists not only of the price of its goods component but also of the cost of the time needed to produce it. This price can be written

$$\pi_i = \Sigma x_j p_j + t_i w,$$

where π_i is the unit price of commodity i,
   x_j is the amount of purchased good j required per unit of i;
   p_j is the price of a unit of j;
   t_i is the amount of time required to produce a unit of i;
   w is the value of time per unit.

It is clear from this definition that the price of a commodity will vary depending upon how it is produced and by whom. "Dinner" can be produced in a goods-intensive manner—by using little time and a lot of market goods (heating a TV dinner is an example)—or it can be produced in a time-intensive manner—by preparing the raw ingredients in one's own kitchen.

The household's consumption of commodities is limited by its resources and by its "consumption technology." The primary resource of the family is its time. Time can be used either to produce commodities at home or to earn money with which to purchase market goods. Time, unlike other factors of production, cannot be stored or saved for use at a later date. Households may also draw upon nonlabor income (bequests, government transfer payments, property income) to purchase market goods; but for most families the principal resource is time.

Economists assume that families allocate their limited resources so as to get the most output. An efficient allocation requires that several relationships among the inputs hold true. It is these relationships which prove useful in analyzing the household's behavior. An efficient allocation requires that: [6]

1. The marginal value of time in producing one commodity equals its value in producing any other commodity consumed by the household. If this were not true, time could be shifted from one production activity to a second with a resulting increase in total output. Thus the value of the time of a given person is equal to the value of the marginal product of his time in the production of each commodity. Hence,

$$\hat{W} = \pi_1 MP_{t1} = \pi_2 MP_{t2} = \ldots = \pi_n MP_{tn},$$

   where $\hat{W}$ is the value of time in home production, π_i is the unit price of the i-th commodity, and MP_{ti} is the marginal product of time in the i-th commodity (i.e., the additional amount of each household commodity produced with an additional unit of time).

2. The marginal value of a dollar's worth of market goods must also be equated over all activities.

$$\hat{P} = \pi_1 MP_{x1} = \ldots = \pi_n MP_{xn}$$

where MP_{xj} is the additional amount of each household commodity produced with an additional unit of market good x.

3. From the above two equations it is clear that the following must hold for all commodities:

$$\hat{W}/\hat{P} = MP_{t1}/MP_{x1}$$

That is, the ratio of the marginal productivities of time and goods in producing any one commodity should equal the ratio of their respective opportunity costs.

4. Similarly, the ratio of the marginal productivities of time of any two family members in producing a given commodity should equal the ratio of their respective opportunity costs of time.

5. The value of the marginal product of time in home production must equal the value of an hour's work in the labor market. If the value of the marginal product of an hour's time in home production did not equal the value of marginal product of the goods purchased with an hour's wage, a reallocation of time could lead to greater output.[7]

These relationships can be used to forecast many aspects of household behavior, such as family size or the goods-intensity of home production, from a knowledge of the factors which alter the productivity and prices of inputs. Examples of these factors are education, age, location of residence, climate, and relative wages of husband and wife.

How can these basic relationships explain a married woman's time allocation? It is clear that, holding other factors constant, an increase in the husband's earnings will tend to increase a woman's time input to home production and decrease her working time, for two reasons. First, more goods being available tends to increase the marginal product of each unit of time relative to that of each unit of goods; to restore the ratios between marginal products and prices of goods and time, more time must be spent in home production. Second, since the market value of husband's time has risen relative to the wife's, she will spend more time in-home production. Consequently, the wife's labor market time will fall.[8] A rise in her own wage will have both income and price effects. An increase in the value of her time in market work will cause changes in the relative prices of commodities if some commodities are produced more time-intensively than others. Those household commodities in which the time cost component (wt_i/π) is larger than average will rise in price relative to household commodities with exactly average time intensity. A fundamental theorem of demand theory states that a change in relative prices, other factors affecting demand being unchanged, will induce households to consume less of the commodity rising in price. Therefore, a rise in the wife's earnings, assuming total family income is unchanged, will cause a shift away from time-intensive commodities and toward household commodities whose production is more intensive in market goods. Within the production of any commodity, goods will also be substituted for time. The net result will be that less time is used in home production and more is devoted to work in the market. The total effect of an increase in the wife's earnings on hours used in home production cannot be determined a priori. Not only does an increase in the wife's wage change the relative prices of household commodities but it also increases family income if the wife is working. The net result of a rise in the wife's wage on time spent in home production will depend on the relative strength of the substitution effect, tending to reduce hours spent in home production, and the income effect, tending to increase them. It is clear that, if both home and market productivity rose by the same amount, the condition described by 5 would be undisturbed, and the only incentive for changing the allocation of time would be the effect of the increase of the wife's wage rate on family income.

A woman's schooling level is positively related to her productivity in the market and in the home, as well as to family income. What is the net effect of schooling on time spent at home and in the market? Empirically, students of female labor force behavior have consistently found that women with more education are more likely to be in the labor force.[9] This is true in a classification of participation rates by years of schooling, and the relationship is even stronger when the comparison is made among women with similar family incomes.

The most widely accepted explanation for this association is that education has a nonneutral effect on the productivity of time, raising the

value of labor market time more than that of time spent in home production.[10] As discussed above, this will cause women to shift to market
work. It follows that because women with more schooling spend a greater
proportion of their lifetime in the labor market, they must ordinarily
spend a smaller proportion of their time in home production. This, of
course, is the result one would predict directly from household production
analysis, because the opportunity cost of time rises with the level of
schooling.

Not only do women with more schooling supply more time to the labor
market, but their lifetime pattern of labor supply differs from that of

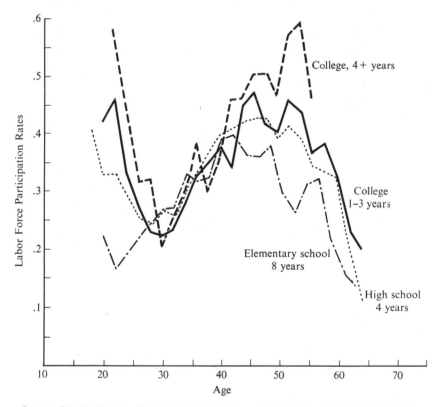

SOURCE: Calculated from the 1/1000 sample of the 1960 Census, using biennial averages for women who are
not enrolled in school, who have married only once, and who are living with their husbands.
FIGURE 9.1.   Labor Force Participation Rates for Married Women,
by Age and Education, 1960

women with less schooling. Figure 9.1 shows that the supply of labor to the market is greater the higher the level of schooling attained by the woman, except that between the ages of 25 and 40 all women supply nearly the same amount of labor to the market.[11] This indicates that relative to other women, more educated women average more time in the market and less time in home production except during the ages when young children are in the home. All home production is more costly for more educated women, due to their higher opportunity cost of time. Thus, they are induced to substitute goods or services for their time in home production and spend more time in the labor market. The care of preschool children is widely believed to be a time-intensive activity as compared with other forms of home production. Thus the relative cost of producing child care at home is greater for more educated women. This is one rationale for the lesser number of children desired (and produced) by more educated women.[12]

Yet the labor supply profiles point to a paradox: in spite of the fact that the price of child care relative to that of other household production is greater for more educated women, they appear to spend more time at it. This would appear to contradict the fundamental law of demand theory that states that one consumes less of the commodity whose relative price rises, unless some other factors are at work. Because labor supply is assumed to be determined as the result of a process which optimizes the utility of household production over the lifetime, we can make some fairly strong statements about what those other factors may be. In particular, we can state that if home production behavior is consistent with known labor force behavior, child care must differ from other home production by one or more of the following characteristics:[13] (1) smaller elasticity of substitution between time and goods in household production; (2) greater income elasticity; (3) greater increases in home productivity relative to market productivity with increases in education. The first condition states that it may be more difficult to substitute market goods or other people's time for the mother's time in child care. The belief that there are no good substitutes for the mother has been reinforced by such influential sources as Dr. Spock, who writes:

Some mothers *have* to work to make a living. Usually their children turn out all right, because some reasonably good arrangement is made for their care. But others grow up neglected and maladjusted. . . . . If a mother realizes clearly how vital this kind of care is to a small child, it may make it easier for her to decide that the extra money she might earn, or the satisfaction she might receive from an outside job, is not so important, after all.[14]

Here Spock is also implicitly making a judgment about the high income elasticity of demand for child care (condition 2): namely, that, given sufficient family income, women would want to take care of their own children. Whereas child care is a superior good, some other household activities, such as housecleaning, are clearly inferior goods, that is, as income rises, women do less housecleaning with their own hands.

The third condition states that additional years of education increase women's productivity in child care even more than in other household activities. Many educated mothers believe that their schooling allows them to be more productive in child care, just as Grossman and Benham have shown schooling has a positive influence in other areas of home production. Indeed, psychologists have shown that more educated mothers interact with their children in a way that is more likely to generate language skills and logical processes.[15] This I will call the productivity effect of schooling.

In the discussion that follows, I will show that time budget data are consistent with the labor force data: that is, more educated women do have smaller time inputs to household production carried on throughout the life cycle but greater time inputs to child care. In a final section, I will try to examine the factors causing this difference.

Average Time Inputs to Household Activities by Education

Time inputs to various domestic activities were calculated by the author from time budgets collected by Kathryn Walker in 1967–68 from 1,296 two-parent families in the Syracuse, New York, area.[16]

Table 9.1 presents average time inputs to various household activities by women of differing educational attainments. The low-education group consists of women with up to four years of high school; the high-education group comprises women who have attended at least one year of college or training beyond high school. Two household activities carried on throughout the lifetime—meal preparation and laundry work—are represented in this table. Two kinds of child care are distinguished in this

TABLE 9.1   Time Inputs (number of minutes for two days) to Household
Activities

	High-Education Group	Low-Education Group
A. Time Inputs to General Household Production		
Meal Preparation		
By wife	153.41	154.39
By husband	12.85	10.53
Laundry (minutes over one day)		
By wife	27.26	31.12
B. Total Time Inputs to Child Care		
Physical Care		
By wife	129.51	116.40
By husband	14.90	12.26
By others	5.67	4.41
Other Care		
By wife	90.96 *	79.17
By husband	40.77 *	31.51
By others	44.74	36.38
C. Per-Child Time Inputs to Child Care		
Physical Care		
By wife	59.6	48.3
By husband	6.9	5.1
By others	2.6	1.8
Other Care		
By wife	41.9	32.9
By husband	18.8	13.1
By others	20.6	15.1
D. Number of Children	2.17	2.41
E. Wife's Preference Rating [a]		
Physical care	6.78	6.84
Other care	7.43	7.28

NOTE: Sample sizes for meal preparation and laundry time inputs were 627 and 667 for high- and low-education groups, respectively. Since child care averages were calculated only for families with children, sample sizes were 493 and 591, respectively.

For definitions of "physical care" and "other care," see text, p. 232.

[a] Preference ratings are averages of ratings of activities by homemakers on a scale from 1 (extremely dislike) to 9 (like exceptionally). See text, p. 235.

* Significantly greater at the 1 percent level than the low-education group.

table as well. "Physical care" includes time spent in bathing, feeding, and dressing children and in caring for a sick child. "Other care" was defined as "all activities related to the social and educational development of family members, such as: helping with lessons, reading to children, taking children to social and educational functions." [17]

The low-education group spent as much or more of their own time in meal preparation and laundry work as did the high-education group. In addition, the husbands of women with more schooling spent greater amounts of time in meal preparation, substituting their own time for that of their wives. Both these facts are consistent with the greater price of time of more educated women.

In spite of their greater price of time, however, more educated mothers spent more time in child care. The difference was particularly striking with respect to educational care. This phenomenon is not due to a substitution of the mothers' time for the fathers' or that of other persons, since husbands of more educated women also spent more time with their children. More educated mothers also used more of the time of other adults and older children in providing care for their children. Section C of Table 9.1 verifies that these greater time inputs are not the result of more educated women having more children, since children of the high-education group received more hours of care—both total and per child—than children whose mothers had less schooling.

A similar pattern was found in a study of time use by Indiana families in 1961–62.[18] As in the Cornell study, the greater the education of the wife, the more time she spent in child care. Table 9.2 shows that women with college degrees spent more than twice as many hours in child care as

TABLE 9.2   Hours per Week Spent on Household Tasks
by Women of Various Schooling Levels

	Years of Schooling of Wife			
	Less than 12	*12*	*13–15*	*16 or more*
Meal preparation	10.4	9.0	9.0	9.4
Laundry	4.3	4.3	3.5	4.0
Physical care of children	4.8	5.3	6.1	9.7
All tasks	49.7	48.1	46.9	54.3
Number of observations	10	47	35	19

SOURCE: Sarah L. Manning, unpublished calculations.

women with less than twelve years of schooling, 83 percent more time than high-school graduates, and 59 percent more time than women with one to three years of college completed. Greater time expenditures on the part of more educated women are observed within age categories of children as well as over all families.

Detailed Analysis of Time Inputs

In spite of the higher relative cost of child care faced by more educated women, they spend more time, both total and per child, in child care, as shown above. Child care must thus be differentiated from other home production activities by at least one of the above-mentioned three factors: smaller elasticity of substitution among inputs, greater income elasticity, or greater increases in home productivity relative to market productivity with increases in schooling.

To determine what combination of these factors operates to counteract the relatively greater cost of child care for more educated women, a more detailed analysis of the Cornell data was undertaken. For each of four activities, time inputs were regressed on (1) demand factors, which increase the value of marginal productivity of time in the home, and should be positively related to time inputs; (2) productivity factors; and (3) presence of substitutes.

Variables Used in the Regression Analysis

1. *Measures of Time Inputs.* The dependent variables covered time inputs to two child-care activities and to two other household activities. The dependent variables were defined as follows:
   (a) *Physical care*—Number of minutes used in a two-day period in the physical care of children (bathing, feeding, dressing, first aid, etc.).
   (b) *Other care*—Number of minutes used in a two-day period in all activities related to the social and educational development of family members, such as helping with lessons, reading to children, taking children to social and educational functions.
   (c) *Food preparation*—Number of minutes used in a two-day period in preparation and serving of food for all regular meals. Excludes preparation of food for guest and for future use.

(d) *Laundry work*—Number of minutes used in *one* day in all activities necessary to wash laundry at home or in a laundromat.

2. *Demand Factors*. The greater the demand for time in home production (more children, bigger house to clean, more income), the greater the value of the marginal product of time spent in the home, all other things being equal.

(a) *Number of children*—In this study we were looking at women at various stages of their life cycles, and the number and ages of children in the home have an important influence on the amount of time spent in child care, meal preparation, washing, etc. Thus, in the regressions measuring time inputs to meal preparation and child care, five variables measuring the number of children in various age groups were included to see how other variables affected time inputs while holding family size and composition constant.

(b) *Income variables*—No direct questions in the survey concerned income, so a variety of variables positively associated with family income were used as proxies: (i) Education of the husband is closely related to his earnings; (ii) Age of husband is also related to earnings at a point in time; (iii) The number of rooms per family member in the dwelling occupied by the family was used as an index of income, since Margaret G. Reid has presented evidence that the demand for rooms rises, although not very rapidly, with income.[19]

3. *Productivity Factors*. Age and education were hypothesized to affect productivity. Greater time inputs with age and years of schooling, holding output constant, would indicate that older and more educated persons are less productive.

4. *Substitutes*.

(a) *Husband's time*—A good substitute for the wife's time in producing many commodities. Thus it was expected that the greater the husband's time input to a given activity, the less the wife's, all other things being equal.

(b) *Hours per week worked by husband*—An index of the availability of his time. The more hours the husband worked, the less available is a good substitute for the wife's time and the greater will be her time input to home production, all other things being equal. This may also be a proxy for income, with greater hours worked indicating more transitory income. Both interpretations lead to an expectation of a positive relationship.

(c) *Time inputs*—By other adults (either hired or not, although none of the families had other adults living with them) and by children over six. These were allocated to each of the activities they participated in.

(d) *Data on quantities of goods and purchased services used*—Not collected in this sample, but there is some information on the kinds of household capital available. Availability of a dishwasher, disposal, and freezer were used in studies of meal preparation. Differences in the quality of capital goods available were also incorporated into the study. For example, it was assumed that an automatic washing machine provided more capital service than a nonautomatic one. Thus, the kind of washing machine (automatic/nonautomatic) and its location (at home or in a laundromat), as well as the availability of an automatic dryer, were used in analyses of time spent in washing.

5. *Other Factors.*

(a) *Prices of goods*—Important decision variables in the household production model described above. The absence of data on prices of goods is not too serious, however, since all consumers in the sample lived in the same geographical area and faced the same prices.

(b) *Differences in tastes*—Not usually considered by economists in statistical analysis. However, one preference measure was available in this sample which could be used to represent differences in tastes between individuals. Each woman sampled was asked to rate her preference for each of the activities she engaged in on a scale from 1 (representing great dislike) to 9 (representing exceptional liking). The rating of each individual for each activity was included in the regressions for that activity. It should be pointed out that expressed preferences may reflect opportunities as well as innate likes and dislikes.

TABLE 9.3 Time Inputs by the Wife to Meal Preparation
and Laundry Activities: A Regression Analysis of
Factors Affecting Time Spent

	Meal Preparation (Minutes for two days)	Laundry Work (Minutes for one day)
No. of children under 1 year	22.73 (4.67)	
No. of children 1 year old	20.39 (4.13)	
No. of children aged 2–5	18.28 (7.58)	
No. of children aged 6–11	16.14 (8.52)	
No. of children aged 12–18	6.52 (2.78)	
Wife's education	.02 (.01)	−2.29 (1.96)
Husband's education	1.16 (.70)	−.75 (−.81)
Age of wife	.92 (3.95)	
Husband's time input	−.51 (−5.74)	
Rooms per capita	1.61 (.40)	.35 (.23)
Nonautomatic washer used [a]		38.53 (7.8)
Dryer used [a]		−9.69 (−4.51)
Washer–dryer used [a]		8.01 (.95)
No. of loads of wash [b]		13.69 (21.7)
Laundromat used [a]		6.59 (1.89)
C	94.72 (7.61)	11.92 (2.40)
R^2	.14	.46

NOTE: t-values in parentheses.

[a] Dummy variable: equal to 1 if statement is true, 0 otherwise. The coefficients represent additional time expenditures relative to average time spent by women who washed at home with automatic washer and no dryer.

[b] A more accurate measure of demand than number of children for the laundry work regression.

Results of Regression Analysis

Table 9.3 shows that time inputs to meal preparation depend on demand factors, with time inputs decreasing monotonically with increasing age of children. The income proxies, rooms per capita and husband's education, are positively but not significantly related to time inputs.

As for substitutes, each ten minutes spent by the husband in preparing meals reduces the wife's time input by five minutes. However, the presence of capital goods (dishwasher, disposal, and freezer) had no effect on meal preparation time (regression not shown). Among the productivity of time variables, we see that education has no significant impact on time inputs to meal preparation, but that older women spend more time at this activity than younger women.

Capital goods significantly affect time inputs to laundry work. Holding constant the number of loads washed, the housewife who used a nonautomatic washer spent thirty-nine minutes more in washing than one who used an automatic washer. Having a dryer saved ten minutes of laundry time, and using a washer at home rather than a laundromat saved time. More educated women have more and better-quality capital goods, but even holding these factors constant in the regression, the net effect of education was to decrease time inputs to laundry work.

Table 9.4 shows that time inputs to physical care of children are closely related to the number and ages of children. While children under one year require an additional 208 minutes of care per two-day period from their mothers, one-year-olds require an additional 112 minutes, while each two-to-five-year-old adds only 26 minutes to the total time spent in physical care of children. The presence of older children may actually reduce the demands on the mother's time, presumably because they can help with the feeding and dressing of younger brothers and sisters.

The wife's education has a positive but not very significant effect on time inputs. Since education is also a proxy for the value of time in the market, a substitution effect due to the rise in the price of time may partially offset the positive income effect. Also, if education increased the productivity of time in child care relative to other activities, there would be no incentive to replace own time with other inputs if spending own time in child care had high income elasticity.

The income proxies, husband's education and rooms per capita, are not

TABLE 9.4 Time Inputs by the Wife to Child Care:
A Regression Analysis of Factors
Affecting Time Spent
(in minutes) over a Two-Day Period

	Physical Care			Other Care		
		High-education	Low-education		High-education	Low-education
Schooling Group:	All	group	group	All	group	group
Number of children under 1 year	207.6	214.8	204.9	23.42	6.62	46.84
	(26.24)	(19.02)	(19.97)	(3.50)	(.71)	(4.84)
Number of children 1 year old	111.6	114.88	114.81	30.53	36.70	29.78
	(14.52)	(9.99)	(11.63)	(4.52)	(3.71)	(3.19)
Number of children aged 2–5	26.34	19.81	36.55	18.03	15.13	21.96
	(6.92)	(3.59)	(7.55)	(5.40)	(3.26)	(4.55)
Number of children aged 6–11	−4.91	−4.03	−.48	15.47	17.99	14.14
	(−1.25)	(−.96)	(−.13)	(5.84)	(4.77)	(3.78)
Number of children aged 12–18	−6.99	−5.00	−4.41	.91	−.73	3.27
	(−1.88)	(−.93)	(−.99)	(.28)	(−.15)	(.74)
Wife's education	2.96	6.90	5.70	.35	−5.45	−2.95
	(.91)	(.97)	(.85)	(.12)	(−.95)	(−.48)
Husband's education	.1.62	.60	2.08	3.48	−2.19	−3.54
	(.64)	(.05)	(.66)	(1.57)	(−.65)	(1.20)
Age of wife	1.45	.77	2.03	.32	−.79	1.23
	(1.82)	(.57)	(2.08)	(.46)	(−.72)	(1.36)
Husband's time input	.389	.53	.27	.287	.25	.344
	(4.18)	(3.91)	(2.05)	(7.46)	(4.73)	(6.24)
Rooms per capita	−11.84	.25	−.42	617	3.08	9.47
	(−1.41)	(.34)	(−.66)	(.84)	(.29)	(.93)
Husband's age	−1.65	−1.63	−1.74	−.68	.22	−1.44
	(−2.21)	(−1.31)	(−1.87)	(−1.05)	(.22)	(−1.67)
Care by others	−.005	.20	−.14	−.04	.010	−.123
	(−.05)	(1.18)	(−1.07)	(−1.74)	(.33)	(−3.40)
Wife's Preference Rating	3.94	3.96	3.83	.55	−.78	1.14
	(3.03)	(1.99)	(2.20)	(.38)	(−.36)	(.57)
C	68.92	71.52	46.53	53.27	84.01	32.28
	(2.45)	(1.70)	(1.170)	(2.04)	(2.11)	(.55)
R^2	.65	.68	.63	.15	.163	.179

NOTE: t-values in parentheses.

significantly different from zero. The latter has the wrong sign, which may be due to the fact that a greater number of rooms indicates not only greater income but also greater demand for time in such activities as cleaning. A variable which reflects the housewife's preference for child care indicates that women who prefer physical care do, in fact, spend more time at it than women who rate it less highly.

Husband's time was shown to be a substitute for the wife's in meal preparation but not in physical care. The significantly positive coefficient on husband's time inputs indicates that for each ten minutes the husband spends in physical care, the wife puts in an additional four minutes. This is not merely an indication of the family's tastes (since these are controlled for by the "preference" variable), but may indicate true complementarity—increased inputs of husband's time increasing the marginal productivity of the wife's time inputs. Time spent by others in the care of children had no significant effect on the mother's time inputs.

The sample was again divided into high- and low-education subsamples, defined as above. A comparison of the regression coefficients indicates that husband's time is more complementary for the high-education group, because each 10 minutes of husband's time elicits another 5.3 minutes of wife's time in the high-education group but only 2.7 minutes more in the low-education group. Time inputs by others—older children and adults other than the parents—seem to act as a substitute for own time in the low-education group only.

The next three equations deal with time inputs to social and educational activities with children. As with physical care, time inputs are clearly related to the number and ages of children. Again the husband's time inputs appear as a complementary factor to the wife's time, while time inputs by others are only weak substitutes for the wife's time. For each 100 minutes of care by others, the wife reduces her own time inputs by only four minutes. The positive coefficient on husband's education may reflect a positive income effect, but rooms per capita, the second income proxy, is not significantly related to time inputs. Preferences are less strong a determinant of time use here than with respect to physical care.

When the data is again split into high- and low-schooling subsamples, there are some interesting differences between the two groups. First, there seem to be differences in the age pattern of time inputs: the low-education group spends decreasing amounts of time as the children age, whereas time inputs peak for one-year-old children in the high-education group.

The most important difference concerns time inputs by others, whose coefficient has become significant at the 1-percent level in the low-schooling group, while having an insignificant effect on time inputs by mothers with more schooling. That is, for mothers with less schooling time inputs by older children and other adults are seen as a better substitute for their own time than is the case with more educated mothers.

The baby sitters, grandmothers and other children over six who are most likely to provide child care, are more similar in education and ability to the mothers with little schooling, and therefore provide good substitutes for their time. However, if education increases the productivity of time in child care, more educated women would find these other workers relatively unsatisfactory substitutes. In fact, mothers in the high-education group spent the same amount of time in child care whether or not other workers also cared for their children.

Stafford and Hill concluded that in high-status families (defined by husband's education or occupation) time inputs to preschool children are invariant with the number of other children in the family, while in low-status families mothers reduce their time inputs to preschool children as family size increases.[20] Thus the child of a more educated mother or a child growing up in a high-status family suffers less of a reduction in time inputs from his mother than a less privileged child when he is taken care of by others or when there are more children in the family. This behavior on the part of more educated mothers increases the "cost" to them of working when small children are in the home, and this is reflected in the greater reduction in labor supply shown by these women when they have young children.

The fact that more educated women spend more time in child care, even though their children also receive more time from their fathers and from other workers as well, implies a high income elasticity for spending own time in child care or increased productivity of time in child care with increased education. There is clear evidence for the income effect, since greater productivity of more educated women's time in child care could not account for the greater time inputs by husbands and other adults in families where the wife is highly educated.

The historical evidence also supports the hypothesis of high income elasticity for using own time in child care. Vanek, working with samples ranging back to 1926, found that women of higher socio-economic status spent more time in child care than low status women and that "contemporary non-employed women spend about ten hours a week more in family care than women in earlier samples." [21] That the income elasticity of demand for child care exceeds that for other housework can be inferred from Vanek's finding that contemporary women lower their standards for housework when child care demands are highest.

What do these findings imply for the future? Time allocation theory suggests that women's increasing schooling levels will continue to draw them into the labor force in ever greater numbers. Women can thus be expected to spend less of their increasingly valuable time in home production. Due to increases in both income and schooling, however, women will spend even more of their time with children.

NOTES

[1] Estimates for married women, husband present, in March of the year cited. U.S. Department of Labor, Bureau of Labor Statistics, *Special Labor Force Reports,* Nos. 13, 94, 130, and 153 (April 1961, April 1968, March 1971, April 1973). U.S. Bureau of the Census, 1950, *Current Population Reports,* Series P-50, Nos. 22 and 29.

[2] Joann Vanek, "Keeping Busy: Time Spent in Housework, United States, 1920–1970" (Ph.D. diss., University of Michigan, 1973), pp. 160–86.

[3] Jacob Mincer, "Labor Force Participation of Married Women: A Study of Labor Supply," in Universities-National Bureau Committee of Economic Research, *Aspects of Labor Economics* (Princeton, N.J., 1962), pp. 63–105.

[4] Michael Grossman, "The Correlation between Health and Schooling" (Paper presented at National Bureau of Economic Research Conference on Research in Income and Wealth, November 1973).

[5] See Lee Benham's paper, "Nonmarket Returns to Women's Investment in Education," in this volume.

[6] The following relationships are proved by Gary S. Becker in "A Theory of the Allocation of Time," *Economic Journal,* LXXV (September 1965): 493–517.

[7] This statement assumes no depreciation and also assumes that marginal products equal wages.

[8] Hours worked could rise only if relatively time-intensive commodities were sufficiently inferior.

[9] See William G. Bowen and T. Aldrich Finegan, *The Economics of Labor Force Participation* (Princeton, N.J., 1969); and Glen G. Cain, *Married Women in the Labor Force* (Chicago, 1966).

[10] Yoram Ben-Porath, "The Production of Human Capital Over Time," in W. Lee Hansen, ed., *Education: Income and Human Capital* (New York, 1970).

[11] Arleen Leibowitz, "Women's Allocation of Time to Market and Non-Market Activities: Differences by Education" (Ph.D. diss., Columbia University, 1972).

[12] Robert Willis, "A New Approach to the Economic Theory of Fertility Behavior," *Journal of Political Economy,* LXXXI, Part II, (March/April 1973): S14–S64.

[13] For the derivation of these results, see Leibowitz, "Women's Allocation of Time," pp. 22–27.

[14] Benjamin Spock, *Baby and Child Care* (New York, 1961), pp. 569–70.

[15] C. Cazden, "Subcultural Differences in Child Language: An Interdisciplinary Review," in J. Nellmuth, ed., *Disadvantaged Child,* (New York, 1968), II, 217–56.

[16] The data were collected for a research project on "Use of Time for Household Work" in the Department of Consumer Economics and Public Policy, New York College of Human Ecology, Cornell University, Ithaca, N.Y. I am indebted to Dr. Walker and Mrs. Irma Telling for providing these data.

[17] Kathryn Walker, "Definition of Household Activities" (mimeographed), prepared for research project on "Use of Time for Household Work."

[18] I am grateful to Sarah L. Manning, Agricultural Experiment Station, Purdue University, Lafayette, Ind., for providing me with these unpublished results. A description of the study is found in her paper "Time Use in Household Tasks in Indiana Families," *Purdue University Agricultural Experiment Station Research Bulletin No. 837* (January 1968).

[19] Margaret G. Reid, *Housing and Income* (Chicago, 1962), p. 348.

[20] Frank P. Stafford and C. Russell Hill, "Family Background and Lifetime Earnings," Paper presented at the National Bureau of Economic Research Conference on the Distribution of Economic Well-Being, May 1974.

[21] Vanek, "Keeping Busy," p. 179.

10

The Economics of Marital Status

FREDRICKA PICKFORD SANTOS

GONE ARE THE DAYS when a female's marital credentials provided a barometer of her social and economic success. Whereas, previously, a divorcée or single female over 30 was regarded with misgivings, today in the United States she is often referred to as "liberated"—her status not only accepted but very much in vogue.

To what may we attribute the changed attitude toward the unattached female? Has there been a structural transformation within society leading to a growing number of females whose life-style negates such pejorative nomenclature as "spinster" or "divorcée"? Could it be that fewer women are interested in defining themselves via their husband's profession and income—rather they seek their own professional fulfillment and identity? If this is so, what factors have made this comparatively recent phenomenon both physically and psychologically possible?

As technological progess led to a rise in real wages at all levels of education, an increasing number of women were induced to enter the labor force. Furthermore, technological advances meant that the role of homemaker evolved into a far less specialized and time-consuming activity, since such equipment as dishwashers, washing machines, and pre-prepared foods provided good substitutes for home-produced goods. Thus the substantial increase in female labor force participation which occurred

This paper is an outgrowth of my doctoral dissertation, written under the sponsorship of Jacob Mincer at Columbia University. Comments on this paper by Jacob Mincer were much appreciated, as were those of the editor, Cynthia B. Lloyd. I am also indebted to Gary S. Becker and Barry R. Chiswick for their encouragement during the initial phase of my effort to study the economics of marital status.

between 1940 and 1970 (see Table 10.1) would imply that women are devoting fewer hours to production in the home and, furthermore, that the clearly defined productive association common to most marriages—breadwinner-homemakers—is on the wane.

Economic phenomena of this nature are bound to be accompanied by social repercussions, since, if the traditional male–female complementarity is declining, one important rationale for marrying is disappearing. With a decrease in the economic interdependency generally associated with marriage, it would not be surprising to observe a greater reluctance

TABLE 10.1   Labor Force Participation Rate

	1940	1950	1960	1970
All Females [a]	.27	.31	.35	.43
Married Females [b]	.17	.25	.32	.41

SOURCE: U.S. Census, *Statistical Abstract of the United States: 1972*, Table 346, p. 219.

NOTE: Rates, 1940 through 1960, refer to females 14 years old and over. For 1970, they refer to the age group 16 years old and over.

[a] Female labor force as a percentage of total female population.
[b] Married women in the labor force as a percentage of married women in the population.

to marry, remarry, or stay married on the part of females whose market potential has undergone a significant change. Indeed, an inverse relationship is apparent in the postwar period (1947 to 1971) between the relative market potential of married females (as measured by their wage relative to men's) and the proportion of the female population married. Figure 10.1 indicates that the relationship is strongest among prime-age females (between the ages of 20 and 34).

On the other hand, real family income has risen over time in the United States, making it possible for more young couples to afford the "set-up" costs of marriage. If a rise in real income reduces any proclivities toward "swinging" in favor of a march down the aisle, it could also be expected to lead to a decline in the age at first marriage and an expansion in the desired number of children per married couple as well as in expenditures per child. Furthermore, within a marriage more income makes a higher standard of living possible, which in itself would soothe any major conjugal difficulties. For example, individual privacy, independence, romance, and prestige could all be better maintained through such things as

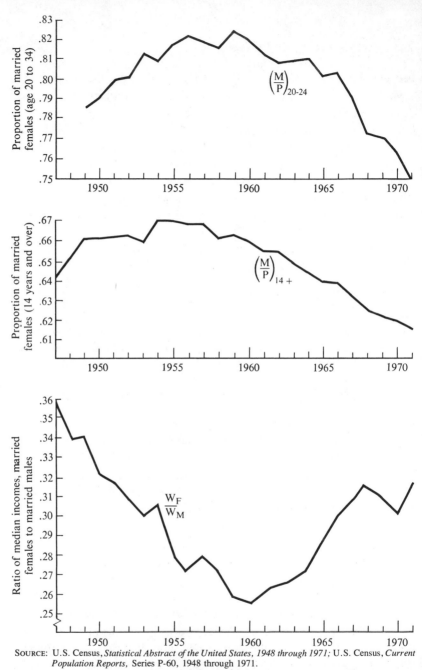

SOURCE: U.S. Census, *Statistical Abstract of the United States, 1948 through 1971;* U.S. Census, *Current Population Reports,* Series P-60, 1948 through 1971.

FIGURE 10.1.   Proportion of Married Females (age 20 to 34); Proportion of Married
Females (age 14 +); Ratio of Median Incomes, Married Females
(spouse present) to Married Males (wife present), 1947–1971

SOURCE: U.S. Census, *Statistical Abstract of the United States, 1948 through 1971*.

FIGURE 10.2.   Marriages per 1,000 Unmarried Females,
14 Years and Older, 1947–1970

spacious living quarters, two cars in the garage, foreign travel, and fancy schools for the children.

Despite what might have been expected, the growth of real income in the United States has not been accompanied over time by a rising trend in marriage rates. On the contrary, Figure 10.2 indicates that marriages per thousand unmarried females (14 years old and over) have declined.[1] There is reason to believe that the marriage rate fell owing to a decrease in the number of eligible [2] males, since the ratio of eligible females (aged 14 to 24) to eligible males (aged 14 to 34), portrayed in Figure 10.3 indicates an inverse relationship to the relative number of marriages. However, these statistics provide estimates only for the *civilian* population. Therefore the number of eligible males would have been underestimated with the advent of the Korean and Vietnam wars, resulting in an exaggeration of the increase in the ratio of eligible females to males during the early 1950s and again in the late 1960s.

Expectations as to the age at first marriage and the birthrate are also not supported statistically. Table 10.2 reveals that the age at first marriage did decline for women until 1956, but then rose, exhibiting a U-shaped pattern. The opposite was true for birthrates. The number of births per

TABLE 10.2   Median Age at First Marriage for Females
and Births per Thousand Females
Aged 15 to 44, 1947–1970

Year	Median Age at First Marriage	Live Births per Thousand
1947	20.5	113.3
1948	20.4	107.3
1949	20.3	107.1
1950	20.3	106.2
1951	20.4	111.3
1952	20.2	113.5
1953	20.2	114.7
1954	20.3	117.6
1955	20.2	118.0
1956	20.1	120.8
1957	20.3	122.7
1958	20.2	120.1
1959	20.2	120.1
1960	20.3	118.0
1961	20.3	117.2
1962	20.3	112.1
1963	20.5	108.4
1964	20.5	105.0
1965	20.6	96.0
1966	20.5	91.3
1967	20.6	87.6
1968	20.8	85.7
1969	20.8	85.8
1970	20.8	87.6

SOURCE: U.S. Census, *Historical Statistics of the United States, Colonial Times to 1957;*
and U.S. Census, *Statistical Abstract of the United States: 1958 through 1972.*

thousand females (aged 15 to 44) rose until 1957 and then fell precipitously.

The dwindling interest in raising children is probably associated with the same forces that caused a decline in both the *proportion* married (Figure 10.1) and the *rate* of marriage (Figure 10.2). That is, the increase in female market capacity, tending to discourage matrimony, predominated over the positive effect of the rise in real family income. Had men become better substitutes in household activities, including child care, the effect of female market opportunities would probably not have been as strong.

Marital status has been described as the net result of two economic

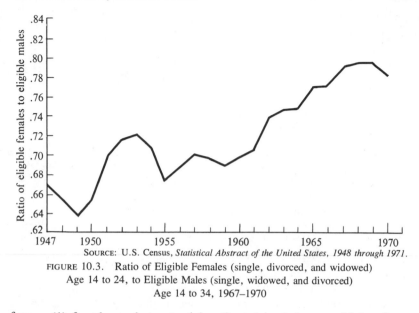

SOURCE: U.S. Census, *Statistical Abstract of the United States, 1948 through 1971.*

FIGURE 10.3.   Ratio of Eligible Females (single, divorced, and widowed)
Age 14 to 24, to Eligible Males (single, widowed, and divorced)
Age 14 to 34, 1967–1970

forces: (1) female market potential, reflected in their rate of labor force participation; and (2) real family income. In the next section of the paper, these same forces will be analyzed within a more rigorous theoretical framework so as to provide a basis for investigating changes in marital status within the population.

Conceptual Framework

The efficiency with which an individual can produce in the home (for example, prepare a meal) or in the market (measured in terms of earnings) can be shown graphically. The shape and position of the production-possibility frontier (p–p) expresses the productive capacity of the individual, while the preference function (I) reflects personal tastes (see Figures 10.4 and 10.5). The individual operates optimally at the point where the two curves are tangent to one another. That is, we may say that the individual is in equilibrium at point X and allocates his or her time to producing M market goods and H home goods. The inclination at the point of tangency measures the individual's relative efficiency in the two areas of activity $\left(\frac{\text{efficiency in the market}}{\text{efficiency in the home}}\right)$. Generally, owing to biological and cultural cir-

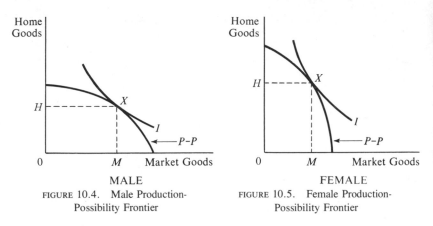

FIGURE 10.4.   Male Production-
Possibility Frontier

FIGURE 10.5.   Female Production-
Possibility Frontier

cumstances, the investment patterns of males and females in training and education have tended to differ, resulting in production-possibility frontiers differentiated by sex.

As marriage implies some degree of mutually beneficial specialization, the relative efficiencies of the partners entering the marital contract are an important consideration. If their equilibrium productivities were similar before marriage, indicating a duplication of training and ability, matrimony would not lead to greater allocative efficiency. However, if

$$\left(\frac{\text{his efficiency in the market}}{\text{his efficiency in the home}} \right) > \left(\frac{\text{her efficiency in the market}}{\text{her efficiency in the home}} \right),$$ and if

this inequality is the result of a greater market productivity (wage rate) and a smaller home productivity on the part of a male in comparison with his prospective mate, then marriage would provide a means of shifting time inputs so as to rearrange production and consumption to the advantage of both parties. The rewards to be expected from union, in terms of additional home and market goods produced, depend on the degree to which a couple's talents and resources differ. How effective the marriage has been in bringing about an optimal reallocation of time is measured by the extent to which the relative productivities equalize after marriage. That is, assuming diminishing marginal productivity, more time allocated to the market on the part of the male will lower his relative efficiency in the market. By the same token, the female's relative efficiency in the market will rise if she devotes more of her working hours to home production.

Similar tastes are an important consideration as well, since common backgrounds and experience are emphasized in the literature as important criteria for marrying and staying married.[3] The preference functions (*I*) of two compatible individuals would tend to have the same shape, indicating a similar ordering of preferences. Thus, a marriage is viable to the extent that tastes coincide and productivities differ.[4]

If a wife earns a substantial proportion of the family income, complementarity between marriage partners tends to be minimal.[5] In such cases, the wife has less to lose financially from termination of the contract than if she were relatively more productive in the home. Similarly, a professionally capable single woman has less to gain materially from matrimony than if she were a debutante looking for a wealthy bachelor. Thus, it may be hypothesized that duplication of skills between the sexes is causally associated with becoming and/or remaining a "divorcée" or "spinster."

The effect of a change in market efficiency on male–female complementarity differs by sex. A rise in the market wage of a male, income held constant, implies a decrease for him in the price of market goods relative to the price of home-produced goods and leisure. Rationally, the male will increase time spent in the market and barter goods resulting from his market activities (that is, his earnings) in return for his desired level of home goods. Since from the cradle he has been led to expect that this is most easily accomplished through taking a wife, his natural predisposition is to marry, for, besides facilitating the identification of heirs, it avoids certain transaction costs. That is, a young man might simply live with his girl friend, in which case there is generally a cost imposed by society, or he might hire a servant, in which case an inconvenience cost is attached to the formal or informal contract stating that she is available for only a limited number of hours per week.[6] Thus, all other things being equal, a rise in the market efficiency of a male implies a greater incentive to specialize and find a wife who will produce effectively in the home.

The results of an increase in relative market productivity would tend to be quite different for females. The female is not preconditioned to seek a male who willingly would or effectively could substitute his time for hers in home activities. Furthermore, since she would, as a wife be under cultural pressure to discharge home-oriented duties, marriage would suggest the probability of a less-than-optimal allocation of her time. Thus, a rise in the female's relative market potential, tending to equalize male–female relative productivities, would, if anything, discourage matrimony. For those females already married, an increase in market capacity would encourage a reallocation of time toward the market, implying greater economic independence and a declining interest in the role of "homemaker."

The effect of a change on the female's relative market efficiency was described holding real income constant. However, a rise in the wage rate of a female, assuming that she is working, usually means an increase in her real income as well. Thus, we have two economic effects in operation: the income effect, tending to increase the consumption of goods (like marriage) generally assumed to be positively associated with income; and a relative wage effect, which would tend to discourage matrimony. The net outcome of these two economic forces would determine female marital status, providing other factors affecting consumption and production were unchanged.

Obviously, however, other factors are not held constant. Individuals differ by age, education, race, religion, and other variables that influence marital status. In view of this, let us consider some of the more important of these.

Take, for instance, unemployment. Most men would find it difficult to assume or fulfill their role as "breadwinner" if they could not find and retain a job. Thus, it is not surprising that marital dissolution has been found to be more prevalent where the husband has experienced considerable unsteadiness of employment.[7]

Children provide a rationale not only for marrying[8] but for parental unity as well, in terms of both preferences and production. Representing an area of mutual concern, children and child-related activities would tend to figure prominently in the ordering of parental preferences. Furthermore, since good substitutes for a mother's care are not easily obtained, division of labor within the marriage becomes more of a necessity. Would marriages tend to dissolve more frequently if children were not present? Studies point in that direction,[9] but it is debatable whether children deter marital dissolution or whether the anticipation of disruption curtails procreation.

The age composition of the population is also relevant, since the prevalence of a particular marital status may result from a population being highly concentrated in a specific age category. For example, Table 10.3 indicates that in 1963 first marriages were more likely to occur among

TABLE 10.3 Percentage Distribution of
Brides and Grooms by Age According
to Previous Marital Status:
Marriage Registration Area, 1963

Previous Marital Status and Age	Bride	Groom
Single	Percentage distribution	
All ages	100.0	100.0
< 18 years	14.8	1.6
18–19	30.7	14.7
20–24	42.6	56.3
25–29	6.7	16.7
30–34	2.3	5.4
35–44	1.9	3.6
45 +	1.0	1.7
Previously married		
All ages	100.0	100.0
< 25 years	18.9	8.3
25–34	29.5	28.2
35–44	24.1	25.9
45–54	16.0	17.7
55–64	7.8	11.0
65 +	3.6	8.9

SOURCE: National Center for Health Statistics, *Marriage Statistics Analysis: United States, 1963*, Series 21, No. 16, Table K, p. 17.

persons 20 to 24 years old than in other age categories, while remarriages were more prevalent at slightly older ages. Marital instability, on the other hand, was most apparent at younger ages (see Table 10.4).

Besides the flow of marriages and divorces in a given year, the absolute number (or stock) of individuals who comprise a specific age and marital category should also be considered. Table 10.5 provides an estimate, but it can only be considered an imprecise approximation, since the data fails to exclude the flow of newlyweds and divorcées, a component which was shown above to differ in importance according to age category. Table 10.5 reveals that the proportion married is greatest in the age category 35 to 44, while the relative number divorced is greatest in the next age group, 45 to 54.

Black males may find particular difficulty in assuming their "masculine role," since it is probable that they encounter less favorable market

TABLE 10.4   Divorce Decrees per 1,000
Married Persons, by Age and Sex in 1962

	Divorce Rate	
Age at Divorce	Men	Women
Total	7.5	7.5
< 20 years	24.8	29.0
20–24	22.0	18.9
25–29	15.5	11.1
30–34	10.2	9.0
35–39	7.5	7.1
40–44	6.9	5.9
45–49	5.6	4.2
50 +	2.5	1.8

SOURCE: National Center for Health Statistics, *Divorce Statistics Analysis: United States, 1962,* Series 21, No. 7, Table 4.

TABLE 10.5   Percentage Distribution of the Population
Aged 14+ According to
Marital Status, 1962

Age and Sex	Total	Single	Married	Widowed	Divorced
Male	100.0	25.3	69.2	3.4	2.1
14–19 years	100.0	91.0	2.9	—	0.1
20–24	100.0	52.4	47.0	—	0.7
25–29	100.0	21.4	76.8	0.2	1.7
30–34	100.0	10.2	86.9	0.3	2.6
35–44	100.0	8.4	88.8	0.6	2.2
45–54	100.0	7.7	86.6	2.0	3.6
55–65	100.0	7.7	84.6	4.6	3.1
65–74	100.0	6.0	79.6	12.4	2.0
75+	100.0	7.0	59.4	32.4	1.2
Female	100.0	19.6	65.3	12.5	2.7
14–19 years	100.0	88.0	11.8	0.1	0.2
20–24	100.0	29.3	68.8	0.3	1.7
25–29	100.0	9.8	86.6	0.6	3.0
30–34	100.0	7.5	87.5	1.3	3.6
35–44	100.0	5.3	88.2	2.8	3.7
45–54	100.0	6.4	80.4	9.1	4.1
55–64	100.0	6.8	67.2	22.6	3.4
65–74	100.0	7.3	48.3	42.9	1.6
75+	100.0	7.0	20.8	71.6	0.7

SOURCE: U.S. Census, *Current Population Reports,* Series P-20, No. 122, cited in U.S. Census, *Statistical Abstract of the United States: 1963,* Table 32, p. 36.

opportunities relative to black females, especially at higher occupation levels.[10] Table 10.6 (column 4) reveals that the relative earnings capacity of black females rose with the education level of the husband, while the opposite was true for white wives. Furthermore, at all levels of education

TABLE 10.6 Family Income and Wife's Earnings by Race, Home-Ownership, and Education of Husband, 1960

Race, Home-Ownership, Education of Husband (years) (1)	Family Income Minus Wife's Earnings (2)	Working Wife's Average Weekly Earnings (3)	Ratio of Wife's Earnings to column 2 [a] (4)
White homeowners			
0–4 years education	$5,242	$56.52	54
5–8	6,030	59.92	50
9–11	6,649	66.54	50
12	7,317	65.69	45
13–15	8,663	69.80	40
16 +	11,410	75.07	33
White renters			
0–4	4,137	55.73	67
5–8	4,765	57.50	60
9–11	5,109	60.44	59
12	5,266	62.58	59
13–15	6,013	70.56	59
16 +	7,064	76.80	54
Black homeowners			
0–4	3,538	39.97	56
5–8	4,092	44.48	54
9–11	4,465	53.89	60
12	4,727	55.03	58
13 +	5,397	78.56	73
Black renters			
0–4	2,848	40.86	72
5–8	3,432	43.38	63
9–11	3,663	48.60	66
12	3,993	66.39	83
13 +	4,085	82.59	101

SOURCE: See Glen Cain, *Married Women in the Labor Force* (Chicago, 1966), Table 30, Columns 5, 6, 7, p. 102.

NOTE: Based on summary statistics for U.S. Census, 1960, 1/1000 sample.

[a] Column 3 was first multiplied by 50 before division by column 2.

the earnings capacity of black wives relative to black family income was greater than that of their white counterparts. This suggests that, in the case of black couples, the market structure may tend to discourage the standard male–female division of labor, a situation conducive to the higher rate of marital instability among blacks of all occupation and education levels.[11]

Residential location can affect marital status. For example, a well-defined division of labor between husband and wife is essential to the joint productive effort characteristic of a farm. A comparison of ten different occupations reveals that, in 1960, farmers consistently had the lowest proportion of persons separated, divorced, or remarried.[12] On the other hand, Table 10.7 indicates that divorced and separated individuals

TABLE 10.7   Percentage of Marriages Disrupted
in the Population Aged 14+ by Residence, 1960

	Males	Females
Residence	Total marriage Disrupted (percent)	Total marriage Disrupted (percent)
Total	3.6	4.8
Urban	3.9	5.6
Rural	2.8	2.7

SOURCE: Computed from 1960 census data by Hugh Carter and Alexander Plateris, in "Trends in Divorce and Family Disruption," *Health, Education, and Welfare Indicators* (September 1963), p. xi.

abound in urban centers, where a joint economic enterprise involving a high degree of family cooperation is rare. However, since census statistics provide place of residence only at the time of census enumeration, it cannot be stated with certainty whether instability is actually more prevalent in cities or whether rural residents who divorce move to urban centers to avoid provincial censure. What can be said is that, owing to greater population density, the cost of searching for another mate tends to be less in urban centers.

Certain types of welfare payments, such as Aid to Families with Dependent Children, may actually foster family disruption, since such relief is more accessible if the husband has left the household. Indeed, the existence of the AFDC program has been shown to be a significant factor affecting the desertion rate in the population.[13] One interpretation of this phenomenon suggests that welfare serves as a form of government-subsidized alimony, reducing the costs of marital disruption among low-income groups.[14]

Do marriage and divorce laws, which are under the separate jurisdiction of the states, create strong barriers to entrance into or exit from marriage? Marriage legislation generally seems to be characterized by poor enforcement, probably owing to the structure of county budgets, which are designed with the assumption that officials will receive a substantial part of their income from license fees.[15] Divorce legislation, on the other hand, has been more rigorously applied, so that migration to Nevada, for example, for the purpose of obtaining a "quickie," is quite common and reflects the short residence requirements and tractable grounds for divorce found in that state. Such a situation would tend to discriminate against low-income groups, making legal dissolution of marriage more accessible to wealthier couples. Increasing public pressure, however, has led to a modification of some of the strictest state laws, the 1966 liberalization of the New York State divorce law being a case in point. Thus, the inhibiting effect of divorce legislation appears to be diminishing in answer to public pressure for a lowering of the cost of a conjugal error.

Empirical Analysis

A supply function of married women may be most simply specified as follows:

$$M_F = \beta_1 Y + \beta_2 W_F + u, \tag{1}$$

where M_F provides an approximation of the number of married females, Y measures family income, W_F expresses the earnings capacity of wives, and u includes other relevant factors determining marital status.

The variables in equation (1) are expressed as long-run magnitudes, since we are seeking results useful in interpreting changes over time. Thus the sign of the income coefficient β_1 indicates in which direction (positive or negative) a change in long-run income would affect the relative number of married women, holding the earnings of married women constant. β_2 reflects the effect of the market productivity of married females on the relative size of the married female population, keeping family income constant. Theoretically, we would expect β_1 to be positive and β_2 negative.

In view of the prevalence of the nuclear family in the United States, it may be argued that husband's income (W_M) is a reasonable approximation for total family income excluding the earnings of the wife. This simplification makes it possible to write equation (1) as follows:

$$M_F = \beta_1(W_M + W_F) + \beta_2 W_F + u$$
$$= \beta_1 W_M + \alpha W_F + u \tag{2}$$

Since $\alpha = \beta_1 + \beta_2$, equation (1) may be estimated statistically using the more readily available data required for equation (2).

It is certainly an oversimplification to formulate a female's productivity in terms of her market wage W_F, when what is relevant is marked efficiency in relation to home productivity $W_F/(MP_H)_F$. This variable, although more precise, presents a problem in estimation, since the opportunity cost of a woman's time spent in home production is not easily measured. However, if income is held constant (as it is in our equation), a change in the labor force participation of married females should approximate a change in relative productivity, since participation is a function of family income and relative efficiency, i.e., $LFP = f(Y, W_F/(MP_H)_F)$.

Equation (3) then provides the final version of our supply equation:

$$M_F = \beta_1 W_M + \gamma(LFP) + u. \tag{3}$$

The income coefficient in equation (3), when estimated using cross-sectional data, may be interpreted as the average effect of a change in husbands' income on the relative number of women who choose to be married, their market capacity being held constant. Thus a rise in husband's income, assuming marriage is positively associated with income, implies a greater tendency for adult females to be married, rather than single or divorced. In equation (3), γ is a relative price effect *uncompensated* by a change in income. A rise in the relative market potential of a wife would be conductive to her greater independence and would imply that the gains from marriage resulting from economic complementarity have declined. On the other hand, a rise in family income owing to an increase in the female's earning power would mean that the set-up and maintenance costs of marriage could be met with greater ease. The net effect resulting from these opposing forces—the price effect discouraging matrimony and the income effect favoring it—on the proportion of married females will be reflected in the sign of γ and is not predictable a priori.

By using aggregate cross-sectional data—that is, state statistics derived from the 1960 U.S. census of population—we are provided with averages which can be interpreted as approximations for long-run or permanent levels of the variables included in our model.[16] Since the average levels of these variables in a particular geographic area tend to be quite stable, census estimates of husbands' income or the labor force participation of wives at a point in time could be considered equivalent to trend-free averages over the life cycle. Statistics on a state basis provide the further advantage that differences in divorce legislation and religious affiliation can be taken into account.[17]

Although state averages do not reflect individual fluctuations in income, they do reflect deviations in income for the whole group attributable to sharp changes in economic conditions within the state. Both marriage and divorce rates have been found to respond positively and significantly to the business cycle.[18] It seems reasonable to suppose, therefore, that both rates would decline with increasing unemployment. That is, couples considering matrimony would be less able to confront the costs of marrying and setting up a household, while couples contemplating divorce would find even a relatively small attorney's fee and court costs a formidable barrier.

Regression analysis allows us to take into account area unemployment and provides a means of testing whether the relationship between marital status and the female's market capacity (as expressed in equation 3) is statistically significant. At the same time it permits us to include other factors in an effort to control for the relevant social and economic variables discussed above, which may influence marital status. The dependent variable used, the proportion of married females (14 years old and over), is essentially a stock concept, although it includes the inflow of new marriages in any given year. However the flow of new entrants, i.e., the marriage rate, cannot be employed as an additional variable, since those entering marriage are never classified by income, level of education, employment, race, etc.[19] Table 10.8 provides a summary of all theoretical variables and their empirical counterparts.

The weighted regression results,[20] presented in Table 10.9, indicate

TABLE 10.8   Variables Used in Regression Equation,
48 States, 1960

Theoretical Variable	*Empirical Counterpart*
Dependent Variable	
Number of married females	Proportion of married females (14 years old and over)
Independent Variables	
Relative market potential of married females, spouse present	Married females in the labor force, spouse present, divided by total married females, spouse present
Husband's income	Median income of married males, spouse present
Female education level	Median number of school years (females 25 years old and over)
Male education level	Median number of school years (males 25 years old and over)
Relative city size	Proportion of urban females (14 years old and over) living in central cities (population 50,000+)
Rural-farm population	Proportion of females (14 years old and over) living in rural-farm areas
Age composition	Proportion of the female population (14 years old and over) in the age group 20 to 34
Color composition	Proportion of the female population white
Female employment opportunities	Ratio of unemployed to employed females
Male employment opportunities	Ratio of unemployed to employed males
Welfare assistance	Proportion of families receiving AFDC payments
Aversion to divorce based on religious conviction	Proportion of the population Catholic
Divorce legislation	Dummy variable: strict legislation = 1, liberal legislation = 0
Family size	Proportion of families with no own children less than 18
Market demand	Net migration of females in the age group 15–24 during the period 1950–60. "Net migration" is defined as immigration minus outmigration
Ratio of eligibles	Single, divorced, and widowed females (aged 15 to 44) divided by single, divorced, and widowed males (aged 15 to 44)

Table 10.8 (continued)
NOTES: Alaska and Hawaii were excluded in the interest of greater demographic homogeneity.

All variables are derived from the *U.S. Census of Population, 1960,* with the following exceptions: Proportion of families receiving AFDC payments—*Social Security Bulletin,* Vol. 24, No. 1 (January 1961); Percentage Catholic—*National Catholic Almanac, 1960,* pp. 443–45; Net migration of females aged 15–24—Gladys Bowles and James D. Tarver, *Net Migration of the Population, 1950–1960* (Washington, D.C., 1965); Divorce legislation—for a more detailed analysis of the determination of the dummy variable used, see Fredricka Pickford Santos, ''Some Economic Determinants of Marital Status'' (Ph.D. diss., Columbia University, 1972).

that the net effect of female market potential, as measured by the labor force participation of married females (spouse present), on the relative size of the married female population is negative and significant.[21] What is more, the effect of husband's income is positive and significant. Employment opportunities within a state appear to play a significant role in determining a female's decision as to her marital status; that is, the

TABLE 10.9   Weighted Regression Explaining the Proportion
of Married Females, 48 States, 1960

Independent Variables [a]	Regression Coefficients	t Values
Labor force participation of married females, spouse present	−0.25	−3.61 *
Husband's income [b]	0.05	2.42 *
Ratio of eligible females to males	−0.15	−3.88 *
Female unemployment rate	0.75	2.71 *
Male unemployment rate	−0.43	−1.48
Female net migration (aged 15 to 24)	-10^{-6}	−2.24 *
Percentage Catholic	−0.06	−3.84 *
Proportion of female population (14+) aged 20 to 34	0.38	2.13 *
Adjusted R^2	0.78	

NOTE: Alaska and Hawaii were excluded in the interests of greater demographic homogeneity.

[a] All other variables listed in Table 10.8 (female education level, male education level, family size, divorce legislation, color composition, relative city size, rural-farm population, welfare assistance) were held constant. Although accompanied by the expected signs, they were not significant.

[b] Variable run in log form.

* Significant at the 5 percent level.

female unemployment rate has a positive sign and is significant. For males, the unemployment rate is accompanied by the expected negative sign but is not significant. The net migration variable is negative and significant, suggesting that if opportunities are abundant, so that inmigration into a state greatly exceeds outmigration, the proportion of the female population which is married tends to be relatively small. The variable approximating the age composition of the female population indicates that a larger concentration of females in the age group 20 to 34 results in a greater proportion married. The negative and significant sign associated with the variable "proportion Catholic" suggests that young Catholics spend more time in search of a mate and are more cautious about matrimony than non-Catholics, a reaction compatible with the well-known position of the Catholic Church on divorce. Finally, the ratio of eligible females to unattached males in a state appears to be a significant factor affecting the proportion of married women and suggests that female marital status is not always a matter of choice. Other variables included in the regression equation were accompanied by the theoretically expected sign but lacked statistical significance. According to the coefficient of determination (adjusted R^2), the variables in our equation explain 78 percent of the observed variation in the relative number of married females among states in 1960.

Conclusions

Findings, based on multiple regression analysis, suggest that the rise in female market potential is a significant factor explaining the decline in the proportion of married females which has occurred in the United States over time despite the rise in real family income over time. However, if female market capacity is a determining factor leading more women to select alternatives other than marriage, what are the social and economic implications of this phenomenon?

As was mentioned in the introduction, singles and divorcées, once social outcasts, have not only become acceptable; they have acquired an aura of glamour and adventure. They comprise a new and growing market which has enticed shrewd entrepreneurs to enter into such profitable ventures as singles' bars, apartments, country clubs, exotic vacations, etc.

Furthermore, owing to the large numbers of individuals involved in the process of disengaging themselves from unsatisfactory marriages, a strong pressure group has emerged capable of bringing about more liberal divorce legislation. Thus the cost accruing from a conjugal error is declining and ceases to be prohibitive in either social or economic terms.

One may question whether marriage represents an obsolete and dying institution in the United States. For the time being, it continues to be the statistical norm. But what the future holds depends very much on how the marital ground rules are modified in the light of increasingly similar male–female productive capacity. To the extent that the old institutional guidelines change, relaxing highly structured role concepts and emphasizing psychic rather than economic gains, marriage will certainly continue as a life-style, but one which is no longer so all-pervasive.

APPENDIX

An individual allocates his (or her) time optimally by maximizing his (or her) preference function, subject to his (or her) production-possibility frontier and a time constraint.[22] That is:

$$U = U(M, H, L); \tag{A1}$$
$$M = f_M(T_M), \tag{A2}$$

where f_M depends on the real wage rate.

$$H = f_H(T_H), \tag{A3}$$

where f_H depends on natural ability, formal and informal education, and capital inputs.

$$T_M + T_H = T_X; \tag{A4}$$
$$T_X + L = T_0, \tag{A5}$$

where L = leisure;
  M = goods produced in the market (i.e., earnings);
  H = goods produced in the home;
  T_M = time spent working in the market;
  T_H = time devoted to home production;
  T_X = total time spent working; and
  T_0 = total time available.

Given a limited amount of work time, the production possibility frontier of market and home goods may be described by the following function:

$$g(M, H; T_X) = 0. \tag{A6}$$

Maximize $U(M, H. L)$, subject to the following restrictions:

$$g(M, H; T_X) = 0;$$
$$T_X + L = T_0.$$

Thus,

$$U^* = U(M, H, L) - \lambda[g(M, H, T_0 - L)];$$

$$\frac{\partial U^*}{\partial M} = \frac{\partial U}{\partial M} - \lambda \frac{\partial M}{\partial T_M} = 0;$$

$$\frac{\partial U^*}{\partial H} = \frac{\partial U}{\partial H} - \lambda \frac{\partial H}{\partial T_H} = 0;$$

$$\frac{\partial U^*}{\partial L} = \frac{\partial U}{\partial L} - \lambda \frac{\partial L}{\partial T_L} = 0.$$

Thus, the optimal allocation of time inputs for an individual occurs when:

$$\frac{\frac{\partial U}{\partial M}}{\frac{\partial M}{\partial T_M}} = \frac{\frac{\partial U}{\partial H}}{\frac{\partial H}{\partial T_H}} = \frac{\frac{\partial U}{\partial L}}{\frac{\partial L}{\partial T_L}}, \tag{A7}$$

or:

$$-\frac{\frac{\partial H}{\partial M}}{} = \frac{\frac{\partial M}{\partial T_M}}{\frac{\partial H}{\partial T_H}} = \frac{\left(\frac{\partial M}{\partial I}\right)\left(\frac{\partial I}{\partial T_M}\right)}{\frac{\partial H}{\partial T_H}} = \frac{\frac{W}{\bar{p}}}{MP_H}, \tag{A8}$$

where $I = W \cdot T_M$, that is, earnings derived from time spent working in the market;

$\dfrac{W}{\bar{p}}$ = Real wage, i.e., the market wage of the individual divided by the average price of market goods; and

MP_H = Marginal productivity in the production of home goods.

NOTES

[1] It would be both interesting and enlightening to observe marriage rates according to prime-age categories (e.g., 14 to 24 or 20 to 34). These are not available over time, however.

[2] "Eligible" is defined to include single, widowed, and divorced males.

[3] See Charles Ackerman, "Affiliations: Structural Determinants of Differential Divorce Rates," *American Journal of Sociology,* LXIX (July 1963): 12–20; Harvey J. Locke, *Predicting Adjustment in Marriage: A Comparison of a Divorced and a Happily Married Group* (New York, 1951).

[4] The individual is considered here as both a producer and a utility maximizer. A derivation of his or her equilibrium position is presented in the appendix.

[5] There exists a somewhat remote possibility that the husband is relatively more efficient in the home. This, however, is unlikely since the upbringing of the male continues to be geared toward stifling the possible development of talents related to home production.

[6] One might argue that several wives would provide additional rewards for the male and present no problems with respect to the identification of heirs. Gary Becker has pointed out, however, that in societies where the sex ratio is close to unity, and where men and women do not differ greatly in wealth and ability, and assuming diminishing returns to additional wives, monogamy is the most efficient marital form in terms of maximizing the community's total output. See Gary S. Becker, "A Theory of Marriage: Part I," *Journal of Political Economy,* LXXXI (July/August 1973): 820.

[7] See William J. Goode, *Women in Divorce* (Glencoe, Ill., 1956), p. 75.

[8] Gary Becker explains marriage in terms of the desire to raise one's own children. See his "A Theory of Marriage: Part I," p. 818.

[9] Paul H. Jacobson and Thomas P. Monahan made studies holding the duration of marriage constant, and showed some excess of divorce frequency among childless groups. See Paul H. Jacobson, "Differentials in Divorce by Duration of Marriage and Size of Family," *American Sociological Review,* V (April 1950): 235–44; Thomas P. Monahan, "Is Childlessness Related to Family Stability?" *American Sociological Review,* XX (August 1955): 446–56.

[10] This has been suggested by Glen Cain in his investigation of black and white married women in 1960. See Glen Cain, *Married Women in the Labor Force* (Chicago, 1966), pp. 102–5. However, it is possible that efforts in the past decade to create more favorable market conditions for blacks of both sexes have changed the relative earnings position of black males considerably.

[11] See Richard J. Udry, "Marital Instability by Race, Sex, Education, and Occupation Using 1960 Census Data," *American Journal of Sociology,* LXXII (September 1966): 205–9; Karen G. Hillman, "Marital Instability and Its Relation to Education, Income, and Occupation: An Analysis Based on Census Data," in Robert F. Winch, Robert McGinnis, and Hubert R. Barringer, eds., *Selected Studies in Marriage and the Family* (New York, 1962), pp. 602–8.

[12] See Hugh Carter and Paul C. Glick, *Marriage and Divorce: A Social and Economic Study* (Cambridge, Mass., 1970), Table 7.19, p. 209.

[13] See Marjorie H. Honig, "Work and Welfare: An Analysis of Consumer Choice" (Ph.D. diss., Columbia University, 1971).

[14] See Robert D. Reischauer, "The Impact of the Welfare System on Migration and Marital Stability" (Ph.D. diss., Columbia University, 1971).

[15] Hugh Carter provides evidence that local clerks even assist young applicants in circumventing the law in order to enable them to qualify for a marriage license; see H. Carter and P. Glick, *Marriage and Divorce* (Cambridge, 1970), pp. 362–63. See also Dale L. Womble, "Trends in Falsification of Age at Marriage in Ohio," *Journal of Marriage and the Family,* XXVIII (February 1966): 54–56.

[16] The term "permanent income" was conceived by Milton Friedman to express the normal income position of a family devoid of transitory variations. According to Friedman's theory, consumption varies with income only to the extent that income changes represent a change in permanent income. Friedman observed that permanent income results from such observable factors as age, level of education, occupation, etc. See Milton Friedman, *A Theory of the Consumption Function* (Princeton, N.J., 1957), pp. 215–16. For further discussions of the use of cross-sectional data to explain trends over time see Robert Eisner, "The Permanent Income Hypothesis: Comment," *American Economic Review,* XLVIII (December 1958): 972–80, and Jacob Mincer, "Labor Force Participation of Married Women: A Study of Labor Supply," in Universities-National Bureau Committee for Economic Research, *Aspects of Labor Economics* (Princeton, N.J., 1962), pp. 69–71.

[17] The National Catholic Almanac provides statistics as to number of Catholics on a state basis. Unfortunately, this statistic does not discriminate between practicing and nominal Catholics.

[18] For an empirical analysis of the cyclical response of marriage and divorce rates, see Morris Silver, "Births, Marriages, and Business Cycles in the United States," *Journal of Political Economy,* LXXIII (June 1965): 237–55, and Fredricka Pickford Santos, "Some Economic Determinants of Marital Status" (Ph.D. diss., Columbia University, 1972), pp. 154–57.

[19] Owing to the lack of appropriate independent variables, efforts on the part of the author to use the marriage rate as a dependent variable were in vain. See Santos, "Some Economic Determinants of Marital Status," pp. 49, 72–77.

[20] Since a large state contains a smaller amount of random variation than a small state, reliability varies according to state size. To take account of different reliability, weighted regressions were used. That is, each variable was multiplied by the square root of the female population (14 years old and over). Weighting the regression assured that the variance of the residual was the same for each observation, thus satisfying the homoscedasticity assumption.

[21] Our hypothesis is also confirmed using similar variables for 1950. See Santos, "Some Economic Determinants of Marital Status," pp. 57–58.

[22] Equations A1 through A7 are those developed by Ruben Gronau in his unpublished paper "The Allocation of Time between Work in the Market, Work at Home, and Leisure." See also Gary S. Becker, "A Theory of the Allocation of Time," *Economic Journal,* LXXV (September 1965): 493–517.

11

Child Investment and Women

MARK R. ROSENZWEIG

THE ALLOCATION of resources to children within the family, often called child investment, is one important activity that has only recently received the attention of economists.[1] Since it is women who have largely taken on the function of "raising" children, at least in most western societies, the analysis of child investment is an important part of any study of women's role in the household. Moreover, because child investment has two dimensions—the number of children and the amount of resources devoted to each child—the study of women as investors in children may shed light on the relationship between the changing economic activities of women and recent trends in fertility, expenditures on children, and school investment. In addition, the amount of resources invested in children within the household may have an important influence on the future roles of children as adults in society at large. Thus, some part of the differential roles of men and women in society may be traced to differential investments, according to sex, at the household level.

Some evidence of such family-oriented differentials can be found in the sociological literature. Sewell and Shah found that parental encouragement, one component of household child investment, is positively associated with the college plans, attendance, and achievement of children. They have concluded that "males [are] in a more favorable position than females" [2] with respect to all three of the alternative measures of the quality of children. Adams and Meidam have shown that family economic variables are the crucial determinants of college attendance and

I am indebted to Harriet S. Zellner for her encouragement and perceptive criticism, and to Cynthia B. Lloyd for her patience and substantial assistance in the preparation of this paper.

that "sex differences favor males." [3] The significantly different teenage school enrollment rates for males and females, as displayed for 1960 and 1970 in Table 11.1, may be additional evidence of household-level sex-specific differential child investment, though not necessarily of household "discrimination." Such differentials may also be the product of societal influences external to the family, such as subtle social pressures or various laws and institutions. Compulsory schooling laws are examples of the latter that may have a direct effect on school enrollment. Their role in child investment must also be examined.

TABLE 11.1   Urban Teenage School Enrollment
Rates, Male and Females Aged 15–18

	1960	*1970*	*Percent-age Change*
Male	.7586	.8436	11.0
Female	.6979	.8023	17.5

SOURCES: U.S. Census, 1960, PC(1) 2D-52D, Table 103; U.S. Census, 1970, "Special Report: School Enrollment."

The theory of the allocation of time (originally formulated by Becker),[4] with its emphasis on production activities within the household, is a useful framework within which to study the role of women in child investment. In this paper, the relationship between the recent decline in birthrate, the differential levels of and changes in male and female teenage school enrollment rates, and the rise in per-pupil schooling expenditures [5] will be shown to be predominantly the result of changes in the factors affecting child investment decisions of women in the home. In the first part, the theoretical approach to the family's child investment behavior is outlined. The analysis explicitly considers the possibility of differential allocation of resources to male and female children. Within this framework, the differential influences of the husband's and wife's educational attainment and opportunity costs on the quality and quantity of children desired and on the derived demand for the goods used in child investment will be analyzed. In the second part, the implications derived from the preceding discussion will be tested empirically with aggregate state data from the 1960 census of population. Household variables are related to the average completed family size, the male and female teenage school enrollment rates, and the public school expenditures of residents of urban areas.

Theoretical Framework

The Quantity and Quality of Children

The fundamental insight of household production analysis in its general form is that the ultimate objects of consumer satisfaction, called "commodities," are produced in the home with various combinations of goods purchased in the market and the time of family members. In order to highlight the child investment decisions of the household, a set of four possible household commodities is chosen for this analysis: 1) the quantity of children, 2) the quality per child of female children, 3) the quality per child of male children, and 4) a composite commodity which represents all the other commodities produced in the home, which are alternative sources of satisfaction for the family. It should be noted here that the use of the rubric "child quality" in no way implies that some children are superior to others. The term is used to convey in one expression all the many dimensions of children (such as behavior, appearance, education, athletic ability, etc.) which are subject to at least some parental influence. It is assumed that the two parents desire to maximize their joint lifetime utility with respect to these four kinds of household commodities, subject to the constraint of limited family resources.

It is important to note also that the total number of children and the two sex-specific quality-per-child commodities each have an independent influence on the level of parental satisfaction. Thus it is assumed that parents can increase their satisfaction from children, or increase the total level of "services" that their children provide, in two ways: 1) by simply increasing family size; or 2) by enhancing the quality of each child. It is further assumed that parents are able to influence the level of these commodities by controlling their fertility and by investing more or less family resources in each male or female child. The desired amount of each of the commodities is determined both by parental preferences and by the relative costs, or prices, of the resources necessary for their production.

Family resources are of two kinds—the available time of each parent, which can be used either to help produce household commodities or to

earn money income, and purchased market goods and services. En-
cyclopedias, books, memberships in child organizations, etc., are examples of market inputs which increase child quality. Such household
"enrichment" factors have been found by Keller to have had a significant
effect on the scholastic achievement of children.[6] Expenditures on the
schooling of children, through the tax system and/or by paying for private
schooling, are an additional kind of child investment input, one which
will be examined empirically in the second part of the paper.

   The notion that parental time and market goods are used as inputs to
improve the quality of children means that the relationship between the
amounts of these inputs and the output, child quality, may differ among
families according to the abilities and experience of the parents. This
relationship may also differ within families according to the innate characteristics of children. Thus it is important to note that the devotion of
equal amounts of parental time and goods to male and female children
does not automatically imply that each male and female child will attain
the same level of quality or that identical levels of satisfaction will be experienced by the family.[7] If raising male and female children efficiently
to the same level of quality requires different amounts (and combinations)
of inputs, particularly of parental time, then the amount of inputs required
per unit of male and female quality will differ. Moreover, the educational
attainment of the parents may have differing effects on the relationship
between the resources used in child investment and the quality of male
and female children respectively. Evidence of the different effects of
parental time on sex-specific child quality has been observed by social
scientists. Walters and Stinnet, in a review of sociological studies of
parent–child relationships, noted that, "concerning the differential impact
of parents upon children according to the sex of the child, various studies
have shown that boys are perhaps more susceptible than girls to parental
influence." [8]

   The existence of innate or "technological" differences in the household production of the sex-specific child quality commodities would also
be reflected in the price or cost of producing comparable levels of male
and female child quality. Since increasing one's satisfaction from children requires additional resources, the cost of an additional amount of
child services would be equal to the sum of the costs of these required
resources, parental time and purchased goods. In a market economy, the

prices of market inputs such as books, clothing, lessons, etc., would presumably be the same for all families,[9] but the expenditure components of the prices of total child services (male and female) would vary among families. Each household would choose different combinations of market goods inputs to produce the desired level of child quality in accordance with their childrearing abilities and training.

The other component of the cost of total child services, parental time, also has a price, but this price differs among families. The "price" of a unit of time for each parent is equal to the income lost by devoting that unit of time to household production rather than to market work. The rate at which time can be traded for income is conventionally defined as the wage rate. The price of time or the opportunity cost of time of the wife is thus the wage she could earn, or earns, by working, that of the husband is his market wage. Thus the total time-cost component in the price of child services is the sum of the husband's and wife's marginal time inputs valued at their respective wages. If the level and mixture of the per-unit inputs, wife's time, husband's time, and market goods, differ between children according to sex, the prices of sex-specific child services will also differ. Similarly, an alternative nonchild commodity produced in the home will also have its own price.

The important assumption of this analysis, already mentioned, is that parents can alter the total level of satisfaction received from their children by increasing either the number of children or the level of services provided by each child, child quality, for either sex. Moreover, these components of child services have their own prices, which are in turn related to the prices of male and female child quality. The price of quality per female child, for instance, is the increase in total expenditures on female children necessitated by a unit increase in the quality of *each* female child, assuming that the total number of female children within the family remains the same. If π_M and π_F are denoted as the previously defined prices of a unit increase in male and female child quality, the price of a one-unit increase in the quality of *every* female child is π_F multiplied by the number of female children. Thus the larger the number of girls in the family, the more "expensive" is female quality per child, since the additional unit of quality must be allocated among all female children. Similarly, the price of quality per male child is π_M times the number of male children.

The price of an additional child can be defined in a similar manner. It is the increase in expenditures on children induced by an additional child *for given levels of quality per male and female child and for an unchanged sex ratio*. If the additional child receives the same amount of resources as other, already existing, children,[10] the price of that child would be the average number of units of child quality desired per child times the cost of each unit, π_F or π_M. The higher the level of quality per child chosen, therefore, the more costly are increases in family size.

The dependence of the price of sex-specific quality per child on the relative numbers of male and female children and the relationship between the price of an additional child and the desired levels of quality per child have three implications for household child investment behavior. Two of these implications will be tested in the second part of this essay.

The first implication is that those families with a greater proportion of female (male) children will desire a higher level of male (female) than female (male) quality per child. This would be true even if there were no innate differences in male and female children (so that $\pi_F = \pi_M$) and no relative parental preferences for male or female child services. If the number of females (males) exceeds the number of males (females) in a family, the price of female (male) quality per child would be higher than that of male (female) quality per child, since the resources associated with a unit of female (male) quality would have to be spread over more children. Thus, it would be expected that among families with the same number of children those with a higher proportion of boys would tend to invest less per male child and more per female child than those families with a higher proportion of female children, *in the absence of discrimination*. However, Adams and Meidam found that, for a given family size, the number of male siblings was negatively correlated with the likelihood that *female* children would attend college in blue-collar families,[11] which would appear to support the alternative hypothesis that parents tend to favor males over females with respect to child investment. Given that their desired amount of resources to be devoted to children remains relatively unchanged, parents with a larger number of boys transfer market goods and time which might otherwise be devoted to girls to male children in order not to reduce quality per male child. These researchers did not report, however, whether the higher male–female ratio also reduced the college attendance of males, as is implied by this analysis.

A second implication which can be derived from these price relationships is that any phenomenon which reduces fertility (the quantity of children) would diminish the cost of child quality and thus should raise the amount of resources devoted to each child. For example, if the use of more efficient birth-control techniques lowers actual fertility, then the greater the efficiency with which contraception is utilized, the higher will be the level of quality per child. Michael has shown that more educated women are more successful in averting the birth of "unwanted" children because they choose more efficient contraceptive techniques.[12] Thus the schooling of women should not only be negatively associated with fertility but should be positively correlated with child quality. The human capital of the parents, however, may have other influences on child investment, and these are discussed in the next section.

The third price implication concerns a nonhousehold influence on the levels of quality per child—compulsory schooling legislation. These laws, to the extent that they are effective, should reduce family size, since the price of child quantity would be increased. This assumes, of course, that these laws actually induce a rise in quality per child by forcing parents to "educate" their children beyond the level otherwise deemed optimal. Such legislated enhancements of the quality of children thus make children more "expensive," as long as parents have to bear some of the costs of the additional schooling. Moreover, these laws may have a differential impact on male and female quality levels if they are enforced differentially with respect to sex.[13] This phenomenon, the existence of which is tested in the second part of the paper, would be an example of societal, not familial, bias.

Changes in the prices of the components of π_M and π_F may also influence decisions concerning child investment. In the next section, the relationships between the wages and schooling levels of the two parents and fertility, quality per male and per female child, and mixture of inputs used in the production of these commodities will be discussed.

Child Investment and the Parents

PARENTAL WAGES, CHILD QUALITY, AND FERTILITY

The principal assumption that enables economists to make predictions about child investment behavior in the family is that the activity of child-rearing requires more parental time than the production of any other household commodity. Specifically, it is assumed that women tend to specialize in child investment and that therefore the share of the wife's time-cost component in the price of child services exceeds her share in the prices of alternative commodities. This assumption of the wife's time-intensity with respect to household child investment is not only intuitively appealing but is consistent with the findings of several economists that women who choose to bear more children spend more time in the home.[14]

Because wives allocate a larger proportion of their time to childrearing than to other household production activities, an increase in the wife's wage would raise the price of child services *more* than the price of other commodities. In other words, the activity requiring the most time becomes relatively more expensive. Thus, it is hypothesized that, among families with the same total income, those in which wives have relatively higher market wages would tend to devote relatively less time to child investment and relatively more time to other pursuits. What cannot be predicted as clearly is how the reduction in child investment due to an increase in the wife's opportunity cost of time is allocated between child quantity and quality per child, the two components of total child services. It is possible that both the number of children and the resources devoted to each child would decrease. However, it is likely that higher-wage women would choose a smaller family size but higher-quality children. However, given the assumption of the time-intensity of child investment, it is not expected that relatively high-wage women would have both larger families and higher quality children when their total family income is no different from that of low-wage women.

If the husband does not specialize in any particular household activity, or if he devotes little of his time to household production generally, the relationship between variations in his wage and changes in either fertility or quality per child would be weak. Smith provides evidence that husbands tend to spend somewhat more time in the production of nonchild commodities than in child investment, because the presence of children appears to increase rather than inhibit the labor force participation of married men.[15] Thus, an increase in the husband's wage may have a small positive effect on family size and on the time-intensity of children even when total family income is unchanged.

Because of the greater overall commitment of wives' time to household production and the greater relative time-intensity of wives' investment in children, variations in the wife's price of time will also dominate any differential changes in the levels of investment per male and female child. Walters and Stinnet report that a number of sociological studies of the home have shown that the intelligence of male children is more closely associated with maternal behavior than is the intelligence of female children and that paternal behavior has only a small effect on the aptitude of both sexes.[16] Moreover, Sewell and Shah found that the educational attainment of mothers had a stronger effect on males than on females with respect to college attendance.[17] In the framework of the analysis outlined here, these findings are consistent with either of two alternative characteristics of household child investment. Mothers spend more time with male children than female children either because 1) women prefer male children; or 2) male children require more time to raise to the same level of quality as female children. The latter hypothesis corresponds to the notion that male children are more rambunctious than female children and require more (maternal) effort to discipline: to get Johnny to sit down and learn the alphabet consumes more time than does teaching "well-behaved" Mary the ABCs. The first hypothesis is an assertion that sex discrimination occurs within the household, and also that the primary agent is the mother! [18] Whatever the underlying causes, the sociological evidence predicts that measures of the quality of male children should be more sensitive than those of female child quality to variations in the wages of women.

PARENTAL WAGES AND MARKET INPUTS

Changes in the value of the wife's price of time will not only influence the relative amounts of commodities consumed but will also affect the mixture of inputs used in household production, including child investment. An increase in the wife's wage, for instance, would induce her to substitute market goods for her more expensive time per unit of child quality. Child investment and all other household activities would become less time-intensive. For example, instead of teaching songs to their children, high-wage mothers might purchase market goods such as records and record players for them so that they could learn on their own. Alternatively, they could purchase market services in the form of lessons as a way of substituting for their own time. Thus, higher levels of women's wages should be associated with greater expenditures on market goods and services per unit of child quality. As a result, child investment should become more goods-intensive. The relationship between female wages and the amounts of market inputs used in child investment, however, would also depend on the desired levels of quality per child and family size. Given the assumption that child investment requires more time than other household activities, an increase in the price of the wife's time would therefore have two offsetting effects on the demand for child investment goods. The demand for total child services would decline, but the amount of goods used to produce a particular level of child quality would increase. Thus, a rise in the wage rates of women could result in a decline in the demand for child quality but an increase in money expenditures on children. This would follow if the rate of substitution of goods for time in household production exceeded the rate of substitution of other commodities for child quality in consumption.

PARENTAL SCHOOLING, CHILD QUALITY, AND FERTILITY

The human capital embodied in the parents may also influence the amount and combination of resources invested in children. The household production framework, with its emphasis on the use of parental time in household activities, highlights an important role of schooling, as one component of human capital, in its effect on the productivity of time used in household production. If formal education not only serves to enhance the market skills of individuals but also increases their nonmarket productivity, then the educational attainment of parents may affect the relative prices of commodities. If the acquisition of household skills meant that the average amounts of time needed to produce every household commodity were reduced by some percentage,[19] the prices of time-intensive commodities like child services would decline relative to other commodities requiring less time. Thus, if the wage rates of women are negatively correlated with both fertility and quality per child, female schooling should be positively associated with these child investment measures. The positive child investment-women's education relationship may also result from possible biases in the schooling of women, if the education of women is directed more toward making them better mothers than toward improving their productivity in the labor market.

However, the prediction that high levels of female schooling will be associated with higher fertility, based on the child investment efficiency hypothesis, contradicts the prediction arising from the notion that contraceptive efficiency and the wife's educational attainment are positively correlated, as discussed in the preceding section. The level of the husband's schooling, if increased household production efficiency were the only influence of education, should have little effect on child investment, given the small amount and relatively even distribution of the time devoted to household production by married men.

SCHOOLING AND MARKET INPUTS

More educated women might also be observed to spend greater amounts of time per unit of child services produced than do their less educated counterparts, at given wage rate levels, if schooling improves the productivity of time used in child investment. Therefore, female educational attainment should be negatively correlated with the per-unit amount of goods used in the production of child services. Time as the more productive input would be substituted for inputs purchased in the market. High-wage women who were also highly educated might thus be more reluctant to purchase substitutes for their time in raising their children. The net effect of the schooling of women on the derived demand for total child expenditures is ambiguous. Although child investment becomes more time-intensive, an increase in the education of the wife leads to an increase in the desired level of child quality and, therefore, an increase in expenditures on market inputs.

Before proceeding to the data, it may be useful to review some of the empirical "predictions" derived from the theoretical framework:

1) The wage level and the educational attainment of the wife should have a greater impact on the level of child investment and the total resources expended per child than these same characteristics of the husband.

2) For women with similar levels of education, the female wage should have a negative impact on fertility and on both male and female child quality, if women specialize in child investment. The effect of women's wages on sex-specific measures of child quality may differ if either preferences ("tastes") for male and female child quality differ or the production characteristics ("technologies") of sex-specific child quality commodities are dissimilar.

3) The relative numbers of male and female children in a family should affect the relative amount of resources invested in children along sex lines. The higher the ratio of female to male children, the lower

would be the ratio of resources per child invested in female children to those invested in male children, since in this case, an increment in female quality per child would have to be spread over relatively more children. This predicted inverse relationship between sex-specific quality and sex ratios would be symmetric in the absence of parental sex preferences or innate differences between the sexes.

4) The influence of female education on fertility depends on the relative strengths of the contraceptive knowledge and home productivity effects of schooling. If the schooling of the wife and her knowledge of efficient birth-control techniques are positively associated, then female education will have a negative impact on the birthrate and a positive impact on quality per child. If schooling increases the productivity of the wife's time in home production, then female educational attainment should be positively correlated with both fertility and child quality. If both effects are operative, the effect of female schooling on family size should be less than its effect on child quality.

5) The relationship between the wife's wage and the derived demand for total market expenditures per child may be positive even if the demand for quality per child declines with increases in the wife's price of time, if there is strong substitution of goods for time in the household production of child services. The relationship between the wife's schooling and child expenditures will depend on both the substitutability of time and goods in child investment and the strength of the household productivity effect of education.

6) Compulsory schooling laws, if they succeed in raising child quality above the levels otherwise desired by parents, should have a negative influence on family size and may also be an institutional, or nonhousehold, source of bias with respect to sex-specific child investment if they are enforced in a discriminatory manner.

Empirical Analysis

The Data and the Dependent Variables

The preceding framework implied that family size, male and female child quality, and expenditures on the market goods and services used as inputs in child quality production are all dimensions of child investment that are related to important characteristics of parental decision makers. Thus, to test the implications of the analysis, empirical counterparts to these theoretical constructs are used in four separate, ordinary-least-squares regression equations corresponding to these four child investment measures: i.e., family size, female child quality, male child quality, and total expenditures on market goods and services per child.

While the household production model of child investment has been formulated in terms of an individual family, the model is tested on cross-sectional aggregate state data for urban residents [20] from the 1960 census of population because aggregate samples have two important advantages over data consisting of individual observations.[21] First, the price of women's time in individual families is often unknown and is affected by the level of desired child investment, because many women, at a given point in time, are not in the labor market. The existence of separate labor markets in urban areas provides estimates of female wage rates and thus the average opportunity cost of time for women in each state. Second, although tastes vary considerably across individual families, these variations are insignificant when aggregate population averages are compared. This phenomenon is important because, among individual families, preferences for child services influence labor force participation and thus the relevant opportunity costs of child investment.[22]

Of the four dependent variables representing different aspects of child investment, that used in the fertility regression is the number of children ever born per 1,000 urban married women aged 35–44 (CEB). This age cohort was chosen because these women are likely to have completed their childbearing, and thus the fertility measure corresponds closely to completed family size. Measures of the completed fertility of older cohorts were not used because the effects of mortality on these women might produce biases in the estimated regression coefficients.

The sex-specific child quality variables are measured by the school enrollment rates of male and female urban teenagers aged 15–18 (ENRM, ENRF).[23] The theory of human capital investment [24] suggests that those parents who desire high-quality children will invest more in them at every stage of the child's life cycle, at home and in school. Thus children's schooling and the household investment in children should be positively correlated. To the extent that schooling and time-intensive household child investment are substitutes, however, the coefficients of the wife's wage variables will be biased upwards.

Aggregate current state public school expenditures per pupil in average daily attendance in urban districts (EXP) is the measure used to represent one component of the goods input in the production of child quality and is the fourth dependent variable. It is assumed that families are able to influence the level of these expenditures on education through either the political process or migration. The omission of private-school expenditures from this educational expenditure measure may bias toward zero all the estimated coefficients of the variables in the expenditure regression equations if public school expenditures understate total expenditures on schooling more for high- than for low-expenditure demand states.

Independent Variables

The measure of the opportunity cost of time for women aged 35–44 used in all the regressions (FW) is the average weekly wage of all women in that age group who worked—their annual income divided by an estimate of the number of weeks worked during the year. This computed wage is preferable to annual female earnings because time spent in the labor force and thus total female income will be negatively correlated with child investment, since such activity is time-intensive. Thus a negative correlation between female *earnings* and child investment variables would not represent the effect of the wife's price of time on fertility or child quality but rather the influence of tastes for children on earnings.

The male price of time (MW) is constructed in the same manner as the female variable. The parental education measures (EDF, EDM) are the number of years of schooling completed by males and females aged 35–44. These wage and schooling variables represent the basic household production parameters and are included in all four regressions.

Finally, to assess the strength of compulsory schooling laws on sex-specific teenage school enrollment (child quality), and thus on family size, the minimum lawful school-leaving age for each state (EDLAW) is also entered in all regressions.

All the variables used, including those added to control for the effects of other influences on the child investment measures, and the results obtained, are described in Table 11.2.

TABLE 11.2 Regression Results
(*t*-values in parentheses)

Independent Variables	Dependent Variables			
	CEB	ENRM	ENRF	EXP
FW	−5.865 ‡	−.01092 ‡	−.00421 ‡	3.07015 ‡
	(1.66)	(3.07)	(2.149)	(3.46)
MW	3.259	.00127	.00024	.22782
	(0.63)	(0.14)	(0.05)	(0.16)
EDF	−495.3 ‡	.30837 ‡	.23979 ‡	− 19.7702
	(1.84)	(1.28)	(1.34)	(0.25)
EDM	337.8 ‡	−.01299	.00022	21.9366
	(1.63)	(0.05)	(0.00)	(0.37)
EDLAW	−3.613	.01399 ‡	−.002373	−2.70668
	(0.92)	(1.33)	(0.47)	(1.06)
R^2	.5323	.6471	.6323	.6455

SOURCES: Children ever born—U.S. Census, 1960, PC(1) 2D-52D, Table 113
    Enrollment rates—*Ibid.*, Tables 101 and 102
    School expenditures—U.S. Office of Education, *Biennial Survey of Education in the United States, 1954–56,* "Statistics of Local School Systems: Staff, Pupils, and Finances," ch. 3, sec. IV, Table 0 for thirty-eight states; ch. 3, sec. II, Tables 3 and 4 for six states having country-unit systems, groups I and II.
    Weekly wages—U.S. Census, 1960, PC(1) 2D-52D
    Median income—*Ibid.*, Table 134
    Weeks worked—Computed from *ibid.*, Table 118
    Schooling—*Ibid.*, Table 103
    Compulsory schooling—U.S. Office of Education, *State Law on Compulsory Attendance,* circular No. 793
    Infant mortality—U.S. Census, *Vital Statistics,* "National Summaries," 1950–59
    Proportion nonwhite—U.S. Census, 1960, PC(1) 2D-52D, Table 103
    Age—*Ibid.*, Table 187
    Unemployment rate—*Ibid.*, Table 176
    Opportunity wage—U.S. Department of Labor, *Statistical Yearbook, 1960*

NOTE: *t*-values in parenthesis. Number of observations = 47; Rhode Island, Alaska, Hawaii excluded

    Variables also included: infant mortality rate in urban areas, 1950–59; percentage of urban population aged 35–44 nonwhite; median age of nonagricultural employed males; unemployment rate of urban population aged 15–24 (enrollment equations only); wage rate of nonagricultural unskilled workers, average for 1950–59 (enrollment equations only).

‡ Significant at the 10 percent level, one-tailed test.

The Results

In general, the household production parameters, together with the selected control variables, account for over 50 percent of the interstate variation in each of the four measures of child investment, and the signs and statistical significance of the coefficients are consistent with the implications derived from the theoretical analysis in the first part of the paper. The most striking characteristic of the set of equations is the dominance of female over male variables. In all cases but one, the schooling and wage coefficients pertaining to males are not significantly different from zero, while all of the coefficients of the household production parameters pertaining to women at least approach statistical significance. Thus, the results confirm the notion that it is women who supply the most time to child investment in the home.

CHILD QUANTITY—FERTILITY

The significant negative effect of the female wage on family size is consistent with the assumption that child services require more of the wife's time per unit of output than other commodities produced in the household. High levels of the wife's education are also associated with lower fertility, a result which seems to support the hypothesis that female schooling and contraceptive efficiency are positively correlated. The recent decline in birthrate can thus be attributed to increases in both female educational attainment, which would shrink discrepancies between desired and actual fertility, and female wage rates, which would lead to a decline in the desired number of children, who require relatively large amounts of more expensive female time.

While the wage of the husband has no effect on fertility, because of the small participation of the husband in household production and the relatively even distribution of his time among consumption activities in the household, male schooling levels are positively, but weakly, correlated with family size. Increases in the educational attainment of both males and females by 10 percent results in a net reduction in fertility of 7.5 percent; the negative female education effect dominates the positive influence of male schooling.

The effect of the compulsory schooling laws on family size, while in the predicted negative direction, is not significantly different from zero. The reason for the lack of influence of these laws on fertility may be their failure to raise school enrollment rates, and thus child quality, by significant amounts.

MALE AND FEMALE CHILD QUALITY—SEX-SPECIFIC SCHOOL ENROLLMENT RATES

Female wages are also negatively and significantly correlated with the sex-specific child quality variables, indicating that an increase in the wage of women will lower the demand for the quality of children because of the wife's time-intensity of child investment. The observed upward trend in school enrollment rates is due to the much stronger positive influence of the schooling level of women. The relatively strong positive effect of female educational attainment (EDF) may be due to 1) the negative impact of female schooling on the quantity of children, as was found in the CEB regression, which would raise desired levels of quality per child; 2) the positive effect of schooling on the productivity of the wife's time in household production, which would lower the cost of time-intensive child investment more than other commodities; and/or 3) a positive correlation between schooling and tastes for high-quality children. Because of the strength of the positive education effect, increases in both the schooling and earnings of women would, on balance, result in an increase in the demand for child quality. The increase in both male and female teenage enrollment rates from 1960 to 1970, depicted in Table 11.1, can thus be explained by the influence of increases in the schooling of female parents.

The higher level of male and the greater increase in female school enrollment rates during this period can also be accounted for by the results obtained. Only two variables in the male and female quality equations have significantly different coefficients—the female wage (FW) and the compulsory schooling law variable (EDLAW). Compulsory schooling laws appear to affect only male teenage school enrollment. The coefficient of this variable is positive and significant in the male enrollment equation, but is not significantly different from zero in the female enrollment regression. Thus the impact of compulsory schooling legislation may account somewhat for the higher *level* of the urban male school enrollment rate. The differential impact of these laws on male and female teenagers can be interpreted in two ways, since minimum laws of this kind can be ineffective for two reasons: 1) the law is not enforced; or 2) the law is not a binding constraint on behavior because the desired level of the variable exceeds the lawful requirement. The acceptance of the latter reason, however, as an explanation for the ineffectiveness of the school laws with respect to urban teenage females but not males requires the assumption that the desired level of quality per child for females exceeds that for males, which contradicts the sociological evidence cited. Thus it appears that the differential effect of compulsory schooling legislation is most likely due to discriminatory enforcement. In that case, these laws exacerbate the household differences in sex-specific child investment.

The differential impact of the wife's wage rate on male and female school enrollment is supportive of the hypothesis that male and female children are treated differently in the home. This result, it will be recalled, is consistent with the findings of sociologists that male child quality is more sensitive than female child quality to the behavior of mothers and, in terms of the economic analysis of the first part of this paper, with the assumption of the greater time-intensity of male than female child quality. Whatever the reason for this result, an important implication is that as the wages of women rise, the discrepancy between the levels of male and female child quality will be diminished, since male child investment, utilizing more of women's time per unit of quality produced, will become relatively more expensive than female child investment.[25]

INPUTS TO CHILD QUALITY—SCHOOL EXPENDITURES

The EXP equation represents the derived demand for one type of input used in child investment, expenditures on formal schooling. The positive and significant effect of the wife's wage on this variable thus appears to reflect the strength of the substitution effect in the production of child quality. Increases in the price of time of women lead to the substitution of purchased market goods for time per unit of child quality produced, which more than offsets the weak negative relation between women's wages and the demand for the level of child quality. In a sense, more highly paid teachers are substituted for mother's time as the labor force participation rates of women rise.

The insignificance of the female education coefficient in this equation may be due to the strong offsetting influence of the positive consumption effect of the wife's education, as evidenced in the child quality regressions. Increases in the schooling of women both strongly increase the demand for the level of child quality and, given the positive effect of education on the productivity of time in the home, induce substitution away from goods toward more productive time in the production of each unit of child quality. The level and input substitution effects of female schooling, of opposite sign and, perhaps, of equal strength, may thus offset each other.

That the coefficients of the male wage and schooling variables in the EXP regression are not significantly different from zero, however, is further evidence of the small amount of time supplied by the husband to household child investment, since the effects of these variables on the level of child quality were also insignificant. Increases in schooling expenditures per pupil may thus be attributed to the substitution of wives' household child investment time for goods as women's wages have risen.

Conclusions

The principal general conclusions that can be made on the basis of the foregoing theoretical and empirical analysis are that the levels of and changes in family size, male and female enrollment rates, and per-pupil school expenditures are the joint manifestations of child investment decisions made within the family; that it is the variables associated with the wife's time, principally her wage rate and education, which dominate these decisions; and that some differential investment in children with respect to sex occurs within the household. Evidence was also found that these differences are exacerbated by societal forces. A continuation of the upward trends in the education and wage rates of women should result in further declines in fertility, a continued rise in educational expenditures, and continued increases in school enrollment rates, particularly of female teenagers. The latter conclusion is most important because it means that the greater participation of women in the market economy will tend, in the future, to alter the level of sex-specific household child investment in favor of females.

These results must remain tentative, however, because the male–female allocation of time between household production activities and the division of labor between home and market work may change in the future so that women cease to be dominant in household child investment. In addition, the evidence of child investment differences between male and female children requires further exploration, particularly as regards whether those differences can be attributed to technological factors in child quality production or are the result of the preferences of the parents. If it is parental choice that is predominantly responsible for sex differentials in child investment, additional study is required to measure the extent to which this behavior represents a rational response on the part of parents to sex differentials in the rates of return to child quality that derive from the economic structure of society.

NOTES

[1] Gary Becker was the first to consider the demand for the quantity and quality of children in the context of the family, in "An Economic Analysis of Fertility," in Universities-National Bureau Committee for Economic Research, *Demographic and Economic Change in Developed Countries* (Princeton, N.J., 1960), 209–31. More recently Robert Willis, Gary Becker and H. L. Lewis, and Dennis DeTray have developed models of child investment in papers published in the *Journal of Political Economy*, LXXXI, Part II (March/April 1973). DeTray has been the only economist, however, to subject the child-quality implications of his theory to rigorous empirical analysis.

[2] W. H. Sewell and V. P. Shah, "Parent's Education and Children's Educational Aspirations and Achievements," *American Sociological Review*, XXXIII (April 1968): 201.

[3] B. N. Adams and M. T. Meidam, "Economics, Family Structure, and College Attendance," *American Journal of Sociology*, LXXIV (November 1968): 238.

[4] Gary S. Becker, "A Theory of the Allocation of Time," *Economic Journal*, LXXV (September 1965): 493–517.

[5] In terms of constant purchasing power, current expenditures per pupil in average daily attendance in all U.S. public elementary and secondary schools rose from $525 in 1959–60 to $889 in 1969–70. U.S. Department of Health, Education and Welfare, Office of Education, *Digest of Educational Statistics,* 1972, Table 77.

[6] F. E. Keller, "A Comparative Study of Selected Background Factors Related to Achievement of Mentally Able Fifth and Sixth Grade Children," *Dissertation Abstracts*, 29: 3327–28. These goods may also serve as inputs in household activities unrelated to children.

[7] The possibility that birth order affects the satisfaction parents receive from the quality of each child is not considered here. See note 11.

[8] J. Walters and N. Stinnet, "Parent–Child Relationships: A Decade Review of Research," *Journal of Marriage and the Family*, XXXIII (February 1971): 101.

[9] Families may choose goods of different quality and thus may be observed to

pay different prices for the same "type" of input, but presumably all parents face the same market price structure.

[10] Adams and Meidam concluded in their study that the order of birth had no effect on the likelihood of either a male or a female child attending college. See "Economics, Family Structure, and College Attendance," pp. 230–39. B. Barger and E. Hall, in their paper "The Interrelationship of Family Size and Socioeconomic Status for Parents of College Students," *Journal of Marriage and the Family,* XXVIII (May 1966): 186–88, also found that ordinal position was not significantly related to the educational achievement of children.

[11] Adams and Meidam, "Economics, Family Structure, and College Attendance."

[12] Robert Michael, "Education and the Derived Demand for Children," *Journal of Political Economy,* LXXXI, Part II (March/April 1973): 128–64.

[13] Linda Edwards, in "Investment in Human Capital: A Study of the Teenage Demand for Schooling in the United States" (Ph.D. diss., Columbia University, 1971), found that these laws have had different effects on teenage male and female school enrollment rates, being more effective in boosting the rates of teenage males.

[14] Evidence is provided in William G. Bowen and T. Aldrich Finegan, *The Economics of Labor Force Participation* (Princeton, N.J., 1969); J. Mincer, "Labor Force Participation of Married Women: A Study of Labor Supply," in Universities-National Bureau Committee for Economic Research, *Aspects of Labor Economics* (Princeton, N.J., 1962), pp. 63–105; and J. P. Smith, "The Life Cycle Allocation of Time in a Family Context" (Ph.D. diss., University of Chicago, 1972).

[15] Smith, "The Life Cycle Allocation of Time in a Family Context."

[16] Walters and Stinnet, "Parent–Child Relationships: A Decade Review of Research."

[17] Sewell and Shah, "Parents' Education and Children's Educational Aspirations and Achievements," p. 208.

[18] Her behavior may, however, reflect the preferences of the husband.

[19] This particular kind of home productivity effect of education is thus neutral between commodities but nonneutral between production inputs; the marginal productivities of the goods inputs are assumed to be unaffected by the wife's schooling.

[20] The child investment behavior of farm families is significantly different from that of urban families, and urban income variables are not compatible with those pertaining to the farm population. For evidence see Mark R. Rosenzweig, "Economic Aspects of Rural-Farm Fertility: A Comment," *Southern Economic Journal,* XL (April 1974): 675–79.

[21] For a detailed discussion of the advantages (and shortcomings) of using aggregate data to estimate fertility behavior, see G. Cain and A. Weininger, "Economic Determinants of Fertility: Results from Cross-sectional Aggregate Data," *Demography,* X (May 1973): 205–24.

[22] See R. Willis, "A New Approach to the Economic Theory of Fertility Behavior," *Journal of Political Economy,* LXXXI, Part II (March/April 1973): 14–64, for a detailed analysis of this point.

[23] The enrollment rates of these age groups were chosen because the interstate variation in the rates of the school-age population below the age of 15 was negligible.

[24] See Y. Ben-Porath, "The Production of Human Capital and the Life Cycle of Earnings," *Journal of Political Economy,* LXXV, Part I (August 1967): 352–65.

[25] Russell Hill and Frank P. Stafford, in "Time Inputs to Children" (unpublished manuscript), using a sample of families compiled by the U.S. Office of Educational Opportunity in 1969, found that when wives had at least some college education, for given levels of the husband's schooling, they spent more time with female children less than seven years of age than with male children in the same age group, while the reverse was true for families in which the wife had not attended college. These results appear to indicate that, in the cross section, the greater time-intensity of male child quality may have led to a reversal in the sex-specific child quality differential among families with highly educated mothers.

12

Nonmarket Returns to Women's Investment in Education

LEE BENHAM

ECONOMISTS have generally argued that increases in market earnings constitute an important component of the benefits derived from formal education. Almost without exception, past studies of the returns to education for men have examined the relationship between men's level of schooling attainment and their market earnings. It has been well recognized, however, at least since the time of Adam Smith, that the benefits of schooling are not limited to improvements in earnings; rather, a wide range of benefits may be derived from schooling. In this paper, several components of the returns to education for women are examined. These include the returns through women's own market earnings, those returns derived through marriage, and certain family benefits associated with the presence of a more highly educated wife.

In the first section, the returns through earnings and marriage are estimated. The remainder of the paper is concerned with the extent to which the benefits of women's education through marriage result from women marrying more productive men vs. the extent to which men who marry more educated women become more productive.

Returns through Earnings and Marriage

It has frequently been asserted that access to a better marriage market is the principal "benefit" of higher education for women. Since the eco-

I would like to thank T. W. Schultz for generous permission to excerpt material from my article, "Benefits of Women's Education within Marriage," *Journal of Political Economy*, LXXXII, Part II (March/April 1974).

nomic returns to women from their own earnings have appeared to be low, the marriage-market argument offers one hypothesis as to why women have obtained higher education in such large numbers.

To provide some evidence on the relative importance of marriage and own earnings for women, estimates are made here of women's earnings and husbands' income in 1960 and 1970 by years of schooling completed.[1] The estimates for these two dates permit an examination of changes over the decade in the importance of marriage for women's overall economic welfare.

The results for 1960 are shown in Table 12.1.[2] It is not surprising that

TABLE 12.1 White Women's Mean Earnings, Husbands' Income, and Family Income in 1959, by Women's Education

	Years of Schooling Completed				
	11	*12*	*13–15*	*16*	*17 +*
Mean 1959 Earnings of All Women ($) [a]	884	1,104	1,291	1,722	3,243
Mean 1959 Earnings of Women Working Full-Time ($) [b]	2,861	3,116	3,560	4,283	5,184
Mean 1959 Earnings of Never-Married Women ($) [a]	1,931	2,322	2,595	3,442	4,085
Percentage of Women Married with Husband Present	76.0	76.6	73.8	72.3	51.7
Mean 1959 Total Income of Husbands, for Women with Husbands ($)	5,897	6,684	8,449	10,634	10,415
Mean 1959 Family Income [c] Including Weighted Husbands' Income ($)	5,366	6,224	7,526	9,410	8,628
Mean 1959 Family Income Including ½ of Weighted Husbands' Income ($)	3,125	3,664	4,409	5,566	5,935
Sample Size	2,792	16,259	4,905	2,206	812

NOTE: Data from U.S. Census, 1960, 1/1000 sample. Calculated for women aged 18–65 not enrolled in school at the time of the census. Women with Spanish surnames were excluded.

[a] Mean wage and salary and self-employment income.

[b] Worked at least 30 hours during week prior to 1960 census and at least 48 weeks during 1959.

[c] Earnings of woman plus total income of husband weighted for probability at each age of women that husband is present.

women's own earnings, here measured three ways, increased with their own schooling. The incomes of husbands also rose consistently with wife's education, except for women with graduate education (more than 16 years). The most striking feature of these results is that increases in women's own earnings as a function of their own education were small relative to the increases in their husbands' income. This can be seen in several ways. As women's schooling increased from 12 to 16 years, their husbands' income (for women who were married) increased 59 percent, while women's own full-time earnings increased only 37 percent. The difference ($3,950) in the annual incomes of husbands of high-school and college graduates in 1959 was almost as large as the level ($4,283) of full-time earnings of female college graduates.

Two measures of family income are examined: the first is the mean earnings of women in each educational group plus the total mean income of their husbands, weighted by the percentage of women in each educational group who are married. This measure attributes the income of both spouses to the wife. Since income is shared within the family, it is unlikely that any individual within the family receives the full benefit of an increment in family income. Hence, this measure is likely to overstate the pecuniary benefits the wife derives from marriage.[3] The second measure examined provides one adjustment for this overstatement in that only half of the husbands' income is included. This pair of measures provides alternative estimates of the expected lifetime family income associated with each level of women's educational attainment. These measures of family income show the same patterns as husbands' income by level of women's schooling. Increases in family income were large relative to increases in women's own earnings through 16 years of schooling.

The estimates for 1970, shown in Table 12.2, permit an examination of the changes which took place during the 1960s. The pecuniary returns from higher education for women in 1969, as in 1959, were predominantly associated with husbands' income. The basic patterns were also similar.[4] Husband's income increased with wife's schooling up until graduate training and then fell.[5] However, there were substantial changes between 1960 and 1970 in the relative importance of husbands' income. Over the decade, women's full-time earnings generally increased more rapidly than their husbands' incomes. The greatest increases in women's earnings relative to husbands' income occurred at the highest levels of

TABLE 12.2 White Women's Mean Earnings, Husbands' Income, and Family Income in 1969, by Women's Education

	Years of Schooling Completed				
	11	*12*	*13–15*	*16*	*17 +*
Mean 1969 Earnings of All Women ($) [a]	1,758	2,105	2,122	2,966	6,060
Mean 1969 Earnings of Women Working Full-Time ($) [b]	4,651	5,317	5,667	7,507	9,067
Mean 1969 Earnings of Never-Married Women ($) [a]	2,354	3,001	1,956	3,558	7,265
Percentage of Women Married with Husband Present	75.9	74.3	62.6	72.3	60.0
Mean 1969 Total Income of Husbands, for Women with Husbands ($)	8,556	9,812	13,728	15,352	14,617
Mean 1969 Family Income [c] Including Weighted Husbands' Income ($)	8,252	9,395	10,716	10,465	8 14,830
Mean 1969 Family Income Including ½ of Weighted Husbands' Income ($)	5,005	5,750	6,419	8,516	10,445
Sample Size	328	2,123	843	343	155

NOTE: Data from U.S. Census, 1970, 1/10,000 sample. Calculated for non-black women aged 18–65.

[a] Mean wage, farm and self-employment income.
[b] Worked at least 30 hours during week prior to 1970 census and at least 48 weeks during 1969.
[c] Earnings of woman plus total income of husband weighted for probability that husband is present.

schooling. For example, women's full-time earnings at 12, 16, and 17 + years of schooling increased 71, 75, and 75 percent, respectively, over the decade while those of husbands of women with 12, 16, and 17 + years of schooling increased 47, 44, and 40 percent. This is reflected in changes in the relative importance of husbands' income associated with wives' college education. Whereas the 1960 husbands' income increased 3.38 times as much as women's own full-time earnings for women with 16 as against 12 years of schooling, in 1970 this ratio had fallen to 2.53.

In sum, women do appear to receive substantial economic returns from higher education through marriage, although the importance of marriage declined somewhat over the past decade.[6]

Nonmarket Productivity

The most obvious explanation for the observed relationship between women's schooling and husbands' income is that college serves as a marriage market and that women who attend college marry more productive men. This process of assortative mating is doubtless an important reason why husbands' income rises with women's schooling. Assortative mating is not, however, the only hypothesis consistent with the results in Tables 12.1–12.2. One alternative hypothesis is that the productivity of family members is affected by the knowledge and ability of all members of the family. Hence, in this context, men who marry more highly educated women become more productive.

An individual's knowledge about the world and ability to cope effectively may be positively influenced by the knowledge and ability of those with whom the person associates—including his or her spouse. There are several ways in which associates can contribute to a person's effective education. These include: 1) providing a close substitute for the person's own formal education by providing information and advice; 2) helping the person acquire specific skills; and 3) helping the person acquire general skills related to information acquisition and assimilation and adaptability to change.

Marriage provides an interesting opportunity to examine the benefits from association, for several reasons. There are greater incentives in marriage to share acquired abilities than in most other nonmarket associations, because marriage usually involves a long-term association wherein both current and future benefits of increased knowledge by either family member are shared. The costs of sharing would also appear to be lower, since the transactions cost of communication within the household, given the proximity of spouses, is likely to be less than in other types of association.

The general hypothesis is that the knowledge and ability of each spouse within a marriage will be reflected in the market and nonmarket productivity of both spouses. The specific issue examined here is the extent to which the positive relationship between women's schooling and husbands' market productivity (earnings) is related to increased productivity resulting from association with a more educated spouse. The level of schooling is assumed to reflect or at least to be positively correlated with knowledge and ability.

Several models have been developed to obtain estimates of the relationship between wife's schooling and husband's earnings. In the first model, the logarithm of husband's earnings is estimated to be a function of years of formal education of each spouse and the years of husband's employment experience.

$$\ln EARN = f(EDH, EDW, EXP),[7] \tag{1}$$

where $\ln EARN =$ log annual earnings of husband in family with husband and wife;

$EDH =$ years of schooling completed by husband;
$EDW =$ years of schooling completed by wife; and
$EXP =$ years of work experience of husband.

The coefficient estimates of husband's and wife's education (*EDH, EDW*) from this model have a simple interpretation. They are estimates of the percentage increase in husband's earnings associated with a year's increase in husband's (or wife's) schooling, given the other spouse's years of formal education and the husband's work experience.

If the positive relationship between husband's earnings and wife's schooling is due entirely to the positive relationship between husband's and wife's schooling, then after taking into account husband's schooling and work experience, wife's education should be unrelated to husband's earnings. That is, the partial relationship between husband's earnings and wife's education should be essentially zero. Such a finding would be strong evidence that the previously discussed results were due to assortative mating.

Data

Four samples of the United States population were used to estimate this model: the 1/1000 sample of the U.S. Census for 1960, a 1963 health survey conducted by the Center for Health Administration Studies of the University of Chicago, the 1967 Survey of Economic Opportunity conducted by the Bureau of the Census for the Office of Economic Opportunity, and the 1/10,000 sample of the U.S. Census for 1970. The sub-

TABLE 12.3   Estimated Percentage Differentials
in Husband's Earnings with
Husband's and Wife's Schooling

Sample	Dependent Variable	Husband's Schooling	Wife's Schooling	R^2	Sample Size
	1	2	3	4	5
1) 1/1000 Sample, 1960 census	ln EARN	.070 (19.0)	.041 (9.7)	.22	4780
2) CHAS, 1963	ln EARN	.064 (9.8)	.035 (4.3)	.22	967
3) SEO, 1967	ln EARN	.063 (24.3)	.035 (11.5)	.20	8055
4) 1/10,000 Sample, 1970 census	ln EARN	.066 (15.0)	.036 (6.6)	.22	3427

SOURCES: 1/1000 Sample, 1960 census. These data are from a 20 percent random sub-sample of the 1/1000 sample of the U.S. Census for 1960. The data used here are for males aged 18–64, married once with spouse present, husbands of once-married women, non-black, nonfarm residents, not in school, having positive number of weeks worked, positive earnings, and positive total income in 1959.

CHAS, 1963: These data are from a 1963 national survey conducted by the Center for Health Administration Studies of the University of Chicago and the National Opinion Research Center. The subsample used here includes only males aged 18–64, married with spouse present, heads of household, nonfarm residents, having positive number of weeks worked and positive earnings in 1963. Observations were excluded if there were indeterminate values for any of these variables. Information was not included in this survey that would allow estimation of length of marriage or exclusion of those individuals who had remarried.

SEO, 1967: These data are from the 1967 Survey of Economic Opportunity conducted by the Bureau of the Census for the Office of Economic Opportunity. The subsample used here includes only males aged 18–64, married with spouse present, white, nonfarm residents, not in school, not in army, having positive earnings in 1966. Observations were excluded if there were indeterminate values for any of these variables. The observations were unweighted.

1/10,000 Sample, 1970 census: These data are from the 1/10,000 sample of the 1970 census. The data used here are for husbands of non-black women aged 18–65 who were not in school. The husbands had to have positive earnings in 1969.

samples used in these tables include only married white males with spouse present who had positive earnings in the survey year.[8]

Results

The results of estimating the model with these data are shown in Table 12.3. The partial coefficients listed in columns 2 and 3 are the percentage differentials in husband's earnings associated with husband's and wife's schooling, given the other spouse's schooling and husband's work experience. For example, in Table 12.3 the estimate for sample 1, column 2 (.070), shows that when husband's schooling increases one year, leaving unchanged wife's schooling and husband's work experience, his earnings increase 7 percent. Column 3 for this first sample indicates that an increase in wife's schooling (leaving unchanged husband's schooling and work experience) results in a 4.1 percent increase in his earnings.

The hypothesis that wife's schooling is unrelated to husband's earnings, given his schooling and work experience, can be rejected. The partial relationship between wife's schooling and husband's earnings in Table 12.3 is positive and statistically significant in all cases. Considering that four separate data sources are used, the results are remarkably stable. Given the level of husband's schooling and his years of work experience, the coefficients of wife's schooling in samples (1)–(4) imply that his earnings increase between 3.5 percent and 4.1 percent for each year of his wife's schooling. This compares with increases in husband's earnings of from 6.3 percent to 7.0 percent for each year of his own schooling, given his wife's education. In other words, husband's earnings increase at a rate over half as fast with each year of wife's schooling as with his own schooling.

For purposes of comparison, husband's schooling is excluded from the estimating equation in the second model.

$$ln\ \text{EARN} = f(EDW,\ EXP) \qquad (2)$$

NOTES: The estimating equation used to obtain these results was $ln\text{EARN} + \alpha_1 + \beta_1\ \text{EDH} + \beta_2\ \text{EDW} + \beta_3\ \text{EXP} + \beta_4\ \text{EXP}^2$.

Only the β_1 and β_2 coefficients are listed in this table.

t-value (numbers in parentheses) indicates the degree of confidence with which the coefficients can be considered statistically different from zero.

The results in Table 12.4 show that husband's earnings increased approximately 8.7 percent in 1960 and 8.0 percent in 1970 for each year of wife's schooling when the effects of husband's own schooling were not taken into account. From Table 12.3, we know that husband's earnings increased 4.1 percent in 1960 and 3.6 percent in 1970 for each year of wife's schooling when husband's schooling *was* taken into account. These combined results indicate that increases in husband's own schooling alone account for slightly more than half of the gross increase in hus-

TABLE 12.4   Estimated Returns to Wife's Education in Terms
of Husband's Earnings (husband's education omitted)

Sample	Dependent Variable	Wife's Education	R^2	Sample Size
1/1000 Sample, 1960 census	ln EARN	.087 (24.3)	.16	4780
1/10,000 Sample, 1970 census	ln EARN	.080 (17.0)	.17	3427

SOURCES: See Table 12.3.

NOTES: The model used to estimate these coefficients was ln EARN $= \alpha_1 + \delta_1 EDW + \delta_2 EXP + \delta_3 EXP^2$.

t-values in parentheses.

band's earnings associated with increases in wife's schooling.[9] The remainder is associated with the independent effects of wife's schooling.

While these results are open to alternative interpretations, a strong partial relationship between wife's schooling and husband's earnings has been established. These results are consistent with the productivity hypothesis; that is, the husband benefits from his wife's schooling. However, these results are not inconsistent with an alternative (selective-mating) hypothesis that, within a schooling cohort of males, the more productive males marry more highly educated females. Some evidence will now be developed to examine the consistency of the results with the implications of these two hypotheses.

There are several reasons for believing that the benefits of association are a cumulative process and hence that the full benefits of association would not be observed at the time of marriage. It takes time to communicate information. It also takes time for improved knowledge and ability to be reflected in improved earnings. Improvements in productivity are likely to lead to more on-the-job training, which in turn increases relative earnings during the first years of marriage. These productivity arguments would suggest that relative earnings would increase, at least initially, with the length of marriage, with earnings increasing more for those with more knowledgeable spouses. The selective-mating hypothesis has different implications. If marriage were based on the productivity of the spouse at the time of marriage, then husband's relative earnings should not increase over time as a function of wife's schooling and could decline.

To examine the life-cycle patterns of husband's earnings as a function of wife's schooling, separate estimates were made of equation (1) for four ten-year length-of-marriage intervals, using the 1960 Census data and the 1967 SEO data. In both sets of estimates, shown in Table 12.5, the differential in husband's earnings as a function of wife's schooling increases after the first decade of marriage and declines again during the latter years. The full benefits from association within the household are, therefore, not observed at the time of marriage. These results are consistent with the hypothesis that husband's productivity increases during the first years of marriage as a positive function of wife's schooling, and that productivity benefits diminish at older ages.

An alternative method of examining the productivity-versus-selectivity

TABLE 12.5 Estimated Percentage Differentials in Husband's Earnings Associated with Wife's Education by Length of Marriage

Sample	0–10 Years of Marriage	10–20 Years of Marriage	20–30 Years of Marriage	30–40 Years of Marriage
1/1000 Sample, 1960 census	.032 (4.1) N = 1549	.041 (6.5) N = 1614	.060 (5.9) N = 980	.024 (2.1) N = 558
SEO, 1967	.031 (6.0) N = 2610	.044 (8.3) N = 2432	.036 (5.6) N = 2056	.031 (3.0) N = 833

SOURCES: See Table 12.3.

NOTES: Given education of husband, husband's years of experience, and square of husband's years of experience.

t-values in parentheses.

issue is to separate the effects of wife's premarriage and postmarriage schooling. If more productive males marry females who are more highly educated at the time of marriage, husband's earnings should be more strongly associated with wife's premarriage than with wife's postmarriage schooling.

The educational attainment of wife at time of marriage is not indicated in any of the data samples used, but wife's age at time of marriage is included in the U.S. Census and SEO data, and from these two indirect tests can be made. First, an examination is made of the relationship be-

TABLE 12.6   Estimated Effect of Wife's Age
at Marriage on Husband's Earnings

Sample	Dependent Variable	Husband's Schooling	Wife's Schooling	Wife's Age at Marriage	R^2	Sample Size
1/1000 Sample,	ln EARN	.076	.032	−.0061		
1960 census		(21.2)	(7.7)	(−3.1)	.207	4625
SEO, 1967	ln EARN	.065	.036	−.0034		
		(24.7)	(11.6)	(−3.2)	.202	8055
SEO, 1967	ln EARN	.066	.032	−.0032		
		(23.4)	(9.6)	(−2.2)	.207	7052

SOURCE: See Table 12.3. SEO, 1967, is also the same except that families were included
   only if husbands were married only once.

NOTE: The model used to obtain these estimates was ln EARN = $\alpha_1 + \gamma_1 EDH + \gamma_2 EDW$
   $+ \gamma_3 EXP + \gamma_4 EXP^2 + \gamma_5 AGEMAR$.

t-values in parentheses.

tween wife's age at marriage and husband's earnings, in 1960 and 1967. The argument is that for any given level of wife's schooling, the younger she is at the time of marriage, the less likely she is to have completed her education; hence, according to the selective-mating hypothesis proposed above, the less likely she is to marry a highly productive male. This hypothesis is not supported by Table 12.6, which shows the *partial* relationship between wife's age at marriage and husband's earnings to be consistently negative.

An alternative way of examining this same question is to estimate the years of schooling completed by the wife at the time of marriage and to examine the husband's earnings differentials associated with wife's pre- and postmarriage schooling. The estimates in Table 12.7 suggest that the

TABLE 12.7 Estimated Percentage Differentials in Husband's Earnings Associated with Wife's Premarriage and Postmarriage Education

Dependent Variable	Husband's Education	Wife's Years of Pre- Marriage Education	Wife's Years of Post- Marriage Education	R^2	Sample Size
ln EARN	.070	.041	.043	.22	4780
	(17.5)	(10.3)	(6.1)		
ln EARN for subset of husbands whose wives have some postmarriage education	.079 (8.7)	.043 (3.6)	.044 (3.1)	.27	982

NOTES: See Table 12.3, source for 1/1000 sample, 1960 census. Wives' years of pre- and postmarriage education were determined by comparing their age at marriage with an age assigned to their corresponding level of education completed. Values were assigned as follows: for years of wife's education ≤ 16.5, age at completion = years of education $+ 6$. For years of wife's education > 16.5, age at completion $= 22.5 + 2$ (years of education $- 16.5$). (The highest category for schooling completed is 18 years.)

In the subsample used for the first equation above, for husband's education, wife's premarriage education, and wife's postmarriage education, means are 11.328, 11.056, and .341 and standard deviations are 3.521, 3.126, and 1.63, respectively. In the subsample used for the second equation, the corresponding means are 12.589, 11.507, and 1.660 and standard deviations are 3.232, 3.930, and 3.274.

t-values in parentheses.

relationships between wife's pre- and postmarriage schooling and husband's earnings are very similar, that women's postmarriage schooling is at least as strongly associated with husbands' earnings as is their premarriage schooling. These results, therefore, do not support the hypothesis that husband's earnings increase with wife's schooling because of selective mating based on wife's premarriage schooling.

Another basis for questioning the productivity hypothesis is that wife's schooling may be only a proxy for other background characteristics of both spouses, such as intelligence and social class. Should these latter variables be associated both with husband's earnings and with wife's own schooling, then the association noted between wife's schooling and husband's earnings may be spurious. This argument has its counterpart in the recurring question of the extent to which an individual's education itself results in higher earnings as against the extent to which education is merely a proxy for intelligence, social background, and so forth.

Data on background variables were not available in the samples used for Tables 12.1–12.7. However, this issue has been examined in another context by Duncan, Featherman, and Duncan[10] in a study of the relationship between the occupational status of husbands and the background characteristics (including education) of both spouses. A multiple regression was computed of husband's occupational status in 1956 as a function of his background characteristics, including his education, his occupational status at marriage, and his father's occupational status, and his wife's background characteristics, including her education, her father's occupational status, her intelligence, and a psychological index of her drive to "get ahead." Of all the wife's characteristics examined, only education was significantly related to husband's occupational attainment. This is consistent with the hypothesis that a wife's education has a significant independent effect on a husband's productivity.

These results, however, are not directly comparable with those presented in Tables 12.1–12.7, since occupational status rather than earnings was the dependent variable. Using another data set developed by Blau and Duncan,[11] it is possible to obtain more directly comparable results by estimating the relationship between husband's income in 1961 and both spouses' education, given several of husband's background characteristics, including occupational status of his first job and his father's occupation and education.

The following three specifications were used to estimate the impact of including husband's background characteristics using these data:

$$\text{INCOME} = f(EDH,\ EDW); \tag{3}$$
$$\text{INCOME} = f(EDH,\ EDW,\ EDHF,\ OCHF); \tag{4}$$
$$\text{INCOME} = f(EDH,\ EDW,\ EDHF,\ OCHF,\ OCHJ), \tag{5}$$

where INCOME = husband's income in 1961;
    EDH = husband's schooling;
    EDW = wife's schooling;
    EDHF = husband's father's schooling;
    OCHF = husband's father's occupation;
    OCHJ = husband's occupational status on first job.

Due to the nature of the available data,[12] these specifications differ from the earlier ones in this paper in that income rather than ln earnings is the dependent variable and husband's work experience is not included.[13] Nevertheless, they provide qualitative estimates of the relative importance of husband's background characteristics.

Table 12.8 shows the relative impact of wife's as compared with husband's education on husband's income by age of wife. These estimates are consistent with those presented earlier. There is a substantial relationship between wife's schooling and husband's income in most years. For wives aged 22–26, husband's income increases 37 percent as much with a given increase in wife's schooling as with a similar increase in husband's own schooling. This ratio increases to 80 percent for wives aged 32–36 and then declines at older ages, a pattern similar to that shown in Table 12.5.

TABLE 12.8   Ratio of Increase in Husband's Income as a Function of Wife's Schooling to Increase in Husband's Income as a Function of Husband's Schooling for Intact White Couples by Age of Wife in 1962

Independent Variables Included	Age of Wife							
	22–26	27–31	32–36	37–41	42–46	47–51	52–56	57–61
Husband's and wife's schooling [a]	.37 [b]	.51 [c]	.80 [c]	.46 [c]	.25 [c]	.35 [c]	.16 [c]	.14 [b]
Husband's and wife's schooling, husband's father's schooling and occupation [d]	.36 [b]	.57 [c]	.93 [c]	.49 [c]	.24 [c]	.33 [c]	.14 [b]	.05
Husband's and wife's schooling, husband's father's schooling and occupation, and husband's occupational status on first job [e]	.41 [b]	.62 [c]	1.22 [c]	.52 [c]	.26 [c]	.37 [c]	.18 [b]	.04

The model estimated was INCOME = $\alpha_1 + \beta_1 EDH + \beta_2 EDW$. The ratios β_2/β_1 for each age group are shown in line 1.

Coefficient of wife's schooling greater than its standard error but less than twice as great (in absolute value).

Coefficient of wife's schooling greater than twice its standard error (in absolute value).

The model estimated was INCOME = $\alpha_2 + \delta_1 EDH + \delta_2 EDW + \delta_3 EDHF + \delta_4 OCHF$. The ratios δ_2/δ_1 for each age group are shown in line 2.

The model estimated was INCOME = $\alpha_3 + \gamma_1 EDH + \gamma_2 EDW + \gamma_4 EDHF + \gamma_5 OCHF + \gamma_6 OCHJ$. The ratios γ_2/γ_1 for each age group are shown in line 3.

When husband's father's occupation and schooling are included, the pattern is very similar. Except for the oldest age group, these results are not consistent with the hypothesis that the association between wife's education and husband's income is predominantly due to assortative mating based on background characteristics of the husband.

When husband's occupational status on first job is included, wife's education remains statistically significant for wives aged 27–51. Assortative mating based upon husband's occupational status on first job does not provide an explanation of the association between husband's income and wife's education.

Obviously, other evidence will be required before the relative importance of selective mating versus benefits of wife's schooling within the family can be determined. However, a significant positive relationship between husband's earnings and wife's schooling, given the husband's own schooling and work experience, has been found, and further evidence has been examined which might have contradicted the hypothesis that wife's schooling increases husband's market productivity but instead was found to be consistent with it.

Conclusions

In 1960, a college education for a woman was associated with a much larger increase in her husband's expected income than in her own full-time earnings. In 1970, the pattern was the same, although women's own earnings increased relative to their husbands' over the decade.

A substantial proportion of these returns through marriage appear not to be due to any simple process of assortative mating. The partial association between wife's schooling and husband's earnings, given his schooling and work experience, was found to be positive and statistically significant in the four separate data samples analyzed. These results are consistent with the view that a substantial fraction of the increase in the husband's earnings associated with wife's schooling is due to increases in his productivity through his association with a more highly educated wife.

These results suggest that both the social and the private returns to women's education may be higher than heretofore realized. Labor market benefits to men appear to be associated with their marrying well-educated women. These benefits have implications not only for earnings but also for the likelihood of marriage, the characteristics of marriage partners selected, labor force participation rates and fertility patterns after marriage, and the stability of marriages.

NOTES

[1] The few studies which have investigated women's returns to education have been limited to studies of women's earnings alone. See Stefan N. Hoffer, "Rates of Return to Higher Education for Women," *Review of Economics and Statistics,* LV (November 1973): 482–86; E. F. Renshaw, "Estimating the Returns to Education," *Review of Economics and Statistics,* XLII (August 1960): 318–24.

[2] Originally, a separate analysis was planned for both blacks and whites. Preliminary analysis of the 1960 census data showed substantial differences in the patterns of husbands' and wives' income for these two groups. The samples were small for blacks, particularly when the 1/10,000 1970 census data were used. For these reasons the analysis here is limited to whites.

[3] If the view is taken that pecuniary returns alone should be considered in these calculations, then care must be taken to avoid attributing the same income to both husband and wife. However, if a measure of full income also includes the returns to nonmarket activity, then including all the husband's pecuniary earnings in a measure of the returns to the wife's education is not necessarily double-counting, provided that the nonmarket productivity of the husband is positively related to his earnings and his wife shares this nonmarket productivity. The returns to women's education may even be some multiple of the total pecuniary returns of both husband and wife. I am grateful to Gary Becker for assistance on this point.

[4] Since income early in the life cycle is generally preferred to the same income later, and since life-cycle patterns of earnings may vary as a function of wife's education, mean annual earnings and income in Tables 12.1 and 12.2 may inaccurately reflect the relative pecuniary returns associated with levels of schooling. In addition, education requires resources both because of the direct outlays and because an individual in school is foregoing earnings to attend school, and annual earnings do not reflect the variation in investment costs across levels of schooling attainment. If education is thus viewed as an investment, and the lifetime earnings associated with each level of education as the return on that investment, then estimates can be made on the rate of return to schooling. This is the conventional method used to summarize the economic returns to an investment.

Estimates were made of the rates of return to women from their own earnings and their husbands' income using the 1959 and 1969 data. The results were very similar to those shown in Tables 12.1 and 12.2. The rate of return to college education from husbands' income was higher in both years than from their own earnings; the returns through marriage from graduate education were negative in both years.

[5] In 1970, but not in 1960, it was possible to obtain separate estimates for 17 and 18 + years of schooling. As wife's education increased from 16 to 17 years (for women with husband present), husband's income increased from \$15,379 to \$16,579. For women with 18 or more years of schooling, husband's income declined sharply to \$12,429.

[6] The increase in the relative importance of women's own full-time earnings during the 1960s may be one of the reasons for the decline in the fertility rates over this same period.

[7] The specification of the model is as follows: ln EARN $= \alpha + \beta_1$ $EDH + \beta_2$ $EDW + \beta_3$ EXP $+ \beta_4$ EXP$^2 + \mu$. Husband's work experience is entered in quadratic form to approximate the postschool investment pattern usually assumed. The model presented here is discussed in more detail in Lee Benham, "Benefits of Women's Education within Marriage," *Journal of Political Economy,* LXXXII, Part II (May/June 1974).

[8] The characteristics of the subsamples differed in some minor details; a complete description of the characteristics of each subsample appears in the footnotes to Table 12.3. Note that the data used in these estimates are not restricted to women with eleven or more years of schooling. Hence, these results cannot be directly compared with those in Table 12.1.

[9] These percentages were obtained by dividing the women's schooling coefficient in Table 12.3 by the women's schooling coefficient in Table 12.4.

[10] Otis Dudley Duncan, David Featherman, and Beverly Duncan, *Socioeconomic Background and Achievement* (New York, 1972).

[11] Data were collected from 20,700 respondents representing men between the ages of 20 and 64 in the United States civilian noninstitutional population in March 1962. See Peter Blau and Otis Dudley Duncan, *The American Occupational Structure* (New York, 1967).

[12] Professor Otis Dudley Duncan generously provided the correlation matrices that he had developed for Table 8.16 in Duncan, Featherman, and Duncan (p. 240). The estimates shown here were calculated from those matrices.

[13] The consequences of excluding the husband's work experience variables are less severe here, since separate estimates are made for each of eight age-of-wife categories.

Part 4

The Effect of
Some Government Policies
on Women's Economic Position

13

The Vicious Cycle of Welfare: Problems of the Female-Headed Household in New York City

ELIZABETH DURBIN

It is a subject often started in conversation, and mentioned always as a matter of great surprise, that, notwithstanding the immense sum which is annually collected for the poor in this country, there is still so much distress among them.

T. R. Malthus,
An Essay on the Principles of Population

WELFARE EXPENDITURES in New York City have more than quadrupled over the last decade, creating a fiscal and social crisis for the city administration. A major factor in this increase has been the tripling of the caseload for Aid to Families with Dependent Children (AFDC), the program for mothers and children without a father's support. This phenomenon has strengthened the belief that the welfare system has been encouraging fathers to desert their families. It has also led to speculation that the system, by providing higher levels of welfare income to individuals than they could otherwise earn, has discouraged both men and women from working.

Although nineteenth-century economists, notably the Reverend Malthus, were considerably concerned with the effects of public-assis-

The chapter is based on work completed by the author at the New York RAND Institute under contract from New York City's Economic Development Administration. Kenneth Leeson of New York University provided invaluable assistance in updating the statistics.

tance programs on family formation and the incentive to work, little systematic work on these problems has been conducted since then. More recently, sociologists and anthropologists have explored the culture of poverty in its effects on the relationships of poor people within the family and to society at large. The existence of public assistance, particularly the overwhelming importance of AFDC, has been viewed as one factor contributing to the maintenance of this culture and to the inability of families to advance economically and socially. Probably the best-known hypothesis relating to these problems has been the one formulated by Moynihan, which states that welfare actually encourages desertion by the father and consequent family dependence on public assistance.

This paper presents a somewhat different perspective on the continued cycle of poverty and dependence on public assistance. Rather than concentrating on the effects of cultural values and family structure, this analysis explores the economic realities of families faced, on the one hand, with little skills, low earning capacity, and high probability of unemployment and, on the other hand, with public assistance. Indeed, the economic connections between family formation, the welfare alternative, and incentives to work are considerably more complex than simple explanations—such as that welfare causes family breakups and creates loafers unwilling to work—allow for.

The purpose of this article is twofold: first, to provide a framework for understanding the factors determining (1) the decision to seek welfare, (2) the decision to marry and to stay together, and (3) the decision to work, and the connections between the three; and, second, to explore the relative impact of factors affecting these decisions in New York City. I have focused on the AFDC program first because by far the largest number of welfare recipients are currently on this program—in New York City there were 1,478,778 separate persons on welfare in 1972, of which 984,144 were on AFDC—and, second, because it is this program which, by providing government assistance to families without a male provider, is most likely to affect the incentives to form traditional family units in which fathers support mothers during their childbearing and childrearing years.[1]

It is important to remember that the traditional escape from poverty for families in this country has been for mothers to work as second earners supplementing their husbands' earnings, in addition to the unpaid work they perform at home. Thus, the effect of welfare on the willingness to work, particularly on the part of mothers, has a crucial impact on the ability of families to rise from poverty. Recent improvements in the benefits and coverage provided by welfare programs in New York have raised serious questions about the extent to which welfare income has now become a viable alternative to labor market earnings, particularly for the lowest-paid workers. For example, in 1970, the annual basic allowance for a family of four in New York City was about $4,000, not including free medical care, various special grants, and other social services available to recipients. The gross annual income from a job paying a minimum wage of $1.60 per hour is $3,200. From this income, social security, taxes, transportation, and other costs incurred because of employment must be deducted in order to make a valid comparison with welfare income. In terms of income alone, then, welfare would clearly, be preferable to employment for the marginal worker.

Many would argue that there can be little connection between labor market conditions and the number of AFDC recipients, because 95 percent of the latter are mothers and children, who can receive public assistance only because they are without a working father. Yet the majority of women and children in this country are supported by their own labor market earnings in addition to the earnings of other family members, whether or not the family is separated. Therefore, the fundamental question still remains: why has there been such a startling increase in the number of families not supported by family members, but instead seeking government assistance? This has been particularly surprising in New York City over the past ten years, because during that time, except for the 1970 recession, unemployment fell drastically, income rose, and presumably it was easier for families to be supported by labor market earnings.

Framework of Analysis

Decisions about family formation are clearly determined by many factors other than the existence of public assistance. Only those families for whom welfare constitutes a possible alternative to work can conceivably be influenced by the AFDC program. Furthermore, although working or going on welfare are often thought of as simple alternatives, the choice need not be mutually exclusive. State programs vary as to which recipients are eligible and the extent to which they are allowed or even required to work; hence the effect of AFDC on labor supply is complex. In seeking to clarify the relationship between welfare, family formation, and labor supply, I will first examine the factors affecting the decision to seek AFDC, then examine the relationship between family formation and welfare, and finally trace the effects of these decisions on the labor supply of both men and women.

The Demand for Welfare

Before a family goes on welfare, it must first apply for assistance and then be accepted by the welfare agency. The first step represents the demand for welfare; the second, the supply of welfare funds by the government. The actual number of families on welfare at any given time will depend on the interaction between these supply and demand conditions. On the one hand, demand for welfare will be affected by the relationship between the supply factors and alternative sources of income. In the following analysis I have concentrated on the labor market alternative, although there may well be others—for example criminal activities. The supply of welfare, on the other hand, will basically be influenced by the willingness of society to raise and to allocate the necessary tax money to welfare programs, decisions made through the legislative and administrative processes of government. It is also probable that just as demand is influenced by supply, so the availability of funds may be affected by demand conditions. If the number seeking public assistance increases too much, both the welfare administration and the taxpayers may react by curtailing supply.

This analysis concentrates on understanding the demand side of the welfare market and does not attempt to explain the supply of public assistance. Because the demand for welfare will be influenced by the prevailing supply conditions, however, it is important to understand which are the important supply factors from the point of view of potential welfare recipients. The supply factors to which families are expected to respond fall into three categories. First, there are the eligibility criteria of the program. For example, a family must include dependent children and be without an ablebodied father to be eligible for AFDC. Second, a qualified family will be given welfare assistance only if its total resources are less than the basic monthly welfare allowance for that family's size. Third, the degree to which the rules and regulations governing program requirements and definitions of need are strictly interpreted and enforced will affect the supply of public assistance funds. This, as well as the treatment of welfare applicants and recipients, may also have an important impact on the willingness to seek welfare. For convenience, I refer to this third category as the degree of administrative stringency exercised by the welfare agency. Clearly, the broader the coverage, the higher the welfare allowance, and the more lenient the administrative policy, the more families are likely to seek welfare assistance.

Because families with savings and other assets will not be accepted as welfare recipients, the only alternative source of income is the labor market earnings of family members. Therefore, one of the crucial factors in the decision to seek welfare is the relationship between expected earnings and the expected value of welfare income. The term "expected" is used to adjust for the likelihood of receiving income from either source. For instance, high unemployment rates will reduce the likelihood of finding a job, while a stringent welfare administration will reduce the likelihood of receiving public assistance. The higher expected earnings are relative to expected welfare benefits, the less likely it is that a family will seek welfare.

For families deprived of an ablebodied male supporter, the only likely earner is the mother. In addition to her wage rate and her likelihood of finding a job, a mother's ability to work will be affected by the availability of child-care facilities. Also, assuming the mother is not required to work by welfare regulations, the time spent at work necessarily involves curtailment of the services she can perform for her family at home. Therefore, her labor market earnings must more than compensate for these losses if she is to be willing to work to support her family. Clearly, if all of her earnings are deducted from welfare benefits, there is no incentive for a mother to work unless she can earn substantially more than the welfare allowance for her family. More precisely, such a deduction rule represents a 100 percent tax rate on labor market earnings up to the welfare allowance level and, furthermore, means that the opportunity cost of a mother's time spent at home will be her earnings minus her welfare allowance. This is negative if her earnings are less than her allowance and very low until she earns a lot more. This is not to argue that AFDC mothers should be forced to work, however, because the social and administrative costs of compelling welfare mothers to work and providing sufficient child-care facilities may well outweigh any tax savings derived from a reduction in welfare expenditures. Although New York City did have the 100 percent tax rate rule throughout the period of my study, recent amendments to the Social Security Act were adopted because the work disincentive effect was explicitly recognized by Congress. These amendments allow welfare agencies to ''disregard'' one third of an AFDC mother's earnings in calculating her welfare allowance: in other words, the tax rate is reduced to 67 percent.

Welfare and Family Formation

So far, only the relationship between the labor force participation of mothers and their decision to seek welfare has been considered. The other important, and perhaps crucial, relationship is that between the labor supply of fathers and the decision of their families to seek public assistance. A large proportion of AFDC families in New York City either have been deserted or have never had a legal father. Obviously, the actual value of the welfare check will be sensitive to the degree of enforcement of rules which require mothers to assist in finding the father, obtaining court orders for the support of their children, and ensuring payment. Of more basic importance, however, is the possible effect of both benefit levels and administrative stringency on the decisions of men and women to marry and to stay together. If the expected welfare income for a mother and her children is higher than the expected earnings of the father less his living expenses, then there is little financial incentive to maintain a marriage. If, in addition, it is relatively easy to get on AFDC, the steady income from welfare may well be preferred to the low, and perhaps intermittent, earnings which an unskilled father facing high unemployment rates may be able to contribute.

In examining the relationship of employment conditions to the numbers on public assistance, Moynihan found that

during the 1950's, there were quite astonishingly strong correlations between nonwhite male unemployment rates and such phenomena as the number of new AFDC cases opened and the number of nonwhite married women separated from their husbands, but . . . with the onset of the 1960's, these relations seemed to disappear, so that, for example, the unemployment rate would decline but the number of new AFDC cases would rise.

In trying to explain this phenomenon, Moynihan suggested the following hypothesis:

Developments in the 1950's would have made it apparent to anyone closely involved that, despite burgeoning prosperity, patterns of income, employment, housing, discrimination, and social services—*very possibly including the welfare system itself*—were somehow undermining stability of family life among the poor, particularly the urban Negro poor.[2]

Such an hypothesis is impossible to prove or disprove without an explanation which takes into account (a) the other factors which explain the rise in AFDC caseloads, (b) the other factors which explain family instability in the society at large, and (c) the phenomenon that whereas increased welfare availability may affect family stability, increases in desertion will increase demand for AFDC. For example, there is evidence that many families without a father present are eligible for but do not seek public assistance. To the extent that improved benefits or access to welfare encourages such families to apply, AFDC caseloads will increase, but not family instability. Furthermore, the general increase in family instability in the United States must be taken into account as well as the fact that black families have always experienced greater family instability, even without the benefit of public assistance. Few social scientists would attribute increasing divorce rates to the availability of public assistance, and most agree that black family instability is due to the total disruption of black family life caused by slavery and its aftermath. Indeed, some sociologists have gone further to suggest that family stability, in the sense of both parents present, "does not guarantee good experiences for children," that the matrifocal family system typical of American urban ghettoes is a source of strength, and that public concern over black family instability is not only a reflection of middle-class mores but may actually arise out of the tensions produced by the "formal" stability of nuclear middle-class families.[3] In short, simple correlations explain nothing; only a model which properly identifies and measures all the relevant factors can attempt to assess the relationship between welfare and family formation.

In general, there will always be an incentive for welfare families to disguise either part-time earnings or supplements to income from any other source. Indeed, since all regular financial contributions to a family's support are deducted from the welfare benefit, the present system encourages contributions in kind, at irregular intervals, from other friends and relatives as well as from absent fathers. In this way, the system does seem to distort the usual incentives by which the wider family circle can help to support a small dependent unit through a period of hardship. The most extreme reaction to such disincentives is suggested in the "fiscal abandonment" thesis. This argues that fathers desert only in the eyes of the welfare investigator and actually live either with the family or around the corner. In such cases, the family is much better off, because the father can provide supplemental income from his employment without adjustments being made in the welfare allowance. This thesis is extremely hard to prove or disprove because such behavior might reflect deliberate cheating, as suggested by the proponents of the thesis, or might reflect a general social pattern of loser marriage ties among some segments of the population of welfare recipients. Accordingly many mothers and children may be supported fairly permanently on welfare, while men may maintain casual liaisons with one or more families and contribute from their earnings on a casual basis.

The Supply of Labor

Economists view the individual's decision to work as a choice between leisure, treated as one consumption good, and all the other goods that can be purchased with the earnings from work. This choice will depend, in part, on the individual's relative preferences for work and leisure, which economic analysis takes as given. In addition, there are two basic economic factors to be considered. First, for all goods, the higher their price, the less the inclination to acquire them and the greater the tendency to find substitutes for them. This is referred to as the substitution effect of a price change. The price of leisure time is measured as the amount of income which could have been earned by working during that time instead. For this reason, the higher the individual's wage rate, the more he will be willing to give up leisure hours and supply more hours of work. Second, as individual or family wealth increases, people are likely to demand more goods of all kinds, including leisure. This tendency is called the income effect, and works in the opposite direction of the substitution effect. In other words, as income rises, hours of leisure will increase and hours of work will decrease.

Analysis of the effect of changes in the wage rate on the actual amount of labor supplied is consequently complicated because, apart from any income from unearned assets, a given change in wage rates will also change the income of the individual. Therefore, the adjustment in hours of work supplied to an increase in the opportunity cost of working will depend on the relative strengths of the income and substitution effects: if the income effect is stronger, hours worked will decrease; if the substitution effect is stronger, hours worked will increase. Consequently, the response of labor supply to the wage level can be determined empirically only by estimating the net effect of the income and substitution effects.

Obviously, different groups in the population will react differently to these labor supply factors. Furthermore, these reactions may vary over time. Perhaps most important are the differences in the reactions of different family members. Those family members who have alternative means of support open to them are more likely to respond to changes in wage rates; that is to say, they have a relatively strong substitution effect. A good example is the housewife who can work at home or in the labor market. Thus, one explanation for the dramatic increase in the labor supply of married women over the last fifty years is the improvement in the value of market work relative to work performed at home for women.[4]

In addition, some family members are able to vary their labor supply in the short run, while others are not. For instance, it has been found that married women, young people, and old people, who are often referred to as the secondary labor force, have a tendency to enter the labor force when wage rates increase and unemployment decreases, and to drop out when unemployment increases and expected earnings decrease. This reaction to deteriorating economic conditions is called the "discouraged worker" effect. In contrast, primary male earners are normally expected to work, or to look for work, no matter what their wage rate or chance of employment. Therefore, although their hours of work may change, their labor force participation rate does not, at least in the short run. In the long run, however, the income effect from rising real incomes may lead to a reduction in the lifetime labor supply of men, as reflected, for example, in lower retirement ages and lower labor force participation rates among older age groups.

Individuals from families in different income groups may also react differently to the incentives to work, quite apart from any dissimilarities in tastes or attitudes. Thus, it is thought that the labor supply behavior of ablebodied men of working age is not substantially different in different income groups; but, the labor supply responses of women may well vary much more. The lower the women's earning potential, so long as her husband is working, the more likely she is to be more valuable to the family by remaining out of the labor force and performing household services. The less the husband earns, however, or the longer he remains unemployed, the more likely it is that his wife will also look for work to supplement his income. The tendency of a secondary worker to come into the labor force in this manner is sometimes referred to as the "additional worker" effect, in contrast to the "discouraged worker" effect described above. There is considerable controversy over which effect predominates in the behavior of the female labor force. The extent to which mothers can enter the labor force will also be affected by the number and ages of children and whether there are alternative means of caring for them. If the husband is unemployed or has left home, the mother is likely to go to work to support her family; indeed, in the event that she has no other means of support, she then becomes the primary earner.[5]

Interaction between Welfare Demand, Family Formation, and Labor Supply

In theory, the existence of welfare programs affects labor supply behavior in a number of ways. First, the relationship between welfare benefits and wage rates may lead to substitution between hours of leisure and hours of work, if welfare is viewed as an alternative to work by the actual or potential recipient. The labor supply of women of working age, particularly those with children, is thought to be especially sensitive to changes in this relationship. Second, the labor supply of those welfare recipients who are not required to work is also most likely to be affected by the welfare alternative. Indeed, for mothers with limited earning power, welfare will often be a perfect substitute for work, because welfare income is greater than earnings. Third, although, in theory, the labor force participation rate of ablebodied men on welfare will not be affected by welfare because they are required either to work or to look for work, it is likely that the actual number of hours spent searching for work may be reduced. It is possible that more men will try to appear unemployable, and in this way in effect drop out of the labor force. Fourth, the less stringently work requirements are enforced, the more likely it is that withdrawals from the labor force will occur. The labor supply of teenagers and the elderly is more likely to be reduced by the welfare alternative, both because they have alternatives to work in the form of school or retirement and because welfare administrators are less likely to enforce work regulations on them. Finally, any income effect of increases in welfare benefits will also reinforce these substitution effects. Insofar as receipt of public assistance raises family income, both income and substitution effects will tend to reduce hours of work and labor force participation rates.

There is also an important relationship between labor supply behavior and the incidence of female-headed families. Once a family has been deserted by the father and is accepted on welfare, the welfare department takes on the role of "primary earner." This has two important effects. First, it enables the woman to continue to behave as a secondary member of the labor force, and thus to work only when the relative price conditions are favorable. It is also clear that the tax on earnings, which results from deducting earnings from welfare allowance levels, will considerably reduce [in the case of the 100 percent tax rate, totally remove] any incentive for a mother to supplement family income through work. Second, men, whether actually separated from welfare families or not, are no longer the primary supporters. Insofar as they do contribute to the family's income, it is on a supplemental basis. In terms of labor supply, this means that the substitution effect for men is likely to grow in importance if the men maintain some attachment to welfare families. In essence, these men are expected to behave more as secondary workers because the family has viable alternatives to their earnings as primary sources of income. The rates of labor force participation of men would, therefore, become more sensitive to fluctuations in their earning power, even though the men themselves may not be on welfare.

Pursuing this analysis, a new perspective on the so-called vicious cycle of welfare can be gained by highlighting the economic difficulties for a family once on welfare to get off. In the first place, to quality for welfare, any source of savings or other outside resources must be depleted. Therefore, in the situation where no support is required from relatives, and assuming that families do not cheat, the family by definition has no assets. Thus, the only way to raise the family's income is through the earnings of family members. If these earnings are already low and unlikely to rise above the welfare benefit level, and/or there are no family members required to work, then the family may be a welfare case fairly permanently. If, in addition, the family has gone on welfare by dissolving the tie with the father, the likelihood of the family ever being supported off welfare is even further reduced. Furthermore, both the rules about deducting any earnings of teenage members of welfare families and familiarity with the welfare system itself may also influence the attitudes and behavior of the second generation, contributing to their subsequent dependence on welfare as well. Other income maintenance programs available by right, which support families in the event of unemployment or sickness, may be important ways of reducing welfare dependency, because they do not require the exhaustion of all other resources or irreversible changes in family patterns likely to ensure long-run dependence on welfare income.

Developments in New York City

Before assessing the impact of these complex relationships on conditions in New York City, a brief overview of what has happened to family formation, to the Aid to Families with Dependent Children program, and to labor force participation rates will provide a helpful background.[6]

Family Instability in New York City

There are no continuous data for New York City on marital status, but national figures indicate a growth in divorce rates and in the proportion of female-headed households, particularly among nonwhites.[7] Indeed, by 1970, more than half the nonwhite children in this country lived in homes headed by a female. Nonwhite families have traditionally had a higher proportion of female-headed households than whites; this proportion would be expected to increase, therefore, wherever the proportion of nonwhites increased, as has been the case in New York City.

Table 13.1 reflects these trends in New York by summarizing census information on the proportion of female-headed households from 1940 to 1970. Since 1950, the overall proportion of female-headed households has increased by roughly a third each decade. However, because the 1950 figures include suburban New York counties, they somewhat underestimate the percentage figures for that year, and therefore overstate the rate of change between 1950 and 1960. In short, it is in the most recent de-

TABLE 13.1   Female-Headed Households, New York City, 1940–70 (percentages)

	1940	*1950* [a]	*1960*	*1970*
White				
Female heads as percent of all household heads	16.6	16.6	21.7	27.6
Female heads as percent of all household heads by age:				
Aged 14–24	15.5	15.2	17.8	28.8
Aged 25–44	10.3	9.4	13.5	19.4
Aged 45 and over	22.1	21.9	26.4	31.8
Nonwhite				
Female heads as percent of all household heads	32.3	32.1	33.6	39.6 [b]
Female heads as percent of all household heads by age:				
Aged 14–24	34.7	32.9	32.6	44.8 [b]
Aged 25–44	31.2	30.0	30.9	36.6 [b]
Aged 45 and over	33.8	34.8	36.7	42.2 [b]
Total				
Female heads as percent of all household heads	17.5	17.8	23.3	29.8
Female heads as percent of all household heads by age:				
Aged 14–24	17.4	15.3	20.8	32.6
Aged 25–44	11.9	11.5	16.7	23.7
Aged 45 and over	22.6	22.7	27.4	33.3

SOURCE: U.S. Department of Commerce, Bureau of the Census, *Census of Population, 1940, 1950, 1960,* and *1970.*

[a] New York City portion of Standard Metropolitan Statistical Area (SMSA).

[b] 1970 data for blacks only.

cade that the proportion of female-headed households has increased fastest. The most dramatic increase has been in the younger age groups, particularly among those under 25, both white and nonwhite. The oldest age group, 45 and over, includes relatively more widows, and thus reflects demographic changes in relative mortality rates of men and women as well as increased family separation.

Apart from the conceptual difficulties, which were discussed previously (see p. 319), of using the proportion of female-headed families as a measure of family instability, there are also statistical problems. First, these figures do not include families which separate and in which the mother remarries. Second, and more interestingly, it has been shown that many families, particularly poorer black families, have changed their statistical status rather than their marital status.[8] That is to say, a black woman who had been left by her husband was more likely to live with other relatives (normally her parents) in 1950, and thus be counted as a secondary, not a primary, household unit. By contrast, in 1969 such women were more likely to have set up their own households and be counted as primary female-headed units. In short, it could be argued that public assistance, if it has encouraged anything, has encouraged the formation of independent family units and not desertion.

The figures for New York City show that, as expected, the nonwhite proportion of female heads is almost twice that of whites, in families where the head of household is below 45.[9] Although the nonwhite proportion has increased, the rate of increase has been *less* than that for whites, who were starting from a lower base. This not only contradicts the generally held view that family instability has increased most among nonwhites, but also, in light of the statistical discussion above, suggests that separations in nonwhite families certainly increased significantly less than whites and perhaps even declined in New York City, because it would be the poorer black family without a father who previously lived with relatives which public assistance has now enabled to live as a separate household unit. In conclusion, analysis of these statistics underscores the dangers of blaming public assistance for increases in black family instability simply because AFDC caseloads and the proportion of nonwhite female-headed families have risen at the same time.

There are two sources of continuous data on the marital status of AFDC mothers: (1) monthly information on the reasons for acceptance of AFDC cases, including as reasons "departure of parent," which in the vast majority of cases means the departure of the man supporting the family; (2) monthly information on the marital status of accepted mothers. Annual averages of the proportion such cases constitute of incoming AFDC caseloads are summarized in Table 13.2.

"Departure of parent" has consistently been one of the major reasons for accepting an AFDC case, accounting for around 30 percent of all cases. This proportion has not changed greatly in ten years; but the rise in caseloads means that the absolute number of such families has risen considerably. Such figures, however, measure the impact of desertion only as

TABLE 13.2 Marital Status of Mothers on AFDC in New York City, 1960–70
(Annual Averages of Monthly Data)

	1960	1961	1962	1963	1964	1965	1966	1967	1968	1969	1970
Status of Mother Accepted in Cases with No Father Present [a]											
(percentages of total acceptances)											
No legal marriage	30.1	30.6	31.7	32.8	33.0	33.7	33.9	31.8	30.8	30.2	30.6
Father dead	2.5	2.8	2.7	2.6	2.8	2.9	2.9	3.1	3.1	3.0	2.7
Divorced/legally separated	7.0	6.2	6.6	6.8	6.5	6.4	6.7	7.0	6.7	6.0	5.9
Father deserted	29.7	31.7	32.5	32.8	34.2	35.7	35.4	38.2	39.0	37.1	39.3
Father in an institution	10.3	10.4	10.1	9.1	8.6	7.5	6.9	5.4	4.4	4.5	4.1
Other	.9	1.1	1.3	1.6	1.7	1.8	2.3	2.6	3.0	3.1	2.9
Total	80.5	82.8	84.5	85.7	86.8	88.0	88.1	88.1	87.0	83.9	85.2
Departure of Parent as a Reason for Acceptance on AFDC											
(percentages of total acceptances)											
Divorce/separation	4.6	4.8	5.1	5.0	4.0	3.9	4.1	3.9	3.4	3.7	3.5
Desertion	16.5	15.9	15.9	16.9	18.3	19.3	20.0	21.7	23.2	21.4	23.8
Other	7.2	7.2	6.9	5.8	5.6	4.8	4.5	3.4	2.7	2.7	2.2
Total	28.3	27.9	27.9	27.7	27.9	28.0	28.6	29.0	29.3	27.8	29.5
Total Acceptances on AFDC	2342	2179	2172	2537	2768	3007	3801	4994	6011	4937	5835

SOURCE: New York City, Department of Social Services, *Monthly Statistical Report* (1960–70)

[a] Excludes families with father present but totally disabled and families with no mother.

an *immediate* reason for opening a case; in fact, the process by which desertion leads to an application for public assistance may take some time if the deserted mother has some short-term resources or tries to support the family by working. The data on the marital status of the mother in incoming cases indicates that the proportion of mothers that have been deserted has increased. These data refer only to the marital status of mothers coming onto welfare, and not to the whole caseload. A government study of AFDC mothers in New York City, which presents comparative survey information of the whole AFDC caseload, confirms the view that the proportion of AFDC families deserted by the father has increased. But at the same time, the proportion of unmarried mothers in the total caseload fell from 39 percent to 30 percent between 1961 and 1967.[10] These trends suggest that an increasing proportion of separations are taking place after marriage.

Aid to Families with Dependent Children in New York City, 1960–70

Table 13.3 brings together the pertinent data for the AFDC program. The program has grown fourfold in the decade, whether viewed in terms of recipients or caseloads (an AFDC case includes the dependent children as recipients of public assistance). It is also clear that until the end of the decade this increase derived mainly from the increase in openings, rather than from a dramatic increase in applications or decline in closings. The increase in the acceptance rate (openings divided by applications) reflects the increased availability of AFDC to families seeking assistance. This increase arose from two sources: (1) the increased number of eligible families, indicated by the rise in the basic welfare allowance for a family of four, and (2) the increased willingness of the welfare administration to accept eligibles for the program.

Table 13.4 provides an overall view of labor market conditions in New York City in the previous decade. The substantial decline in unemployment rate, until the 1970 recession, was not matched by any significant gain in employment. In other words, the number of job opportunities in the city did not increase, as a fall in unemployment rate usually suggests. Average weekly earnings rose substantially over the period, but the weekly welfare allowance for a family of four rose even more, particularly between 1966 and 1970. The crucial relationship for those consider-

TABLE 13.3 Trends in AFDC Caseloads in New York City, 1960–70

	1960	1961	1962	1963	1964	1965	1966	1967	1968	1969	1970
Caseload trends											
Numbers											
Recipients	195,155	209,130	220,643	245,563	280,761	321,650	377,496	472,508	596,123	701,969	772,331
Caseload	47,497	50,477	52,898	59,082	68,084	78,538	93,516	120,316	155,857	187,336	208,740
Applications	4,326	4,182	4,156	4,620	4,632	4,713	5,021	6,034	6,796	5,965	7,321
Openings	2,342	2,179	2,172	2,537	2,768	3,007	3,801	4,994	6,011	4,937	5,835
Closings	2,168	1,947	1,899	1,854	1,978	2,104	2,300	2,449	2,897	3,706	3,459
Rates (percentages)											
Acceptance rate	52	50	48	52	57	60	67	74	77	69	70
Opening rate	4.9	4.3	4.1	4.3	4.1	3.8	4.1	4.2	3.8	2.6	2.8
Closing rate	4.6	3.9	3.6	3.1	2.9	2.7	2.5	2.0	1.8	2.0	1.7
Basic welfare allowance											
for family of four	$177.55	182.15	182.15	182.15	196.35	196.35	257.75	263.40	272.50	301.25	356.00

SOURCES: Caseload trends New York City, Department of Social Services, *Monthly Statistical Report* (annual averages of monthly data).
Basic welfare allowance New York City, Department of Social Services, *Budget Schedules* (as of July 1st each year).

NOTES: Acceptance rate = Openings/Applications. (These figures include adjustments for reclassification which are not included in application figures above.)

Opening rate = Openings/Caseload.
Closing rate = Closings/Caseload.

TABLE 13.4 Labor Market Conditions in New York City, 1960–72

	1960	1961	1962	1963	1964	1965	1966	1967	1968	1969	1970	1971	1972
A. *Employment and Unemployment*													
Total employment (thousands)	3,954	3,949	3,973	3,925	3,946	3,952	3,966	3,996	4,048	4,119	4,078	3,919	3,836
Total unemployment (thousands)	209	236	208	219	205	191	175	154	135	132	208	213	215
Unemployment rate (percentage)	5.0	5.6	4.9	5.3	4.9	4.6	4.2	3.7	3.2	3.1	3.9	5.1	5.3
B. *Weekly Earnings and Welfare Benefits*													
Average weekly earnings in total manufacturing ($)	84.36	87.10	89.86	95.25	95.25	97.88	101.95	106.60	112.94	119.51	126.82	135.76	142.13
Weekly welfare allowance for family of four ($)	41.01	42.03	42.03	42.03	45.31	45.31	59.47	60.78	62.86	69.50	82.13	76.80	76.80
Ratio of welfare benefits to average earnings	.49	.48	.47	.46	.48	.46	.58	.57	.55	.58	.64	.56	.54
C. *Equivalent Weekly Income at Minimum Wage* [a]													
New York State ($)	40	40	46	46	46	50	50	60	60	64	64	74	74
U.S. ($)	40	40	46	46	50	50	50	56	64	64	64	64	64
Ratio of welfare benefits to: New York State minimum-wage income	1.03	1.05	.91	.91	.99	.91	1.19	1.01	1.05	1.09	1.28	1.04	1.04
Federal minimum-wage income	1.03	1.05	.91	.91	.91	.91	1.19	1.09	.98	1.09	1.28	1.20	1.20

SOURCES: Employment and unemployment—New York State Department of Labor, *Employment Review* (data for 1970–72 unrevised). Weekly earnings and welfare benefits—See *ibid.*, and Table 13.3. Equivalent Weekly Income at Minimum wage—New York State Department of Labor, Division of Employment, Research and Statistics Office. Information acquired and checked by telephone to this office at sucessive dates, 1967 to 1974.

[a] As of July 1st each year (equivalent weekly income = 40 hours per week times prevailing minimum wage).

ing the effects of welfare assistance is the ratio of welfare benefits to labor market earnings. Weekly welfare allowances were less than half the average earnings in manufacturing for the first half of the decade, but rose to two-thirds of same by 1970. In late 1970, the New York State legislature, alarmed by the rapid increases in public assistance expenditures, cut welfare allowances roughly 10 percent. Since average labor earnings continued to rise, the crucial ratio fell in 1971 and 1972.

The prevalent minimum wage may be more relevant than average manufacturing earnings as an indicator of the earnings alternative for welfare families, because their members are usually low-wage earners. The equivalent weekly incomes from New York State and federal minimum wages are therefore included in Table 13.4. Apart from the period 1962 through 1965, the welfare allowance for a family of four was higher than the equivalent income from a minimum-wage job; indeed, by 1970 welfare allowances were roughly 30 percent higher. An increase in the state minimum wage along with the cut in welfare allowances brought the two back to parity, but the welfare allowance remained 20 percent higher than the federal minimum. In conclusion, it is clear that income from public assistance gained substantially as an alternative to labor market earnings for low-wage workers in New York City, particularly from 1966 to 1970. One explanation for part of the lag in employment as unemployment fell is that workers dropped out of the labor force; the increase in AFDC caseloads from 50,000 to 200,000 suggests that many of these may have been welfare mothers.

Labor Force Participation Rates in New York City

Tables 13.5 and 13.6 present census data on the labor force participation rates for different age, race, and sex groups in New York City from 1940 to 1970. The most striking phenomenon is the large increase in the labor force participation rates of all women over the age of 14, although in the last decade there was a slight decline in the much higher rates of nonwhite women. In the prime age group 35–54, nonwhite women have labor force participation rates as high as 60 percent, and in all age groups except teenagers nonwhite women's labor force participation exceeds that of white women. This possibly reflects the use of nonwhite teenagers as babysitters for younger siblings while their mothers work. It is worth not-

TABLE 13.5 Female Labor Force Participation Rates,
New York City, 1940–70

		Age Group	1940	1950	1960	1970
White females		14–15	.4	1.0	3.7	4.1
(including Puerto Ricans)		16–17	16.6	18.3	24.3	21.2
		18–19	64.6	64.8	63.8	50.2
		14–19	28.7	30.6	30.1	25.5
		20–24	67.7	60.4	57.5	59.5
		25–34	71.9	35.5	39.7	43.4
		35–44	29.9	35.7	43.8	47.4
		45–54	23.7	34.7	49.2	....
		55–59	18.2	27.5	43.0	50.2 [a]
		60–64	13.9	21.6	32.6	....
		65+	5.7	8.5	12.1	11.8
	Total	14+	32.6	33.0	38.2	39.9
Nonwhite females		14–15	.8	1.3	3.7	4.0
		16–17	15.1	10.2	15.7	13.1
		18–19	53.2	44.4	52.4	38.4
		14–19	24.2	20.1	24.3	17.7
		20–24	65.6	52.4	54.3	51.2
		25–34	60.6	53.5	52.4	48.7
		35–44	54.8	57.0	59.2	54.2
		45–54	47.1	42.2	61.4	....
		55–59	36.2	40.5	50.5	54.0 [a]
		60–64	25.7	30.0	41.6	....
		65+	9.5	12.8	18.8	14.9
	Total	14+	50.4	47.6	49.9	44.0
Puerto Rican females		14–15			4.0	3.4
		16–17			18.0	13.5
		18–19			54.0	33.6
		14–19			24.0	16.1
		20–24			48.4	35.1
		25–34	n.a.	n.a.	41.2	24.5
		35–44			46.1	31.7
		45–54			40.0	....
		55–59			29.0	31.6 [a]
		60–64			20.0	....
		65+			4.9	7.5
	Total	14+			37.8	26.5
Total females		14–15	.4	1.0	3.6	4.1
		16–17	16.6	17.4	23.2	19.1
		18–19	63.8	62.6	62.0	47.2
		14–19	28.5	29.5	29.3	23.5
		20–24	67.5	59.3	57.0	57.6
		25–34	43.5	37.9	42.2	44.9
		35–44	31.8	38.0	46.4	49.3
		45–54	25.0	36.2	50.7	....
		55–59	19.0	28.4	43.7	50.9 [a]
		60–64	14.4	22.1	33.3	....
		65+	5.9	8.8	12.6	12.1
	Total	14+	33.8	34.5	39.9	40.8

SOURCE: U.S. Census, 1940, 1950, 1960, and 1970.

[a] Average for age group 45–64.

TABLE 13.6   Male Labor Force Participation Rates,
New York City, 1940–70

	Age Group	1940	1950	1960	1970
White males	14–15	.6	4.0	7.1	6.7
(including	16–17	18.8	18.8	28.7	24.1
Puerto	18–19	65.6	58.5	64.2	48.2
Ricans)	14–19	29.3	27.7	31.0	25.8
	20–24	88.7	77.9	84.3	74.1
	25–34	96.2	91.6	94.9	91.9
	35–44	95.6	94.3	97.4	93.4
	45–54	92.3	92.3	93.4	....
	55–59	85.6	88.2	90.4	88.4 [a]
	60–64	73.7	79.9	82.9	....
	65+	36.7	42.7	36.8	30.3
Total	14+	81.0	79.6	77.9	71.8
Nonwhite	14–15	.8	2.6	6.4	5.2
males	16–17	17.5	17.4	25.2	16.3
	18–19	62.3	58.5	67.9	42.5
	14–19	26.1	25.8	31.0	19.5
	20–24	88.6	76.3	85.1	70.2
	25–34	93.3	85.6	90.0	86.6
	35–44	92.1	88.0	92.0	86.9
	45–54	88.2	85.5	89.4	....
	55–59	81.2	81.3	84.2	81.3 [a]
	60–64	68.2	70.4	73.3	....
	65+	34.6	39.0	37.2	25.4
Total	14+	81.2	76.6	78.9	67.2
Puerto Rican	14–15			7.0	4.3
males	16–17			33.0	16.5
	18–19			72.0	44.1
	14–19			36.4	19.5
	20–24			90.4	61.4
	25–34	n.a.	n.a.	92.1	85.8
	35–44			91.2	85.9
	45–54			84.0	....
	55–59			79.0	75.5 [a]
	60–64			69.0	....
	65+			24.6	18.4
Total	14+			79.0	66.2
Total males	14–15	.6	3.9	7.0	6.3
	16–17	18.6	18.7	28.2	22.1
	18–19	65.5	58.5	64.6	46.6
	14–19	29.1	27.5	31.2	24.2
	20–24	88.7	77.7	84.4	73.1
	25–34	96.0	90.9	94.1	90.7
	35–44	94.6	93.8	96.5	92.0
	45–54	92.1	91.8	92.8	....
	55–59	85.5	87.8	89.8	87.3 [a]
	60–64	73.5	79.5	82.1	....
	65+	36.6	42.6	36.7	29.8
Total	14+	81.1	78.3	78.1	71.0

SOURCES: U.S. Census, 1940, 1950, 1960, and 1970.

[a] Average for age group 45–64.

ing that the labor force participation rates of white women aged 25–44 are two-thirds the rates of the 20–24 age group, while nonwhite women maintain practically the same rates across these age groups.

The total labor force participation rate of men in New York City shows a significant decline between 1960 and 1970. In contrast to nonwhite women, nonwhite men appear to have slightly lower labor force participation rates than white men in all age groups. This may possibly reflect an adjustment to the lower expected earnings of nonwhite men relative to those of nonwhite women. The labor force participation rates of older men do not appear until recently to have fallen to the same extent in New York City as they have nationwide. This is undoubtedly due to the fact that New Yorkers retire out of the city, so that only those who are still working remain. The labor force participation rates of teenagers in New York increased slightly until 1960 but have dropped sharply since, nonwhites and Puerto Ricans falling fastest. The trends are not significantly different for young girls and boys.

To summarize labor supply behavior in New York City since 1960, the aggregate male labor force participation rate for the population over 14 fell from 78 percent to 71 percent, and the aggregate female rate rose slightly from 40 percent to 41 percent. The major factor contributing to the decline in male labor force participation rate was the decline in the rates of teenagers and older men, that is, secondary members of the labor force. The decline was less for whites than for nonwhites and Puerto Ricans. The labor force participation rates of nonwhite women, for the most part, are still higher than those of white women. However, all nonwhite female age groups registered a decline in their participation rates. Rates for Puerto Rican women fell drastically from rates similar to those of white women in 1960 to rates only half those of white women. In short, these trends are consistent with the arguments presented earlier. Specifically, it is the low-wage secondary workers who are most likely to drop out of the labor force when the welfare alternative improves, as it did in New York City during the sixties.

It should be noted, however, that 1970 was a recession year, which may have contributed to the large declines in the labor force participation rates of teenagers, older people, and minority groups. These groups are the ones most likely to get discouraged in the search for work and, therefore, most likely to be sharply affected by increasing unemployment.

A survey in New York City conducted by the Office of Economic Opportunity in 1967, when unemployment was falling fastest, showed a slight increase in the total male labor force participation rate and a substantial increase in the female rate as compared with 1960. Teenagers and non-white males aged 25–55 also showed gains. The sample size was rather small, so that the results may not be reliable for specific age, sex, and ethnic groups; nevertheless, the trends are consistent with the predicted cyclical effect of low unemployment on the secondary labor force.

The Vicious Cycle of Welfare in New York City

So far I have described the vicious cycle of welfare and outlined a theoretical framework for its analysis. To estimate the impact of the important variables, a statistical evaluation which takes all the relevant factors into account in an appropriate explanatory model is necessary. In previous work, I attempted to build a cross-sectional model with 1960 census data using three hundred health areas in New York City as the units of observation. The full details are reported elsewhere.[11] In this paper I shall discuss the usefulness of my approach in predicting welfare demand, the proportion of female-headed households, and labor supply in New York City.

The Incidence of AFDC and Female-Headed Households in New York City

The usual method for predicting welfare caseloads is to use detailed breakdowns of income distribution to estimate the numbers of persons and families below the relevant welfare budget allowance.[12] Although there is nothing wrong with the basic concept involved, there are some basic methodological problems to this approach.[13] First, a prediction of welfare caseloads obtained in this manner will only be as good as the income distribution estimates themselves. When these are required according to detailed breakdowns by family size, race, sex, and age of family head for New York City, the available data sources are inadequate. Second, without a meaningful explanatory model it is extremely difficult to make useful predictions concerning behavioral response. Even if there were reasonable estimates of population change by race, age, sex of family head, and family size, there would still be no way to predict that portion of the rate of growth of female-headed families relative to male-headed families which results from anything other than these demographic changes. Yet, explanatory factors may be crucial to predicting the number of female-headed families and the incidence of AFDC.

In my work, therefore I built regression models using the 1960 cross-sectional data to estimate the relative importance of different factors, and then used the estimated regression coefficients to make projections of AFDC incidence and the proportion of female-headed families using 1967 values of the relevant variables. The regression equations used are described in the Appendix. The equations predicted 5.1 percent for AFDC incidence in 1967 and 24.7 percent for the proportion of female-headed households. Actually AFDC incidence was 5.9 percent in 1967, a substantial increase over the 1960 figure of 2.7 percent. There are no estimates of the proportion of female-headed households aged 25–44 for 1967, but Table 13.1 shows an increase from 16.7 percent in 1960 to 23.7 in 1970.

In an earlier set of equations I used the proportion of families with incomes below \$2,000 as the relevant variable to test the eligibility for AFDC, because this was roughly the basic allowance for a family of four in 1960. By 1967, however, the basic allowance was actually above \$3,000, and this accordingly seemed the more appropriate figure to use. Thus, while the proportion of families with incomes below \$2,000 fell from 8.4 percent in 1960 to 5.0 percent in 1967, the proportion of families with incomes below \$3,000 in 1967 was 11.8 percent. In short, increased welfare allowances was one major factor leading to an increase in both AFDC incidence and the proportion of female-headed households. Other factors leading to the increases were the increase in acceptance rates noted earlier and increases in the proportions of dependent children and of nonwhites. The only major offsetting factor was the increase in the proportion of old people. Increases in median family income, the proxy for long-term earning capacity, slightly decreased AFDC incidence.

Since the prediction of AFDC incidence remains short of actual incidence, it is useful to examine some of the possible reasons. First, because there were no estimates of female wage or skill variables in 1967, it was not possible to include the effect of these factors on AFDC incidence, although other equations showed that female earning capacity had an added impact on AFDC incidence. Female earning capacity obviously affects the extent to which women without male support can earn enough to maintain their families themselves. The trend data for New York City discussed above showed that earnings in the labor market did not keep pace with welfare allowances from 1960 to 1967. The decrease in the number of women working as domestics also suggests that more women are preferring to seek welfare assistance rather than struggle to support their families by working at earning rates below welfare allowances.

Another possible reason for the underestimate of AFDC incidence is that the observed relationship between AFDC incidence and acceptance rates does not adequately represent the total buildup of cases after acceptance rates started to increase in 1964 and more eligibles were admitted to the welfare rolls. In my earlier work, I estimated that, if acceptance rates had remained constant, AFDC caseloads would have risen only about 50 percent since 1962 instead of the actual 127 percent increase as of 1967. Improved access to the system may well have increased the propensity of low-income families to seek AFDC as the increased application rate also suggests.

Labor Force Participation Rates and the Impact of AFDC in New York City

I have also developed and tested two models explaining male and female labor supply, respectively, which are also described in detail in the Appendix. As proxies for male and female labor supply, I used the relevant labor force participation rates for the population over the age of 14, unfortunately the only available measures. However, I was able to control to some extent for the effects of differences in labor force participation rate by age by using age correction factors in the regression equations. To estimate the extent to which the existence of the AFDC program reduces the willingness of men and women to work, I introduced AFDC incidence as an independent factor in each equation. Although there are problems in the use of this variable as a measure of the effect of welfare, its use does provide a quantitative estimate of the relationship between the numbers on AFDC and the reductions in the male and female labor force.

Unfortunately the results of the predictions are difficult to assess, because there are conflicts in the available statistics on labor force participation rates in 1967. The findings are not inconsistent with my argument, however. In fact, when I used the estimate of the proportion of female-headed households based on the $3,000 welfare eligibility measure in the equation for female labor force participation rates, I obtained the slight increase in participation rates between 1960 and 1970 noted in Table 13:5. Since the use of this higher estimate also predicts AFDC incidence more accurately, this result supports the basic hypothesis concerning the importance of the interrelationship between female labor supply, AFDC incidence, and family instability.

Another interesting result was the predicted impact of AFDC incidence on the male and female labor supply in New York City. The estimated coefficient indicates that an increase of 1 percent in AFDC incidence (approximately 17,000 mothers, using 1960 as a base) leads to a maximum withdrawal of 7,506 females and 7,603 males from the city's labor force. Put differently, for every hundred mothers coming on AFDC, roughly forty women and forty men withdraw from the labor force. However, these results cannot be interpreted solely as a measure of voluntary withdrawal from the labor force. Roughly 20 percent of AFDC families in New York City had incapacitated fathers living at home in 1960. In addition, of AFDC cases opening in 1960, roughly 20 percent were accepted because the father had been laid off or discharged and another 18 percent were accepted because of the illness or injury of the father, which led to a decrease in resources.[14] Clearly, there is overlap between these cases, so that a precise estimate of involuntary withdrawal cannot be made. Since AFDC mothers were not required to work or, therefore, to register as unemployed during the period 1960 to 1970, the cases which opened because the mother was laid off or discharged (cases in which a father was laid off or discharged would be eligible for a different program) probably did lead to a voluntary withdrawal. It also seems reasonable to assume that the cases which were accepted because of a decrease in resources due to illness or injury were also families in which someone had been working, although one cannot tell whether this was the mother or father. In conclusion, while some of the estimated labor market dropouts were involuntary (possibly as many as half the men), there were still a sizable number who dropped out voluntarily because the welfare alternative was preferable. It is particularly interesting that I did find a significant number of men voluntarily withdrawing even after accounting for involuntary withdrawals. This is the one piece of evidence to support the earlier argument that the labor supply behavior of men will be affected by the AFDC program even if they are not on the program themselves. In short, the existence of AFDC does increase the substitution effect for men.

AFDC incidence increased from 2.7 percent to 5.9 percent between 1960 and 1967. My results suggest that as a consequence a maximum of 23,000 women and a minimum of 12,000 men dropped out of the labor force during those seven years, if the estimates for men are adjusted downwards by one-half to account for involuntary withdrawals and the estimates for women are not adjusted at all. In a total labor force (in New York City) of four million, this seems an insignificant number. Furthermore, since the male labor force is twice the female, the relative impact of the increase in AFDC on the male labor supply is one-fourth that of the impact on female labor supply. However, it is also obvious that the effect on the supply of low-wage workers has been more significant than the effect on the total labor force. In addition, the total labor force has grown very little in New York since 1960, probably only by about 125,000. In other words, my findings suggest that the labor force could have grown by as much as one-third more had AFDC incidence not increased. Inasmuch as those dropping out of the labor force because of AFDC are predominantly low-wage workers, their supply must actually have fallen. Finally, these results suggest that the further increase in AFDC incidence since 1967 has led to further labor force withdrawals and decreases in the supply of workers willing to work at low wage rates in New York City.

Table 13.5 shows that, while the overall labor force participation rate of women in New York City increased slightly between 1960 and 1970, the participation of black and Puerto Rican women aged 20–44 fell and that of white women of the same age rose. One of the important factors contributing to the overall increase is the estimated increase in the proportion of female-headed households. In other words, it is the women at the higher end of the income scale who are entering the labor market when their families split up. My regression results also showed that higher family income was a major factor in accounting for increases in the proportion of female-headed households. In short, higher incomes make it possible for richer families to afford the maintenance of separate households. At the same time, the higher earnings capacity of more skilled women has encouraged them to supplement their incomes. But for low-skilled black and Puerto Rican women the improvement in welfare benefits has outweighed any improvements in earnings. It therefore seems reasonable to suppose that unskilled women may prefer welfare to work. The decrease in the employment of domestics, despite a probable increase in demand, also supports the view that the labor supply of unskilled women has shifted downward.

As a final point, it also seems that, insofar as the welfare administration has been accepting more eligibles on AFDC, the increase has come mainly from female-headed families—mothers earning low wages who previously would have supported their children themselves. Inasmuch as one of the purposes of AFDC is to help to maintain the family in a situation where the mother is not compelled to work for survival, the program appears to have worked. Therefore, the primary impact is the extent to which the 100 percent tax rate on earnings has discouraged women from working to supplement family income, as they might have if a primary male wage earner had been present. The figures imply that in terms of total productive capacity this loss has been insignificant. Indeed, any such loss may well be outweighed by other considerations of social equity. On the other hand, if the long-run goal of AFDC is to break the cycle of poverty, then the program is a failure. A major conclusion of this study is that the chief effect has been to the standard of living of those poor families whose income might well have been raised above the poverty line by the supplemental earnings of the mother. However, to the extent that public assistance is less stringently administered and family ties are looser, AFDC families may in fact supplement their welfare income with part-time earnings and voluntary contributions from fathers, friends, and relatives which are not reported. But the problem still remains that the AFDC program does encourage families to continue to collect public assistance and thus to remain locked in the vicious cycle of poverty and welfare dependence outlined earlier.

APPENDIX

This appendix contains the regression equations used to predict the proportion of female-headed households, AFDC incidence, and the impact of AFDC on male and female labor force participation rates in New York City. Equations were chosen that contained independent variables for which estimates were available in 1967. All the coefficients were statistically significant except where indicated by an asterisk.

The Incidence of AFDC and Female-Headed Households

To predict AFDC incidence I used a two-equation recursive system. Thus, in the first equation the proportion of female-headed households is explained, with a number of independent variables. In the second, the incidence of AFDC is explained with the proportion of female-headed households itself introduced as an independent variable. The results for these two structural equations are reported below. The first equation was run as a regression equation as it stands. To obtain the second, however, it is necessary to calculate a reduced form of the AFDC equation, excluding the proportion of female-headed households as an independent variable but including an exogenous variable which, it is assumed, affects the proportion of female-headed families but not AFDC incidence. The coefficients for those variables which appear in the two regression equations are adjusted in the AFDC equation to take account of their estimated effect on the proportion of female-headed households so as to calculate the structural equation for AFDC incidence.

The full details are explained elsewhere (see footnote 11 for sources). The effect of this procedure is to obtain an explanation of the proportion of female-headed households separate from the explanation of AFDC incidence. This then makes it possible to adjust for the independent effect of other variables which influence both AFDC incidence and the proportion of female-headed households in the estimated structural equation for AFDC incidence.

The estimated structural equations are as follows:

$$F = 14.3 - .11(R) - .28(C) - .13(O)* + 1.40(P) + 1.31(Y) + .20(NW);$$
$$AFDC = -4.91 - .01(R) + .10(C) - .10(O) + .32(P) - .03(Y) + .15(F),$$

where:

F = proportion of female-headed households aged 25–44;
$AFDC$ = proportion of *AFDC* recipients in the population;
R = rejection rate of *AFDC* applicants = 100 − Acceptance Rate;
C = proportion of dependent children, or the population under 18 divided by the population aged 18–64;
O = proportion of aged persons aged 65 and over in the population;
P = proportion of families with incomes below $2,000;
Y = median family income; and
NW = proportion of nonwhites in the population.

The R^2 in the first equation is .83, and in the reduced form for calculating the second it is .81.

The Male and Female Labor Force Participation Rates

Separate equations were estimated for male and female labor force participation rates in the population over the age of 14; age correction factors were included. Although I experimented with many different measures as proxies for the independent variables, the results were inconclusive (for a detailed discussion, see sources cited in footnote 11). The basic problem was that the income and substitution effects could not be adequately specified. Similarly, it was not possible to distinguish between the "discouraged" and "additional" worker effects. However, as the equations below suggest, two hypotheses were confirmed in the case of female labor supply. First, the care of children, as measured by the dependency ratio, reduces female labor force participation. Second, the absence of a male head, as measured by the proportion of female-headed households, significantly increases participation.

In addition, AFDC incidence was found to have an independent effect on labor force participation rates. From the coefficient of AFDC in these equations, elasticities and the estimated numerical impact of AFDC on labor supply were calculated. The equations from which the coefficients for AFDC were taken are given below. It should be noted that I used the equations showing the strongest effect of AFDC, in terms of both the size of the coefficient and its statistical significance. In short, I have estimated the maximum impact of AFDC on labor force participation in both cases.

1. Male labor force participation in New York City:

$$MLFP = +93.6 + .32(Y) - .22(S_M) - .61(O) - .37(T) - .27(AFDC) + .02(PR)* - .02(NW) + .50(M),$$

where $Y, O, AFDC,$ and NW are the same as the variables described above;

$MLFP$ = male labor force participation rate for those 14 years of age and over;

S_M = proprotion of unskilled males in the employed labor force;

T = proportion of the population aged 15–25;

PR = proportion of Puerto Ricans in the population; and

M = proportion of the population moved to New York City from the South since 1955.

R^2 is .65.

2. Female labor force participation in New York City:

$$FLFP = +44.2 - .71(P) - .17(S_F) + .48(U_M) - .25(C) - .17(O) + .19(T) + .54(F) - .23(AFDC) + .10(NW) + .09(PR) + .26(M),$$

where $P, C, O, T, F, AFDC, NW, PR,$ and M are the same as the variables described above;

$FLFP$ = female labor force participation rate for those 14 years of age and over;

S_F = proportion of unskilled females in the employed labor force; and

U_M = unemployment rate for males.

R^2 is .87.

NOTES

[1] There is a program, AFDC–UP, available for families with an unemployed father, which has remained small compared to AFDC (less than 19,000 persons in 1972) and which has not been included in this study. Statistics from C. Peter Rydell, Thelma Palmerio, Gerald Blais and Dan Brown, "The Dynamics of New York City's Welfare Caseload," New York City RAND Institute and Office of Policy Research, Department of Social Services, Human Resources Administration, Draft R-1441-NYC, November 1973.

[2] David P. Moynihan, "The Crises in Welfare," *Public Interest,* X (Winter 1968): 16, 17. (Italics mine)

[3] S. M. Miller and Ronnie Steinberg Ratner, "The American Resignation: The New Assault on Equality," *Social Policy* (May/June 1972), p. 10.

[4] See T. Aldrich Finegan's paper, "Participation of Married Women in the Labor Force," in this volume, for further discussion.

[5] *Ibid.*

[6] For fuller details, see Elizabeth Durbin, *Welfare Income and Employment* (New York, 1969), and "Family Instability, Labor Supply, and the Incidence of Aid to Families with Dependent Children" (Ph.D. diss., Columbia University, 1971).

[7] See Fredricka Pickford Santos, "The Economics of Marital Status," and Shirley B. Johnson, "The Impact of Women's Liberation on Marriage, Divorce, and Family Life-Style," in this volume, for further discussion.

[8] Reynolds Farley, "Family Types and Family Headship: A Comparison of Trends among Blacks and Whites," *Journal of Human Resources,* VI (Summer 1971): 275–96.

[9] A slight discrepancy in the 1970 figures, which are for Negroes only and exclude other nonwhites, suggests that the changes between 1960 and 1970 may even overestimate the increase in the nonwhite proportions. The effect is very slight, however. In 1970, there were 353,692 female-headed households in New York City: 220,299 were white, 127,243 Negro, and 6,150 other nonwhites.

[10] U.S. Congress, House of Representatives, Committee on Ways and Means, "Report of Findings of Special Review of Aid to Families with Dependent Chil-

dren in New York City," 91st Cong., 1st sess., No. 34-557-0, September 24, 1969, Tables 6–7, pp. 64–65.

[11] Durbin, "Family Instability," and "Work and Welfare: The Case of Aid in Families with Dependent Children," *Journal of Human Resources,* VIII (Supplement, 1973): 103–25.

[12] David M. Gordon, "Income and Welfare in New York City," *Public Interest,* XVI (Summer 1969): 64–88; Blanche Bernstein, "Welfare in New York City," *City Almanac,* IV (February 1970): 1–4; and "The Distribution of Income in New York City," *Public Interest,* XX (Summer 1970): Table I, p. 103.

[13] For a full discussion, see Durbin, "Family Instability," chapter VII and appendix C.

[14] Durbin, *Welfare Income and Employment,* Tables 20 and 22, pp. 109 and 115.

14

Formal Extrafamily Child Care—
Some Economic Observations

MYRA H. STROBER

IN MARCH 1972, the labor force participation rate of married women, husband present, with children less than six years old, was 30 percent.[1] In the same survey month, the labor force participation rate for divorced women with children under six was even higher, 62 percent.[2] The labor force participation rate for mothers with preschool children increased by ten percentage points from 1960 to 1972[3] and has been the most rapidly rising labor force participation rate of the past decade.[4] Or, looking at it from the children's standpoint, in March 1972, 5.6 million children under six had working mothers.[5] If trends continue, and it looks as though they will,[6] the problem of how best to provide extrafamily child care and the economic ramifications of such care will become increasingly important. Yet, as of 1971 these questions had gone virtually unnoticed by economists;[7] it is not surprising that in vetoing a comprehensive Child Development Bill in 1971, President Nixon expressed concern that the concept of child care centers had not been sufficiently analyzed. Since 1971, however, several economists have begun to examine child care issues.[8] It is in the spirit of contributing to the emerging discussion that this paper and its proposals are offered. The first part of the paper examines the supply and cost of and demand for formal child care. The second part analyzes the economic rationale for government subsidization of child care. The

This paper was originally prepared for delivery at the Western Economic Association Meetings in Santa Clara, California, in August 1972. The author wishes to acknowledge helpful suggestions from Curtis Aller, Michael Boskin, Phyllis Craig, Robert Flanagan, Patricia Greenfield, James E. Howell, Cynthia Lloyd, Philip Robins, and Warren Sanderson. None of these persons, of course, bears any responsibility for the analysis contained herein.

final part of the paper examines the issues of "optimum" product, and the organization and financing of a child care system.

Supply, Cost, and Demand

A child care or day care center may be defined as any facility open full-day (but not necessarily twenty-four hours per day), year-round, which cares for groups of seven or more children up to the age of 14 outside of their own home, for pay. Nursery schools and other schools which are open only part-day and part-year are not part of the child care center network. Care inside the child's own home by a relative, a nurse, or a housekeeper and care outside the home by a relative is also excluded from the child care center network; this type of care will be referred to, loosely, as informal care. Foster homes are completely disregarded in our discussion. However, private homes which care for no more than six children for a fee may be viewed as a particular type of child care center. These homes are usually called family day care homes. Family day care homes and child care centers are referred to here as formal extrafamily child care.

Much of what we know about the child care industry comes from the Westinghouse Day Care Survey, carried out in 1970 by the Westinghouse Learning Corporation and Westat Research, Inc., for the Office of Economic Opportunity.[9] The Westinghouse study surveyed three samples: an area sample, which is a nationwide general population survey of families with annual incomes of less than $8,000 and at least one child aged 9 or under; a sample of formal child care facilities; and a user sample, which is a survey of families of children enrolled in the sample of formal child care facilities.

A second major source of information on child care comes from the Keyserling Study (also known as the National Council of Jewish Women Study).[10] The sample for this study was not scientifically drawn. Rather, members of local chapters of the National Council of Jewish Women simply went out into their communities and surveyed parents and care-givers. While this study is subject to all of the usual reservations regarding nonrandom samples, the large number of cases studied and the wealth of descriptive material provided make this a valuable source of child care information.

Supply

The supply issue may best be put into perspective by noting that the vast majority of preschool children of working mothers are *not* cared for in either family day care homes or child care centers. A 1965 study of the child care arrangements of working mothers found that 48 percent of preschoolers were cared for in their own homes—14 percent by their fathers, about 18 percent by another relative, approximately 15 percent by a nonrelative and about 1 percent by their own mothers who worked only during childs' school hours. About 31 percent were cared for in someone else's home—15 percent by a relative and 16 percent by a nonrelative (i.e., in a family day care home). Only about 5 percent were cared for in a child care center.[11] The 1970 Westinghouse study, looking at families with annual incomes of less than $8,000 a year, found basically the same patterns. Fifty percent of preschoolers were cared for in their own homes; 34.5 percent in someone else's home—15.5 percent by a relative and 19 percent by a nonrelative. 10.5 percent were cared for in child care centers.[12] Both the 1965 and 1970 studies found only about 5 to 6 percent of the school-age children of working mothers in formal child care arrangements. The vast majority of these children received after-school care in their own homes (66 percent for the 1965 study, 80 percent for the 1970 study).

The Westinghouse survey of child care facilities estimated that for the country as a whole, about 575,000 children received full-day care in about 17,500 centers. Sixty percent of these centers were proprietary (i.e., they sought to make a profit), and they cared for about one-half of the children enrolled in centers.[13] About 90 percent of all centers were licensed. The Keyserling study, using HEW data, estimated that in 1970, 625,000 children were cared for in centers; however, many of these were cared for only part-day.[14] Family day care homes provided the remainder of child care slots, but the number of such slots was uncertain, since less than 2 percent of the estimated 450,000 homes were licensed.[15] Westinghouse judged that family day care homes provided full-time care for 695,000 children in 1970,[16] while the Keyserling study calculated that 2 million children were cared for either full- or part-day in such homes.[17] A 1973 Women's Bureau publication [18] reported that, according to several surveys made in the late 1960s and early 1970s, several companies,[19] hospitals,[20] unions, federal agencies, and federal employee organizations operated child care centers. On the whole, however, the number of children served by these innovative centers was very small.

Cost

Studies "by the experts" indicate that extrafamily child care is expensive. We have cost figures from three sources for the 1968–71 period: a joint study by the Children's Bureau and the Day Care and Child Development Council of America (CB–DCCDC), a study by Abt Associates of Cambridge, Massachusetts, and a budget proposed by the National Capital Area Day Care Association.[21] We also have some 1972 cost estimates prepared by Donald Ogilvie for the Inner City Fund.[22]

The 1968–71 studies place the annual cost per child in a "desirable" day care program, eight and one-half hours per day, five days per week, 250 days per year (fifty-two weeks less ten holidays) at $2,300 to $2,400. (The cost of "desirable" care for 6-to-14-year-olds before and after school and during the summer is estimated by CB–DCCDC at $653 per year per child.) "Desirable" day care was defined by CB–DCCDC as "including the full range of general and specialized developmental activities suitable to *individualized* development." [23] The Abt Study budgets provide for quality, developmental care with a teacher–child ratio of 1:5. The National Capital Area Day Care Association teacher–child ratio is 1:6. "Minimum-quality" (custodial) and "acceptable-quality" day care can be obtained for less, with minimum-quality care costing about $1,300 and acceptable-quality care about $1,900 per year per child under six in 1968.[24] Almost all of the difference in cost between the three types of care is attributable to differences in teacher–child ratio.[25] The cost per child of acceptable or desirable care in family day care homes is not, contrary to what one might expect, any less expensive than the cost per child for such care in ordinary child care centers. This is because the cost for care in family day care homes is based on a very high 1:4 adult–child ratio (1:5 for minimum-quality care), and because the budgeted wage rates are the same for family day care mothers and classroom nonprofessionals.

Why is child care so expensive? In particular, why is it so much more costly than per pupil expenditures by school districts, which averaged $783 a year in 1970? [26] First, the child care centers discussed above have very high teacher–child ratios,[27] and since about 80 percent of child care center budgets are for personnel, high ratios lead to high costs. In most public schools the teacher–child ratios are 1:25 or 1:30. A recent study of San Francisco Bay Area nursery schools found staff–child ratios of 1:10.[28]

Second, in the studies quoted, figures for child care centers (and family day care homes) include the cost of medical and dental care, meals and snacks, clothing and emergency needs, parent activities and counseling, the employment of a social service professional, and training—items often not included in school district budgets. I have calculated that about $400 per year per child is devoted to these items in the CB-DCCDC budgets. Finally, child care centers operate for three or four hours more per day and for 80 days more per year than do traditional public school systems.

A recent effort by Donald Ogilvie of the Inner City Fund to calculate child care costs provides figures for annual cost per child that are lower than the earlier estimates. These new estimates are based on staff–child ratios of slightly less than 1:7 for children between the ages of 3 and 4½ and slightly less than 1:10 for children aged 4½ to 6.[29] These new estimates also omit or decrease expenditures for transportation, medical and dental services, parent activities and counseling, the employment of a social service professional, clothing and other emergency items, special resource personnel, and staff training and equipment.[30] They are, then, obviously "bare-bones" estimates; they amount to $1,554 per year per child for children aged 3 to 4½ and $1,311 per year per child for children aged 4½ to 6.[31]

Yet the amount which parents actually spend on formal extrafamily child care is even lower than the Ogilvie estimates. The Keyserling study found that the average annual fee in proprietary centers was about $960 per child, in family day care homes about $860 per child.[32] Using Westinghouse data, William R. Prosser has recently calculated that family day care mothers receive average payments of about 60¢ per hour, 45 hours per week ($1,404 per year based on a 52-week year) for caring for *two or three* children.[33] Most parents are not purchasing the kind of care envisioned in the "expert's" estimates.[34] For example, the CB–DCCDC study budgets $6,600 per year for a classroom professional. But the Westinghouse study indicates that most directors and teachers have neither college degrees nor special training for child care work, and it reports that the median annual salary for directors and teachers is about $5,300.[35]

Which of the figures presented is the "appropriate" one to use in determining child care costs depends to some extent on the level of quality one wishes to provide and on one's estimate of what particular levels of quality require. Because staff costs are such an important component of child care cost, the desired staff–child ratio is a crucial determinant of total cost. The level of education (and hence the salary) of the staff is also a primary cost determinant. The system presented in the third part of this paper attempts to economize on these two elements of cost without compromising quality.

Clearly, before a single cost figure is accepted as appropriate, more research is required on the level of "quality" required to produce certain developmental benefits and on the effect on quality of different staffing patterns. At present we have to be content with cost ranges. If we include imputed costs for all resources used in child care as well as costs of actual expenditures, the annual cost of child care per child appears to lie somewhere between $1,300 and $2,400 depending on the type of care provided.

In concluding our discussion of costs, it should be noted that many parents are already being subsidized for child care services—some directly, some indirectly. As Westinghouse points out, in 1970 only 22 percent of the revenue of nonproprietary centers came from parents.[36] Federal, state, and local funds and donations of buildings and services by community groups have all been used to subsidize child care services.

Demand

Actual and potential users of formal day care come from the following different constituencies: first, children under the age of 6 with working mothers (5.6 million in March 1972); second, working mothers' children between the ages of 6 and 14 (18 million in 1971),[37] who might use after-school and/or vacation care; third, children under the age of 6, whose families are "in poverty" and whose mothers are not employed (2.5 million in 1971),[38] who might use part-time care in order to derive educational or developmental benefits; fourth, children whose mothers are ill or handicapped or in school; and fifth, children of mothers not now in the labor force, whose mothers might be induced to work if "appropriate" child care existed.[39]

Cataloging potential users of formal child care services is, of course, quite different from determining the demand for these services. The demand for extrafamily child care is extremely difficult to ascertain, in large part because the "product" varies so greatly from place to place and because the perception of "product" varies so greatly from mind to mind. But, given any particular product specification, including quality, location, hours of service, and degree of parental control of program, the demand for slots or hours of care may be expected to depend on the following: number and age of children, family income and wealth, market wage or potential market wage of mother, "taste" (including, among other things, mother's commitment to employment, behavior of friends, and perceived desirability of preschool education), and, of course, price.

We have insufficient data to draw a definitive demand curve for formal child care. But we do have several pieces of information which help somewhat to improve our understanding of the demand side of the child care market. When Westinghouse asked working mothers with family incomes under $8,000 per year what they would be willing to pay for the child care arrangements of their choice, 16 percent indicated that they could pay nothing. Of those who could pay something toward child care, $520 was the median annual fee which working mothers said they were willing to pay for the kind of child care they desired.[40] Mary Rowe's study, which includes higher-income families, suggests that less than 5 percent of families would pay more than about $1,000 per year per child for child care services.[41] Given the cost figures discussed earlier (those found in the Keyserling study as well as those estimated by the "experts"), it is clear that most families find it impossible to translate their desire for child care services into effective demand for those services. As one might expect, a certain amount of dissatisfaction results.

Responses to survey questions probing satisfaction with existing child care arrangements indicate that when children of all ages are considered together, families appear satisfied with their child care arrangements. But when preschool children only are considered, the level of satisfaction decreases. In the Westinghouse area survey, 63 percent of working mothers reported that they desired a change in the child care arrangements for their preschool children, and of those who desired a change, 60 percent wished to move to formal day care.[42] In addition, the Westinghouse survey indicates that, overall, the level of satisfaction with child care arrangements is positively related to their cost.[43] The Keyserling study describes parents' dissatisfaction with informal care arrangements requiring parents to work different shifts, or older siblings to care for younger siblings, or children to care for themselves. It is also true that parents are sometimes dissatisfied with formal care. Keyserling discusses instances in which mothers fear child abuse as a result of their day care arrangements. And many parents are dissatisfied with center hours (very few centers operate during evening or nighttime hours), center locations, and the absence of sick care in formal programs.

Dissatisfaction also results from the inability of some mothers to work as a result of the absence of "affordable," reliable child care. However, the question of how many mothers might begin to work if affordable child care became available remains unanswered. Westinghouse found an estimated 124,000 children on center waiting lists—about 16 percent of total enrollment.[44] Some of the children on these lists are undoubtedly those of nonworking mothers who are waiting for a child care opening before seeking work. When center operators were asked by Westinghouse about the need for child care in their communities, 45 percent saw a need for care on the part of working mothers and, significantly, 34 percent perceived additional needs on the part of nonworking mothers.[45] However, when nonworking mothers themselves are asked about the importance of child care as an impediment to their working, interpretation of their answers is difficult, mostly because some women who say they are out of the labor force for child care–related reasons may also be out because of their preference to remain at home. In the Westinghouse survey, day care problems constituted 18 percent of the reasons given for not working.[46] A high percentage of AFDC mothers indicated that child care was a barrier to work. For example, a six-state study done in 1969 reported that 52 to 63 percent of nonemployed AFDC women indicated that they would like to work in a steady job provided adequate child care were available.[47] But, of course, for most of these women inadequate child care is only one of many job-related problems. Low levels of education would undoubtedly make it difficult for many of these women to obtain jobs even if adequate child care became available.[48]

In summary, the intersection of supply and demand in the formal child care market leaves many families unable to satisfy their desire to purchase formal child care. Is this something about which we should worry? It is true, for example, that the demand and supply curves for Cadillacs intersect at a price too high for most families to afford Cadillacs. We don't worry about that; we don't talk about a shortage of Cadillacs. Is there a shortage of formal child care? Strictly speaking, there can never be a shortage if supply and demand are equated. Shortages, defined precisely, can occur only if price is held down artificially, or if price has not yet had time to rise sufficiently to equate supply and demand. Nevertheless, when a good is deemed "important" or "necessary" (as, for example, food, fuel in winter, medical care, education) and when the price of that food is so high that many people are unable to purchase it, we do speak of "shortages," and we speak of them with concern, regardless of whether or not price is being held down artificially.

I believe we should be concerned about the inability of most families to purchase formal child care. And I believe that this concern should be translated into partial government subsidization of formal child care services. Private industry, in the absence of subsidization, is unable to remedy the current "shortage" of child care slots. By and large, private companies cannot profitably run centers of reasonable quality if they charge the prices which most demanders of child care services are willing to pay. At one time there was considerable interest among private companies in running child care centers for profit; that bubble of interest has now burst.[49]

If we are to provide child care services for those who cannot afford them at current prices, increased government subsidies will be required.

The Case for Subsidization of Child Care Centers

There are two major arguments for subsidization—the equity argument and the externality argument. Primary reliance is placed here on externalities. However, the reader is warned that it is virtually impossible to quantify the external benefits in order to weight them against subsidization costs. So in the end, one's decision on the merits of subsidization depends to some degree on one's subjective estimate of the importance of the particular externalities.

Equity

Direct benefits from subsidization accrue to three groups—children of eligible mothers, the mothers themselves, and potential employees of child care systems. All other things being equal, the lower the family income and the greater the number of young children, the higher the subsidy (and hence the direct benefits) should be to eligible families. The equity argument is that a redistribution of income and services in favor of these groups ought to take place because these groups have been "wronged" in the past and/or because they are not as well-off as other groups in the nation.

That children have been "wronged" in the past is not difficult to document. We are supposedly a youth-oriented culture, but in terms of programs for nutrition, health, or education, our record of public interest in or expenditures on very young children has been poor. For example, while only 10 percent of American states provide universal kindergarten, Israel, with a per-capita gross national product only slightly more than one-third of ours in 1969, provides kindergarten for all five-year-olds.[50]

As for mothers or women in general, it is clear that they have not been afforded equal opportunity or treatment—in education, in jobs, or under the law. The perpetrators of the discrimination are not particular educators or employers but rather the society as a whole. A system of quality child care, it is argued, will move toward giving women equality in the working world.

With regard to teachers, it is contended that through no fault of their own, but rather as a result of a falling birthrate, an oversupply of people (mainly women) are trained for elementary-school teaching. These people, many of whom are unable to utilize their training in the current job market, would benefit from the new job opportunities created by an extensive system of child care centers. The benefits to society of utilizing these teachers' training are, of course, also considerable.

External Benefits

A positive externality arises when, as a by-product of some firm's or individual's activity, another firm's or individual's production or utility is increased.[51] Stated as simply as possible, the externality argument is that where externalities exist (i.e., where private benefits are less than social benefits), private production is likely to be less than socially optimal; government should therefore "encourage" increased output until marginal social cost is equal to marginal social benefit. There are at least five external benefits associated with expenditures on child care centers, and each will be discussed in turn.

Education clearly produces externalities, and the first, and probably least controversial, argument in favor of government subsidization is that part of what is being proposed in quality child care is education. Recent studies have reported that increases in achievement or I.Q. scores as a result of preschool education tend to fade as children grow older.[52] It is probably unavoidable that I.Q. and achievement scores have been the measures chosen to assess preschool effectiveness; these aspects of learning are the easiest to quantify. But there are many other educational benefits from a good preschool experience; specifically, the early detection of mental and physical difficulties, the introduction of alternative forms of information and a wider scope of experiences, and the early opportunity for the child to enhance his or her self-confidence and self-esteem. Undoubtedly, I.Q. tests and achievement scores fail to reflect many of these preschool educational benefits. Moreover, the fact is that I.Q. and achievement scores *do* rise as a result of good preschool experience. That these scores tend to drop back after exposure to our "regular" school system should perhaps lead not to decreased investment in preschool education but rather to improved education for school-age children.

The second external benefit of expenditures on child care centers is long-range and likely to affect young women and girls. As a visible system of high-quality extrafamily child care develops, it will become possible for many young women to consider a new option: market work as a permanent feature of their adult lives. These women will then be able to make realistic human capital investments in themselves. This type of external benefit is, in Meade's terminology, due to "creation of atmosphere"—the fact that one group's activity may provide an atmosphere favorable to the activities of another. The example Meade uses concerns the favorable atmosphere created for the production of wheat in a particular district when the production of timber (afforestation) increases local rainfall.[53]

It is already true that work is a substantial part of women's lives, but because the childrearing years frequently require an interruption of market work, work horizons are often short and educational investments designed to maximize the return from work are substantially below what they might be.[54] This is not to say that all women would wish to utilize extrafamily child care. And surely we should take care not to put pressures,[55] subtle or explicit, on women to commit themselves to market work during their childrearing years. Our national social welfare function, at least at the present time, still has a place for women who wish to pursue full-time childrearing.[56] It is the option to do otherwise (to prepare for and engage in permanent market work) which is important. And it is through making this option possible for large numbers of women that extrafamily child care provides an external benefit. It is, of course, also true that increased educational investment by some women not only would benefit the women involved, but would also allow society to employ its human resources more efficiently.

A third external benefit of extrafamily child care would accrue to teenagers. An "optimum" system of child care centers (see the third part of this paper) would make provision for teenagers to obtain child care training in centers through formal coursework arrangements with high schools. Such training would clearly be helpful to teenagers in their later roles as parents, and possibly also in their vocational-choice process. Obviously, not only the teenagers but society as a whole would benefit from their training. In addition, the opportunity to volunteer in a child care center might well provide teenagers with a sense of usefulness—a sense which many teenagers today claim they lack.

Employers constitute a fourth group of external-benefit recipients. By and large, employers have sought to "protect themselves" from presumed high rates of turnover and high absentee rates on the part of women by paying women lower wages, and keeping them in the kinds of jobs usually performed by women (which typically require little in the way of employer-financed on-the-job training). With regard to turnover, more research is clearly required, but it appears that separation rates for men and women of similar age and skill, employed on similar jobs, are about the same.[57] And in at least one recent California study, separation rates for men and women were found to be similar even when age and occupation were not held constant.[58] So employer efforts to "protect themselves" from higher turnover by women may well have been unjustified.

Indeed, it may be that by keeping women in low-level jobs at low pay, employers have increased female turnover beyond what it otherwise might have been. With regard to absenteeism, however, there does seem to be some evidence that women with children tend to have more absences than women without children.[59]

Employers are being required by law both to pay men and women equal pay for equal work *and* to open up heretofore virtually all-male jobs to women. The financial penalties for noncompliance are becoming considerable. Given these legal requirements (and the inability therefore, legally, to "discount" higher absentee rates for women with children), employers will benefit from a child care program—and in particular from a program which provides care for sick children.

It is sometimes alleged that if child care centers increase the supply of labor, employers will also benefit by being able to lower wages. Questions regarding the effects of increases in labor supply on wages and employment need considerably more attention. In order to determine which employers might benefit (and which workers might be harmed), one would have to specify the supply price of the new entrants, their quality, the kinds of jobs they seek, and the degree of competition in each labor market.[60] However, far more important, and usually overlooked by those who fear increased labor force participation by women, is the demand side of the picture. The child care system will, itself, generate jobs; and the increased demand for goods and services associated with an increase in the labor force participation of mothers is also likely to be job-creating. It is not at all certain, therefore, that employers would lower wages or lay off existing personnel in the face of an increase in labor supply.

Assuming that the availability of extrafamily child care increases the educational level and/or the labor force participation of mothers, it is likely that a fifth external benefit will develop. In the long run, the existence of child care centers will probably result in further declines in the birthrate—thus increasing utility for all who find themselves already too crowded or who fear crowding in the future. Let us review the circumstances under which such an external benefit would evolve.

As noted earlier, the option to work in the market without interruption may well induce girls (and women) to invest more heavily in themselves. And increases in educational investment would probably decrease fertility by changing tastes in at least two ways[61]—by changing the quantity-quality trade-off for children and by encouraging labor force participation. In addition, increases in labor force participation, even in the absence of increases in educational attainment, would probably have antinatal effects. A note on the use of the term ''quality of children'' is appropriate here. It is probably impossible to measure objectively the quality of a human being, and it is certainly impossible to do so from afar. ''Quality,'' as used here, refers simply to the quantity of inputs (time, money, education, etc.) received by the child.

It is, of course, true that subsidizing child care would lower the price (in both money and time) of raising children and that the substitution effect of this price change would be negative (i.e., a fall in price would result in an increase in the purchase of child care services). In addition, unless child services were an inferior good, the income effect of the price change would also operate toward increasing the quantity purchased. But purchasing more child services as a result of the subsidization of child care centers does not by any means imply increasing the number of children born. Total child care services is determined not only by number of children but also by quality of children.

A negative relationship between quality and number of children is frequently observed. Gary Becker and H. Gregg Lewis have shown recently that, assuming parents desire an equal quality level for all their children, a negative correlation between quantity and quality will exist in consumption even if, in the household's utility or production functions, quality and quantity are no more closely related than any two commodities chosen at random.[62] In other words, there is a quantity–quality trade-off. Investment in children can be ''widening'' or ''deepening.'' And there is evidence that higher educational attainment results in a preference for ''deepening'' investment.

In a recent article on child quality and the demand for children, Dennis De Tray, like many before him, found a significant negative relationship between level of female education and number of children born.[63] Unlike others, De Tray attempted to remove opportunity cost effects from this correlation. De Tray has shown that even with such effects removed, a significant correlation between the variables remains. In addition, he has shown that quality per child (though admittedly measured rather crudely as expected public-school investment per child) is positively related to female education. The hypothesis that more highly educated women become more efficient at the production of quality and thereby reduce the quantity of children they produce thus finds some support in De Tray's work.

Arleen Leibowitz, using household activity data, has also shown that there is a positive relationship between a woman's level of education and quality of children.[64] The quality measure in this case is number of hours spent on care of children (both total time spent and time spent per child). In families where the mother's educational level is relatively high (twelfth grade or better), mothers, fathers and also "other helpers" spend more time with children (and per child) than in families where mother's educational level is relatively low.

The second effect of education—an increase in labor force participation—will also tend to decrease women's taste for number of children. Increases in education are likely to increase labor force participation for several reasons. First, education increases the opportunity cost of a woman's time (by increasing her potential market wage rate). Second, a greater initial stock of human capital increases the cost of depreciating that capital by withdrawing from the labor market. Third, a greater initial stock of human capital, when combined with new legal requirements, may induce employers to provide additional on-the-job training for women, thus further increasing the opportunity cost of women's time. Finally, education may increase women's desire for certain of the psychological satisfactions associated with market work.

But even if the existence of child care centers does *not* encourage substantial increases in women's educational attainment, it will encourage increases in women's labor force participation rate.[65] And greater labor force participation, per se, would probably be antinatal.

We know that there is a negative relationship between wife's labor force participation and the number of children she bears.[66] We also know that increases in women's earnings are negatively related to number of children-ever-born.[67] (Even in the absence of increased educational attainment, increases in women's earnings can result from increased labor force experience through the effect of job experience on earnings.) Increased earnings certainly make it easier for a woman to have more children (for example, by allowing her to employ household help). But while De Tray found a weak *positive* relationship between an increase in *male* earnings and children-ever-born,[68] it is important to note the strong *negative* relationship between an increase in *female* earnings and fertility.

Of course, we do not know the direction of causality in these relationships. However, it seems plausible that women who are committed to labor force participation are more likely to become less efficient at the rearing of children and to develop tastes for "satisfactions" other than children. Or, as Glen Cain has put it, some women may, after working, become addicted to market goods.[69] Finally, given a particular level of child quality desired, and assuming that most women regard a certain amount of their *own* time as an essential, unsubstitutable, input in the quality-production function, the fewer hours a woman personally has available for child care (due to market work), the less likely she probably will be to dilute her quality input by having additional children.

To summarize, it is of course true that, all other things being equal, a child-care-center subsidy will increase the purchase of child care services. But all other things are not equal, because in the long run such a subsidy also changes tastes—for education and for labor force participation. And increases in educational level and/or labor force participation decrease the taste for children (assuming a taste for at least one child existed to begin with), while increases in educational level also change the composition of child care services purchased (toward quality and away from quantity). It is true that the amount of child care services purchased would be smaller if education and labor force participation increased without a child care subsidy. But such a situation is probably unattainable, for it is likely that the centers are required in the first place if we are to have further substantial increases in education and labor force aspirations. On balance, the taste changes described will almost surely outweigh the pure price effects of the subsidy.

"Optimum" Product and Issues
in Organization and Financing of Child Care

In the first two sections of the paper, we have, in several places, alluded to questions of "optimum" product and to questions of organization and financing of child care systems. It is now time to examine each of these topics in some detail.

"Optimum" Product

There are, it would appear, at least three criteria for optimality in the design of the child care product. First, given a particular price, the product should conform as much as possible to parents' desires. Second, given a particular level of desired quality, this level should be achieved at a minimum cost. And third, given price and quality, external benefits should be maximized. The system described below, I believe, meets these criteria.

I would envision an "optimum" system as a three-tier community system. The nucleus of the program would be a core child care center which would function very much the way nursery schools function for the children of nonworking mothers. The core center could accommodate 25, 75, or more children, depending on the community need, and would provide the major "educational" component of the system. Surrounding the core center would be a network of family day care homes run by what I shall call "community parents"—mothers and/or fathers who take care of children for part of the day. These community parents would be closely associated with the core center. They would receive training there,[70] work there several hours each week, and have a supervisor from the center come to their homes to provide frequent assistance and evaluation. Association with a child care center would, it is hoped, greatly improve the quality of family day care homes. Moreover, community parents would have an opportunity to embark upon new careers—with training, prestige, colleagues, and the possibility of further upward mobility.

Very young children (less than one year or eighteen months) and older children unable to adapt to two child care environments would probably spend all of the time away from their own parents at the home of a community parent. Other older preschoolers would spend several hours per day in the core center in a preschool education program, and the remainder of the time away from their own parents with a community parent. Disadvantaged children of nonworking mothers would utilize the educational program of the core center for several hours each day and then spend the remainder of the day with one of their own parents. This type of product would be in accordance with many parents' desire to have their children cared for in private homes[71] and would raise the quality of care in such homes, but would also provide the benefits of preschool education to children of working mothers. Napping, for younger children, could take place in a private home, and, parents who dislike institutional napping will, of course, prefer this arrangement. Lunch, too, could take place at the community parent's home, although, in some low-income areas, centers might wish to provide lunch in order to pay particularly close attention to their children's nutrition.

Parents might well take their children to the center in the morning but call for them at the community parent's home in the afternoon or evening, or vice versa. Transportation between the center and the private home might be minimal, as in large cities, where the core center and private homes might be in the same building. Or transportation might be provided by the community parents or the center. The cost of such transportation would seem worthwhile; the turnover among community parents is likely to be less than the turnover among professional center personnel whose services have a wider market, and the stability of relationship with the community parent might well be beneficial for the children. Moreover, transportation costs could easily be covered by savings in personnel costs as a result of a "mixed" system, since each child would make less intensive use of the high-cost services of professionals at the core center. In addition, if children did not stay all day at a child care center, the staff–child ratios at the center could probably be lower than those now mandated. Presumably we could utilize nursery-school-type ratios (1:7 or 1:10) in the core center if some of the personal attention required by children came from the community parent setting, where the adult–child ratio would be quite high (e.g., 1:4), and where perhaps not all of the children would be preschoolers. Additional savings could also be effected if child care centers did not have to be equipped with nap rooms, kitchens, and cooks.

The location of child care centers in the community has important consequences.[72] Studies show that parents want child care near their own homes.[73] It is difficult for parents to travel long distances with young children, particularly in cold weather or in early or late hours. Moreover, nearby care makes it possible for older children to join preschoolers during vacations and after school hours.[74] Finally, local care makes it easier to enlist members of the community to volunteer their services.

For all of the reasons given earlier, teenagers should certainly be brought into the child care system. High schools (and junior high schools) should probably have formal programs which teach child development (to men as well as women), and teenagers should have an opportunity to put their training into practice, both during school time, under the supervision of their teachers, and after school, by volunteering. In some communities, where it seemed appropriate, teenagers might earn a training wage.

Senior citizens might also be utilized as volunteers, although certainly many of them might wish to be employees in the system. In conversations with child-care-center personnel I have learned that many centers find it difficult to utilize volunteer senior citizens effectively. Methods of better utilization of all volunteers should be researched and the findings well publicized, for optimum utilization will be important in lowering child care costs.

The feasibility of establishing internships at child care centers for persons in college programs of early childhood education should also be investigated. Intern (or practice teacher) programs are not only a source of low-cost (or zero-cost) labor, but also provide an ongoing supply of trained personnel.

The third tier of an optimum child care system would consist of "practical parents." [75] These would be persons trained in child care and in some practical nursing who could care for sick children while the children's parents work; they might be licensed by the states. Practical parents could also care for very young infants of working mothers in the child's own home and act as vacation or illness "substitutes" for community parents or child-care-center staff.

One reason why parents are reluctant to rely on child care centers is because such centers seldom make arrangements for the care of sick children. Parents are understandably reluctant to call upon unknown adults, whose qualifications they cannot assess, to care for their sick children. It is also obviously extremely difficult for parents to arrange for sick-child care on very short notice (e.g., an hour or so after the family awakens in the morning). If child care centers could "stand behind" practical parents, attesting to their qualifications and introducing them to parents and children prior to illness, and could also arrange for the dispatch of these persons on short notice, they would be performing a crucial service for their clients as well as for their clients' employers.

The costs of practical parents' services to sick children could be paid on a fee-for-service basis, or they could be pooled, with each family paying, in effect, an insurance premium. The two major factors determining the cost of practical parents are: (a) the wage rate for such persons and (b) the frequency of illness among groups of children. The wage rate could be fairly easily determined. However, until some research is done regarding frequency and duration of illness among groups of preschool children,[76] or until we begin operating practical parent programs which impute costs to all resources used, the cost of sick-child services will be very difficult to estimate.

One alternative to practical parents, of course, is to set up an infirmary at the core center. If such an infirmary required the effective isolation of children with different kinds of diseases, it would undoubtedly be more expensive than sending practical parents to sick children's homes. However, if transmission of most children's illness occurs before symptoms appear, it may be that children can be cared for in centers or at community parents' homes without precautions against contagion being required.[77] Clearly, the feasibility and implications of the infirmary model merit further investigation.

Financing

While I believe there is a case for government subsidization of child care, based on the equity and externality arguments, I also believe that since the direct benefits of child care are substantial, parents should pay for a portion of the service wherever possible. Moreover, for reasons of equity, the benefits to employers should probably be appropriated through a tax. Funds for the system, therefore, should come from three sources— general revenues, parents, and a tax on employers.

General revenues (mainly federal, but possibly also state) would be required not only to support low-income children and partially support middle-income children but also to set standards and evaluate quality, to provide technical assistance and overall planning, to support training and research programs, and to furnish initial equipment and construction or renovation funds. Thus all families would receive some government subsidization.

General revenue support for low- and middle-income children can probably be most easily administered in the form of vouchers. The criteria for voucher eligibility, and in particular for the amount of the voucher, would have to be carefully worked out in order to avoid work disincentives. (This is similar to the negative-income-tax problem but even more difficult, because several vouchers may be involved in any one family.) The amount of the voucher should probably be related negatively to family income and positively to the number of hours worked by the mother and the number of preschool children in the family. An upper limit could be set on the number of children per family who could be subsidized, if that seemed desirable. A sliding-scale arrangement on the first two criteria would obviously be required, but given the demand information cited earlier, in order to satisfy desires for child care we may well be partially subsidizing care for families with incomes as high as $12,000 per year.

We should not make the mistake of subsidizing AFDC mothers only. If the sole motivation for child care centers is to reduce welfare costs by getting AFDC mothers to work, legislators may be unwilling to spend any more on child care than they currently spend on welfare. In February 1970, the average annual AFDC payment per family was $2,140.[78] If we include imputed costs for all resources used in child care as well as costs of actual expenditures, day care for two preschool children, using the figures cited earlier, is greater than that figure. Also, as noted earlier, given labor market conditions and the low educational level of most AFDC mothers, it is unlikely that merely providing child care will substantially reduce welfare dependency in the short run. The issues of child care and welfare, rather than being tied together, should be separated—especially since many AFDC children are in the "disadvantaged" group and should probably spend part of each day obtaining the educational benefits of child care centers regardless of their mother's labor force status. The only realistic relationship between child care and welfare is of a long-run nature. If potential AFDC mothers grow up knowing that they will one day utilize child care systems, they may well increase their level of education, make more appropriate vocational decisions, and thus be less likely to require AFDC.

It is also clear that providing child care systems for AFDC children only may well have some serious negative effects for young women who do *not* consider themselves potential AFDC mothers. For these women there would, of course, be no positive incentive toward improved career planning; but even worse, if child care systems came to be thought of as "for poor children only," young women who would ordinarily use these systems might become reluctant to do so.

The total governmental cost of a comprehensive child care program will, obviously, be highly sensitive to the particular income and hours formulae utilized for determining voucher eligibility. I am not prepared to say precisely what these formulae ought to be. The various alternatives and their costs require considerably more research. In particular, detailed estimates of likely utilization patterns and demand elasticities have to be worked out. Most probably, such information will have to come from pilot studies in particular communities, so that the operation of the "demonstration effect" may be observed. In addition, more information needs to be obtained regarding administrative, construction, and renovation costs.[79] Finally, it is, of course, true that program costs will vary from community to community. In communities with large numbers of disadvantaged children, child-care-center systems would probably include elements budgeted for in the studies reviewed earlier, such as additional food, medical and dental services, clothing and emergency needs, social service professionals, and expanded parent counseling. In other communities, such services might not be required. Wages, transportation costs, rent, volunteer availability, illness patterns, and infant populations can also be expected to vary by community, thus influencing total costs of particular programs. In all cases, of course, budgets should be submitted in advance and approved budgets adhered to by centers. Automatic passing on of increased costs, a problem which has so adversely affected other programs (for example, Medicare), should be avoided through a system of prior budgetary review.

The tax on employers, referred to earlier, should be designed only to appropriate employer benefits from a child care system; this tax, therefore, should fund only a small portion of the total. If we wish to encourage the utilization of womanpower, the tax should be on *all* employers, not merely on those who employ women. The particular form which the employer tax should take needs to be examined, particularly with reference to who bears the real burden of the tax.

Ownership and Control

There are several possible ways in which systems of child care centers could be organized. Senator Long, for example, has suggested the establishment of a Federal Child Care Corporation.[80] The Department of Health, Education, and Welfare, on the other hand, seems to prefer appending child care to existing school systems, thus giving primary ownership and control to state governments and local school boards.[81] I would suggest that at this early stage we might well experiment with several different forms of ownership and control.

One form, which presents some very interesting prospects, is that of a cooperative—a system owned by the parents who use it. The system might, for example, be modeled on the Group Health Cooperative of Puget Sound, in Seattle, where the individual subscribers own the cooperative, hire physicians, make policy decisions, etc. Under a parent-owned system, parents, through elected officials, would hire a director, make basic decisions as to core center program and, in general, control the environments to which they send their children. Clearly, this experiment would not take place everywhere; not all parents would be willing or able to set up cooperatives. However, there is some evidence that interest in cooperative child care centers is growing and that cooperatives are a feasible form of day care.[82] Certainly, a full analysis of this economic form ought to be encouraged.

Accompanying a system of cooperatives (or perhaps even accompanying a Federal Child Care Corporation) should be a system of local planning and evaluation boards. Ideally these boards would consist of parents, child-development specialists, pediatricians, employer representatives with management expertise, and local officials with knowledge of community resources; they could be city- or county-wide organizations. The local boards would work with state agencies on matters of licensing and inspection; setting standards in conjunction with federal regulations; assisting in locating appropriate core facilities or, if such are unavailable, in applying for capital grants from the federal government; aiding in recruiting of personnel; approving center-system budgets; working with existing community services, including local school boards; and providing for areawide child-care-center planning.

There are advantages to tying child care to existing school systems, but there are also disadvantages.[83] Before irrevocable decisions are reached, new types of educational organization, such as the one suggested here, should surely be tried, experimentally, in some areas.

Conclusions

The decision to launch an extrafamily child care system must, of course, be made in the political, not the economic, arena. For economists alone cannot make decisions balancing equities, determining priorities, or evaluating the importance of particular externalities. Economists can, however, clarify issues, thereby contributing toward a more enlightened decision-making environment. A beginning has been made here; but, needless to say, there are additional economic matters to be investigated. Many of them have already been mentioned. Others concern the manpower (and womanpower) implications of the program. It is hoped that this paper will serve to stimulate some of this additional research.

NOTES

[1] Howard Hayghe, "Labor Force Activity of Married Women," *Monthly Labor Review,* XCVI (April 1973): 33.

[2] *Ibid.,* p. 35.

[3] The rate in 1960 was 20 percent. See U.S. Department of Labor, Women's Bureau, *Handbook on Women Workers* (Washington, D.C., 1969), p. 41.

[4] *Ibid.*

[5] Anne M. Young, "Children of Working Mothers," *Monthly Labor Review,* XCVI (April 1973): 37.

[6] For projections to 1980, see U.S. Department of Labor, Women's Bureau, *Working Mothers and the Need for Child Care Services* (Washington, D.C., 1967).

[7] Two exceptions to the general lack of notice were a working paper by Richard R. Nelson and Michael Krashinsky, "Some Questions of Optimal Economic Organization: The Case of Day Care for Children," prepared for The Urban Institute, December 1971; and a paper by Mary P. Rowe, "Economics of Child Care," in U.S. Congress, Senate, Committee on Finance, *Child Care: Hearings on S. 2003, Child Care Provisions of H.R. 1, and Title VI of Printed Amendment 318 to H.R. 1,* 92d Cong., 1st Sess., September 22, 23, and 24, 1971, pp. 235–313.

[8] See, in particular, Alice M. Rivlin, "Child Care," in Charles L. Schultze et al., *Setting National Priorities: The 1973 Budget* (Washington, D.C., 1972), pp. 252–90; a working paper by Philip Robins, "The Demand for Child Care by DIME Families," prepared for Stanford Research Institute, May 1973; papers by Vivian Lewis, "Day Care: Needs, Costs, Benefits, Alternatives," pp. 102–65, and Michael Brashinsky, "Day Care and Welfare," pp. 166–220 in U.S. Congress, *Studies in Public Welfare, Paper No. 7: Issues in the Coordination of Public Welfare Programs,* prepared for the use of the Subcommittee on Fiscal Policy of the Joint Economic Committee, 93d Cong., 1st Sess., July 1973; and Mary P. Rowe and Ralph D. Husby, "Economics of Child Care: Costs, Needs and Issues," in Pamela Roby, ed., *Child Care: Who Cares?* (New York, 1973), pp. 98–122.

[9] Westinghouse Learning Corporation and Westat Research, Inc., *Day Care*

Survey, 1970: Summary Report and Basic Analysis, prepared for Evaluation Division, Office of Economic Opportunity (Washington, D.C., 1971).

[10] Mary D. Keyserling, *Windows on Day Care* (New York, 1972), p. 3.

[11] The remaining 16 percent received "no special care," defined as: child looked after self, mother looked after child while working, and other. Seth Low and Pearl G. Spindler, *Child Care Arrangements of Working Mothers in the United States* (Washington, D.C., 1968), pp. 71–72.

[12] The remaining 5 percent received "no special care." Westinghouse and Westat, *Day Care Survey,* pp. 175, 178–80.

[13] *Ibid.,* p. vii.

[14] Keyserling, *Windows,* p. 3.

[15] Westinghouse and Westat, *Day Care Survey,* p. vii.

[16] *Ibid.,* p. vi.

[17] Keyserling, *Windows,* p. 5.

[18] U.S. Department of Labor, Employment Standards Administration, Women's Bureau, *Day Care Facts* Pamphlet 16 (Rev.), (Washington, D.C., 1973), pp. 7–12.

[19] U.S. Department of Labor, Workplace Standards Administration, Women's Bureau, *Day Care Services: Industry's Involvement* (Washington, D.C., 1971), pp. 11–12.

[20] U.S. Department of Labor, Wage and Labor Standards Administration, Women's Bureau, *Child Care Services Provided by Hospitals* (Washington, D.C., 1971), p. 7.

[21] See U.S. Department of Health, Education and Welfare, Children's Bureau, and Day Care and Child Development Council of America (CB–DCCDC), "Standards and Costs for Day Care" (unpublished study, Washington, D.C., 1968), as quoted in Rowe, "Economics of Child Care," p. 280; Abt Associates, Inc., *A Study in Child Care, 1970–71* (Cambridge, Mass., 1971); and budget of National Capital Area Day Care Association, Inc. (Washington, D.C., August 1968), cited in Gilbert Y. Steiner, *The State of Welfare* (Washington, D.C., 1971).

[22] Donald G. Ogilvie, "Estimated Costs of the Federal Day Care Requirements" (Washington, D.C., 1973), as quoted in Lewis, "Day Care."

[23] CB–DCCDC, "Standards and Costs," as quoted in Rowe, "Economics of Child Care," p. 280. (Italics in original)

[24] *Ibid.* "Minimum quality" denotes "the level essential to maintain the health and safety of the child, but with relatively little attention to his developmental needs." "Acceptable quality" means providing "a basic program of developmental activities as well as providing minimum custodial care."

[25] There appear to be some minor economies of scale in operating centers caring for 50 or 75 children as opposed to those with 25 children. The cost of "desirable" care drops from $2,349 per child in a 25-child center to $2,223 in a 50-child center to $2,189 in a 75-child center. The services of administrative and nonteaching personnel are used more efficiently in the larger centers. See Rowe, "Economics of Child Care," p. 287.

[26] U.S. Department of Health, Education and Welfare, Office of Education, National Center for Educational Statistics, *Digest of Educational Statistics, 1970* (Washington, D.C., 1970), Table 77, p. 58.

[27] The Federal Interagency Day Care Requirements, which center programs must meet if they are receiving federal funds, until recently mandated a 1:5 ratio for 3-to-4-year-olds, a 1:7 ratio for 4-to-6-year-olds, and a 1:10 ratio for summer or after-school care for 6-to-14-year olds. See "Federal Interagency Day Care Requirements," in U.S. Congress, Senate, Committee on Finance, *Child Care Data and Materials,* 92d Cong. 1st sess., June 1971, p. 149.

[28] See Henry M. Levin, *Survey of Day Care and Preschool Operations in San Francisco, San Mateo, Santa Clara, and Alameda Counties* (unpublished study, Stanford University, School of Education, November 1971).

[29] Ogilvie, "Estimated Costs" as quoted in Lewis, "Day Care," p. 129.

[30] *Ibid.,* p. 123.

[31] *Ibid.,* p. 120.

[32] Keyserling, *Windows,* pp. 3, 142.

[33] William R. Prosser, "Day Care In The Seventies: Some Thoughts," Office of Economic Opportunity (unpublished working paper, Washington, D.C.), p. 6, as quoted in Lewis, "Day Care," p. 129.

[34] For example, at the prices which families paid for child care in the Keyserling sample they were not obtaining very good care. Council members rated 11 percent of family day care homes, 50 percent of proprietary centers, and 10 percent of nonprofit centers as "poor," i.e., as not even meeting children's basic physical needs. Fifty percent of day care homes, 35 percent of proprietary centers, and 50 percent of nonprofit centers were rated as "fair," i.e., as meeting basic physical needs but providing very little, if any, developmental services. See Keyserling, *Windows,* p. 5.

[35] Westinghouse and Westat, *Day Care Survey,* p. ix.

[36] *Ibid.,* p. 204.

[37] Rivlin, "Child Care," p. 260.

[38] Keyserling, *Windows,* p. 2.

[39] In addition, there are some who believe that *all* children ought to be counted as potential child care users. This view is based on the belief that universal child care availability is required in order that women may develop as individuals in addition to being mothers. For an excellent defense of this position, see Constantina Safilios–Rothschild, "Parents' Need for Child Care," in Roby, ed., *Child Care,* pp. 37–45.

[40] Westinghouse and Westat, *Day Care Survey,* p. 206.

[41] Rowe, "Economics of Child Care," p. 270.

[42] Westinghouse and Westat, *Day Care Survey,* p. 163.

[43] *Ibid.,* pp. 126, 199.

[44] *Ibid.,* p. 25. However, there were also 63,000 unfilled spaces available, indicating that "type of product," including location, is important to potential users.

[45] *Ibid.*, p. 203.

[46] *Ibid.*, p. xvi. I am indebted to Lewis for this interpretation of the Westinghouse figure.

[47] Betty Burnside, "The Employment Potential of AFDC Mothers in Six States," *Welfare in Review* (July/August 1971): 18. The states included were California, Maine, Maryland, Minnesota, New York, and Oklahoma.

[48] For a discussion of the way in which education affects employability of AFDC women, see Perry Levinson, "How Employable Are AFDC Women?" *Welfare in Review* VIII (July/August 1970): 12–16.

[49] For a discussion of the difficulties which proprietary operators encounter, see Joann S. Lublin, "Growing Pains," *Wall Street Journal,* November 27, 1972; and "Where Day Care Helps to Sell Apartments," *Business Week,* September 30, 1972, pp. 60–61.

[50] See Pamela Roby, "What Other Nations Are Doing," in Roby, ed., *Child Care,* p. 299.

[51] For a review of the externality concept, see E. J. Mishan, "The Postwar Literature on Externalities: An Interpretive Essay," *Journal of Economic Literature,* IX (March 1971): 2.

[52] For some evidence regarding fading, see Thomas I. Ribich, *Education and Poverty* (Washington, D.C., 1968), pp. 78–82.

[53] James E. Meade, "External Economies and Diseconomies in a Competitive Situation," *The Economic Journal,* LXII (March 1952): 61.

[54] For example, although the number of women and men graduating from high school is about the same, with slightly more women graduating than men, women in 1967 accounted for only 40 percent of the college and university enrollment, 40 percent of the bachelor's or first professional degrees earned, 35 percent of the master's degrees earned, and only 12 percent of the doctor's degrees earned. See *Handbook on Women Workers,* pp. 187–91. It is assumed here that lower levels of educational investment for women do *not* stem from lesser abilities of women.

[55] It is, of course, true that if subsidizing child care raises tax rates, some pressure is put on women to work in order to maintain a particular level of disposable income.

[56] It would appear that with regard to welfare mothers our social welfare function may be changing. I would argue on equity grounds that all women should be treated equally and that the option to pursue full-time childrearing should be open to all—including welfare mothers.

[57] See U.S. Department of Labor, Wage and Labor Standards Administration, Women's Bureau, *Facts About Women's Absenteeism and Labor Turnover* (Washington, D.C., 1969).

[58] Merchants and Manufacturers Association, *Labor Turnover Handbook* (Los Angeles, 1970).

[59] *Facts About Women's Absenteeism,* p. 6.

[60] For example, if the new entrants to the labor force seek mainly "women's jobs," if their supply price is lower than the going wage rate, if no attempt is

made by employers to diminish job segregation, and if the labor market for women's jobs is sufficiently competitive, then the average wage rate for women's jobs (and hence the average wage rate for most women) will be decreased.

[61] This is not meant to be a complete discussion of the relationship between education and fertility. For a more exhaustive treatment, see, for example, Robert T. Michael, "Education and the Derived Demand for Children," *Journal of Political Economy,* LXXXI (March/April 1973): S128–S164.

[62] Gary S. Becker and H. Gregg Lewis, "On The Interaction Between the Quantity and Quality of Children," *ibid.,* pp. S279–S288.

[63] Dennis N. De Tray, "Child Quality and the Demand for Children," *ibid.,* pp. S70–S95.

[64] Arleen Leibowitz, "Women's Work in the Home," in this volume.

[65] It may be that some women will reduce the number of hours they work if they regard subsidized child care as a wage rate increase. However, the number of women who work (or seek work) is likely to increase as a result of child care availability.

[66] See, for example, U.S. Census, 1970, *Current Population Reports,* Special Studies: *Fertility Indicators, 1970,* Series P-23, No. 36, April 16, 1971, Table 15, p. 29.

[67] De Tray, "Child Quality," p. 589.

[68] *Ibid.*

[69] Glen G. Cain, "The Effect of Income Maintenance Laws on Fertility in the United States," Discussion Paper #117, Institute for Research on Poverty (Madison, Wisc., 1972), p. 28. It is important to note that Cain believes the effect of taste changes will *not* outweigh the subsidy effect. However, many of the taste changes considered here are not analyzed by Cain.

[70] Researchers in education have already had success in training mothers as paraprofessional teachers. See Merle B. Karnes, R. Reid Zehrback, and James A. Teska, "A New Professional Role in Early Childhood Education," *Interchange,* Vol. 2, No. 2 (1971), pp. 89–105.

[71] See Rowe, "Economics of Child Care," pp. 265–68.

[72] One unfortunate consequence is that, as a community-based scheme, it does nothing to further racial integration. However, several members of minority groups who have read this paper have applauded the proposed scheme because it permits communities to maintain "ethnic identity" in child care programs.

[73] Rowe, "Economics of Child Care," p. 262.

[74] However, better use of existing school buildings for care of school-age children during these periods should also be investigated by the community.

[75] The term "practical mother" was used by Alice S. Rossi in her "Equality between the Sexes: An Immodest Proposal," in Robert Jay Lifton, ed. *The Woman in America* (Boston, 1967).

[76] There are some figures on frequency of respiratory illness in preschool children at one center and other figures on home illness in a middle-class population in one city. See Ann De Huff Peters, "Health Support in Day Care," in

Edith Grotberg, ed., *Day Care: Resources for Decisions,* (Washington, D.C., 1971), pp. 321–22. But these figures are not comprehensive enough to warrant generalizations.

[77] *Ibid.,* for a discussion of some limited evidence on this question.

[78] See "Public Assistance in January and February 1970," *Welfare in Review* VIII (July/August 1970): 23.

[79] According to the Women's Bureau study of industry's involvement in day care (see note 18), the cost of building a facility in the three cases noted there varied widely, from $36,000 for a center for 50 children to $56,000 for 49 children and $98,000 for 118 children.

[80] Senator Long, *Child Care: Hearings,* p. 9.

[81] Elliot L. Richardson, *Child Care: Hearings,* p. 96.

[82] See Elizabeth Lewicki, "A Study of Cooperative Full-Day Care Centers in the Mid-Peninsula Area," (mimeographed, Stanford Graduate School of Business, 1972).

[83] Acquisition of excess space and administrative personnel of school systems, teacher training, provision of care for school-age children, and follow-up of preschool education programs might be easier if child care systems were tied to school systems. On the other hand, critics of school systems would not want to see what they regard as current bureaucratic and educational deficiencies transferred to younger children's programs.

Part 5
The Economics of Women's Liberation

15

Income and Employment
Effects of Women's Liberation

ESTELLE JAMES

WHAT WILL the world look like after women have achieved economic equality with men? This paper explores some of the income and employment effects of women's liberation and their implications for economic efficiency and equity.

We would expect that economic equality might mean sexual integration of jobs, so that men and women would be represented in each occupation in proportion to their participation in the labor force. We would also expect wage parity for men and women who are doing the same work. The first part of this paper sets forth a model which helps us to analyze sexual integration and its impact on output and income. The distribution of gains and losses is particularly instructive: the conflicting interests do not lie along simple sexual lines, and attitudes toward integration are similarly complex.

The second part of the paper focuses on the impact of sexual integration on the female labor supply. Induced increases in the female participation rate may profoundly influence the division of labor within and between the market and nonmarket sectors of our economy. As economists, we can only speculate on the changes in family structure and in social and individual values that may ensue.

I wish to thank my colleagues Egon Neuberger and H. O. Stekler for their helpful comments on an earlier version of this paper. I particularly appreciate the contribution of my research assistant, Edith Becvar Nozick, who performed the computations presented in this paper very competently and conscientiously.

Occupational Segregation and Integration

A Model of Occupational Segregation

It is readily observed that many occupations are balkanized by sex. The percentage of secretaries, nurses, and elementary school teachers who are women is much higher than the female share in the labor force, while the female proportion of executives, doctors, and professors is much lower.[1] It is also well known that women earn lower wages than men; Table 15.1 shows this to be true at every educational level and for both races.

One approach that has recently been developed by Barbara Bergmann uses the former observation to explain the latter. That is, labor market barriers are assumed to keep women out of the high-wage male occupa-

TABLE 15.1   Income and Employment by
Education, Sex, and Race, 1967
(For Persons Twenty-five Years of Age and Over)

Sex and Race	*Years of School Completed*					
	0–7	*8*	*9–11*	*12*	*13–15*	*16+*
White Males:						
Income ($)	5,450	6,708	7,462	8,511	9,860	13,087
Employment						
(Millions)	4.066	4.851	6.261	11.915	4.057	5.701
White Females:						
Income ($)	3,289	3,772	4,045	4,664	5,587	7,295
Employment						
(Millions)	1.647	1.944	2.765	6.116	1.707	1.772
Black Males:						
Income ($)	3,535	4,337	4,567	5,257	6,072	7,959
Employment						
(Millions)	1.290	0.371	0.820	0.790	0.220	0.146
Black Females:						
Income ($)	1,943	2,397	2,744	3,387	4,207	6,269
Employment						
(Millions)	0.751	0.314	0.668	0.640	0.143	0.172

SOURCE: U.S. Bureau of the Census. *Current Population Reports, Consumer Income.* Series P-60. Washington, D.C.: Government Printing Office, 1969. Data converted to full-time equivalents by Barbara Bergmann in "The Effect on White Incomes of Discrimination in Employment," *Journal of Political Economy,* 79 (March/April 1971) pp. 294–313. The income figures used in this and the following tables include nonlabor income.

tions and, instead, crowd large numbers of females into their own narrow occupations, producing a relatively low marginal product for these groups. The corresponding low wage rate may then be viewed as stemming from job segregation and a relatively high degree of crowding in the female occupations, rather than from payment below marginal productivity, as in other studies of discrimination.[2]

In this model, which we call the occupational segregation model (and which is presented more formally in Appendix 15.1), national income depends on employment in various occupational categories, with the relationship represented by a production function which assumes a constant elasticity of substitution between factors of production (or between workers in different occupations). Each occupation is initially staffed by a different demographic group, defined in terms of race, sex, and education. Due to exogènous social or cultural forces, complete segregation prevails, and every population group in the labor force is confined to work in its own sector of the economy. Within each occupation, labor markets are competitive, so that wages are uniform and equal to the marginal product. However, in equilibrium productivity and wage differentials may exist between black and white or male and female occupations even when education is held constant; there is no automatic economic mechanism to eliminate this inequality.

Suppose now that these barriers to labor mobility are eliminated and sexual integration is introduced. If we assume that both sexes have equal ability to perform all jobs associated with a given level of schooling, employment will be redistributed and marginal products will adjust until wages are equalized for men and women with the same degree of education.

I have used Bergmann's model to derive the new pattern of employment and the corresponding levels of national income and wages. In my calculations, racial segregation was retained but employment was redistributed to equalize marginal productivities of men and women with equal education. Initially, the labor force was taken as a constant; this assumption is relaxed in the second part of the paper and the impact on labor supply is explored. The results are presented in Tables 15.2 and 15.3, for an elasticity of substitution of 1 among the different occupational categories.

TABLE 15.2 Effects of Sexual Integration: Percentage Change in Income of Year-Round, Full-Time Workers

Sex and Race	Years of School Completed					
	0–7	8	9–11	12	13–15	16+
White:						
Male	−9.2	−10.3	−11.8	−13.2	−10.6	−8.2
Female	50.6	59.5	62.7	58.5	57.7	64.6
Black:						
Male	−14.4	−18.3	−15.9	−13.7	−9.7	−8.7
Female	55.6	47.1	40.4	33.7	29.8	14.6

NOTE: Racial segregation assumed to remain. The elasticity of substitution is assumed to equal 1.

Resulting percentage change in national income = 2.57 percent.

TABLE 15.3 Effects of Sexual Integration: Employment in Occupational Categories (millions of year-round, full-time equivalent workers)

Occupational categories defined by race and sex	Occupational Categories Defined by Number of School Years Completed						
	0–7	8	9–11	12	13–15	16+	Total
Previously white male jobs							
Actual, 1967	4.066	4.851	6.261	11.915	4.057	5.701	36.851
After integration	4.591	5.545	7.283	14.073	4.654	6.369	42.515
Previously white female jobs							
Actual, 1967	1.647	1.944	2.765	6.116	1.707	1.772	15.951
After integration	1.122	1.250	1.743	3.958	1.110	1.	10.287
Previously black male jobs							
Actual, 1967	1.290	0.371	0.820	0.790	0.220	0.146	3.637
After integration	1.546	.466	1.000	.939	.250	.164	4.365
Previously black female jobs							
Actual, 1967	0.751	0.314	0.668	0.640	0.143	0.172	2.688
After integration	.495	.219	.488	.491	.113	.154	1.960

NOTE: Racial segregation assumed to remain. The elasticity of substitution is assumed to equal 1.

Effects on National Income and Efficiency

National income has risen, as expected, due to the employment shift into the productive "male" occupations; the product mix has changed, and, in a broader model, the capital–labor ratio would also change. The increased output may or may not represent a movement toward Pareto optimality depending on the underlying causes for the occupational segregation that initially exists.

If we regard the mobility barriers as market imperfections, rather than as evidence of employer or worker preferences or sex-based cost differentials, the increase in Gross National Product permits us to move toward a boundary point on society's utilities–possibilities frontier, where the marginal rate of substitution among goods equals their marginal rate of transformation. With appropriate transfers, it should be possible to make everyone better off.

On the other hand, we may hypothesize that employers in the "male" occupations have a relatively high taste for discrimination and accordingly offer women lower remuneration and that, therefore, the resulting wage structure has dictated a different occupational choice for women than for men. Closely related is the possibility that occupational segregation may be attributed to sexual differences in preferences for work—differences which would indeed need to be sharp and nonoverlapping to produce the observed results. Under these two interpretations, enforced sexual integration does not imply an unambiguous movement toward Pareto optimality, since the increase in GNP must be weighed against a loss of utility stemming from these nonmaterial considerations. The potential gain in real income can, however, be viewed as the opportunity cost of these tastes. It can also be viewed as the material gain which would accrue if these preferences changed—but conventional economic analysis does not allow us to make welfare comparisons in this situation.

We may, alternatively, consider on-the-job training as the source of occupational segregation and wage differentials. This model does not explicitly incorporate training costs, but they are an important part of the broader discrimination problem. Labor market barriers may partially be explained by the greater need for specific training in the male occupations. Employers who expect women to be unstable, short-term employees may be unwilling to hire and invest in them. This reluctance to train may be accentuated by a tendency to predict for each woman the mean performance of the entire sexual group, rather than seeking more individualized information which is costly and even impossible to obtain. Now it may be that specific and general training are jointly supplied, so that the occupations which are thereby reserved for males also entail more general (transferable) training. Then we would expect men to have a steeper age–earnings profile and, all other things being equal, a higher average wage (aggregated across all ages). In this case, complete wage equality across occupations, as postulated in the above model, is no longer a condition for efficiency.

If employers' expectations were correct, and there existed little overlap between the turnover distributions of the male and female groups, giving specific training to women would be both privately and socially nonoptimal. Since, in fact, men and women do not constitute two disjoint sets with respect to turnover, it is inefficient to ration specific training on the basis of sex, and some other, more reliable, means for detecting unstable employees would be preferable. The failure of the private market to develop such informational techniques suggests that collective-good properties, such as nonexcludability, may be present, and government financing may be required.

Whether the amount of on-the-job training is the same or different for male and female occupations, in the short run considerable retraining would be needed to redistribute the entire stock of labor as described above. This means that the primary impact would be on investment in human capital, rather than on consumption. After the initial period, however, the increment to on-the-job training would be much less, since only new female entrants to the labor force would be involved and they would be trained, from the start, for the higher-productivity occupations indicated by the new employment patterns. Thus, the largest part of the additional training costs would be a once-and-for-all effect, while the increased output, reflecting gains in efficiency and potential welfare, would recur every year.

Effects on Distribution

Since economic welfare depends on the distribution of the pie as well as on its size, we proceed now to consider the former. Postintegration wage rates will be positively related to the level of national income and negatively related to the employment totals in each occupation. These effects reinforce each other to produce a wage increase for women and counter- act each other to produce a smaller wage decline for men; the exact amounts, however, vary significantly by race and educational category.

The wage losses to men range from 8 to 18 percent. Black men suffer proportionately more than white (if racial segregation continues). This can be attributed to the greater percentage employment increases in the previously black male occupations, which in turn is due to the relatively large numbers of black women in the labor force. Among white men, those with a high-school diploma (the educational level where white working women are heavily concentrated) lose most, while for black men the greatest damage is inflicted on those with a grade-school education. In any event, the wage deterioration caused by sexual integration can hardly be termed trivial. Apparently, women's liberation poses a real threat to male incomes.

The wage gains to white females vary from 50 to 65 percent, the larg- est increase going to those with a college degree—among whom, inciden- tally, the demand for women's liberation is strongest. In contrast, among black females those in the lowest educational category benefit most. At every other level they benefit less than white females, and those with a college degree gain least. The explanation, apparently, lies in the rela- tively low wages associated with black male occupations, especially at the higher levels of education; black women have nowhere very attractive to go as long as rigid racial segregation is maintained. The smaller antici- pated gains for (articulate) black women, the larger losses for black men, and the consequent widening of the black–white wage differential are consistent with the often-observed hostility within the black community toward women's liberation.[3]

We may also note that the wage increase for women, black or white, always outweighs the decrease for men in percentage terms and, gener- ally, in absolute terms as well (except for cases where the education and hence the salary of the male greatly exceeds that of the female). Con- sequently, in most households where women engage in market work, family (including husband's) purchasing power rises, on balance. On the other hand, in households where the male is the single breadwinner, fam- ily (including wife's) purchasing power falls—in absolute and, even more, in relative terms. Since the dual breadwinners are currently concentrated among white lower-class and black families, the black-white and upper-lower class average family income differential will initially be narrowed by sexual integration, despite the widening wage differential.

It is clear that the income and substitution effects, as well as the demonstration effect, will all operate to draw more women into the labor force, particularly from white upper-class families, changing both the aggregate impact and its distribution, as discussed in the second part of this paper. Thus, it is hardly surprising that those women who prefer to remain at home feel their standard of living and their way of life threatened by their more militant sisters who are clamoring for sexual integration.

Some Policy Implications

It is important to realize that the favorable effect of integration on national income described above stems from increased employment in the productive male occupations as labor market competition pushes down their wages once the sexual barriers are removed. If this wage decline is effectively prohibited—for example, by legislation or union action which induces integration but at the same time prohibits wage cuts—this redistribution of employment and consequent rise in national income will not take place. Marginal productivities and wages will not be equalized across occupations which currently have the same educational requirements, and some form of nonwage, nonsexual rationing would be used to allocate the remunerative ''male'' jobs among the excess supply of applicants from both sexes. ''Job upgrading'' might raise the educational qualifications associated with these jobs, for example, or personal contacts might be necessary. Unemployment, hitherto ignored in our discussion, might show up as a consequence of wage inflexibility. The maximum wage gains and losses from integration would be larger than in our present model, and their distribution within each population group would be uneven rather than uniform, depending on which individuals got the more desirable jobs.

While an actual decline in money wages may seem unlikely given our present institutional arrangements, real wages may decline if money wages remain constant while prices rise. Furthermore, the redistribution of employment may still take place, more slowly, if real wages in the male occupations remain constant through time while demand and technology grow. An immediate employment and output effect with a decline in real wages may thus be translated into a lagged employment and output effect with constant real wages.

Thus, the sign, size, and timing of the changes in income depend critically on the precise way in which integration is achieved. Moreover, they vary considerably by educational background, marital status, race, and sex. These distributional effects, as well as the overall gain in efficiency, must be taken into account in evaluating alternative policies; if a particular redistribution is deemed undesirable, some form of compensation could perhaps be devised. Further disaggregated analyses of the benefits and costs of sexual equality might help us to determine its social value and to understand the disparate attitudes of various population groups toward such change.

Labor Supply and Related Effects

Labor Force Participation Rate and Education

In the above analysis, the labor force was taken as a constant, totally inelastic with respect to wages or education. Recent studies of the female labor force participation rate indicate that this is a heroic assumption to make about the supply of women workers.[4] This section, therefore, discusses briefly the impact of sexual integration on the labor force participation rate; a fuller presentation may be found in Appendix 15.2.

We know that as female wages rise women are likely to substitute market work for home work, and as male wages fall women may do more work of both kinds due to reduced family income. Cross-sectional studies indicate that the elasticity of the female participation rate with respect to own wages is approximately 38 percent and with respect to male wages is approximately 50 percent. The former produces an increase (of 15–20 percent for whites, 4–20 percent for blacks) in the quantity of labor supplied along a given curve as female wages rise due to sexual integration. The latter produces an outward shift (of 2–8 percent) in the entire female labor supply curve as male wages fall. The excess supply which results from these two forces causes wage declines for everyone and a secondary round of participation-rate changes. When a new equilibrium is reached, we might expect an increase of 20–25 percent in the participation rate of white women and 9–25 percent for black women, depending on educational category of the women and their spouses.

In addition to these income and substitution effects, the demonstration effect may also be at work: we have already noted the invidious comparisons likely to be made by families with single versus double breadwinners. All these effects will be particularly strong in drawing more white upper class women into the labor force, since this is the group with the lowest current participation rate and (because it is relatively well-educated) the largest wage gain from integration. While the total share of national income accruing to white upper class families was seen to fall under the assumption of a fixed labor supply in the second part of this paper, it is likely to increase when this shift in labor force participation is taken into account.

The labor supply effect is further reinforced by changes in female education that we might predict as one of the consequences of sexual integration. Females presently receive less education than men, particularly at the college level; this is hardly surprising in view of the fact that their (monetary) rate of return to education is also less.[5] After integration, these rates of return will be equalized for men and women in the labor force, and we can anticipate that the female incentive to acquire schooling and on-the-job training will likewise increase. The human capital embodied in the female population will rise.

Now the female participation rate is a positive function of education, rising from 19 percent (78 percent) for married (single) women with less than four years of schooling to 61 percent (94 percent) for those with more than seventeen years.[6] Bowen and Finegan estimate that about half of this increment is due to nonpecuniary job differentials or taste change and the other half is a response to the higher wages received by better-educated women. Thus, increases in the education of the general female population will be disproportionately reflected in the educational distribution of the labor force and will further increase its size.

After taking into account all of these diverse pressures, it appears that, in the aggregate, female market employment will rise by at least 30 percent. This will, of course, exert a dampening influence upon wages. It will also mean that market output will increase much more than as indicated in Table 15.2. In fact, the output effect of the expansion in labor supply and education will be much greater than the direct output effect of sexual integration.[7]

The Household and the Market Sector

We must also recognize, however, that production in the subsistence household sector will fall when this shift to market employment occurs. In conclusion, then, let us explore the impact of the labor supply changes on the division of responsibilities within the household sector and between the subsistence and market sectors of the economy.

The household is probably the last major vestige of subsistence production in industrialized economies. Currently, the majority of women work exclusively in this nonmarket sector as housewives. Although females make up roughly 50 percent of the population, they do almost all the housework in the country (with only a few specialized tasks reserved for men)—which is the clearest case we have of occupational segregation.

The value of nonmarket services is admittedly difficult to measure. Records of quantity are incomplete and those of quality virtually nonexistent. If we impute values according to prices of equivalent market services we may be overstating the amount which the household would willingly pay, while opportunity cost may understate this amount. However, recent studies on this subject estimate female time spent in the household at 40 to 60 hours weekly and value these services at $5,000–$10,000 annually.[8] Since most women, especially those without a college degree, earn less than this in the labor force, their low participation rate is understandable.

As wages rise for women due to sexual integration, and their participation in the market sector rises, one important consequence is that their production in the household sector will fall; this is the opportunity cost of market employment. Measured GNP will increase, as discussed above, but against this must be offset the nonmeasured loss of services in the subsistence sector. Preliminary evidence from the studies referred to above indicates a 25 percent drop in time spent on household activities when a woman takes an outside job. Her total working time, nevertheless, increases, so that a loss of leisure time must be counted as another opportunity cost of market employment.

Some of the housewife's services will simply disappear from the household's standard of living. Others will be replaced by substitutes from the market sector, where production can benefit from the division of labor and economies of scale currently made impossible by the segmentation of the household market. Familiar examples of such substitutes include prepared foods, commercial housecleaners, and nurseries. Thus, the structure of demand and productivity in the market sector will shift if large numbers of women enter the labor force. This, in turn, will alter the occupational parameters in the aggregate production function and hence the wage and employment effects predicted in this study.[9]

In particular, the demand for children, a major household consumption good, may fall. The cost of children will rise as the marginal value of the woman's time rises: if she stays home she incurs a heavy opportunity cost and if she works she incurs the heavy monetary costs of hiring mother substitutes. Furthermore, children may be an inferior good, whose numbers fall as family income rises. Thus, the income and substitution effects of sexual integration may lead to a decline in population growth but an increase in demand for marketed child-care services.

The division of the remaining household responsibilities among the members of the family may also change. In the past, the household burden was borne by the woman even when she worked; her wages were invariably lower than her husband's and this was her compensating contribution to the family's welfare. Thus, a husband's contribution to the household did not increase when his wife obtained an outside job. As women achieve wage parity with men, more of this responsibility may be shifted to the husband. In fact, some families may opt to have the men stay home as house-husbands, once wage biases have been removed. This also implies a change in the material incentives for marriage: men will no longer be gaining a full-time, nonmarket housekeeper and women will not need a male to give them access to the benefits of the market sector.

As more women enter the labor force, including occupations from which they were previously excluded, the socialization process that prepared them for their traditional role must also change. The higher female wages and labor force participation may lead also to a changed decision-making structure and distribution of utilities within the household, and to possible conflicts of interest between the husband and wife. We are obviously dealing here with far-reaching shifts in social attitudes and family structure, which, one suspects, must imply changes in individual preferences as well. These are ordinarily taken by economists as constant and exogenously given. Thus, we have come to the interface between economics and the other social sciences, to the point where tastes must be regarded as an endogenous variable in a socioeconomic general equilibrium model. We need a theory of preference formation and a welfare analysis of preference changes in order to go beyond this point and fully assess the economic consequences of women's liberation.

APPENDIXES

I. The Occupational Segregation Model

Bergmann's occupational segregation model may be summarized as follows. Aggregate income and wages in each occupation under sexual segregation are given by equations (1) and (2).

$$Y = [\Sigma a_i E_i^{-\beta}]^{-1/\beta} \qquad (1)$$

$$MP_i = R_i = a_i \left(\frac{Y}{E_i}\right)^{\beta+1} = a_i \left(\frac{\Sigma R_i E_i}{E_i}\right)^{\beta+1} \qquad (2)$$

where:

Y = national income, expressed in equation (1) in terms of a constant-elasticity-of-substitution production function with capital and non-labor income ignored;

E_i = employment in each occupational category i, $i = 1, \ldots, 24$; before integration these are equivalent to the twenty-four population groups in the labor force, defined in terms of race, sex, and education;

MP_i = marginal productivity of occupation i, obtained in equation (2) by differentiating equation (1);

R_i = wage rate in occupation i, set equal to MP_i in equation (2);

a_i = a parameter depending on the "narrowness" of occupation i (i.e., indicating the relative height of its MP curve); estimated by inserting wage and employment data from Table 15.1 into equation (2) and solving for the a_i's;

Equation (3) shows that wages in occupations j and k will be equalized by racial and sexual integration.

$$MP^*_j = R^*_j = a_j\left(\frac{Y^*}{E^*_j}\right)^{\beta+1} = MP^*_k = R^*_k = a_k\left(\frac{Y^*}{E^*_k}\right)^{\beta+1} \qquad (3)$$

Equations (4) and (5) allow us to derive the postintegration level of employment for each occupation; equation (5) is obtained by plugging (4) into (3) and solving for E^*_k, thereby yielding the new employment pattern.

$$E^*_j = E_j + E_k - E^*_k \qquad (4)$$

$$E^*_k = \frac{a^\sigma_k}{a^\sigma_k + a^\sigma_j}(E_j + E_k) \qquad (5)$$

where:

$\sigma = 1/(\beta + 1) = $ the elasticity of substitution, assumed to be the same between all occupational categories;

MP^*_j and $MP^*_k = $ marginal productivity and wage rate in occupations j and k, respectively, after they have been integrated;

E^*_j and $E^*_k = $ employment in occupations j and k, respectively, after integration;

Y^* and $R^*_i = $ national income and wages, respectively, in occupation i, after employment has been redistributed by racial or sexual integration.

Equation (6) simply indicates the percentage change in employment in each occupation, and is obtained by dividing equation (5) by E_k.

$$\frac{E^*_k}{E_k} = \frac{a^\sigma_k}{a^\sigma_k + a^\sigma_j}\frac{(E_j + E_k)}{E_k} \qquad (6)$$

Equations (7) and (8), which give us the percentage change in national income and wage rates once all the E^*_i's are known, are of particular interest.

$$\frac{Y^*}{Y} = \left[\frac{\Sigma a_i E^{*-\beta}_i}{\Sigma a_i E^{-\beta}_i}\right]^{-1/\beta} \qquad (7)$$

$$\frac{R^*_i}{R_i} = \frac{MP^*_i}{MP_i} = \left(\frac{Y^*}{Y}\right)^{\beta+1}\left(\frac{E_i}{E^*_i}\right)^{\beta+1} \qquad (8)$$

$\frac{R^*_i}{R_i}$, it is seen, varies positively with national income and inversely with employment for occupation i. The former is, of course, constant over all population groups, but the latter is specific to each occupation. In the case of integration, this term depends on the relationship between the occupational parameters and initial employment of the two groups being integrated, as set forth in equation (6). This latter equation is central to understanding the preceding results, which focus on the uneven distribution of the gains and losses from various reforms across the population.

II. Sexual Integration and Labor Force Participation

Since the supply of labor by females is highly sensitive to their own and their husbands' wages, we may anticipate a positive response to integration, which raises wages for women and reduces them for men. My estimates of a 20–25 percent increase in the participation rate of white women and a 6–25 percent increase for blacks were obtained by using Cain's regression coefficients and Bowen and Finegan's findings in conjunction with the wage rates presented in Table 15.3. While aggregate results are presented here, the same approach could be used to calculate supply changes separately for each educational–racial category, based on their differential wage response to sexual integration.

Cain's regressions indicate that the participation rate of married women goes up .34 percentage points for every $100 increase in annual income of females; it goes down .29 percentage points for each $100 increase in husbands' income. In logarithmic form, the participation rate goes up .42 percent for each 1 percent increase in female income and down .68 percent for each 1 percent increase in male income. Thus, the own-wage effect outweighs the pure income effect (i.e., that stemming from husbands' income) in the arithmetic regression, but the relative size of the two effects is reversed when measuring elasticities in the logarithmic regression.

Bowen and Finegan have shown that the participation rate for single women is less responsive to wage changes. Consequently, the elasticity with respect to own-wages for all women will be somewhat less than 42 percent—perhaps 38 percent—and the elasticity with respect to male wages for all women will be much less than 68 percent—roughly 50 percent.

Using the 38 percent and 50 percent figures, we find the following

sequence, depicted in Figure 15.1, when sexual integration is instituted:
1. We start under segregation with supply curve FLS_0 and demand curve MPF_0 for female labor in a particular educational category, yielding equilibrium wage FR_0 and employment FL_0. The supply and demand curves, equilibrium wage, and employment for males are MLS_0, MPS_0, MR_0, and ML_0, respectively. The supply of labor by men is assumed to remain constant, perfectly inelastic with respect to their own or their wives' wages, in order to focus on changes in female labor supply.
2. Under sexual integration the demand for male and female labor is combined in MP_1, and the merged supply curve is shown as LS_0. If the labor force remains constant at L_0, the equilibrium wage increases from FR_0 to R_1, 50–70 percent for white women and 10–65 percent for blacks, and decreases 5–20 percent, from MR_0 to R_1, for men (see Table 15.2).

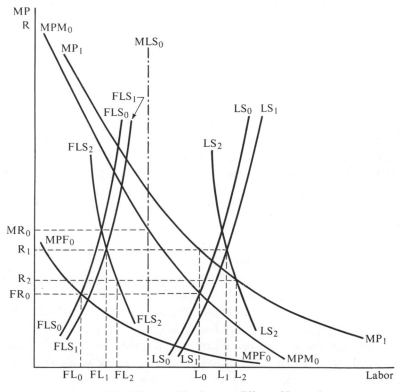

FIGURE 15.1. Wage and Employment Effects of Integration

3. However, in response to these higher wage rates for women, the quantity of female labor supplied along supply curve FLS_0 increases by $.38[2(R_1 - FR_0)/(R_1 + FR_0)]$, or 15–20 percent for whites, 4–20 percent for blacks.

4. The lower male incomes cause the female labor supply curve to shift from FLS_0 to FLS_1, thus increasing by $.5[2(MR_0 - R_1)/(MR_0 + R_1)]$, or 2–8 percent.

5. The combined effects of (3) and (4) imply that the female participation rate and supply of labor at R_1 would be FL_1 instead of FL_0—20–25 percent higher than previously for whites, 6–25 percent higher for blacks, depending on educational category and elasticity of substitution. This produces an excess supply of labor, $L_1 - L_0 = FL_1 - FL_0$, so the wage level will not remain at R_1.

6. As the wage level falls, some women withdraw from the labor force due to their own-wage elasticity; however, this is more than offset by women entering the labor force as their husbands' incomes drop, since 50 percent > 38 percent. If we draw a labor supply curve through (L_1, R_1) taking both these effects into account—that is, a curve which assumes equal earnings for men and women and allows changes in female participation rates due to own-wage and male-wage changes—we find it is (slightly) backward bending, such as LS_2.

7. Therefore, wages will fall until R_2, at which point the expanded labor supply of L_2 is fully absorbed. The final equilibrium R_2 depends, of course, on the elasticity of demand, as does the corresponding L_2. Nevertheless, the overall increase in female market employment, i.e., $(FL_2 - FL_0)/FL_0$, averaged over all educational categories and both races, is clearly seen to exceed 20 percent owing to the income and substitution effects.

The following qualifications must be made for the preceding analysis:

1. Cain's wage and income coefficients seem to vary considerably by geographic area and, particularly, by time period. In 1950, for example, own-wage elasticity was much higher than presented here and was higher than elasticity with respect to husbands' wage.

2. The wage and income coefficients may also vary by educational category and race. Cain does not include interaction terms which would test for the former; he does show a small white–nonwhite differential.

3. Higher wages for women may not only increase their participation rate

but may also, for the same reason, increase the proportion of women who work full-time rather than part-time, thereby raising the labor supply by a larger amount than is here indicated.

4. One may seriously question whether the regressions estimated by Cain can be extrapolated over the wide range of wages discussed in this paper. I have assumed that the coefficients from his logarithmic regressions remain constant. If I had, instead, assumed constant arithmetic coefficients I would have predicted a much larger increase in female labor supplied along FLS_0 and a positively shaped LS_2 curve, with corresponding implications for the final equilibrium R and L.

5. As discussed in the text, sexual integration may also be expected to produce a demonstration effect, a rise in female education, and, possibly, a change in tastes, all of which operate further to expand the labor supply. After taking account of these diverse forces, it seems safe to estimate that the female participation rate will increase by at least 30 percent as a result of sexual integration.

NOTES

[1] For fuller documentation and discussion of the sexual segregation hypothesis, see Valerie K. Oppenheimer, *The Female Labor Force in the United States* (Berkeley, 1970).

[2] Barbara Bergmann, "The Effect on White Incomes of Discrimination in Employment," *Journal of Political Economy,* LXXIX (March/April 1971): 294–313. The alternative approach, which suggests that certain groups may be paid below their marginal productivity because of the employers' taste for discrimination, is most closely associated with Gary Becker, *The Economics of Discrimination,* 2d ed. (Chicago, 1971). The existence of a gap between marginal productivity and wages is also explored by Lester Thurow in "Disequilibrium and the Marginal Productivity of Capital and Labor," *Review of Economics and Statistics,* L (February 1968): 23–31, and *Poverty and Discrimination* (Washington, D.C., 1969).

[3] It is interesting at this point to compare some effects of racial and sexual integration. Bergmann, in "The Effect on White Incomes," has shown that, if racial integration were introduced, the employment shifts and wage increases for blacks would be considerable but the drop in white wages and the change in aggregate output would be trivial. This is hardly the case with respect to sexual integration, which produces a much greater impact on employment and income simply because there are many more underutilized women than blacks in the labor force.

If racial integration should be instituted while sexual segregation is retained, the wage and productivity gains would be greater for black men than for black women, except at the lowest level of schooling. The reason is familiar: the relatively low wages among white women and the large numbers of black women in the labor force. Thus, racial integration increases the male–female wage differential just as sexual integration increases the black–white differential.

Black women, we can see from Table 15.1, are now at the bottom of the totem pole, suffering from both racial and sexual discrimination. Their wages will improve significantly only if both forms of discrimination are removed (i.e., if the two kinds of integration proceed together)—and then they will gain more than any other group. It follows that the expansionary impact on national income of fully utilizing the productivity potential of black women will be realized only when sexual and racial reforms are combined.

[4] The major studies of the female labor force participation rate may be found in Jacob Mincer, "Labor Force Participation of Married Women: A Study of Labor Supply," in Universities-National Bureau Committee for Economic Research, *Aspects of Labor Economics* (Princeton, N.J., 1962), pp. 63–105; Glen Cain, *Married Women in the Labor Force* (Chicago, 1966); and William G. Bowen and T. Aldrich Finegan, *The Economics of Labor Force Participation* (Princeton, N.J., 1969). These are all drawn on in my analysis of labor supply effects here and in Appendix II.

[5] Gary S. Becker, *Human Capital: A Theoretical and Empirical Analysis with Special Reference to Education* (New York, 1964), p. 100.

[6] See Bowen and Finegan, *Economics of Labor Force Participation*, pp. 116, 225. These figures have been adjusted for the effects of color, age, marital status, and children and, particularly important, for other family income. In Cain's regressions (see note 4) the participation rate of married women goes up 1.32 percentage points for every one-year increase in median schooling, holding wages constant; the corresponding elasticity is 53 percent. These labor supply considerations complicate calculation of the social benefits of educating women. If we are interested only in the marketable output flowing from education, those women who are not in the labor force do not contribute to total benefits at all. On the other hand, increased education will cause more women to enter the labor force, and for these new entrants, marketable GNP goes up by the full value of their wages. For example, suppose that the participation rate is 50 percent for female high-school graduates and 70 percent for those with a college degree, as compared with 99 percent for males in both groups, and suppose further that annual wages after college $= Y$ and annual wages after high school $= Y - \Delta Y$ for men and women. Then, the annual benefits of sending a cohort K of male high-school graduates to college $= .99K \Delta Y$, while the comparable benefits from women $= .5K \Delta Y + .2KY$. Of course, if we are also interested in nonmarket benefits, the value of education to women who are not in the labor force must be measured as well, and this is a much more difficult task.

[7] The interaction among these effects is particularly important. For example, if the participation rate were unchanged and sexual segregation were maintained, but women in the labor force were given the same educational distribution as men, this would not have a positive impact on national income. Apparently, educational equality would merely crowd larger numbers of educated women into narrowly restricted occupations, rapidly reducing their productivity and reward and, in the extreme, yielding a negative private and social marginal return to education. On the other hand, if educational equality is combined with integration, the expansionary effect on national income is more than for integration alone. Furthermore, this increment to national income continues through the lifetime of the workers while the pay-off period for the costs of additional schooling is less

than four years. The present value of net benefits thus depends on the social discount rate and the age of the labor force, but clearly it is positive and large. These
calculations are described in detail in E. James, "Integration, Educational Equality and Income Distribution," paper presented at the International Seminar on
Comparative Urban and Grants Economics, Augsburg, August 1972.

[8] See, for example, Kathryn Walker and William Gauger, *The Dollar Value of
Household Work*, Information Bulletin 60, N.Y. State College of Human Ecology, Cornell University, Ithaca, N.Y., 1973; and Wendy Pfeffer, "An Economic
Assessment of the Woman's Productive Services in the Non-Market Sector" (unpublished manuscript, Department of Economics, State University of New York
at Stony Brook, Stony Brook, L.I., N.Y.). These are both drawn on throughout
my discussion of the impact of market employment on the household contributions of men and women.

[9] Our present tax system discourages and penalizes this shift to market employment, since subsistence production is tax-free while the income of a second wage
earner in a household is taxed at a high marginal rate. Furthermore, reductions are
not allowed for additional expenses incurred by the family, such as transportation
and child care. If political pressures from working women led to a change in these
tax laws, we might expect an even greater growth in the female labor supply.

16

The Impact of Women's Liberation on Marriage, Divorce, and Family Life-Style

SHIRLEY B. JOHNSON

THE WOMEN'S LIBERATION MOVEMENT is often dated from the publication of *The Feminine Mystique* in 1963.[1] The new feminism appeals to and is embraced by women with a number of different viewpoints about what should be changed in society. However, almost all of the new feminists would agree that the aims of the Equal Rights Amendment are at the heart of the program of Women's Liberation. Women and men are to have equal opportunities and options open to them both in and out of the labor force.

Although many of the detailed programmatic objectives of the Women's Movement have not yet been accepted by society, the economic impact of changing social attitudes toward women as well as of women's attitudes toward themselves can already be noted. It is this that I shall label the "Women's Liberation effect." Defined in economic terms, the Women's Liberation effect is a change in the preference functions of women in favor of more activities outside the household. This is accompanied by a change in the structure of nonpecuniary or psychic returns which increases the return from labor force participation relative to that from work in the home even with no changes in the pecuniary market wage. It can also be interpreted as an increase in the disutility of work in the home.

The author gratefully acknowledges the assistance of her research assistant, Mr. Bela Feketekuty; of Professor Herbert Parnes, for his permission to use the National Longitudinal Surveys data; of Mr. Arthur Dorfman, Director of the Computer Center, John Jay College of Criminal Justice, for his invaluable help with data processing, and of Professor Cynthia Lloyd, for her unstinting editorial assistance.

This paper will utilize an economic analysis of marriage to study the effects of this attitudinal change in women on household production functions, preference functions of spouses, and patterns of marriage, divorce, and household formation. In a final section, some feminist proposals for further changes in marriage and the married household will be critically evaluated, using the economic model of marriage as a framework of analysis.

An Economic Analysis of Marriage

This section will provide a sketch of an economic model of marriage based on the neoclassical model of market behavior.[2] It includes the theory of household production, in which time and market goods and services are seen as inputs into the production of household commodities. The aim is to provide a framework of analysis which can be used to explain the effect of changes in the preference functions of women on the nature of the married household. The model also provides the groundwork for an analysis of changing patterns of marriage and divorce. It should be noted, before proceeding, that the analysis of marriage within an economic framework is in no way intended to minimize the importance of emotional and psychological factors within individual relationships.

Marriage, considered as a form of economic activity, can be defined by analogy to a business firm. Marriage is a partnership whose aim is to maximize, subject to production constraints, the long-run expected utility (i.e., well-being) of a couple. Clearly, costs and returns are both psychic and monetary, and the consideration of the nonpecuniary aspects of both costs and benefits becomes particularly important when analyzing marriage. A marriage will be entered into by two individuals if each believes that this contractual arrangement will maximize his or her utility relative to costs over time. Individuals will tend to balance the cost of further searching for a mate with the amount of expected satisfaction provided by the best-known alternative at a given point in time.[3]

Divorce, now known as "dissolution of marriage" in no-fault divorce states, can be viewed as analogous to the liquidation of a firm. It will tend to occur when at least one spouse finds the expected future returns relative to the cost of being married smaller than the expected returns from alternative arrangements.

Just as the probability of profitability of a business firm depends, in part, on initial capitalization, so the expected utility of a marriage will be a function of the total resources (material resources as well as human capital) available to the two persons at the time of the marriage. These resources include the ability both to generate income and to produce goods and services within the household.

The material and psychic returns from marriage for either spouse might be expressed more precisely as a function of the income generated by both spouses, the difference in earnings (and wealth) between self and mate, and the unique set of goods which can be produced by the marriage. This set of goods is likely to include intangibles—such as love and companionship—and tangibles—both children, who can be treated as a form of consumer durables, and other household goods and services.

Since the "output" of marriage is largely for home consumption, production functions and utility functions are highly interdependent, although separable in theory. For instance, one may well ask whether choices made about home work versus labor force participation reflect decisions about production functions or utility functions. In fact, they reflect both. The disutility or utility of each form of work has to be balanced against the return from it. The interdependence between consumption and production is particularly true in the case of intangibles—for example, with respect to such activities as playing with one's children and having sexual relations with one's spouse.

However, it is possible when considering marriage as a special kind of firm to analyze its production of output. One can look at what would constitute a production function and a budget constraint for a particular marriage at a particular time. The production function will clearly depend upon the nature of the different "inputs" available to the married couple. Rates of substitution among factors of production will depend upon relative marginal products. Most work done by the married couple, both in the home and in the labor force, probably involves the possibility of substitution among inputs. For work in the home, physical capital can be substituted for human capital, hired labor can be substituted for the inputs of the spouses, and there can be substitution of the time, energy, and skills of one spouse for those of the other. Since it is often very difficult to measure productivity of inputs in the home, the degree of substitutability between male and female inputs is a controversial question. In certain areas of household production, however, particularly the rearing of "own" children,[4] the two spouses are seen as playing complementary roles. "Complementarity" is defined as the ability to provide more output in the form of goods, services, or, more abstractly, utility, jointly than could be produced by both if each were working separately.

Total production possibilities of the marriage are limited by the couple's resources of wealth, earning power, household skills, and time. Choices about inputs are possible only when the constraints on production, which limit market purchases as well as household production, have been properly specified. It is crucial to include time as well as other inputs as limiting factors in the analysis of choices among inputs. This is, of course, true of all budget constraints properly specified.[5] The opportunity costs of time of the husband and wife become the basis for determining the relative costs of the labor inputs in household production and market production. For instance, inflation in the service industries and a decline in the supply of domestics available for hire clearly increase the cost of time in the labor force for many people. Alternatively, an increase in the market wage rate of working women would increase the opportunity cost of their time in household production.

An analogy can also be drawn between the factory or plant established by a business firm and the household set up by a married couple. Both involve fixed costs. The ability to establish a separate household is a very important part of marrying in our culture. All other things being equal, one would therefore expect more marriages to take place in periods of high income and employment than during recessions, just as one would expect more firms to be formed during periods of economic prosperity. This is because initial costs of setting up the household are more easily met during periods of high income and employment and because expectations about income necessary to maintain the separate household and to generate future streams of goods and services are more optimistic.

The married household usually differs from other households established separately or shared by single adults. The contractual arrangement between the spouses creates a more permanent household composition and a relatively permanent budgeting or spending unit. For this reason, and also because marriage usually involves the notion of an expanded production function, the married household is likely to be more capital-intensive than are households formed by single people. One also associates the married household with greater amounts of human capital inputs. In addition to child care and housekeeping, there is the managing of production and consumption activities within the household, which becomes more complex with an increase in the number of interdependent individuals and the level of expenditure.

The incentive to marry and stay married may well vary over time, both over the life cycle of particular families and over time in society as a whole. Variations in returns to marriage relative to costs result from changes in the "output" of marriage, changes in the relative costs of inputs, and taste changes.

The returns to marriage relative to the expenditure on it have traditionally varied over the family life cycle because of changing patterns of household investment and production from one period to another. Just as in the case of business firms, the scale of production can be varied over time. Analyses of the patterns of expenditure on household capital do show significant variations from one life-cycle stage to another. The monetary outlays on the household are highest in the newly-married or family-formation stage, and again after children have entered the family. Purchases of houses are highly correlated with the stage in childrearing when a second child has been produced and/or a first one is entering school.[6] There is the obvious complementarity between marriage, household formation, and the begetting and rearing of children. The household becomes an expanded factory during the childrearing years, with an expansion in the time input of the spouses, particularly the wife.[7] It is also true that the psychic gain from living with one's children is an important part of the return to marriage during these years.

Other examples might be cited which illustrate varying patterns of expenditure and returns over the lifetime of a marriage. If one spouse earns income in order to enable the other to undertake a training program for the purpose of acquiring greater future earnings, this is clearly a period of investment in the marriage partnership with an expectation of future gain.

Insofar as attitudinal changes associated with the new feminism come to influence family life-styles, variations in expenditures and returns within the married household from one life-cycle period to another are likely to be even greater than before. The effect of the new feminism can be seen as a shift in tastes in favor of more labor force activity and less work in the home. Since society has not yet accepted the idea of alternatives to home rearing of children or provided many such alternatives the period in which children are in the home still requires a relatively large input of time-intensive human capital. As a result of new-feminist attitudes, the complementarity in production between spouses, with one primarily earning income and the other managing household production, may tend to disappear both before, after, and in the absence of children.

Over time, a number of additional factors have tended to reduce the average returns to marriage for society as a whole. Such phenomena as the desire for fewer children and other home-produced goods will, assuming other factors unchanged, tend to reduce the gains from marriage. It may well be that the Women's Liberation Movement and the attitudes it has fostered will enhance the declining returns from marriage in a number of ways. However, the effects of the Movement are more complex than they may appear upon superficial examination.

The most obvious effect is that women with marketable skills will tend to shift to more labor force participation as they come to regard the occupation of full-time housewife as less productive and less satisfying. The employed wife may well hire substitutes for herself in household production or persuade her husband to substitute some work in the home for labor force participation. Alternatively, the household may be changed so as to require fewer labor inputs.

There may be a shift away from the consumption of home-produced goods as attitudes change. John Kenneth Galbraith suggests, for instance, that a marriage reflecting "emancipated" attitudes will feature more theatre parties and fewer dinner parties in the home as devices for entertaining guests.[8] This can be viewed as a result of relative cost shifts, in that it is now more expensive, taking psychic costs or the disutility of work into consideration, to produce home-produced goods.

Although this increase in the cost of home-produced goods reduces the gains from marriage, it may represent a net psychic gain (or loss) to individual women. A woman may experience an increase in the nonpecuniary return from her labor force behavior which makes her happier than did her former work in the home, in the era before consciousness raising. This net improvement in her position is clearly not a gain from being married, however.

It is true that an increase in the cost of home produced goods will, all other factors held equal, reduce the gain from marriage. This, of course, assumes that the same basket of goods and services is still desired by the married couple, or at least by the husband. However, given enough taste changes in both men and women, there may be no decline in satisfaction, even though the new feminism definitely downgrades the maintenance and management of consumption as a full-time occupational choice. There may simply be changes in the lifestyle of the married couple. It is possible that changes in the utility functions of married individuals may even permit a shift to greater psychic or non-pecuniary returns to marriage even when there is a net monetary loss or reduction in the amount of goods which can be produced in the home. For instance, an employed woman's salary may not cover the cost of hiring comparable substitutes for her former household production. However, complementarity in *consumption* of married couples may be increased by resulting changes in the division of labor between the sexes.

It should be noted, however, that the attitudinal shifts associated with the new feminism may affect the returns from marriage for some women adversely. For the woman who remains a traditional housewife, but who has now lost the supportive societal myth surrounding her role, there may be a significant utility loss. For her, the gain from marriage has declined with no compensating alternatives. Proposals related to improving the position of the housewife will be discussed in the third part of the paper.

In the next section, changing patterns of marriage, household composition, and divorce will be studied. These changes will be related to the economic model of marriage presented here, and the impact of feminist attitudes will also be analyzed.

Patterns of Marriage and Household Formation, and Divorce and Changes in Household Composition

The above analysis of the impact of feminist attitudes on the nature of marriage leaves open the question of whether or not one would expect shifts in demand for marriage, resulting in less marriage and/or more divorce. It has been shown that strong reasons exist for changes to occur in family life-style because of shifts in production functions, costs of inputs, and utility functions. The economic model of marriage also leads one to expect that some of the changes in the production functions of married households would affect the timing of marriages and the degree of differentiation between the married and single household. But whether or not there has been a net decline in the gain from marriage relative to the cost is undetermined. It may even be the case that the costs, both psychic and monetary, associated with marrying have tended to decline.

This section of the paper will include an examination of historical patterns of marriage and divorce, with particular reference to the past decade. This examination will be related to household formation rates and changes in household composition from 1960 to 1970. Our economic model of marriage will be extended to include a consideration of changes in the alternatives to being married. It will be used to explain observed patterns of marriage, divorce, and household formation that are consistent with, if not engendered by, the new feminist attitudes. Finally, there will be an attempt to evaluate the impact of the new feminist attitudes on marriage and divorce rates.

Marriage and Household Formation

Economists studying marriage over time in the United States have found it to be a normal good (i.e., one with a positive income elasticity). Dorothy Thomas and Thomas Ogburn discovered this historical correlation between marriage rates and income in the 1920s.[9] More recently, Morris Silver found a cyclical income elasticity for marriage rates of about .5 prevailing for the nineteenth century and throughout the first half of the twentieth century in this country.[10] It has also been found that for men, marrying appears to be positively associated with income level in cross-sectional data.[11] However, although real income has risen, the marriage rate in the United States has not risen in the past two decades.[12]

An examination of the percentage distribution of the female population in this country by marital status and age over the time period 1950 to 1970 indicates an increase in the proportion of single women and a decline in the proportion of married women within each of the age groups 14–19 and 20–24 (see Table 16.1). Fredricka Santos has presented a hypothesis and supporting evidence indicating that there has been a decline in the complementarity between men and women in their productive roles within marriage.[13] If this is true, it offers an explanation for the failure of the marriage rate to rise with real income. The positive effect of income on marriage rates has been offset by a decline in the economic gains from specialization within marriage.

An interesting phenomenon accompanying these changing marriage

TABLE 16.1 Percentage Distribution of Female Population
by Marital Status and Age, United States,
1950–70

Age	1950[a]	1955[a]	1960	1965	1970
14–19					
Single	84.8	85.8	88.0	89.5	91.3
Married	14.7	13.8	11.7	10.3	9.4
Divorced	0.2	0.4	0.3	0.2	0.1
20–24					
Single	31.6	29.1	29.9	32.5	35.9
Married	66.1	69.3	69.2	65.6	61.5
Divorced	1.8	1.2	1.6	1.6	2.3
25–29					
Single	10.9	9.3	9.5	8.4	10.7
Married	85.3	87.0	87.3	87.2	84.7
Divorced	2.5	2.7	2.5	3.6	4.3
30–34					
Single	10.9	9.3	6.9	5.3	6.4
Married	85.3	87.0	88.8	90.5	88.3
Divorced	2.5	2.7	3.1	3.1	4.6

SOURCE: U.S. Census, *Statistical Abstracts of the United States, 1951–1971: 1951,* Table
30, p. 24; *1956,* Table 44, p. 46; *1961,* Table 27, p. 34; *1966,* Table 32, p. 31;
1971, Table 38, p. 32.

NOTE: Age categories 25–29 and 30–34 were combined.

rates is the change in household status of married couples and single individuals in this country. Table 16.2 provides data on the household status of United States citizens in 1960 and 1970 for the several age groupings. "Primary households" are physically separate, rented or owned units which are maintained by the members of the household. Households which are not both separate units and self-supporting are defined as "secondary households" or "subhouseholds." For instance, a couple, upon marrying, might receive the gift of a house. If over time they pay the costs associated with running the house they will be regarded as having formed a primary household. If the maintenance of the household is paid by parents or others, or if the couple move into a parental household, they will be defined as a secondary or subhousehold.

There has been a general increase in the proportion of primary households over the past decade in this country. Marriage in the United States has historically been associated with the formation of separate, self-supporting or "primary" households. However, it is interesting to note the

TABLE 16.2   Household Status, United States Citizens

Age of Individual or Head of Household	Proportion of Unrelated Individuals in Primary Households	Proportion of Married Couples in Primary Households
Males and Females, 1961		
18–19	31	Not available
20–24	44	90
25–29	55	97
30–34	60	98
Males, 1970		
18–19	54	62
20–24	58	94
25–29	68	98
30–34	69	99
Females, 1970		
18–19	39	89
20–24	53	96
25–29	72	99
30–34	75	99

SOURCE: Adapted from U.S. Census, *Current Population Reports:* Series P-20, No. 114,
    Tables 6 and 7, p. 11; and Series P-20, No. 212, Table 2, p. 13.

NOTE: "Primary households" are defined as physically separate, self-supporting house-
    holds.

striking increase in the number of single people also forming primary
households between 1960 and 1970. The increase in primary households
composed of females living alone, aged 20–24, was found to be 196 percent for the period 1960–72. This category includes single, widowed,
divorced, and separated women, but this age group is primarily composed
of single women. For men in the same age group and marital cohorts, the
increase in the proportion living alone in primary households was 272
percent over the same time period.[14]

The changing pattern of household formation in the past decade provides an explanation for the decline in response of the marriage rate to income changes. There has been a decline in the relative cost of marrying
due to a decline in the strength of the association between marrying and
forming primary households. It is not that newly married couples fail to
set up separate households, but that many more single people also do so
now. The real association is not between marriage and rises in real income, but rather between rises in real income and the formation of new

households—a phenomenon referred to some time ago by Dorothy Brady as the "undoubling effect." [15] She noted the positive relationship between rises in real income and a decline in multiple-family and multigenerational households. An increase in the proportion of individuals living alone in primary households can also be considered an "undoubling" phenomenon.

Both increases in real income and social changes which make it easier for young people to leave the family home for reasons other than marriage will enhance the "undoubling" effect. If young people characteristically form primary households before marrying, one would expect the association between marrying and increases in expenditure associated with household formation to decline. Marriage might even represent a saving, owing to economies of scale and "doubling." Consequently, one would expect a decline in the income elasticity of the marriage rate.

I studied the complementarity between marriage and expenditure on household formation for the years 1958 and 1959, using Surveys of Consumer Finances of the Survey Research Center at University of Michigan. [16] The results of this study are consistent with the hypothesis presented above that the decline in the initial costs associated with marriage have reduced the responsiveness of marriage rates to changes in income.

Statistically significant differences were found between the household capital expenditures of single primary households and newly married primary households with similar incomes. However, the differences were not of much practical import, amounting to less than one hundred dollars per annum on the average. On the other hand, when persons living in secondary households were included in the comparison, the magnitude of the difference between single and newly married groups became interesting. Single persons and married couples living in secondary households (i.e., at home or in institutional arrangements) were assumed to acquire no household durables. [17] When single and newly married cohorts in each age group were weighted by the proportion of that age group in primary and secondary households in the 1960 census of population, as shown in Table 16.2, the resulting difference in expenditure on household durables between married and single households amounted to between five hundred and one thousand dollars per annum, on the average. [18] Thus, the capital costs associated with marrying were substantial only when change in household status was taken into account.

As the household status of the young changes so that higher proportions are living in primary units, the expectation is that the differential
costs of both forming and maintaining the marriage will decline as single
people also incur rent and mortgage payments. Many people who marry
will already possess a stock of household capital. Even if it is scrapped
and new possessions purchased, the individuals will be accustomed to a
level of expenditure which more nearly approximates that of the married
household.

The decline in responsiveness of the marriage rate to income should
also be enhanced by an increase in the average age of first marriage.
Given the tendency for age–earnings profiles to show increases in income
with age, the cost of setting up the newly married household will be
lower relative to income for older couples.

The longer periods of being single will also tend to affect the household production functions of men and women marrying later. Women
will tend to have more human capital invested in them in both formal education and job experience. This raises the opportunity cost of their time
in the household. Men are likely, if they have lived in primary households, to have acquired some training in household skills. Certainly, it
would appear plausible that both the degree of substitutability and the relative costs of labor inputs of men and women in household production
will shift in response to the social changes outlined above.

Changes in the attitudes of women as to what constitutes their appropriate roles in production may be associated with these same social
changes. In fact, it could be argued that Women's Liberation is a response to such things as increases in real income for women with the at-
tendant increase in higher education and the greater rate of formation of
single-person households. Whether the attitudinal changes among women
are cause or effect, or both, it is true that they tend to reduce the difference between the households formed by two adults living as room-
mates and those of married couples without children, especially when
both members of the couple are employed in the labor force.

Divorce and Changes in Household Composition

Divorce, or the dissolution of marriage, is another kind of undoubling effect. Between the years 1960 and 1970 the real-income elasticity of
divorce was greater than 1 and, therefore, greater than the income elastic-

ity of marriage rates.[19] Table 16.3 shows that divorce rates have risen, particularly sharply between 1965 and 1970, to the highest rate ever recorded in this country since divorce statistics were first tabulated in 1890. There has been not only an increase in the incidence of divorce in the United States but also a change in attitude toward it, involving a wider acceptance of the notion of dissolution of marriage as a rational choice not necessarily accompanied by aberrant behavior or wrongdoing as a justification. The recent adoption of no-fault divorce statutes in California (1971) and several other states reflects this new acceptance.

TABLE 16.3   Annual Rates of Divorce per 1,000
Males and Females United States, 1890–1970

	% Divorced for Females 14 years and older	% Divorced for Males 14 years and older
1890	0.4	0.3
1900	0.5	0.4
1910	0.5	0.6
1920	0.7	0.8
1930	1.1	1.3
1940	1.3	1.6
1950	1.7	2.1
1960	1.9	2.6
1965	2.5	3.3
1970	2.6	4.1

SOURCE: 1890 and 1900—U.S. Census, *Historical Statistics of the United States, Colonial Times to 1957,* Series A210–227, p. 15.
1910 to 1970—*Statistical Abstract of the United States, 1971,* Table 39, p. 33.

Accompanying these startling increases in the rate of divorce in the American population are dramatic increases in the number and proportion of female-headed households. Data from a recent study by Heather L. Ross and Anita MacIntosh at the Urban Institute show the relationship between the two. The percentage increase between 1960 and 1972 in the number of *all* primary families headed by women in the United States was 38.1; [20] however, the increase in the number of families headed by divorced women was 114.8 percent, whereas the number headed by widows increased by only 1.7 percent over the same time period.

Given the greater incidence of divorce and the importance of divorce in the creation of new households, it becomes an important part of the analysis of the effects of Women's Liberation to investigate which women are divorcing. I have undertaken such a study, utilizing the National Longitudinal Surveys of the U.S. Department of Commerce, commonly known as the Parnes data.[21] I was concerned with the relationship between divorce, labor force participation, and attitudes toward work among a group of approximately 5,000 women, sampled in 1967. The hypothesis to be tested was that frequency of divorce is a function of income and wealth, labor force participation of the wife, and attitude of the woman toward working outside the home—interpreted here as the Women's Liberation effect. Other variables which clearly affect the frequency of divorce include age at first marriage of the woman, age of youngest child, length of current marriage, number of marriages, religion, and difficulty (or ease) of obtaining divorce. Unfortunately, a number of the desired control variables were not obtainable from this data pool. However, it was possible to construct an estimating equation with eight explanatory variables, and the results of this regression analysis are presented in Table 16.4.[22] The findings are consistent with the analysis presented thus far in this paper and also with Santos's findings elsewhere in this volume.

The income effect is negative, small, but highly significant. This is as would be expected, since incidence of divorce has usually been found to be inversely related to income in cross-sections. The gains from marriage are likely to be lower at lower levels of income, since the economic returns from marriage are in part a function of the total resources available to the partners. It is important to be cautious in interpreting these results, however, for there was a problem in the response to the income question. Some women gave total income of self plus that of spouse or former spouse. Others gave own earned and asset income plus whatever alimony they received.

The regression coefficient for the wage and salary variable illustrates a small, but significant, positive substitution effect. It suggests that earning income may be to some extent a substitute for "employment" within marriage. This is consistent with Santos's hypothesis of declining complementarity between men and women. A $1,000 increase in wife's wage and salary leads to a 2 percent increase in the probability of divorce. The implied chain of causation is not entirely clear, however, because the separated or divorced woman may be forced to seek a more full-time or higher-paying job in order to make up for loss of income due to loss of husband.

TABLE 16.4 Probability of Divorce among Married Women
Aged 30–44

Explanatory Variable	Regression Coefficients	t-Value
WWS = wife's wage or salary (annual income) in dollars	0.00002	11.58680
INC = total family income from all sources (annual) in dollars	−0.00008	−12.22317
ATW = attitude toward work (1 if positive—"would work even if no economic necessity"; 0 if negative or neutral)	0.02961	3.74906
Control Variable		
NYC = number of years of current marriage, expressed in actual years	−0.00805	−15.93945
AYF = wife's age at her first marriage	−0.00832	−8.63727
AYC = age of youngest child in years (no children coded as 50)	0.00108	4.44146
NM = number of marriages of woman	−0.04719	−4.69677
WE = number of years of schooling of woman	−0.00260	−1.96784
	$R^2 = 0.137$	

SOURCE: U.S. Census, *The National Longitudinal Surveys of Work Experience, 1967 Women Aged 30–44 Years.* (Information available on tape ØM 52343, National Bureau of Economic Research, Inc., New York City.)

NOTE: The probability of divorce is a categorical variable, defined 1 if divorced and 0 if married and living with husband. All women in other categories (separated or widowed) were not included in this sample.

The positive and significant coefficient for attitude toward work is interesting and consistent with what would have been predicted. With wage and salary held constant, attitude toward work can be interpreted as a measure of the psychic components of the return from the job. This indicates that women who take greater interest in and derive greater satisfaction from labor force activity are more likely to leave a marriage, other determining factors unchanged. The fact that this attitude may not be independent of the job experience of the respondent is not in itself very important.

Job experience becomes somewhat more important, however, when we attempt to analyze the impact on divorce rates of autonomous shifts in preferences—the so-called Women's Liberation effect. If these preference shifts are the result of positive labor force experiences, then they are clearly not autonomous. To suggest that labor force experience affects the likelihood of one's embracing changing attitudes, however, does not destroy the notion of a definable change in the preferences of women acting as a separate causal factor in their behavior. Just as educational level may have something to do with the probability of one's accepting new ideas, so may experience outside the household. The regression analysis has not proved that there is an independent Women's Liberation effect, but it is consistent with the existence of one. The results are both significant and in the right direction.

The changes that have been observed in marriage—later marriages, no increase in marriage rates with rises in real income, and less difference in household status between married and single people—all suggest a decline in the income elasticity of marriage. Young people are electing fewer years of marriage, if not less marriage, than formerly. If there had been no impact from the feminist movement, would one expect to have found this result? Income and substitution effects alone could account for a good deal of the observed behavior of the young. The single primary household represents a further "undoubling" as incomes rise. The increased labor force participation of young women results in a substitution to a new kind of employment. It is unlikely that the observed results would be found, however, in the absence of a shift in the relative nonpecuniary returns for women from household and labor market employment. Two decades ago, and to some extent even in the early sixties, lifetime careers would not have been regarded as a reasonable substitute for marriage by many young women. The current change in attitudes toward marriage and careers appears to be highly interdependent with changes in household formation and labor force behavior on the part of young men and women.

Higher divorce rates and the existence of more female-headed families are also consistent with a strong Women's Liberation effect, especially as the propensity to divorce is found to be positively related to a propensity to want to work, even if it is not economically necessary. Again, the income effect cannot be discounted, although cross-sectionally there has been an observed inverse relationship between income and divorce. Divorce also tends to take place in the absence of young children, where the gains from staying married may be less and the cost of breaking up the family unit lower. Over time, then, a decline in family size would also tend to increase the amount of divorce.

Further Aims of the
Women's Liberation Movement

In the preceding sections of this paper, a number of observed phenomena consistent with the views of the new feminists have been discussed. Social and economic changes which affect the nature of marriage and the married household have been analyzed, with particular reference to a taste or preference change which I have identified as the Women's Liberation effect. The focus of attention has been the last decade, roughly coincident with the period of time since the publication of *The Feminine Mystique* helped to launch the Women's Liberation Movement.

Many of the specific programmatic points of that movement, however, have not yet been accepted by society or enacted into law. In this section of the paper, a critical consideration of some proposals for changing the economic position of women engaged primarily in work in the home will be undertaken. Then an attempt will be made to evaluate the impact of these proposals, if realized, on the nature of marriage and on marriage and divorce rates.

If we review the aims of the Women's Liberation Movement, the starting point is equality for men and women, with no a priori difference in productive roles and the same options open to both. We might even restate this goal as a redefinition of men and women as perfect substitutes in all forms of production in and out of the household (except for childbearing). Women should be treated as equals in the labor force and, to quote a current National Organization of Women slogan, as "equal partners in marriage."

The Women's Movement is nonetheless realistic about the fact that for an indefinite period of time, married women are likely to be more intensively employed in the home than are married men. Spokeswomen are also aware of the fact that usually the balance of power within households is determined by who earns the money. Consequently the terminology of "dependent spouse" is still used even though the goal is equality between spouses and complete interdependence.

Three main proposals aimed at improving the position of the housewife and mother are considered here. These proposals have been made in a number of places by feminists and are codified in the various reports of NOW.[23]

(1) Household labor inputs should be priced and housewives should receive a wage or salary. In addition, the occupation of housewife should be covered by Social Security or some other form of retirement benefit.

(2) Housewives should have the opportunity to participate in retraining programs, paid for either by husbands or by society, to permit them to reenter the labor force.

(3) The household sector should be reorganized to permit more efficient use of the labor inputs associated with housekeeping and childrearing.

Compensation for Work in the Home

The first problem in compensating work done in the home would be the determination of wage rates: the market value of the time spent can be measured as the opportunity cost of time in alternative labor force activity. Does this mean that the housewife's wage rate will decline as her unused skills depreciate and become obsolete and her labor force alternatives come to be limited to domestic employment in other homes? [24] An attempt to introduce a wage based on opportunity cost is not likely to lead to a very satisfactory wage bargain for the woman with a long history of housewifery and no labor force participation.

An additional problem associated with "market" determination of household wages is the absence of a competitive market for the household services of spouses once they are married. There is only the implicit threat of divorce or strike (i.e., refusal to perform household services) if the wage bargain is deemed unsatisfactory. The very nature of a long-term marriage contract makes it difficult to negotiate within marriage. The employed spouse might even be described as a monopsonist with respect to his or her "purchase" of the services of the household spouse.

An alternative is the administered wage rate, perhaps a legal minimum wage for time devoted to household production. As different categories of household work and child care are evaluated very differently in the commercial market for domestic services, a single minimum wage for "employment" in the home may be far too simplistic a concept.

Differing levels of productivity may also create problems in wage determination. The woman who is marginally productive in the home but who has high productivity outside the household sector will be able to hire substitutes for herself. For women whose overall productivity is low, however, the minimum wage may be unattainable. In addition, some husbands may not be able to pay the going market rate because of their own low income and employment status. Given a tendency for people of similar ability and/or productivity to marry each other,[25] there will surely be marginal families, like marginal firms, which will not be able to pay the minimum wage. Attempts at enforcement of the minimum wage would result in the same kind of effects that characterize our much-criticized welfare system. Families in the lowest income groups would be forced to dissolve, or men and women forced to live together out of wedlock in order to avoid impossible wage payments. We are led into the policy question of whether some kind of social support is to be provided for the economically marginal family.

Making wage payments for wives' housework explicit points out more clearly factors that have persisted over time. It may be very important to provide women in the home with actual rather than imputed wages in order to give them control over earnings streams. In addition, payment of a money wage may be accompanied by certain psychic benefits. It should also lead to a more rational allocation of time among homemaking duties and between the home and market as marriage partners are made more explicitly aware of alternatives. It is unlikely, however, that a woman's wage will ever be completely disassociated from the level of income and wealth of the family unit. The implicit wage to married women employed in the home has historically been a payment in kind—her standard of living. As long as men are primary earners, the housewife's wage will be tied to the earnings level of the husband. It is really not feasible for different household members to live at vastly different economic levels. In fact, it becomes a matter for the Family Court when attempts are made to impose significant differences in living standards on dependent spouses with children.

The most realistic proposal is probably to assign half of the employed spouse's income to the household spouse.[26] This satisfies the condition of equal partnership, even though it fails to measure the opportunity cost of the household spouse's time. It would tend to encourage high-income earners to marry people of high productivity in the home.

NOW and other women's groups are also advocating pensions and unemployment benefits for housewives. One widely supported proposal is for a Social Security payment for household work. It is proposed that women be insured for both retirement and unemployment (divorce), and that an adjustment in the Social Security deductions for married employed persons be made in acknowledgment of the contribution of the dependent spouse to the productivity of the employed spouse.[27] An adjustment for contribution of the dependent spouse is probably not feasible, however, in that it would force employers to pay a higher rate for married than for single workers of equal productivity performing the same job. Among other things, it would tend to cause justifiable discrimination against married workers by employers.

There are also problems associated with insuring against divorce, insofar as insurance is being extended to cover events of "choice" rather than events of "chance." Such insurance would penalize those with a lower propensity to dissolve marriage unless individuals could be accurately classified as low- and high-risk marriage partners.

Even if we limit our discussion to retirement benefits for housewives, there are thorny questions raised by the notion of housewives' insurance. Uniform rates of forced saving for low- as well as high-income families would impose very different degrees of burden on families of differing socioeconomic status. On the other hand, payments into the fund graduated according to family income would involve a redistribution of income if there were a standard benefit payment to all wives. The welfare implications of proposed social security coverage for wives' work in their own homes need to be investigated in depth. And, of course, certain current criticisms of the existing Social Security system as an inefficient form of savings would apply here.

Retraining Programs for Housewives

Proposed training programs for housewives who have been out of the labor force are based on the assumption that these women suffer from discrimination and therefore should receive reparations. It is argued that not only is there the problem of equity, but there is also the social problem of misallocation of resources. It is alleged that there is an underutilization of highly educated and potentially productive women and that this involves a waste to the economy. Women in the household sector, particularly those without small children, are said to be underemployed in much the same way as are people in the agrarian sectors of less-developed countries.

There is some disagreement as to whether it is the responsibility of husbands or of society to provide the retraining. The proposal that such a program of retraining for divorced or widowed women come under the aegis of the *Manpower Development and Training Act of 1962* makes married women ineligible for such training. Other schemes have been suggested, including marriage insurance that can be used at the time of divorce or cashed in after a number of years of marriage.[28]

Reorganization of the Household Sector

The household sector might be compared to an economy of cottage industries. Productivity increases resulting from economies of scale and greater specialization or professionalization of inputs are ruled out by the inefficiently small units. Furthermore, women, by not organizing, have developed little power to deal with the male-dominated corporate structure. Households are like small competitive firms faced with monopolistic (oligopolistic) or monopsonistic (oligopsonistic) practices in the markets in which they operate. Of course, this characteristic of households affects both men and women, married and single. It is more particularly a married woman's problem only because of the relatively larger proportion of time spent by married women working in households.

The Women's Liberation Movement proposes that women organize into collectives or exchange household services. The need for reorganization has been stressed particularly with respect to child care, which is such a time-intensive activity. Some of the more radical feminists would hope to abolish the institution of marriage altogether or greatly modify it so as to make women less dependent on particular husbands. It has even been proposed that all child care be paid for by the state, as it is an occupation that chiefly benefits society.

The proposals of the Women's Liberation Movement for protection of married women and improvement in their status reflect an ambivalent view of the market mechanism as extended to intramarriage decisions. On the one hand, individual members are to receive wage payments from others for their work in the household. On the other hand, all kinds of guarantees are to be provided to limit the risks associated with marriage. The Women's Liberation model of an improved world is one which is, on the whole, attractive to risk averters. Insurance is to be extended, and like most unions, Women's Liberation opts for fixed rules and involuntary programs rather than discretionary arrangements within marriage. Most of the insurance proposals discussed are feasible only if one accepts the notion that the casualties of broken marriages and financially untenable households are to be supported by society. The wealth and income transfers proposed are not only from men to women but also from richer to poorer families, from married to divorced couples, and from childless couples to those with children.

The several programmatic points of the Women's Movement discussed above appear less contradictory in aim if they are understood to be designed to help women in differing positions of labor market and marriage market strength. The broad range of proposals aims to provide more options for all women, whether they be single, entering marriages, wanting to remain within existing marriages, or leaving marriages.

It remains to be asked whether the programs discussed above do in fact achieve these aims. To answer this question I will return to the model of marriage as a quasi-firm and use it to evaluate the likely effects of the proposals.

If determined through the market mechanism, wages for household labor will reflect the relative costs of labor inputs and will, therefore, leave the distribution of work between husband and wife unchanged in most cases. An administered wage would be likely to have much the same effect. It may even cause a further downgrading of the position of the housewife. The woman's economic position will be improved only if she receives more in wages than she formerly received in support.

Social security payments for housewives' work would tend to increase the gains from marriage to the wife. Once she becomes eligible for a pension, however, it may, reduce the gains of staying married.

Retraining programs for housewives would increase the gain from marriage to all women who are housewives. As the returns from marriage to the couple are a function of the earning power of spouses, such retraining will increase the net return to marriage if it is available to married as well as to divorced and widowed women, and if it is subsidized by society. If retraining programs are available only to divorced women, on the other hand, they might increase the incentive to get divorced. Even if they were available to married women, such programs might, in the long run, increase the likelihood of divorce by increasing both the desire and the ability for labor force participation. They might reduce the gains from marriage after the training program has been completed.

Insofar as the retraining programs are financed by the husband, they increase the cost of the marriage to him, although he may reap a return from his wife's increased earning power.

In general, any forced payment to wives by husbands will tend to lower the desirability of marriage for men. Moreover, the proposals for legislated compensation for women are likely to be realized only if the marriage market becomes a "buyers" market in which women are the buyers. If the attitudinal change in women discussed in this paper were to become strong enough so as to cause a significant shift away from marriage on the part of women, then the proposals might be enacted in order to make marriage more attractive to women, assuming that men still desire wives at more or less the same rate as now. Under such circumstances, wage rates for wives might become extremely high.

Ironically, it is only after a hypothetical shift in the balance of power between men and women that the paying of a wage for household production would be likely to improve the position of the housewife substantially. The only exception to this would be the paying of a wage automatically equal to half the husband's salary.

The one noncontroversial proposal that clearly leads to gains for husbands, wives, and society as a whole is the reorganization of the household sector so as to make it more efficient. The gain to society would result from the freeing of labor and other productive inputs for alternative productive uses. The gain to married couples would be relatively great because married households tend to be larger and more demanding of time-intensive inputs; the only exception would be when tastes have not changed and there are positive psychic benefits associated with the traditional household. The greatest gain of all would probably be to the woman "employed" in her own household. This proposal, then, is eminently sensible, particularly if we view a marriage as a particular kind of firm and one that may be technologically obsolete in the modern world.

Conclusions

The Women's Liberation effect appears to have lowered the economic returns to marriage, at least temporarily. The present demographic situation in the United States, characterized by a decline in the income elasticity of the marriage rate, a rise in the age at marriage, and a high rate of divorce, can be interpreted as reflecting a "disequilibrium" due to changing tastes as well as changing relative productivities of men and women within the context of the traditional marriage. In the long run, however, it is possible that changes in the preference functions of both men and women as well as changes in household production functions will fundamentally alter the way in which the costs and returns from marriage are evaluated.

Although some question the durability of the present level of interest in women's liberation,[29] certain social and economic trends consistent with and supportive of the aims of the Movement are likely to continue. As long as real income continues to rise, there will be an increase in the formation of single-person households as well as an increased investment in education and training, particularly by women. Within the household, a rise in market productivities of men and women will lead to a continued substitution of physical for human capital. Moreover, social factors such as desire for smaller families, concern with population limitation and greater sexual freedom tend to reinforce what I have called the Women's Liberation effect.[30]

In a transition period such as the present one, Social Security for housewives and retraining programs for women may be particularly important, owing to the instability in the institution of marriage. Some form of wage payment in the home may be important in providing a way of evaluating alternative household production functions once traditional ones are questioned. If the programmatic points advocated by the Women's Liberation Movement were to become realities, women would have greater control over income and assets, and this should further reinforce the notion of their being independent persons, free to invest in themselves and to develop interests independent of the household. In my opinion, however, the demands of the Women's Liberation Movement can be seen as relevant only within this present period of "disequilibrium" and will not be applicable if marriage and family life-style are fundamentally changed.

NOTES

[1] Betty Friedan, *The Feminine Mystique* (New York, 1963).

[2] Gary S. Becker, "A Theory of Marriage, Part I," *Journal of Political Economy,* LXXXI (July/August 1973): 813–46; Gary S. Becker, "A Theory of the Allocation of Time," *Economic Journal,* LXXV (September 1965): 493–517; Shirley B. Johnson, "An Economic Analysis of Marriage" (Ph.D. diss., Columbia University, 1966); and Jacob Mincer, "Market Price, Opportunity Costs, and Income Effects," in Carl F. Christ, ed., *Measurement in Economics: Studies in Mathematical Economics and Econometrics, in Memory of Yehuda Grunfeld,* (Palo Alto, 1963).

[3] Romantic love might be defined as the state of belief that no additional amount of searching will lead to a mate selection providing as much utility as the present selection.

[4] Gary S. Becker, "A Theory of Marriage," p. 818.

[5] Gary S. Becker, "A Theory of the Allocation," pp. 493–95.

[6] Shirley B. Johnson, "An Economic Analysis," pp. 34ff.

[7] Arleen Liebowitz, "Women's Work in the Home," in this volume.

[8] John Kenneth Galbraith, *Economics and the Public Purpose* (Boston, 1973), p. 239.

[9] Thomas Ogburn and Dorothy S. Thomas, "The Influence of the Business Cycle and Certain Social Conditions," *Quarterly Publication of the American Statistical Association,* Vol. XVIII (January 1922); and Dorothy S. Thomas, *Social Aspects of the Business Cycle* (New York, 1950).

[10] Morris Silver, "Births, Marriages, and Business Cycles in the United States, *Journal of Political Economy,* LXXIII (June 1965): 237–55; Shirley B. Johnson, "An Economic Analysis," pp. 23–39.

[11] Paul C. Glick, *American Families* (New York, 1959), p. 135.

[12] Fredricka Pickford Santos, "The Economics of Marital Status," in this volume.

[13] *Ibid.*

[14] Heather L. Ross and Anita Macintosh, "The Emergence of Households Headed by Women" (Draft paper, The Urban Institute, June 1973), Tables 3–4, p. 6b.

[15] Dorothy Brady, "Individual Incomes and the Structure of Consumer Units," *American Economic Review,* XLVIII (May 1958): 267–78.

[16] For each year, regressions were run based on approximately 2,000 single and married spending units without children.

[17] Consumer durables such as phonographs, television sets, cameras, and the like are not defined as "household durables."

[18] Shirley B. Johnson, "An Economic Analysis," pp. 86, 106–11.

[19] *Ibid.,* p. 120.

[20] Ross and Macintosh, "The Emergence of Households," p. 7a.

[21] U.S. Census, 1967, National Longitudinal Surveys of Work Experience of Women, Ages 30–44.

[22] Two variables were initially included in the regression but were found to be insignificant: race (coded as 1 if black, 0 if white, all other omitted) and number of years at current job.

[23] National Organization of Women, Report of the Task Force on Marriage, Divorce, and Family Relations, October 1972, and NOW Sixth National Conference Resolutions (1973).

[24] Reuben Gronau, "The Effect of Children on the Housewife's Value of Time," *Journal of Political Economy,* LXXXI (March/April 1973): S168–99.

[25] Paul Jacobson with Pauline Jacobson, *American Marriage and Divorce* (New York, 1959).

[26] This has been proposed by a number of people, including Professor Carolyn Shaw Bell of Wellesley College and Shirley B. Johnson, and is included in the 1974 Proposals of the NOW Conference on Marriage and Divorce, currently being prepared for publication.

[27] Lee Benham, "Non-Market Returns to Women's Investment in Education," in this volume.

[28] NOW Draft Proposal for a Marriage Insurance Plan, presented by Betty Berry at the Third Annual Conference of the Tri State Council on Family Relations, November 14, 1970, p. 6.

[29] Barbara R. Bergmann, "The Economics of Women's Liberation," *Challenge,* XVI (May/June 1973): 17.

[30] It is, of course, true that economists such as Richard Easterlin, studying long cycles in birthrates and other demographic variables, have found evidence of a cycle of approximately twenty years duration. Therefore, one cannot rule out the possibility of a reversal of the current trend. Richard Easterlin, *The American Baby Boom in Historical Perspective* (New York, 1962).

Selected Bibliography

Abbott, Edith. *Women in Industry*. New York, 1924.

American Economic Association, Committee on the Status of Women in the Economics Profession. "Combatting Role Prejudice and Sex Discrimination." *American Economic Review*, LXIII (December 1973): 1049–61.

Baker, Elizabeth F. *Technology and Women's Work*. New York, 1964.

Becker, Gary S. "An Economic Analysis of Fertility." In Universities-National Bureau Committee for Economic Research, *Demographic and Economic Change in Developed Countries*, pp. 209–31. Princeton, N.J., 1960.

—— *The Economics of Discrimination*. 2d ed., Chicago, 1971.

—— *Human Capital: A Theoretical and Empirical Analysis with Special Reference to Education*. New York, 1964.

—— "A Theory of the Allocation of Time." *Economic Journal*, LXXV (September 1965): 493–517.

—— "A Theory of Marriage: Part I." *Journal of Political Economy*, LXXXI (July/August 1973): 813–46.

—— "A Theory of Marriage: Part II," *Journal of Political Economy*, LXXXII, Part II (March/April 1974): S11–S26.

Benham, Lee. "Benefits of Women's Education within Marriage." *Journal of Political Economy*, LXXXII, Part II (March/April 1974): S57–71.

Bergmann, Barbara R. "The Economics of Women's Liberation." *Challenge*, XVI (May/June 1973): 11–17.

—— "The Effect on White Incomes of Discrimination in Employment." *Journal of Political Economy*, LXXIX (March/April 1971): 294–313.

Bergmann, Barbara R., and Adelman, Irma. "The 1973 Report of the President's Council of Economic Advisors: The Economic Role of Women." *American Economic Review,* LXIII (September 1973): 509–14.

Boserup, Ester. *Women's Role in Economic Development.* New York, 1970.

Boskin, Michael J. "The Effect of Government Taxes and Expenditures on Female Labor." *American Economic Review,* LXIV (May 1974): 251–56.

Bowen, William G., and Finegan, T. Aldrich. *The Economics of Labor Force Participation.* Princeton, N.J., 1969.

Butz, Rudolph C., and Ow, Chin Hock. "A Cross-Sectional Analysis of Women's Participation in Professions." *Journal of Political Economy,* LXXXI (January/February 1973): 131–44.

Cain, Glen G. *Married Women in the Labor Force.* Chicago, 1966.

Cain, Glen G., Nicholson, Walter, Mallar, Charles D., Wooldridge, Judith. "The Labor-Supply Response of Married Women, Husband Present." *Journal of Human Resources,* IX (Spring 1974): 201–22.

Cohen, Malcolm S. "Sex Differences in Compensation." *Journal of Human Resources,* VI (Fall 1971): 434–47.

Edgeworth, F. Y. "Equal Pay to Men and Women for Equal Work." *Economic Journal,* XXXII (December 1922): 431–57.

Engels, Frederick. *The Origin of the Family, Private Property, and the State.* Zurich, 1884.

Flanders, Dwight P., and Anderson, Peggy E. "Sex Discrimination in Employment: Theory and Practice." *Industrial and Labor Relations Review,* XXVI (April 1973): 938–55.

Friedan, Betty. *The Feminine Mystique.* New York, 1963.

Fuchs, Victor R. "Differences in Hourly Earnings between Men and Women." *Monthly Labor Review,* XCIV (May 1971): 9–15.

—— "Short-Run and Long-Run Prospects for Female Earnings." *American Economic Review,* LXIV (May 1974): 236–42.

Galbraith, John Kenneth. *Economics and the Public Purpose.* Boston, 1973.

Galenson, Marjorie. *Women and Work: An International Comparison.* Ithaca, N.Y., 1973.

Gilman, Charlotte P. *Women and Economics.* Boston, 1898.

Gordon, Nancy M., Morton, Thomas E., and Braden, Ina C. "Faculty Salaries: Is There Discrimination by Sex, Race, and Discipline?" *American Economic Review,* LXIV (June 1974): 419–27.

Gronau, Reuben. "The Effect of Children on Housewife's Value of Time." *Journal of Political Economy,* LXXXI, Part II, (March/April 1973): S168–S199.

—— "The Intra-family Allocation of Time: The Value of Housewives' Time." *American Economic Review,* LXIII (September 1973): 634–51.

Harrod, Roy F. "Equal Pay for Men and Women." *Economic Essays.* New York, 1952.

Heckman, James J. "Effects of Child-Care Programs on Women's Work Effort." *Journal of Political Economy,* LXXXII, Part II (March/April 1974): S136–S163.

Hoffer, Stefan N. "Rates of Return to Higher Education for Women." *Review of Economics and Statistics,* LV (November 1973): 482–86.

Johnson, George E., and Stafford, Frank P. "The Earnings and Promotion of Women Faculty." *American Economic Review,* LXIII (December 1974).

Kreps, Juanita. *Sex in the Marketplace: American Women at Work.* Baltimore, 1971.

Leibowitz, Arleen. "Education and the Allocation of Women's Time." In *Education and Human Behavior,* edited by F. Thomas Juster. New York, forthcoming.

—— "Production within the Household." *American Economic Review,* LXIV (May 1974): 243–50.

McNulty, Donald. "Differences in Pay between Men and Women Workers." *Monthly Labor Review,* XC (December 1967): 40–43.

Madden, Janice. "The Development of Economic Thought on the 'Woman Problem.' " *Review of Radical Political Economics,* IV (July 1972): 21–39.

Madden, Janice F. *The Economics of Sex Discrimination.* Lexington, Mass., 1973.

Malkiel, Burton G., and Malkiel, Judith A. "Male–Female Pay Differentials in Professional Employment." *American Economic Review,* LXIII (September 1973): 693–705.

Michael, Robert. "Education and the Derived Demand for Children."

Journal of Political Economy, LXXXI, Part II (March/April 1973): S128–S164.

—— "Education in Non-Market Production." *Journal of Political Economy,* LXXXI, Part I (March/April 1973): 306–27.

Mill, John Stuart. *The Subjection of Women.* London, 1869.

Mincer, Jacob. "Labor Force Participation of Married Women: A Study of Labor Supply." In Universities-National Bureau Committee for Economic Research, *Aspects of Labor Economics,* pp. 63–105. Princeton, N.J., 1962.

Mincer, Jacob, and Polachek, Solomon W. "Family Investment in Human Capital and Earnings of Women." *Journal of Political Economy,* LXXXII, Part II (May/June 1974).

Myrdal, Alva, and Klein, Viola. *Women's Two Roles: Home and Work.* London, 1968.

Niemi, Beth. "The Female–Male Differential in Unemployment Rates." *Industrial and Labor Relations Review,* XXVII (April 1974): 331–50.

Oppenheimer, Valerie K. *The Female Labor Force in the United States.* Berkeley, Cal., 1970.

Phelps, Edmund S. "The Statistical Theory of Racism and Sexism." *American Economic Review,* LXII (September 1972): 659–61.

Pinchbeck, Ivy. *Women Workers and the Industrial Revolution, 1770–1850.* London, 1930.

Reid, Margaret. *Economics of Household Production.* New York, 1934.

Sanborn, Henry. "Pay Differences between Men and Women." *Industrial and Labor Relations Review,* XVII (July 1964): 534–50.

Sawhill, Isabel V. "The Economics of Discrimination against Women: Some New Findings." *Journal of Human Resources,* VIII (Summer 1973): 383–96.

Smuts, Robert. *Women and Work in America.* New York, 1959.

Shea, John R. "Welfare Mothers: Barriers to Labor Force Entry." *Journal of Human Resources,* VIII (Supplement, 1973): 90–102.

Smith, Georgina. *Help-Wanted Female: A Study of Demand and Supply in a Local Labor Market for Women.* New Brunswick, N.J., 1964.

Suter, Larry E., and Miller, Herman P. "Income Differences between Men and Career Women." *American Journal of Sociology,* LXXVIII (January 1973): 962–74.

U.S. Congress. House of Representatives. Committee on Education. *Dis-*

crimination against Women: Hearings before a Special Subcommittee on Education. 91st Cong., 2d sess., 1971.

—— Joint Economic Committee. *Economic Problems of Women: Hearings.* 93d Cong., 1st sess., 1973.

U.S. Department of Labor. *Dual Careers: A Longitudinal of Labor Market Experience of Women,* Vol. I. (by Herbert Parnes et al.). Manpower Research Monograph #21, 1970.

—— Wage and Labor Standards Administration, Women's Bureau. *Facts about Women's Absenteeism and Labor Turnover.* Washington, D.C., 1969.

—— Women's Bureau. *1960 Handbook on Women Workers.* Washington, D.C., 1969.

U.S. President's Council of Economic Advisors. "The Economic Role of Women." In *Economic Report of the President.* Washington, D.C., 1973.

Weisskoff, Francine B. " 'Women's Place' in the Labor Market." *American Economic Review,* LXII (May 1972): 161–66.

Willis, Robert. "A New Approach to the Economic Theory of Fertility Behavior." *Journal of Political Economy,* LXXXI, Part II (March/April 1973): S14–S64.

Zellner, Harriet. "Discrimination against Women, Occupational Segregation, and the Relative Wage." *American Economic Review,* LXII (May 1972): 157–60.